GW00775924

Kawasaki ZR550 & 750 Zephyr Fours
Service and Repair Manual

Matthew Coombs

(3382-264-10AR2)

Models covered

ZR550 B Zephyr. 553cc. UK 1991 to 1997
ZR550 B Zephyr. 553cc. US 1990 to 1993
ZR750 C Zephyr. 738cc. UK 1991 to 1996
ZR750 C Zephyr. 738cc. US 1991 to 1993
ZR750 D Zephyr. 738cc. UK 1996 to 1997

© J H Haynes & Co. Ltd. 2018

A book in the **Haynes Service and Repair Manual Series**

ISBN **978 0 85733 864 8**

Library of Congress Catalog Card Number 97-61067

British Library Cataloguing in Publication Data
A catalogue record for this book is available from the British Library.

J H Haynes & Co. Ltd.
Haynes North America, Inc

www.haynes.com

Contents

LIVING WITH YOUR KAWASAKI ZEPHYR

Introduction

Daily (pre-ride) checks

MAINTENANCE

Routine maintenance and servicing

Contents

REPAIRS AND OVERHAUL

REFERENCE

Kawasaki
The Green Meanies

by Julian Ryder

Kawasaki Heavy Industries

Kawasaki is a company of contradictions. It is the smallest of the big four Japanese manufacturers but the biggest company, it was the last of the four to make and market motorcycles yet it owns the oldest name in the Japanese industry, and it was the first to set up a factory in the USA. Kawasaki Heavy Industries, of which the motorcycle operation is but a small component, is a massive company with its heritage firmly in the old heavy industries like shipbuilding and railways; nowadays it is as much involved in aerospace as in motorcycles.

In fact it may be because of this that Kawasaki's motorcycles have always been quirky, you get the impression that they are designed by a small group of enthusiasts who are given an admirably free hand. More realistically, it may be that Kawasaki's designers have experience with techniques and materials from other engineering disciplines. Either way, Kawasaki have managed to be the factory who surprise us more than the rest. Quite often, they do this by totally ignoring a market segment the others are scrabbling over, but more often they hit us with pure, undiluted performance.

The origins of the company, and its name, go back to 1878 when Shozo Kawasaki set up a dockyard in Tokyo. By the late 1930s, the company was making its own steel in massive steelworks and manufacturing railway locos and rolling stock. In the run up to war, the Kawasaki Aircraft Company was set up in 1937 and it was this arm of the now giant operation that would look to motorcycle engine manufacture in post-war Japan.

They bought their high-technology experience to bear first on engines which were sold on to a number of manufacturers as

original equipment. Both two- and four-stroke units were made, a 58 cc and 148 cc OHC unit. One of the customer companies was Meihatsu Heavy Industries, another company within the Kawasaki group, which in 1961 was shaken up and renamed Kawasaki Auto Sales. At the same time, the Akashi factory which was to be Kawasaki's main production facility until the Kobe earthquake of 1995, was opened. Shortly afterwards, Kawasaki took over the ailing Meguro company, Japan's oldest motorcycle maker, thus instantly obtaining a range of bigger bikes which were marketed as Kawasaki-Meguros. The following year, the first bike to be made and sold as a Kawasaki was produced, a 125 cc single called the B8 and in 1963 a motocross version, the B8M appeared.

The three cylinder two-stroke 750

Model development

Kawasaki's first appearance on a road-race circuit came in 1965 with a batch of disc-valve 125 twins. They were no match for the opposition from Japan in the shape of Suzuki and Yamaha or for the fading force of the factory MZs from East Germany. Only after the other Japanese factories had pulled out of the class did Kawasaki win, with British rider Dave Simmonds becoming World 125 GP Champion in 1969 on a bike that looked astonishingly similar to the original racer. That same year Kawasaki reorganised once again, this time merging three companies to form Kawasaki Heavy Industries. One of the new organisation's objectives was to take motorcycle production forward and exploit markets outside Japan.

KHI achieved that target immediately and set out their stall for the future with the astonishing and frightening H1. This three-cylinder air-cooled 500 cc two-stroke was arguably the first modern pure performance bike to hit the market. It hypnotised a whole generation of motorcyclists who'd never before encountered such a ferocious, wheelie inducing power band or such shattering straight-line speed allied to questionable handling. And as for the 750 cc version ...

The triples perfectly suited the late '60s, fitting in well with the student demonstrations of 1968 and the anti-establishment ethos of the Summer of Love. Unfortunately, the oil crisis would put an end to the thirsty strokers but Kawasaki had another high-performance ace up their corporate sleeve. Or rather they thought they did.

The 1968 Tokyo Show saw probably the single most significant new motorcycle ever made unveiled: the Honda CB750. At Kawasaki it caused a major shock, for they also had a 750 cc four, code-named New York Steak, almost ready to roll and it was a double, rather than single, overhead cam motor. Bravely, they took the decision to go ahead - but with the motor taken out to 900 cc. The result was the Z1, unveiled at the 1972 Cologne Show. It was a bike straight out of the same mould as the H1, scare stories spread about unmanageable power, dubious straight-line stability and frightening handling, none of which stopped the sales graph rocketing upwards and led to the coining of the term 'superbike'. While rising fuel prices cut short development of the big two-strokes, the Z1 went on to found a dynasty, indeed its genes can still be detected in Kawasaki's latest products like the ZZ-R1100 (Ninja ZX-11).

This is another characteristic of the way Kawasaki operates. Models quite often have very long lives, or gradually evolve. There is no major difference between that first Z1 and the air-cooled GPz range. Add water-cooling and you have the GPZ900, which in turn metamorphosed into the GPZ1000RX and then the ZX-10 and the ZZ-R1100. Indeed, the

The first Superbike, Kawasaki's 900 cc **Z1**

One of the two-stroke engined KH and KE range - the **KE100B**

The GT750 - a favourite hack for despatch riders

last three models share the same 58 mm stroke. The bikes are obviously very different but it's difficult to put your finger on exactly why.

Other models have remained effectively untouched for over a decade: the KH and KE single-cylinder air-cooled two-stroke learner bikes, the GT550 and 750 shaft-drive hacks favoured by big city despatch riders and the GPz305 being prime examples. It's only when they step outside the performance field that Kawasakis seems less sure. Their first factory

customs were dire, you simply got the impression that the team that designed them didn't have their heart in the job. Only when the Classic range appeared in 1995 did they get it right.

Racing success

Kawasaki also have a more focused approach to racing than the other factories. The policy has always been to race the road bikes and with just a couple of exceptions that's what they've done. Even Simmonds' championship winner bore a strong resemblance to the twins they were selling in the late '60s and racing versions of the 500 and 750 cc triples were also sold as over-the-counter racers, the H1R and H2R. The 500 was in the forefront of the two-stroke assault on MV Agusta but wasn't a Grand Prix winner. It was the 750 that made the impact and carried the factory's image in F750 racing against the Suzuki triples and Yamaha fours.

The factory's decision to use green, usually regarded as an unlucky colour in sport, meant its bikes and personnel stood out and the phrase 'Green Meanies' fitted them perfectly. The Z1 motor soon became a full 1000 cc and powered Kawasaki's assault in F1 racing, notably in endurance which Kawasaki saw as being most closely related to its road bikes.

That didn't stop them dominating 250 and 350 cc GPs with a tandem twin two-stroke in the late '70s and early '80s, but their path-breaking monocoque 500 while a race winner never won a world title. When Superbike arrived, Kawasaki's road 750s weren't as track-friendly as the opposition's out-and-out race replicas. This makes Scott Russell's World title on the ZXR750 in 1993 even more praiseworthy, for the homologation bike, the ZXR750RR, was much heavier and much more of a road bike than the Italian and Japanese competition.

The company's Supersport 600 contenders have similarly been more sports-tourers than race-replicas, yet they too have been competitive on the track. Indeed, the flagship bike, the ZZ-R1100, is most definitely a sports tourer capable of carrying two people and their luggage at high speed in comfort all day and then doing it again the next day. Try that on one of the race replicas and you'll be in need of a course of treatment from a chiropractor.

Through doing it their way Kawasaki developed a brand loyalty for their performance bikes that kept the Z1's derivatives in production until the mid-'80s and turned the bike into a classic in its model life. You could even argue that the Z1 lives on in the shape of the 1100 Zephyr's GPz1100-derived motor. And that's another Kawasaki invention, the retro bike. But when you look at what many commentators refer to as the retro boom, especially in Japan, you find that it is no such thing. It is the Zephyr boom. Just another example of Japan's most surprising motorcycle manufacturer getting it right again.

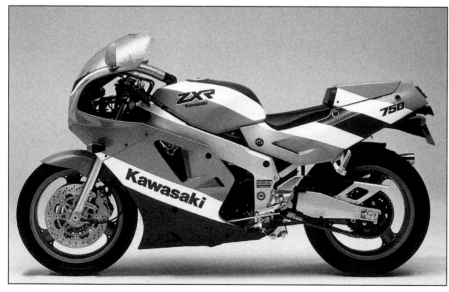

The high-performance ZXR750

The 550 and 750 Zephyrs

The alleged retro boom that swept all before it on the motorcycling scene of the early 1990s didn't really happen. What boom there was in back-to-basics bikes was limited to one family of bikes from one maker: Kawasaki's Zephyrs. In fact the boom really only happened in Japan where the first Zephyr, the 400 cc version, was a major sales success in that very fashion conscious market where a major attraction was the catalogue of after-market parts that could be used personalise a bike.

Kawasaki took the risk of exporting the retro concept for the 1991 model year with a family of three Zephyrs, the closely related ZR550 and 750 and the ZR1100. The idea was to hark back to the glory days of Kawasaki's double-overhead-cam air-cooled fours, the Z650, the GPz750 and of course the mighty Z1000.

The 550 was in fact an overbored version of the Japan-only 400 while the 750 shared the 66 x 54 mm bore and stroke of the old GPz750 and the other three-quarter litre air-cooled Kawasakis. Both were delivered in a cleverly designed package that looked very reminiscent of the old bikes but incorporated the benefits of progress in bike design in the intervening ten years.

The first 550, the B1, got that favourite '80s accessory the four-into-one exhaust as standard along with digital ignition, oil cooler, alloy swinging-arm, piggyback shocks, five-spoke alloy wheels and three disc brakes. Bolting that lot onto a standard Z1 would have cost you a lot of money back in 1980. The 750 got the same goodies but was recognisable by its three-spoke wheels.

The arrival of the Zephyrs coincided with a new type of motorcycle buyer in many countries, the rider returning to bikes after a long absence. These so-called 'born-again bikers' could relate immediately to the Zephyrs and, crucially, found them unthreatening in the way full-on sportsters were not. Other manufacturers scrabbled to

Kawasaki ZR750 D Zephyr

bring out their own retro bikes but Kawasaki had the crucial advantage of being there first and reaped the rewards. No other retro came anywhere near either the 550 or 750 in the sales charts.

The 550 felt comparatively small and was popular with newly qualified riders whereas the 750 came to transcend its image and be regarded as a good basic bike, not just a cute retro. Meanwhile, back in Japan, they'd started racing them in a new class known as Naked Bike.

The formula was basically right first time and the two smaller Zephyrs have remained almost totally unchanged from their launch in 1991 with the 550B1 and 750C1 until the 1996 model year. Even then the 550 escaped and went on to the become the B6 while the 750 got its first important modifications and became the 750D1. Even then the changes were mainly cosmetic. The modern, racy

three-spoked alloy wheels were swapped for a totally retro set of spoked wheels and to emphasise the Z1 heritage there was a paint option of the very same brown and orange two-tone scheme that graced Kawasaki's very first DOHC four, although they called it 'luminous chestnut brown and luminous tangerine orange'. Quite.

No other bike took part in the early '90s retro boom although later models like the Suzuki Bandits and Triumph Speed Triples did re-popularise the idea of an unfaired bike. They are not the same thing. The Zephyr can trace its ancestry directly back to the machines it takes its styling cues and its riding position from, it runs twin shocks, a tubular steel frame and an air-cooled motor. There are one or two other bikes that could truthfully be labelled as retros but the Zephyrs aren't just the only successful retros, they're the most honest retros.

Acknowledgements

Our thanks are due to Paul Branson Motorcycles of Yeovil who supplied the ZR550 and Bridge Motorcycle World of Exeter who supplied the ZR750 featured in the photographs throughout this manual. Thanks are also due to Kawasaki Motors (UK) Ltd for the supply of technical information and permission to use some of the line drawings featured. We would also like to thank the Avon Rubber Company, who kindly supplied information and technical assistance on tyre fitting, and NGK Spark plugs (UK) Ltd for information on spark plug maintenance and electrode conditions.

Thanks are also due to the Kawasaki Information Service and Kel Edge for supplying colour transparencies, and to Phil Flowers for carrying out the cover photography. The introduction, "Kawasaki - The Green Meanies" was written by Julian Ryder.

About this Manual

The aim of this manual is to help you get the best value from your motorcycle. It can do so in several ways. It can help you decide what work must be done, even if you choose to have it done by a dealer; it provides information and procedures for routine maintenance and servicing; and it offers diagnostic and repair procedures to follow when trouble occurs.

We hope you use the manual to tackle the work yourself. For many simpler jobs, doing it yourself may be quicker than arranging an appointment to get the motorcycle into a dealer and making the trips to leave it and

pick it up. More importantly, a lot of money can be saved by avoiding the expense the shop must pass on to you to cover its labour and overhead costs. An added benefit is the sense of satisfaction and accomplishment that you feel after doing the job yourself.

References to the left or right side of the motorcycle assume you are sitting on the seat, facing forward.

We take great pride in the accuracy of information given in this manual, but motorcycle manufacturers make alterations and design changes during the production run of a particular motorcycle of which they do not inform us. No liability can be accepted by the authors or publishers for loss, damage or injury caused by any errors in, or omissions from, the information given.

Professional mechanics are trained in safe working procedures. However enthusiastic you may be about getting on with the job at hand, take the time to ensure that your safety is not put at risk. A moment's lack of attention can result in an accident, as can failure to observe simple precautions.

There will always be new ways of having accidents, and the following is not a comprehensive list of all dangers; it is intended rather to make you aware of the risks and to encourage a safe approach to all work you carry out on your bike.

Asbestos

● Certain friction, insulating, sealing and other products - such as brake pads, clutch linings, gaskets, etc. - contain asbestos. Extreme care must be taken to avoid inhalation of dust from such products since it is hazardous to health. If in doubt, assume that they do contain asbestos.

Fire

● Remember at all times that petrol is highly flammable. Never smoke or have any kind of naked flame around, when working on the vehicle. But the risk does not end there - a spark caused by an electrical short-circuit, by two metal surfaces contacting each other, by careless use of tools, or even by static electricity built up in your body under certain conditions, can ignite petrol vapour, which in a confined space is highly explosive. Never use petrol as a cleaning solvent. Use an approved safety solvent.

● Always disconnect the battery earth terminal before working on any part of the fuel or electrical system, and never risk spilling fuel on to a hot engine or exhaust.

● It is recommended that a fire extinguisher of a type suitable for fuel and electrical fires is kept handy in the garage or workplace at all times. Never try to extinguish a fuel or electrical fire with water.

Fumes

● Certain fumes are highly toxic and can quickly cause unconsciousness and even death if inhaled to any extent. Petrol vapour comes into this category, as do the vapours from certain solvents such as trichloroethylene. Any draining or pouring of such volatile fluids should be done in a well ventilated area.

● When using cleaning fluids and solvents, read the instructions carefully. Never use materials from unmarked containers - they may give off poisonous vapours.

● Never run the engine of a motor vehicle in an enclosed space such as a garage. Exhaust fumes contain carbon monoxide which is extremely poisonous; if you need to run the engine, always do so in the open air or at least have the rear of the vehicle outside the workplace.

The battery

● Never cause a spark, or allow a naked light near the vehicle's battery. It will normally be giving off a certain amount of hydrogen gas, which is highly explosive.

● Always disconnect the battery ground (earth) terminal before working on the fuel or electrical systems (except where noted).

● If possible, loosen the filler plugs or cover when charging the battery from an external source. Do not charge at an excessive rate or the battery may burst.

● Take care when topping up, cleaning or carrying the battery. The acid electrolyte, evenwhen diluted, is very corrosive and should not be allowed to contact the eyes or skin. Always wear rubber gloves and goggles or a face shield. If you ever need to prepare electrolyte yourself, always add the acid slowly to the water; never add the water to the acid.

Electricity

● When using an electric power tool, inspection light etc., always ensure that the appliance is correctly connected to its plug and that, where necessary, it is properly grounded (earthed). Do not use such appliances in damp conditions and, again, beware of creating a spark or applying excessive heat in the vicinity of fuel or fuel vapour. Also ensure that the appliances meet national safety standards.

● A severe electric shock can result from touching certain parts of the electrical system, such as the spark plug wires (HT leads), when the engine is running or being cranked, particularly if components are damp or the insulation is defective. Where an electronic ignition system is used, the secondary (HT) voltage is much higher and could prove fatal.

Remember...

✗ **Don't** start the engine without first ascertaining that the transmission is in neutral.

✗ **Don't** suddenly remove the pressure cap from a hot cooling system - cover it with a cloth and release the pressure gradually first, or you may get scalded by escaping coolant.

✗ **Don't** attempt to drain oil until you are sure it has cooled sufficiently to avoid scalding you.

✗ **Don't** grasp any part of the engine or exhaust system without first ascertaining that it is cool enough not to burn you.

✗ **Don't** allow brake fluid or antifreeze to contact the machine's paintwork or plastic components.

✗ **Don't** siphon toxic liquids such as fuel, hydraulic fluid or antifreeze by mouth, or allow them to remain on your skin.

✗ **Don't** inhale dust - it may be injurious to health (see Asbestos heading).

✗ **Don't** allow any spilled oil or grease to remain on the floor - wipe it up right away, before someone slips on it.

✗ **Don't** use ill-fitting spanners or other tools which may slip and cause injury.

✗ **Don't** lift a heavy component which may be beyond your capability - get assistance.

✗ **Don't** rush to finish a job or take unverified short cuts.

✗ **Don't** allow children or animals in or around an unattended vehicle.

✗ **Don't** inflate a tyre above the recommended pressure. Apart from overstressing the carcass, in extreme cases the tyre may blow off forcibly.

✔ **Do** ensure that the machine is supported securely at all times. This is especially important when the machine is blocked up to aid wheel or fork removal.

✔ **Do** take care when attempting to loosen a stubborn nut or bolt. It is generally better to pull on a spanner, rather than push, so that if you slip, you fall away from the machine rather than onto it.

✔ **Do** wear eye protection when using power tools such as drill, sander, bench grinder etc.

✔ **Do** use a barrier cream on your hands prior to undertaking dirty jobs - it will protect your skin from infection as well as making the dirt easier to remove afterwards; but make sure your hands aren't left slippery. Note that long-term contact with used engine oil can be a health hazard.

✔ **Do** keep loose clothing (cuffs, ties etc. and long hair) well out of the way of moving mechanical parts.

✔ **Do** remove rings, wristwatch etc., before working on the vehicle - especially the electrical system.

✔ **Do** keep your work area tidy - it is only too easy to fall over articles left lying around.

✔ **Do** exercise caution when compressing springs for removal or installation. Ensure that the tension is applied and released in a controlled manner, using suitable tools which preclude the possibility of the spring escaping violently.

✔ **Do** ensure that any lifting tackle used has a safe working load rating adequate for the job.

✔ **Do** get someone to check periodically that all is well, when working alone on the vehicle.

✔ **Do** carry out work in a logical sequence and check that everything is correctly assembled and tightened afterwards.

✔ **Do** remember that your vehicle's safety affects that of yourself and others. If in doubt on any point, get professional advice.

● If in spite of following these precautions, you are unfortunate enough to injure yourself, seek medical attention as soon as possible.

Frame and engine numbers

The frame serial number is stamped into the right-hand side of the steering head. The engine number is stamped into the top of the right-hand side of the crankcase, behind the cylinder block. Both of these numbers should be recorded and kept in a safe place so they can be furnished to law enforcement officials in the event of a theft. There is also a carburettor identification number on the side of each carburettor body.

The frame serial number, engine serial number and carburettor identification number should also be kept in a handy place (such as with your driver's licence) so they are always available when purchasing or ordering parts for your machine.

The procedures in this manual identify the bikes by model code. To determine the model code, refer to the frame numbers given in the accompanying table. Note that the production year may not necessarily coincide with the date of registration. Engine numbers for all 550 models commence KZ550DE060001 and for all 750 models KZ750EE150001.

UK Models	Year	Frame no.
ZR550 B2	1991	ZR550B-004001 to 012000
ZR550 B3	1992	ZR550B-012001 to 022000
ZR550 B4	1993	ZR550B-022001 to 030000
ZR550 B5	1994	ZR550B-030001 to 036000
ZR550 B6	1995/6/7	ZR550B-036001 on
ZR750 C1	1991	ZR750C-000001 to 018500
ZR750 C2	1992	ZR750C-018501 to 035000
ZR750 C3	1993	ZR750C-035001 to 040000
ZR750 C4	1994/5	ZR750C-040001 on
ZR750 C5	1995/6	ZR750C-050001 on
ZR750 D1	1996/7	ZR750D-000001 on

US models	Year	Frame no.
ZR550 B1	1990	JKAZRFB1*LA000001 to 004000
ZR550 B2	1991	JKAZRFB1*MA004001 on
ZR550 B3[†]	1992	JKAZRFB1*NA012001 to 022000
ZR550 B4[†]	1993	JKAZRFB1*PA022001 on
ZR750 C1	1991	JKAZRDC1*MA00001 to 018500
ZR750 C2	1992	JKAZRDC1*NA018501 on
ZR750 C3[†]	1993	JKAZRDC1*PA035001 on

[†]Canada only

The frame number is stamped on the steering head

The engine number is stamped into the top of the crankcase behind the cylinder block

Buying spare parts

Once you have found all the identification numbers, record them for reference when buying parts. Since the manufacturers change specifications, parts and vendors (companies that manufacture various components on the machine), providing the ID numbers is the only way to be reasonably sure that you are buying the correct parts.

Whenever possible, take the worn part to the dealer so direct comparison with the new component can be made. Along the trail from the manufacturer to the parts shelf, there are numerous places that the part can end up with the wrong number or be listed incorrectly.

The two places to purchase new parts for your motorcycle - the accessory store and the franchised dealer - differ in the type of parts they carry. While dealers can obtain virtually every part for your motorcycle, the accessory dealer is usually limited to normal high wear items such as shock absorbers, tune-up parts, various engine gaskets, cables, chains, brake parts, etc. Rarely will an accessory outlet have major suspension components, cylinders, transmission gears, or cases.

Used parts can be obtained for roughly half the price of new ones, but you can't always be sure of what you're getting. Once again, take your worn part to the breaker (wrecking yard) for direct comparison.

Whether buying new, used or rebuilt parts, the best course is to deal with someone who specialises in parts for your particular make.

1 Engine/transmission oil level

Before you start:
✔ Take the motorcycle on a short run to allow it to reach normal operating temperature.

Caution: Do not run the engine in an enclosed space such as a garage or shop.

✔ Stop the engine and support the motorcycle in an upright position on level ground, using an auxiliary stand or an assistant if required. Allow it to stand for a few minutes to allow the oil level to stabilise.

✔ The oil level is viewed through the window in the clutch cover on the right-hand side of the engine. Wipe the glass clean before inspection to make the check easier.

Bike care:
● If you have to add oil frequently, you should check whether you have any oil leaks. If there is no sign of oil leakage from the joints and gaskets the engine could be burning oil (see *Fault Finding*).

The correct oil
● Modern, high-revving engines place great demands on their oil. It is very important that the correct oil for your bike is used.
● Always top up with a good quality oil of the specified type and viscosity and do not overfill the engine.

Oil type	API grade SE, SF or SG
Oil viscosity	SAE 10W/40, 10W/50, 20W/40 or 20W/50

1 Wipe the oil level window in the clutch cover so that it is clean.

2 On 550 models, with the motorcycle held vertical, the oil level should lie between the upper and lower level lines marked on the clutch cover (arrowed).

3 On 750 models, with the motorcycle held vertical, the oil level should lie between the H and L lines marked on the plate behind the window (arrowed).

4 If the level is below the lower line, remove the filler cap from the top of the clutch cover.

5 Top the engine up with the recommended grade and type of oil, to bring the level up to the upper line (550 models) or the H line (750 models) on the window.

2 Suspension, steering and drive chain

Suspension and steering:
● Check that the front and rear suspension operates smoothly without binding.
● Check that the suspension is adjusted as required.
● Check that the steering moves smoothly from lock-to-lock.
● Check that all nuts and bolts, including axles and controls, are properly tightened.

Drive chain:
● Check that the drive chain slack isn't excessive, and adjust if necessary (see Chapter 1).
● If the chain looks dry, lubricate it (see Chapter 1).

3 Brake fluid levels

Bike care:
● The fluid in the front and rear brake master cylinder reservoirs will drop slightly as the brake pads wear down.
● If either fluid reservoir requires repeated topping-up this is an indication of an hydraulic leak somewhere in the system, which should be investigated immediately.

Before you start:
✔ Position the motorcycle on its stand, and turn the handlebars until the top of the master cylinder is as level as possible. If necessary, tilt the motorcycle to make it level. Remove the seat (see Chapter 7) for access to the rear brake fluid reservoir.
✔ Make sure you have the correct hydraulic fluid - DOT 4 is recommended. Wrap a rag around the reservoir being worked on to ensure that any spillage does not come into contact with painted surfaces.

● Check for signs of fluid leakage from the hydraulic hoses and components - if found, rectify immediately.
● Check the operation of both brakes before taking the machine on the road; if there is evidence of air in the system (spongy feel to lever or pedal), it must be bled as described in Chapter 6.

> ⚠ **Warning: Brake and clutch hydraulic fluid can harm your eyes and damage painted surfaces, so use extreme caution when handling and pouring it and cover surrounding surfaces with rag. Do not use fluid that has been standing open for some time, as it absorbs moisture from the air which can cause a dangerous loss of braking effectiveness.**

1 The front brake fluid level is checked via the sightglass in the reservoir - it must be above the low level mark (arrowed).

2 If the level is below the mark, remove the two screws (arrowed) to free the brake fluid reservoir cover, and remove the cover, diaphragm plate and diaphragm.

3 Top up with new clean hydraulic fluid of the recommended type until the level is up to the high level mark on the inside of the reservoir (arrowed). Take care to avoid spills (see **Warning** above).

4 Ensure that the diaphragm is correctly seated before installing the plate and cover.

5 The rear brake fluid level can be seen through the translucent body of the reservoir which is located under the seat. Remove the seat for access (see Chapter 7). The fluid must lie between the UPPER and LOWER level marks (arrowed). To top up, unscrew the cap, then remove the plate and diaphragm.

4 Legal and safety checks

Lighting and signalling:
● Take a minute to check that the headlight, taillight, brake light, instrument lights and turn signals all work correctly.
● Check that the horn sounds when the switch is operated.
● A working speedometer is a statutory requirement in the UK.

Safety:
● Check that the throttle grip rotates smoothly and snaps shut when released,

and that it does so in all steering positions. Also check for the correct amount of freeplay (see Chapter 1).
● Check that the clutch lever operates smoothly and with the correct amount of freeplay (see Chapter 1).
● Check that the brake pads have not worn down to or beyond their wear limit - there must be at least 1 mm of lining left on each brake pad (see Chapter 1).
● Check that the engine shuts off when the kill switch is operated.

● Check that sidestand return spring holds the stand securely up when retracted. The same applies to the centre stand (where fitted).

Fuel:
● This may seem obvious, but check that you have enough fuel to complete your journey. If you notice signs of fuel leakage - rectify the cause immediately.
● Ensure you use the correct grade unleaded fuel - see Chapter 3 Specifications.

5 Tyres

Tyre care:

● Check the tyres carefully for cuts, tears, embedded nails or other sharp objects and excessive wear. Operation of the motorcycle with excessively worn tyres is extremely hazardous, as traction and handling are directly affected.
● Check the condition of the tyre valve and ensure the dust cap is in place.
● Pick out any stones or nails which may have become embedded in the tyre tread. If left, they will eventually penetrate through the casing and cause a puncture.
● If tyre damage is apparent, or unexplained loss of pressure is experienced, seek the advice of a tyre fitting specialist without delay.

Tyre tread depth:

● At the time of writing UK law requires that tread depth must be at least 1 mm over 3/4 of the tread breadth all the way around the tyre, with no bald patches. Many riders, however, consider 2 mm tread depth minimum to be a safer limit. Kawasaki recommend the following minimum tread depths.

Front . . . . .1 mm
Rear - below 80 mph (130 km/h) . . . .2 mm
Rear - above 80 mph (130 km/h) . . . .3 mm

● Many tyres now incorporate wear indicators in the tread. Find the wear indicator pointer on the tyre sidewall (this will vary according to the tyre fitted) to locate the indicator bar; replace the tyre if the tread has worn down to the bar.

1 Check the tyre pressures when the tyres are **cold** and keep them properly inflated.

2 Measure tread depth at the centre of the tyre using a tread depth gauge.

3 Tyre tread wear indicator bar location marking (arrowed) - usually either an arrow, a triangle or the letters TWI on the sidewall.

The correct pressures:

● The tyres must be checked when **cold**, not immediately after riding. Note that low tyre pressures may cause the tyre to slip on the rim or come off. High tyre pressures will cause abnormal tread wear and unsafe handling.

● Use an accurate pressure gauge.
● Proper air pressure will increase tyre life and provide maximum stability and ride comfort.

Front . . . . .28 psi (2.0 Bar)
Rear . . . . .32 psi (2.2 Bar)

Chapter 1
Routine maintenance and servicing

Contents

Degrees of difficulty

| Easy, suitable for novice with little experience | Fairly easy, suitable for beginner with some experience | Fairly difficult, suitable for competent DIY mechanic | Difficult, suitable for experienced DIY mechanic 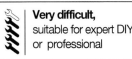 | Very difficult, suitable for expert DIY or professional |

Engine

Spark plugs
  ZR550
    B1 and B2 US models . . . .   NGK D9EA or Nippondenso X27ES-U
    All other models . . . .   NGK DR9EA or Nippondenso X27ESR-U
    Electrode gap . . . .   0.6 to 0.7 mm
  ZR750
    UK C1, C2, C3 and C4 models . . . .   NGK DR8ES or Nippondenso X27ESR-U
    US C1, C2, C3 and C4 models . . . .   NGK D9EA or Nippondenso X27ES-U
    All other models . . . .   NGK DR9EA or Nippondenso X27ESR-U
    Electrode gap . . . .   0.6 to 0.7 mm
Engine idle speed
  ZR550
    UK models . . . .   1300 ± 50 rpm
    US models . . . .   1200 ± 50 rpm
  ZR750 . . . .   1100 ± 50 rpm
Carburettor synchronisation - max difference between carburettors . .   2 cm Hg
Cylinder identification . . . .   from left to right, numbered 1, 2, 3 and 4
Valve clearances (COLD engine)
  ZR550
    Intake valves . . . .   0.10 to 0.20 mm
    Exhaust valves . . . .   0.15 to 0.25 mm
  ZR750 - intake and exhaust . . . .   0.08 to 0.18 mm
Cylinder compression
  ZR550 . . . .   128 to 198 psi (9 to 14 Bar)
  ZR750 . . . .   109 to 170 psi (7.7 to 12 Bar)
Oil pressure (with engine warm - oil at 90°C)
  ZR550 . . . .   31 to 36 psi (2.2 to 2.5 Bar) at 4000 rpm
  ZR750 . . . .   28 to 36 psi (2.0 to 2.5 Bar) at 4000 rpm

Miscellaneous

Drive chain
  Freeplay . . . .   35 to 40 mm
  Stretch limit (21 pin length - see text) . . . .   323 mm
Brake pad friction material minimum thickness . . . .   1 mm
Freeplay adjustments
  Clutch lever . . . .   2.0 to 3.0 mm
  Throttle grip . . . .   2.0 to 3.0 mm (see text)
  Choke lever . . . .   2.0 to 3.0 mm
Brake pedal - distance below top of footrest
  ZR550 . . . .   35 mm
  ZR750 . . . .   40 mm
Tyre pressures (cold)
  Front . . . .   28 psi (2.0 Bar)
  Rear . . . .   32 psi (2.25 Bar)
Tyre tread depth . . . .   see Daily (pre-ride) checks

Recommended lubricants and fluids

Drive chain lubricant . . . .   Heavy motor oil (SAE 90), or aerosol chain lube suitable for O-ring chains
Engine/transmission oil type . . . .   API grade SE, SF or SG motor oil
Engine/transmission oil viscosity . . . .   SAE 10W40, 10W50, 20W40 or 20W50
Engine/transmission oil capacity
  ZR550
    Oil change . . . .   2.6 litres
    Oil and filter change . . . .   2.7 litres
    Following engine overhaul - dry engine, new filter . . . .   3.0 litres
  ZR750
    Oil change . . . .   3.0 litres
    Oil and filter change . . . .   3.5 litres
    Following engine overhaul - dry engine, new filter . . . .   3.6 litres
Brake fluid . . . .   DOT 4

Recommended lubricants and fluids (continued)

Fork oil type	SAE 10W20 fork oil
Fork oil capacity	
ZR550	
Oil change	350 cc
Following fork overhaul (completely dry)	408 to 416 cc
ZR750	
C1 and C2 models	
Oil change	400 cc
Following fork overhaul (completely dry)	466 to 474 cc
C3, C4 and C5 models	
Oil change	417 cc
Following fork overhaul (completely dry)	490 cc
D1 model	
Oil change	400 cc
Following fork overhaul (completely dry)	463 to 471 cc
Fork oil level*	
ZR550	96 to 100 mm*
ZR750	
C1 and C2 models	108 to 112 mm*
C3, C4 and C5 models	88 to 92 mm*
D1 model	111 to 115 mm*

*Oil level is measured from the top of the tube with the fork spring removed and the leg fully compressed.

Miscellaneous

Wheel bearings	Multi-purpose grease
Swingarm bearings	Multi-purpose grease
Steering head bearings	Multi-purpose grease
Inner cables	Cable lubricant
Cable ends	Multi-purpose grease
Lever and stand pivot points	Motor oil
Throttle grip	Multi-purpose grease or dry film lubricant

Torque settings

Chain adjuster clamp bolts	39 Nm
Torque arm nuts	
ZR550	32 Nm
ZR750	34 Nm
Spark plugs	14 Nm
Cylinder head nuts and bolts	
ZR550	
Cylinder head 8 mm nuts	25 Nm
Cylinder head 6 mm bolts	12 Nm
Cylinder head 6 mm nuts	9.8 Nm
ZR750	
Cylinder head bolts	29 Nm
Cylinder head nuts	39 Nm
Oil drain plug	29 Nm
Oil filter bolt	20 Nm
Steering stem bolt	39 Nm
Pulse generator assembly cover bolts	10 Nm
Fork oil drain screw	1.5 Nm
Fork top bolt	23 Nm
Fork clamp bolts	
ZR550	21 Nm
ZR750	20 Nm
Shock absorber lower mounting nuts	39 Nm
Swingarm pivot nut	
ZR550	93 Nm
ZR750	109 Nm
Oil gallery plug	15 Nm

Maintenance schedule - ZR550 B & ZR750 C models

Note: *The daily (pre-ride) checks at the beginning of the manual cover those items which should be inspected on a daily basis. Always perform the pre-ride inspection at every maintenance interval (in addition to the procedures listed). The intervals listed below are the intervals recommended by the manufacturer for the models covered in this manual. Your owner's handbook may have different intervals if your model is not specifically covered by this manual. If in doubt, check with a Kawasaki dealer.*

Daily (pre-ride)

☐ See *'Daily (pre-ride) checks'* at the beginning of this manual.

After the initial 500 miles (800 km)

Note: *This check is usually performed by a Kawasaki dealer after the first 500 miles (800 km) from new. Thereafter, maintenance is carried out according to the following intervals of the schedule.*

Every 200 miles (300 km)

Carry out all the items under the Daily (pre-ride) checks, plus the following

☐ Clean and lubricate the drive chain (Section 1).

Every 500 miles (800 km)

Carry out all the items under the Daily (pre-ride) checks, plus the following

☐ Check and adjust drive chain freeplay (Section 2).

Every 3000 miles (5000 km) or six months

Carry out all the items under the Daily (pre-ride) checks and the 200 mile (300 km) and 500 mile (800 km) check, plus the following

☐ Clean and check the spark plugs (Section 3).
☐ Check the air suction valve (US models only) (Section 4).
☐ Check and adjust the engine idle speed (Section 5).
☐ Check carburettor synchronisation (Section 6).
☐ Check the evaporative emission control (EVAP) system (California models only) (Section 7).
☐ Check and empty the air filter drain reservoir (750 models only) (Section 8).
☐ Change the engine oil (Section 9).
☐ Check the operation of the clutch (Section 10).
☐ Check for drive chain wear and stretch (Section 11).
☐ Check the brake pads for wear (Section 12).
☐ Check the operation of the brakes, and for fluid leakage (Section 13).
☐ Check the steering head bearing freeplay (Section 14).
☐ Check the tyre and wheel condition, and the tyre tread depth (Section 15).
☐ Check and lubricate the stands, lever pivots and cables (Section 16).
☐ Check the battery electrolyte level (ZR550 B1, B2, B3 and B4 models only) (Section 17).

Every 6000 miles (10 000 km) or twelve months

Carry out all the items under the 3000 mile (5000 km) check, plus the following:

☐ Check the valve clearances (Section 18).
☐ Clean the air filter element (Section 21).
☐ Check throttle/choke cable operation and freeplay (Section 22).
☐ Change the engine oil and replace the oil filter (Section 23).
☐ Check the fuel hoses and system components (Section 24).
☐ Tighten the cylinder head nuts (Section 25).
☐ Check the front and rear suspension (Section 26).
☐ Re-grease the swingarm pivot and bearings (Section 27).
☐ Check the tightness of all nuts and bolts (Section 28).

Every 12 000 miles (20 000 km) or two years

Carry out all the items under the 6000 mile (10 000 km) check, plus the following:

☐ Replace the air filter (Section 29).
☐ Change the brake fluid (Section 30).
☐ Re-grease the steering head bearings (Section 31).

Every 18 000 miles (30 000 km) or two years

Carry out all the items under the 6000 mile (10 000 km) check, plus the following:

☐ Change the front fork oil (Section 33).

Every two years

☐ Replace the brake master cylinder and caliper seals (Section 34).

Every four years

☐ Replace the brake hoses (Section 35).
☐ Replace the fuel hoses (Section 36).

Non-scheduled maintenance

☐ Check the headlight aim (Section 37).
☐ Check the wheel bearings (Section 38).
☐ Check the cylinder compression (Section 39).
☐ Check the engine oil pressure (Section 40).

Maintenance schedule - ZR750 D model

Note: *The daily (pre-ride) checks at the beginning of the manual cover those items which should be inspected on a daily basis. Always perform the pre-ride inspection at every maintenance interval (in addition to the procedures listed). The intervals listed below are the intervals recommended by the manufacturer for the models covered in this manual. Your owner's handbook may have different intervals if your model is not specifically covered by this manual. If in doubt, check with a Kawasaki dealer.*

Daily (pre-ride)
☐ See *'Daily (pre-ride) checks'* at the beginning of this manual.

After the initial 600 miles (1000 km)
Note: *This check is usually performed by a Kawasaki dealer after the first 600 miles (1000 km) from new. Thereafter, maintenance is carried out according to the following intervals of the schedule.*

Every 400 miles (600 km)
Carry out all the items under the Daily (pre-ride) checks, plus the following
☐ Clean and lubricate the drive chain (Section 1).

Every 600 miles (1000 km)
Carry out all the items under the Daily (pre-ride) checks, plus the following
☐ Check and adjust drive chain freeplay (Section 2).

Every 4000 miles (6000 km) or six months
Carry out all the items under the Daily (pre-ride) checks and the 400 mile (600 km) and 600 mile (1000 km) check, plus the following
☐ Clean and check the spark plugs (Section 3).
☐ Check the air suction valve (US models only) (Section 4).
☐ Check the evaporative emission control (EVAP) system (California models only) (Section 7).
☐ Check and empty the air filter drain reservoir (Section 8).
☐ Change the engine oil (Section 9).
☐ Check the operation of the clutch (Section 10).
☐ Check for drive chain wear and stretch (Section 11).
☐ Check the brake pads for wear (Section 12).
☐ Check the operation of the brakes, and for fluid leakage (Section 13).
☐ Check the steering head bearing freeplay (Section 14).
☐ Check the tyre and wheel condition, and the tyre tread depth (Section 15).
☐ Check and lubricate the stands, lever pivots and cables (Section 16).

Every 7500 miles (12 000 km) or twelve months
Carry out all the items under the 4000 mile (6000 km) check, plus the following:
☐ Check and adjust the engine idle speed (Section 19).
☐ Check carburettor synchronisation (Section 20).
☐ Check the valve clearances (Section 18).
☐ Clean the air filter element (Section 21).
☐ Check throttle/choke cable operation and freeplay (Section 22).
☐ Change the engine oil and replace the oil filter (Section 23).
☐ Check the fuel hoses and system components (Section 24).
☐ Check the front and rear suspension (Section 26).
☐ Re-grease the swingarm pivot and bearings (Section 27).
☐ Check the tightness of all nuts and bolts (Section 28).

Every 15 000 miles (24 000 km) or two years
Carry out all the items under the 7500 mile (12 000 km) check, plus the following:
☐ Replace the air filter (Section 29).
☐ Change the brake fluid (Section 30).
☐ Re-grease the steering head bearings (Section 31).
☐ Change the front fork oil (Section 32).

Every four years
☐ Replace the brake master cylinder and caliper seals (Section 34).
☐ Replace the brake hoses (Section 35).
☐ Replace the fuel hoses (Section 36).

Non-scheduled maintenance
☐ Check the headlight aim (Section 37).
☐ Check the wheel bearings (Section 38).
☐ Check the cylinder compression (Section 39).
☐ Check the engine oil pressure (Section 40).

Component locations on right-hand side

1   Rear brake fluid reservoir
2   Battery
3   Front brake fluid reservoir
4   Throttle cable upper adjuster

5   Front fork seals
6   Brake pads
7   Engine oil gallery plug
8   Engine oil level window

9   Engine oil filler cap
10 Clutch cable lower adjuster
11 Air filter drain reservoir
    (750 models)

12 Rear brake light switch and
    pedal height adjuster

Component locations on left-hand side

1   Clutch cable upper adjuster
2   Steering head bearings
3   Spark plugs and valves

4   Fuel tap filter
5   Throttle stop screw (idle speed)
6   Air filter

7   Drive chain adjusters
8   Drive chain
9   Swingarm pivot bearings

10 Engine oil filter
11 Engine oil drain plug
12 Front brake pads

Introduction

1 This Chapter is designed to help the home mechanic maintain his/her motorcycle for safety, economy, long life and peak performance.
2 Deciding where to start or plug into the routine maintenance schedule depends on several factors. If the warranty period on your motorcycle has just expired, and if it has been maintained according to the warranty standards, you may want to pick up routine maintenance as it coincides with the next mileage or calendar interval. If you have owned the machine for some time but

have never performed any maintenance on it, then you may want to start at the nearest interval and include some additional procedures to ensure that nothing important is overlooked. If you have just had a major engine overhaul, then you may want to start the maintenance routine from the beginning. If you have a used machine and have no knowledge of its history or maintenance record, you may desire to combine all the checks into one large service initially and then settle into the maintenance schedule prescribed.

3 Before beginning any maintenance or repair, the machine should be cleaned thoroughly, especially around the oil filter, spark plugs, valve cover, side panels, carburettors, etc. Cleaning will help ensure that dirt does not contaminate the engine and will allow you to detect wear and damage that could otherwise easily go unnoticed.
4 Certain maintenance information is sometimes printed on decals attached to the motorcycle. If the information on the decals differs from that included here, use the information on the decal.

Every 200 miles (300 km) - ZR550 B & ZR750 C
Every 400 miles (600 km) - ZR750 D

1 Drive chain -
cleaning and lubrication

1 Place the machine on its centre stand (where fitted), or support the machine on an auxiliary stand so that the rear wheel is off the ground. Rotate the back wheel whilst cleaning and lubricating the chain to access all the links.
2 Wash the chain in paraffin (kerosene), then wipe it off and allow it to dry, using compressed air if available. If the chain is excessively dirty it should be removed from the machine and allowed to soak in the paraffin (see Chapter 5).
Caution: Don't use petrol (gasoline), solvent or other cleaning fluids which

might damage the internal sealing properties of the chain. Don't use high-pressure water. The entire process shouldn't take longer than ten minutes - if it does, the O-rings in the chain rollers could be damaged.
3 The best time to lubricate the chain is after the motorcycle has been ridden, as when the chain is warm the lubricant penetrates the joints between the side plates better than when cold.
4 Apply the specified lubricant (see Specifications at the beginning of the Chapter) to the area where the side plates overlap - not to the middle of the rollers **(see illustration)**. After applying the lubricant, let it soak in for a few minutes before wiping off any excess.
Caution: If you use an aerosol drive chain lubricant, make sure it is marked as being

suitable for O-ring chains, otherwise the O-rings could be damaged by the lubricant solvents and additives.

1.4 Apply the specified lubricant to the overlap between the sideplates

Every 500 miles (800 km) - ZR550 B & ZR750 C
Every 600 miles (1000 km) - ZR750 D

2 Drive chain - freeplay check and adjustment

Check

1 A neglected drive chain won't last long and can quickly damage the sprockets. Routine chain adjustment will ensure maximum chain and sprocket life.
2 To check the chain, shift the transmission into neutral and make sure the ignition switch is OFF. Rotate the rear wheel until the chain is positioned with the tightest point at the centre of its bottom run, then place the machine on its sidestand. Make sure that the adjuster is in

the same position on each side relative to the cut-out in the swingarm.
3 Measure the amount of freeplay on the chain's bottom run, at a point midway between the two sprockets, then compare your measurement to the value listed in this Chapter's Specifications **(see illustration)**. Since the chain will rarely wear evenly, rotate the rear wheel so that another section of chain can be checked; do this several times to check the entire length of chain. In some cases where lubrication has been neglected, corrosion and galling may cause the links to bind and kink, which effectively shortens the chain's length. If the chain is tight between the sprockets, rusty or kinked, or if any of the pins are loose or the rollers damaged, it's time to

replace it with a new one. If you find a tight area, mark it with felt pen or paint, and repeat the measurement after the bike has been

2.3 Measuring drive chain freeplay

2.5a Slacken the chain adjuster clamp bolt (arrowed) on each end of the swingarm . . .

2.5b . . . and the brake torque arm nuts (arrowed)

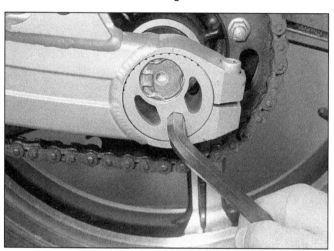

2.6a Turn the adjuster using a 12 mm Allen key

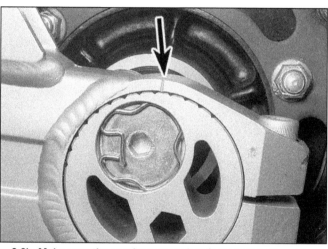

2.6b Make sure the notches on each adjuster are in the same position relative to the cut-out in the swingarm (arrowed)

ridden. If the chain is still tight in the same area, it may be damaged or worn. Because a tight or kinked chain can damage the transmission output shaft bearing, it's a good idea to replace it.

Adjustment

4 Rotate the rear wheel until the chain is positioned with the tightest point at the centre of its bottom run, then place the machine on its sidestand.
5 Slacken the chain adjuster clamp bolt on each end of the swingarm, and the nuts securing the brake torque arm to the swingarm and the rear brake caliper bracket (see illustrations).
6 Using a 12 mm Allen key (one is supplied in the motorcycle's tool kit which is stored under the seat), rotate the chain adjuster on each side of the swingarm evenly until the amount of freeplay specified at the beginning of the Chapter is obtained at the centre of the bottom run of the chain (see illustration). You will probably find that as you turn one adjuster

the other adjuster turns as well. Following chain adjustment, make sure that each adjuster is in the same position relative to the cut-out in each side of the swingarm (see illustration). It is important that the same notch on each adjuster aligns with the swingarm cut-out; if not, the rear wheel will be out of alignment with the front.

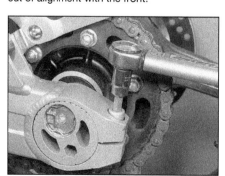

2.8a Tighten the adjuster clamp bolts . . .

7 If there is a discrepancy in the chain adjuster positions, adjust one of the chain adjusters so that its position is exactly the same as the other. Check the chain freeplay as described above and readjust if necessary.
8 Tighten the adjuster clamp bolts and the torque arm nuts to the specified torque setting (see illustrations).

2.8b . . . and the torque arm nuts to the specified torque setting

Every 3000 miles (5000 km) - ZR550 B & ZR750 C
Every 4000 miles (6000 km) - ZR750 D

3 Spark plugs -
gap check and adjustment

1 Make sure your spark plug socket is the correct size before attempting to remove the plugs - a suitable one is supplied in the motorcycle's tool kit which is stored under the seat.
2 Remove the seat (see Chapter 7) and disconnect the battery negative (–) lead.
3 Clean the area around the plug caps to prevent any dirt falling into the spark plug channels.
4 Check that the cylinder location is marked on each plug lead, then pull the spark plug cap off each spark plug (see illustration). Using either the plug removing tool supplied in the bike's toolkit or a socket type wrench,

unscrew the plugs from the cylinder head (see illustration). Lay each plug out in relation to its cylinder; if either plug shows up a problem it will then be easy to identify the troublesome cylinder.
5 Inspect the electrodes for wear. Both the centre and side electrodes should have square edges and the side electrode should be of uniform thickness. Look for excessive deposits and evidence of a cracked or chipped insulator around the centre electrode. Compare your spark plugs to the colour spark plug reading chart on the inside rear cover. Check the threads, the washer and the ceramic insulator body for cracks and other damage.
6 If the electrodes are not excessively worn, and if the deposits can be easily removed with a wire brush, the plugs can be re-gapped and re-used (if no cracks or chips are visible in the

insulator). If in doubt concerning the condition of the plugs, replace them with new ones, as the expense is minimal.
7 Cleaning spark plugs by sandblasting is permitted, provided you clean the plugs with a high flash-point solvent afterwards.
8 Before installing the plugs, make sure they are the correct type and heat range and check the gap between the electrodes (they are not pre-set on new plugs). For best results, use a wire-type gauge rather than a flat (feeler) gauge to check the gap (see illustrations). Compare the gap to that specified and adjust as necessary. If the gap must be adjusted, bend the side electrode only and be very careful not to chip or crack the insulator nose (see illustration). Make sure the washer is in place before installing each plug.
9 Since the cylinder head is made of aluminium, which is soft and easily damaged,

3.4a Pull off the spark plug cap . . .

3.4b . . . then unscrew the spark plug

3.8a A wire type gauge is recommended to measure the spark plug electrode gap

3.8b A blade type feeler gauge can also be used

3.8c Adjust the electrode gap by bending the side electrode only

3.9 Thread the plug in as far as possible by hand

thread the plugs into the heads by hand **(see illustration)**. Once the plugs are finger-tight, the job can be finished with the tool supplied or a socket. Tighten the spark plugs to the specified torque setting; do not over-tighten them.

HAYNES HINT *Stripped plug threads in the cylinder head can be repaired with a Heli-coil insert - see "Tools and workshop tips" in the Reference section.*

10 Reconnect the spark plug caps, making sure they are securely connected to the correct cylinder. Connect the battery negative (–) lead and install the seat.

4 Air suction valves - check (US models)

1 Remove the fuel tank (see Chapter 3).
2 Unscrew the four bolts securing each suction valve cover to the valve cover, then lift the covers off and remove the reed valve assemblies, noting which way up they fit.
3 Check the reeds for cracks, warpage and any other damage or deterioration. Also check the contact areas between the reeds and the

reed holders, and the holders themselves, for any signs of damage or deterioration. Any carbon deposits or other foreign particles can be cleaned off using a high flash-point solvent. Replace the reed valve assemblies if there is any doubt about their condition. On 550 models, also check the condition of the upper and lower gaskets and replace them if necessary.
4 Install the valve assemblies with their gaskets (550 models), making sure the projection on each valve holder faces up, then install the covers and tighten the bolts securely.

5 Idle speed - check and adjustment (ZR550 B and ZR750 C)

1 The idle speed should be checked and adjusted before and after the carburettors are synchronised (balanced) and when it is obviously too high or too low. Before adjusting the idle speed, make sure the valve clearances and spark plug gaps are correct. Also, turn the handlebars back-and-forth and see if the idle speed changes as this is done. If it does, the throttle cable may not be adjusted correctly, or may be worn out. This is a dangerous condition that can cause loss of control of the bike. Be sure to correct this problem before proceeding.
2 The engine should be at normal operating temperature, which is usually reached after 10 to 15 minutes of stop and go riding. Place the motorcycle on its centre stand (where fitted), or support it upright using an auxiliary stand, and make sure the transmission is in neutral.
3 With the engine idling, adjust the idle speed by turning the throttle stop screw in or out until the idle speed listed in this Chapter's Specifications is obtained. The throttle stop screw is located on the left-hand end of the carburettors on 550 models, and under the carburettors in the middle on 750 models **(see illustrations)**.

4 Snap the throttle open and shut a few times, then recheck the idle speed. If necessary, repeat the adjustment procedure.
5 If a smooth, steady idle can't be achieved, the fuel/air mixture may be incorrect (see Chapter 3) or the carburettors may need synchronising (see Section 6). On US models, check the air suction valves (see Section 4).

6 Carburettors - synchronisation (ZR550 B and ZR750 C)

⚠ *Warning: Petrol (gasoline) is extremely flammable, so take extra precautions when you work on any part of the fuel system. Don't smoke or allow open flames or bare light bulbs near the work area, and don't work in a garage where a natural gas-type appliance is present. If you spill any fuel on your skin, rinse it off immediately with soap and water. When you perform any kind of work on the fuel system, wear safety glasses and have a fire extinguisher suitable for a Class B type fire (flammable liquids) on hand.*

⚠ *Warning: Take great care not to burn your hand on the hot engine unit when accessing the gauge take-off points on the intake manifolds. Do not allow exhaust gases to build up in the work area; either perform the check outside or use an exhaust gas extraction system.*

1 Carburettor synchronisation is simply the process of adjusting the carburettors so they pass the same amount of fuel/air mixture to each cylinder. This is done by measuring the vacuum produced in each cylinder. Carburettors that are out of synchronisation will result in decreased fuel mileage, increased engine temperature, less than ideal throttle response and higher vibration levels. Before synchronising the carburettors, make sure the valve clearances are properly set.

5.3a Throttle stop screw - 550 models

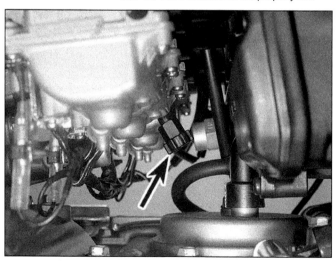

5.3b Throttle stop screw (arrowed) - 750 models

6.5 Pull the hoses or caps off the vacuum take-off stubs (A).
The synchronisation screws (B) are in between each pair of carburettors

2 To properly synchronise the carburettors, you will need some sort of vacuum gauge set-up with a gauge for each cylinder, or a manometer, which is a calibrated tube arrangement that utilises columns of mercury or steel rods to indicate engine vacuum. **Note:** *Due to the nature of the synchronisation procedure and the need for special instruments, most owners leave the task to a Kawasaki dealer.*

3 Start the engine and let it run until it reaches normal operating temperature, then shut it off.

4 Remove the fuel tank (see Chapter 3).

5 Disconnect the fuel tap vacuum hose and remove the blanking caps or hoses (UK models), or EVAP and suction valve hoses or blanking caps as appropriate (US and California models) from the take-off stubs on the carburettors **(see illustration)**. Make a note of which hoses fit where.

6 Connect the gauge hoses to the take-off adapters. Make sure there are no air leaks as false readings will result.

7 Arrange a temporary fuel supply, either by using a small temporary tank or by using extra long fuel pipes to the now remote fuel tank. Alternatively, position the tank on a suitable base on the motorcycle, taking care not to scratch any paintwork, and making sure that the tank is safely and securely supported.

8 Start the engine and let it idle. If the gauges are fitted with damping adjustment, set this so that the needle flutter is just eliminated but so that they can still respond to small changes in pressure.

9 The vacuum readings for all of the cylinders should be the same. If the vacuum readings vary, proceed as follows.

10 The carburettors are adjusted by turning the synchronising screws situated in-between each carburettor, in the throttle linkage **(see illustration 6.5)**. **Note:** *Do not press down on the screws whilst adjusting them, otherwise a false reading will be obtained.* First synchronise the outer left carburettor (no. 1) to the inner left carburettor (no. 2) until the readings are the same. Then synchronise the outer right carburettor (no. 4) to the inner right carburettor (no. 3). Finally synchronise the left-hand carburettors (nos. 1 and 2) to the right-hand carburettors (nos. 3 and 4) using the centre synchronising screw. When all the carburettors are synchronised, open and close the throttle quickly to settle the linkage, and recheck the gauge readings, readjusting if necessary.

11 When the adjustment is complete, recheck the vacuum readings, then adjust the idle speed by turning the throttle stop screw until the idle speed listed in this Chapter's Specifications is obtained. Remove the gauge hoses, then install the fuel tap vacuum hose and the take-off blanking caps or hoses, or EVAP and suction valve hoses onto the carburettors.

12 Detach the temporary fuel supply and install the fuel tank (see Chapter 3).

7 Evaporative emission control (EVAP) system - check (California models)

1 Visually inspect all the EVAP system hoses for kinks and splits and any other damage or deterioration. Make sure that the hoses are securely connected with a clamp on each end. Replace any hoses that are damaged or deteriorated. See Chapter 3 for further information and a diagram of the EVAP system.

8 Air filter reservoir - draining (750 models)

1 The drain hose from the bottom of the air filter housing has a reservoir to store any oil that drains from the housing. The reservoir is located at the back of the clutch cover on the right-hand side of the engine.

2 Lift the rubber boot and check for any oil in the reservoir **(see illustration)**. If any oil is present, remove the drain plug from the bottom of the reservoir hose and allow the oil to drain into a suitable container **(see illustration)**. Make sure the drain plug is securely installed on completion.

8.2a Check for any oil in the reservoir (arrowed)

8.2b Remove the plug and allow any oil to drain out

9.3 Remove the oil filler cap to vent the crankcase (arrowed)

9.4 Remove the drain plug and allow the oil to drain completely

9 Engine - oil change

Warning: Be careful when draining the oil, as the exhaust pipes, the engine, and the oil itself can cause severe burns.

1 Consistent routine oil changes are the single most important maintenance procedure you can perform on a motorcycle. The oil not only lubricates the internal parts of the engine, transmission and clutch, but it also acts as a coolant, a cleaner, a sealant, and a protectant. Because of these demands, the oil takes a terrific amount of abuse and should be replaced often with new oil of the recommended grade and type. Saving a little money on the difference in cost between a good oil and a cheap oil won't pay off if the engine is damaged. **Note:** *The oil filter should be changed with every second oil change.*

2 Before changing the oil, warm up the engine so the oil will drain easily.

3 Put the motorcycle on its centre stand (where fitted), or support it upright using an auxiliary stand, and position a clean drain tray below the engine. Unscrew the oil filler cap on the clutch cover to vent the crankcase and to act as a reminder that there is no oil in the engine **(see illustration)**.

4 Next, unscrew the oil drain plug from the bottom of the engine and allow the oil to flow into the drain tray **(see illustration)**. Discard the sealing washer on the drain plug as it should be replaced whenever the plug is removed.

5 When the oil has completely drained, fit a new sealing washer over the drain plug. Fit the plug to the sump and tighten it to the torque setting specified at the beginning of the Chapter **(see illustration)**. Avoid overtightening, as damage to the sump will result.

6 Refill the crankcase to the proper level using the recommended type and amount of oil (see *Daily (pre-ride) checks*). With the motorcycle held vertical, the oil level should lie between the high and low level lines on the inspection window in the clutch cover (see *Daily (pre-ride) checks*). Install the filler cap. Start the engine and let it run for two or three minutes (make sure that the oil pressure light extinguishes after a few seconds). Shut it off, wait a few minutes, then check the oil level. If necessary, add more oil to bring the level up to the high level line on the inspection window. Check that there are no leaks from around the drain plug.

Saving a little money on the difference between good and cheap oils won't pay off if the engine suffers damage.

7 The old oil drained from the engine cannot be re-used and should be disposed of properly. Check with your local refuse disposal company, disposal facility or environmental agency to see whether they will accept the used oil for recycling. Don't pour used oil into drains or onto the ground.

9.5 Fit a new sealing washer onto the drain plug and tighten it to the specified torque setting

Check the old oil carefully - if it is very metallic coloured, then the engine is experiencing wear from break-in (new engine) or from insufficient lubrication. If there are flakes or chips of metal in the oil, then something is drastically wrong internally and the engine will have to be disassembled for inspection and repair. If there are pieces of fibre-like material in the oil, the clutch is experiencing excessive wear and should be checked.

10 Clutch - check

1 Periodic adjustment of the clutch cable is necessary to compensate for wear in the clutch plates and stretch of the cable. Pull in the clutch lever gently until the cable slack is taken up, then measure the gap between the lever and bracket comparing it with freeplay specification at the beginning of the Chapter **(see illustration)**. If adjustment is required, it

10.1 Measuring clutch lever freeplay

10.2 Lockring (A), adjuster (B) (lever end)

10.4 Slacken the locknuts (arrowed) and move the adjuster as required

can be made at either the lever end of the cable or at the clutch end.

2 To adjust the freeplay at the lever, loosen the locking ring and turn the adjuster in or out until the required amount of freeplay is obtained **(see illustration)**. To increase freeplay, turn the adjuster clockwise. To reduce freeplay, turn the adjuster anti-clockwise. Tighten the locking ring securely.

3 If all the adjustment has been taken up at the lever, reset the adjuster to give the maximum amount of freeplay, then set the correct amount of freeplay using the adjuster at the clutch end of the cable. Subsequent adjustments can then be made using the lever adjuster only.

4 To adjust the freeplay at the clutch, loosen the locknuts and move the adjuster until the required amount of freeplay is obtained, then tighten the locknuts against the bracket **(see illustration)**. To increase freeplay, move the

adjuster down in the bracket. To reduce freeplay, pull the adjuster up in the bracket.

5 The clutch lever has a span adjuster which alters the distance of the lever from the handlebar **(see illustration)**. Pull the lever away from the handlebar and turn the adjuster dial until the setting which best suits the rider is obtained. There are five positions. Align the number for the setting required with the triangular mark on the lever bracket.

11 Drive chain -
wear and stretch check

1 Check the entire length of the chain for damaged rollers, loose links and pins and replace the chain if damage is found. If the chain has reached the end of its adjustment, it must be replaced.

2 The amount of chain stretch can be

measured and compared to the stretch limit specified at the beginning of the Chapter. Place the machine on its sidestand and remove the chain guard (see Chapter 7), then hang a 10 kg (22 lb) weight from the bottom run of the chain. Measure along the top run the length of 21 pins (from the centre of the 1st pin to the centre of the 21st pin) and compare the result with the service limit specified at the beginning of the Chapter **(see illustration)**. Rotate the rear wheel so that several sections of the chain are measured. If any measurement exceeds the service limit the chain must be replaced (see Chapter 5).
Note: It is good practice to replace the chain and sprockets as a set.

3 Check the teeth on the engine sprocket and rear wheel sprocket for wear (see Chapter 5).

4 Inspect the drive chain slider on the swingarm for excessive wear and replace it if necessary (see Chapter 5).

10.5 Set the lever span adjuster as required

11.2 Measure the distance between the 1st and 21st pins to determine chain stretch

12.1a Brake pad wear indicator step - all pad types except 550 B3, B4 and B5 rear, and 750 D front

12.1b Brake pad wear indicator cut-outs - 550 B3, B4 and B5 rear

12 Brake pads - wear check

1 Each brake pad has wear indicator steps, cut-outs or grooves that can be viewed without removing the pads from the caliper **(see illustrations)**. If the pads are worn to or beyond the wear limit, they must be replaced. If the pads are dirty or if you are in doubt as to the amount of friction material remaining, remove them for inspection (see Chapter 6) and measure the thickness of the material. If the thickness of the material remaining is 1 mm or less, the pads must be replaced. **Note:** *Some after-market pads may use different indicators to those on the original equipment pads shown.*

2 Refer to Chapter 6 for details of pad replacement.

13 Brake system - check

1 A routine general check of the brake system will ensure that any problems are discovered and remedied before the rider's safety is jeopardised.

General checks

2 Check the brake lever and pedal for loose connections, improper or rough action, excessive play, bends, and other damage. Replace any damaged parts with new ones (see Chapter 6).

3 Make sure all brake fasteners are tight. Check the brake pads for wear (see Section 12) and make sure the fluid level in the reservoirs is correct (see *Daily (pre-ride) checks*). Look for leaks at the hose connections and check for

cracks in the hoses **(see illustration)**. If the lever or pedal is spongy, bleed the brakes (see Chapter 6).

4 The front brake lever has a span adjuster which alters the distance of the lever from the handlebar **(see illustration)**. Pull the lever away from the handlebar and turn the adjuster dial until the setting which best suits the rider is obtained. There are four positions. Align the number for the setting required with the triangular mark on the lever bracket.

Brake light

5 Make sure the brake light operates when the front brake lever is depressed. The front brake light switch is not adjustable. If it fails to operate properly, check it (see Chapter 8).

6 Make sure the brake light is activated after about 10 mm of brake pedal travel or just before the rear brake takes effect. If adjustment is necessary, hold the switch and turn the adjusting nut on the switch body until

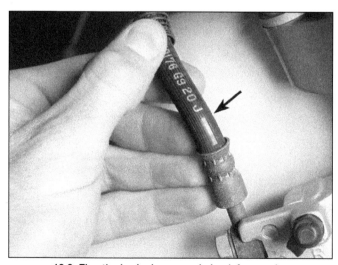

13.3 Flex the brake hoses and check for cracks, bulges and leaking fluid

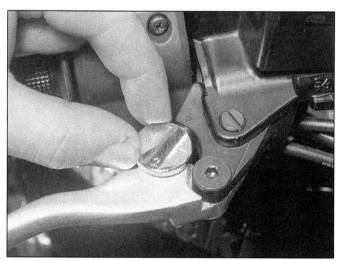

13.4 Adjusting the front brake lever span

13.6 Rear brake light switch adjuster nut (arrowed)

13.7a Measuring rear brake pedal height

the brake light is activated when required (see illustration). If the switch doesn't operate the brake light, check it (see Chapter 8).

Brake pedal height

7 Check the position of the brake pedal. The distance from the top of the brake pedal tip to the top of the rider's footrest should be as specified at the beginning of the Chapter (see illustration). If the pedal height is incorrect, slacken the locknut on the master cylinder pushrod, then turn the pushrod using a spanner on the hex at the top of the rod until the pedal is at the correct height (see illustration).

8 If access to the pushrod is too restricted, remove the footrest bracket mounting bolts and detach the brake light switch spring from the pedal, then draw the bracket away from the frame, taking care not to twist or strain the master cylinder hoses. On completion tighten

the locknut securely. Adjust the rear brake light switch after adjusting the pedal height (see Step 6).

14 Steering head bearings - freeplay check and adjustment

1 This motorcycle is equipped with tapered-roller type steering head bearings which can become dented, rough or loose during normal use of the machine. In extreme cases, worn or loose steering head bearings can cause steering wobble - a condition that is potentially dangerous.

Check

2 Place the motorcycle on its centre stand. Raise the front wheel off the ground either by having an assistant push down on the rear or by placing a support under the engine.

3 Point the front wheel straight-ahead and slowly move the handlebars from side-to-side. Any dents or roughness in the bearing races will be felt and the bars will not move smoothly and freely.

4 Next, grasp the fork sliders and try to move them forward and backward (see illustration). Any looseness in the steering head bearings will be felt as front-to-rear movement of the forks. If play is felt in the bearings, adjust the steering head as follows.

> **HAYNES HiNT** *Freeplay in the fork due to worn fork bushes can be misinterpreted for steering head bearing play - do not confuse the two.*

Adjustment

5 Remove the fuel tank to avoid the possibility of damage should a tool slip while

13.7b Master cylinder pushrod locknut (A) and adjuster hex (B)

14.4 Checking for play in the steering head bearings

14.5a Slacken the steering stem bolt (arrowed) . . .

14.5b . . . and the bottom yoke clamp bolts for each fork (arrowed)

adjustment is being made (see Chapter 3). Slacken the steering stem bolt, then slacken the fork clamp bolts in the bottom yoke **(see illustrations)**. **Note:** *Depending on the tools available, it may be necessary to displace the handlebars in order to provide enough clearance for access to the steering stem bolt (see Chapter 5).* Also slacken the bolt securing the headlight support frame to the bottom yoke, located behind the brake hose union.

6 Using a suitable C-spanner or drift located in one of the notches in the adjuster ring locknut, slacken the locknut slightly **(see illustration)**. Now initially slacken, then tighten or slacken further the adjuster ring as required until all freeplay in the forks is removed, yet the steering is able to move freely from side to side. The object is to set the adjuster ring so that the bearings are under a very light loading, just enough to remove any freeplay. Tighten the locknut against the adjuster ring finger-tight only.

Caution: Take great care not to apply excessive pressure because this will cause premature failure of the bearings.

7 If the bearings cannot be set up properly, or if there is any binding, roughness or

14.6 Using a drift located into one of the notches, slacken the locknut, then adjust the bearings via the adjuster nut below it

notchiness, they will have to be removed for inspection or replacement (see Chapter 5).

8 With the bearings correctly adjusted, tighten the steering stem bolt and the fork clamp bolts to the torque settings specified at the beginning of the Chapter. **Note:** *Depending on the tools available, it may be necessary to displace the handlebars in order to provide enough clearance for a socket and torque wrench on the steering stem bolt (see Chapter 5).*

9 Check the bearing adjustment as described above and re-adjust if necessary.

15 Wheels and tyres - check

Tyres

1 Check the tyre condition and tread depth thoroughly - see *Daily (pre-ride) checks*.

Wheels

2 The cast wheels used on all except ZR750 D models are virtually maintenance free, but they should be kept clean and checked periodically for cracks and other damage. Also check the wheel runout and alignment (see Chapter 6). Never attempt to repair damaged cast wheels; they must be replaced with new ones. Check the valve rubber for signs of damage or deterioration and have it replaced if necessary. Also, make sure the valve stem cap is in place and tight.

3 On ZR750 D models, visually check the spokes for damage, breakage or corrosion. A broken or bent spoke must be renewed immediately because the load taken by it will be transferred to adjacent spokes which may in turn fail.

4 If you suspect that any of the spokes are incorrectly tensioned, tap each one lightly

with a screwdriver and note the sound produced. Properly tensioned spokes will make a sharp pinging sound, loose ones will produce a lower pitch and overtightened ones will be higher pitched. Unevenly tensioned spokes will promote rim misalignment - seek the help of a wheel building expert if this is suspected.

16 Stands, lever pivots and cables - lubrication

1 Since the controls, cables and various other components of a motorcycle are exposed to the elements, they should be lubricated periodically to ensure safe and trouble-free operation.

2 The footrests, clutch and brake levers, brake pedal, gearshift lever linkage and stand pivots should be lubricated frequently. In order for the lubricant to be applied where it will do the most good, the component should be disassembled. However, if chain and cable lubricant is being used, it can be applied to the pivot joint gaps and will usually work its way into the areas where friction occurs. If motor oil or light grease is being used, apply it sparingly as it may attract dirt (which could cause the controls to bind or wear at an accelerated rate). **Note:** *One of the best lubricants for the control lever pivots is a dry-film lubricant (available from many sources by different names).*

3 To lubricate the cables, disconnect the relevant cable at its upper end, then lubricate the cable with a pressure adapter, or if one is not available, using the set-up shown **(see illustrations)**. See Chapter 3 for the choke and throttle cable removal procedures, and Chapter 2 for the clutch cable.

4 The speedometer cable should be removed (see Chapter 8) and the inner cable withdrawn from the outer cable and lubricated with motor oil or cable lubricant. Do not lubricate the upper few inches of the cable as the lubricant may travel up into the instrument head.

17 Battery - electrolyte level check (ZR550 B1, B2, B3 and B4 models only)

Caution: Be extremely careful when handling or working around the battery. The electrolyte is very caustic and an explosive gas (hydrogen) is given off when the battery is charging.
1 Remove the seat (see Chapter 7).
2 The electrolyte level is visible through the translucent battery case - it should be between the UPPER and LOWER level marks.
3 If the electrolyte is low, remove the battery (see Chapter 8), then remove the cell caps and fill each cell to the upper level mark with distilled water. Do not use tap water (except in

16.3a Lubricating a cable with a pressure lubricator. Make sure the tool seals around the inner cable

an emergency), and do not overfill. The cell holes are quite small, so it may help to use a clean plastic squeeze bottle with a small spout to add the water. Install the battery cell caps, tightening them securely, then install the battery.

16.3b Lubricating a cable with a makeshift funnel and motor oil

Every 6000 miles (10 000 km) or 12 months - ZR550 B & ZR750 C

Every 7500 miles (12 000 km) or 12 months - ZR750 D

18 Valve clearances - check and adjustment

1 The engine must be completely cool for this maintenance procedure, so let the machine sit overnight before beginning.
2 Remove the valve cover (see Chapter 2). Unscrew the spark plugs to allow the engine to be turned over easier (see Section 3).
3 Make a chart or sketch of all four valve positions so that a note of each clearance can be made against the relevant valve.
4 Unscrew the bolts securing the pulse generator coil cover to the right-hand side crankcase cover **(see illustration)**. The

engine can be rotated using a 17 mm socket on the timing rotor hex and turning it in a clockwise direction only. Alternatively, place the motorcycle on its centre stand, select a high gear and rotate the rear wheel by hand in its normal direction of rotation.
Caution: DO NOT use the timing rotor bolt to turn the crankshaft - it may snap or strip out. Also be sure to turn the engine in its normal direction of rotation.
5 Rotate the engine until the T mark on the rotor aligns with the static timing mark on the crankcase **(see illustrations)**. At this point either no. 1 cylinder or no. 4 cylinder will be at top dead centre (TDC) on the compression stroke. Check the position of the cam lobes on no. 1 cylinder. If they are facing away from

each other, no. 1 cylinder is at TDC on the compression stroke. If the cam lobes are facing each other, the lobes on no. 4 cylinder will be facing away from each other and no. 4 is at TDC on the compression stroke.
6 With no. 1 cylinder at TDC on the compression stroke, the following valves can be checked:
a) No. 1, intake and exhaust
b) No. 2, exhaust
c) No. 3, intake
7 With no. 4 cylinder at TDC on the compression stroke, the following valves can be checked:
a) No. 2, intake
b) No. 3, exhaust
c) No. 4, intake and exhaust

18.4 The pulse generator assembly cover is secured by two bolts (arrowed)

18.5a Rotate the engine using a 17 mm socket on the timing rotor hex . . .

18.5b . . . so that the T mark on the rotor aligns with the static timing mark on the crankcase (arrowed)

18.8 Check the valve clearance using a feeler gauge

18.12a Lift the follower off its valve . . .

8 Insert a feeler gauge of the same thickness as the correct valve clearance (see Specifications) between the cam base and follower of each valve and check that it is a firm sliding fit - you should feel a slight drag when you pull the gauge out **(see illustration)**. If not , use the feeler gauges to obtain the exact clearance. Record the measured clearance on the chart.

9 Rotate the engine so that the timing rotor turns through 360° and the T mark is once again correctly aligned, then measure the valve clearance of the remaining valves using the method described in Step 8.

10 When all clearances have been measured and charted, identify whether the clearance on any valve falls outside that specified. If it does, the shim between the follower and the valve must be replaced with one of a thickness which will restore the correct clearance.

11 Shim replacement requires removal of the camshafts (see Chapter 2). There is no need to remove both camshafts if shims from only one side of the engine need replacing.

12 With the camshaft removed, remove the cam follower of the valve in question, then prise the shim out of the top of the valve using a small screwdriver and remove it using a pair of pliers **(see illustrations)**.

13 The shim size should be stamped on its face. A shim size of 250 denotes a thickness of 2.50 mm, 245 is 2.45 mm. It is recommended that the shim is measured to check that it has not worn **(see illustration)**. Shims are available in 0.05 mm increments from 2.00 mm to 3.20 mm.

14 Using the appropriate shim selection chart, find where the measured valve clearance and existing shim thickness values intersect and read off the shim size required **(see illustrations)**. Obtain and install the replacement shim, noting that its size marking should be installed downwards and that the shim should be lubricated with molybdenum disulphide grease - this will also hold it in

18.12b . . . then remove the shim

18.13 Measure the shim using a micrometer to confirm its size

PART No. (92025-)	1090	1091	1082	1083	1094	1085	1096	1097	1098	1099	1100	1101	1102	1103	1104	1105	1106	1107	1108	1109	1110	1111	1112	1113	1114
MARK	200	205	210	215	220	225	230	235	240	245	250	255	260	265	270	275	280	285	290	295	300	305	310	315	320
THICKNESS (mm)	2.00	2.05	2.10	2.15	2.20	2.25	2.30	2.35	2.40	2.45	2.50	2.55	2.60	2.65	2.70	2.75	2.80	2.85	2.90	2.95	3.00	3.05	3.10	3.15	3.20
0.00 ~ 0.03		2.00	2.00	2.05	2.10	2.15	2.20	2.25	2.30	2.35	2.40	2.45	2.50	2.55	2.60	2.65	2.70	2.75	2.80	2.85	2.90	2.95	3.00	3.05	
0.04 ~ 0.07		2.00	2.00	2.05	2.10	2.15	2.20	2.25	2.30	2.35	2.40	2.45	2.50	2.55	2.60	2.65	2.70	2.75	2.80	2.85	2.90	2.95	3.00	3.05	3.10
0.08 ~ 0.18	SPECIFIED CLEARANCE / NO CHANGE REQUIRED																								
0.19 ~ 0.22	2.05	2.10	2.15	2.20	2.25	2.30	2.35	2.40	2.45	2.50	2.55	2.60	2.65	2.70	2.75	2.80	2.85	2.90	2.95	3.00	3.05	3.10	3.15	3.20	
0.23 ~ 0.27	2.10	2.15	2.20	2.25	2.30	2.35	2.40	2.45	2.50	2.55	2.60	2.65	2.70	2.75	2.80	2.85	2.90	2.95	3.00	3.05	3.10	3.15	3.20		
0.28 ~ 0.32	2.15	2.20	2.25	2.30	2.35	2.40	2.45	2.50	2.55	2.60	2.65	2.70	2.75	2.80	2.85	2.90	2.95	3.00	3.05	3.10	3.15	3.20			
0.33 ~ 0.37	2.20	2.25	2.30	2.35	2.40	2.45	2.50	2.55	2.60	2.65	2.70	2.75	2.80	2.85	2.90	2.95	3.00	3.05	3.10	3.15	3.20				
0.38 ~ 0.42	2.25	2.30	2.35	2.40	2.45	2.50	2.55	2.60	2.65	2.70	2.75	2.80	2.85	2.90	2.95	3.00	3.05	3.10	3.15	3.20					
0.43 ~ 0.47	2.30	2.35	2.40	2.45	2.50	2.55	2.60	2.65	2.70	2.75	2.80	2.85	2.90	2.95	3.00	3.05	3.10	3.15	3.20						
0.48 ~ 0.52	2.35	2.40	2.45	2.50	2.55	2.60	2.65	2.70	2.75	2.80	2.85	2.90	2.95	3.00	3.05	3.10	3.15	3.20							
0.53 ~ 0.57	2.40	2.45	2.50	2.55	2.60	2.65	2.70	2.75	2.80	2.85	2.90	2.95	3.00	3.05	3.10	3.15	3.20								
0.58 ~ 0.62	2.45	2.50	2.55	2.60	2.65	2.70	2.75	2.80	2.85	2.90	2.95	3.00	3.05	3.10	3.15	3.20									
0.63 ~ 0.67	2.50	2.55	2.60	2.65	2.70	2.75	2.80	2.85	2.90	2.95	3.00	3.05	3.10	3.15	3.20										
0.68 ~ 0.72	2.55	2.60	2.65	2.70	2.75	2.80	2.85	2.90	2.95	3.00	3.05	3.10	3.15	3.20											
0.73 ~ 0.77	2.60	2.65	2.70	2.75	2.80	2.85	2.90	2.95	3.00	3.05	3.10	3.15	3.20												
0.78 ~ 0.82	2.65	2.70	2.75	2.80	2.85	2.90	2.95	3.00	3.05	3.10	3.15	3.20													
0.83 ~ 0.87	2.70	2.75	2.80	2.85	2.90	2.95	3.00	3.05	3.10	3.15	3.20														
0.88 ~ 0.92	2.75	2.80	2.85	2.90	2.95	3.00	3.05	3.10	3.15	3.20															
0.93 ~ 0.97	2.80	2.85	2.90	2.95	3.00	3.05	3.10	3.15	3.20																
0.98 ~ 1.02	2.85	2.90	2.95	3.00	3.05	3.10	3.15	3.20																	
1.03 ~ 1.07	2.90	2.95	3.00	3.05	3.10	3.15	3.20																		
1.08 ~ 1.12	2.95	3.00	3.05	3.10	3.15	3.20																			
1.13 ~ 1.17	3.00	3.05	3.10	3.15	3.20																				
1.18 ~ 1.22	3.05	3.10	3.15	3.20																					
1.23 ~ 1.27	3.10	3.15	3.20																						
1.28 ~ 1.32	3.15	3.20																							
1.33 ~ 1.38	3.20																								

PRESENT SHIM — Example ↓

Example → (left axis) VALVE CLEARANCE MEASUREMENT

INSTALL THE SHIM OF THIS THICKNESS (mm)

18.14a Shim selection chart - ZR750 - intake and exhaust valves

18.14b Shim selection chart - ZR550 - intake valves

Example ↓ / SPECIFIED CLEARANCE / NO CHANGE REQUIRED / INSTALL THE SHIM OF THIS THICKNESS (mm)

VALVE CLEARANCE (mm)	2.00	2.05	2.10	2.15	2.20	2.25	2.30	2.35	2.40	2.45	2.50	2.55	2.60	2.65	2.70	2.75	2.80	2.85	2.90	2.95	3.00	3.05	3.10	3.15	3.20
PART No. (92025-)	1090	1091	1092	1093	1094	1095	1096	1097	1098	1099	1100	1101	1102	1103	1104	1105	1106	1107	1108	1109	1110	1111	1112	1113	1114
MARK	200	205	210	215	220	225	230	235	240	245	250	255	260	265	270	275	280	285	290	295	300	305	310	315	320
0.00 ~ 0.02				2.00	2.05	2.10	2.15	2.20	2.25	2.30	2.35	2.40	2.45	2.50	2.55	2.60	2.65	2.70	2.75	2.80	2.85	2.90	2.95	3.00	3.05
0.03 ~ 0.07			2.00	2.05	2.10	2.15	2.20	2.25	2.30	2.35	2.40	2.45	2.50	2.55	2.60	2.65	2.70	2.75	2.80	2.85	2.90	2.95	3.00	3.05	3.10
0.08 ~ 0.09		2.00	2.05	2.10	2.15	2.20	2.25	2.30	2.35	2.40	2.45	2.50	2.55	2.60	2.65	2.70	2.75	2.80	2.85	2.90	2.95	3.00	3.05	3.10	3.15
0.10 ~ 0.20	SPECIFIED CLEARANCE / NO CHANGE REQUIRED																								
0.21 ~ 0.22	2.05	2.10	2.15	2.20	2.25	2.30	2.35	2.40	2.45	2.50	2.55	2.60	2.65	2.70	2.75	2.80	2.85	2.90	2.95	3.00	3.05	3.10	3.15	3.20	
0.23 ~ 0.27	2.10	2.15	2.20	2.25	2.30	2.35	2.40	2.45	2.50	2.55	2.60	2.65	2.70	2.75	2.80	2.85	2.90	2.95	3.00	3.05	3.10	3.15	3.20		
0.28 ~ 0.32	2.15	2.20	2.25	2.30	2.35	2.40	2.45	2.50	2.55	2.60	2.65	2.70	2.75	2.80	2.85	2.90	2.95	3.00	3.05	3.10	3.15	3.20			
0.33 ~ 0.37	2.20	2.25	2.30	2.35	2.40	2.45	2.50	2.55	2.60	2.65	2.70	2.75	2.80	2.85	2.90	2.95	3.00	3.05	3.10	3.15	3.20				
0.38 ~ 0.42	2.25	2.30	2.35	2.40	2.45	2.50	2.55	2.60	2.65	2.70	2.75	2.80	2.85	2.90	2.95	3.00	3.05	3.10	3.15	3.20					
0.43 ~ 0.47	2.30	2.35	2.40	2.45	2.50	2.55	2.60	2.65	2.70	2.75	2.80	2.85	2.90	2.95	3.00	3.05	3.10	3.15	3.20						
0.48 ~ 0.52	2.35	2.40	2.45	2.50	2.55	2.60	2.65	2.70	2.75	2.80	2.85	2.90	2.95	3.00	3.05	3.10	3.15	3.20							
0.53 ~ 0.57	2.40	2.45	2.50	2.55	2.60	2.65	2.70	2.75	2.80	2.85	2.90	2.95	3.00	3.05	3.10	3.15	3.20								
0.58 ~ 0.62	2.45	2.50	2.55	2.60	2.65	2.70	2.75	2.80	2.85	2.90	2.95	3.00	3.05	3.10	3.15	3.20									
0.63 ~ 0.67	2.50	2.55	2.60	2.65	2.70	2.75	2.80	2.85	2.90	2.95	3.00	3.05	3.10	3.15	3.20										
0.68 ~ 0.72	2.55	2.60	2.65	2.70	2.75	2.80	2.85	2.90	2.95	3.00	3.05	3.10	3.15	3.20											
0.73 ~ 0.77	2.60	2.65	2.70	2.75	2.80	2.85	2.90	2.95	3.00	3.05	3.10	3.15	3.20												
0.78 ~ 0.82	2.65	2.70	2.75	2.80	2.85	2.90	2.95	3.00	3.05	3.10	3.15	3.20													
0.83 ~ 0.87	2.70	2.75	2.80	2.85	2.90	2.95	3.00	3.05	3.10	3.15	3.20														
0.88 ~ 0.92	2.75	2.80	2.85	2.90	2.95	3.00	3.05	3.10	3.15	3.20															
0.93 ~ 0.97	2.80	2.85	2.90	2.95	3.00	3.05	3.10	3.15	3.20																
0.98 ~ 1.02	2.85	2.90	2.95	3.00	3.05	3.10	3.15	3.20																	
1.03 ~ 1.07	2.90	2.95	3.00	3.05	3.10	3.15	3.20																		
1.08 ~ 1.12	2.95	3.00	3.05	3.10	3.15	3.20																			
1.13 ~ 1.17	3.00	3.05	3.10	3.15	3.20																				
1.18 ~ 1.22	3.05	3.10	3.15	3.20																					
1.23 ~ 1.27	3.10	3.15	3.20																						
1.28 ~ 1.32	3.15	3.20																							
1.33 ~ 1.37	3.20																								

18.14c Shim selection chart - ZR550 - exhaust valves

Example ↓ / SPECIFIED CLEARANCE / NO CHANGE REQUIRED / INSTALL THE SHIM OF THIS THICKNESS (mm)

VALVE CLEARANCE (mm)	2.00	2.05	2.10	2.15	2.20	2.25	2.30	2.35	2.40	2.45	2.50	2.55	2.60	2.65	2.70	2.75	2.80	2.85	2.90	2.95	3.00	3.05	3.10	3.15	3.20
PART No. (92025-)	1090	1091	1092	1093	1094	1095	1096	1097	1098	1099	1100	1101	1102	1103	1104	1105	1106	1107	1108	1109	1110	1111	1112	1113	1114
MARK	200	205	210	215	220	225	230	235	240	245	250	255	260	265	270	275	280	285	290	295	300	305	310	315	320
0.00 ~ 0.02					2.00	2.05	2.10	2.15	2.20	2.25	2.30	2.35	2.40	2.45	2.50	2.55	2.60	2.65	2.70	2.75	2.80	2.85	2.90	2.95	3.00
0.03 ~ 0.07				2.00	2.05	2.10	2.15	2.20	2.25	2.30	2.35	2.40	2.45	2.50	2.55	2.60	2.65	2.70	2.75	2.80	2.85	2.90	2.95	3.00	3.05
0.08 ~ 0.12			2.00	2.05	2.10	2.15	2.20	2.25	2.30	2.35	2.40	2.45	2.50	2.55	2.60	2.65	2.70	2.75	2.80	2.85	2.90	2.95	3.00	3.05	3.10
0.13 ~ 0.14		2.00	2.05	2.10	2.15	2.20	2.25	2.30	2.35	2.40	2.45	2.50	2.55	2.60	2.65	2.70	2.75	2.80	2.85	2.90	2.95	3.00	3.05	3.10	3.15
0.15 ~ 0.25	SPECIFIED CLEARANCE / NO CHANGE REQUIRED																								
0.26 ~ 0.27	2.05	2.10	2.15	2.20	2.25	2.30	2.35	2.40	2.45	2.50	2.55	2.60	2.65	2.70	2.75	2.80	2.85	2.90	2.95	3.00	3.05	3.10	3.15	3.20	
0.28 ~ 0.32	2.10	2.15	2.20	2.25	2.30	2.35	2.40	2.45	2.50	2.55	2.60	2.65	2.70	2.75	2.80	2.85	2.90	2.95	3.00	3.05	3.10	3.15	3.20		
0.33 ~ 0.37	2.15	2.20	2.25	2.30	2.35	2.40	2.45	2.50	2.55	2.60	2.65	2.70	2.75	2.80	2.85	2.90	2.95	3.00	3.05	3.10	3.15	3.20			
0.38 ~ 0.42	2.20	2.25	2.30	2.35	2.40	2.45	2.50	2.55	2.60	2.65	2.70	2.75	2.80	2.85	2.90	2.95	3.00	3.05	3.10	3.15	3.20				
0.43 ~ 0.47	2.25	2.30	2.35	2.40	2.45	2.50	2.55	2.60	2.65	2.70	2.75	2.80	2.85	2.90	2.95	3.00	3.05	3.10	3.15	3.20					
0.48 ~ 0.52	2.30	2.35	2.40	2.45	2.50	2.55	2.60	2.65	2.70	2.75	2.80	2.85	2.90	2.95	3.00	3.05	3.10	3.15	3.20						
0.53 ~ 0.57	2.35	2.40	2.45	2.50	2.55	2.60	2.65	2.70	2.75	2.80	2.85	2.90	2.95	3.00	3.05	3.10	3.15	3.20							
0.58 ~ 0.62	2.40	2.45	2.50	2.55	2.60	2.65	2.70	2.75	2.80	2.85	2.90	2.95	3.00	3.05	3.10	3.15	3.20								
0.63 ~ 0.67	2.45	2.50	2.55	2.60	2.65	2.70	2.75	2.80	2.85	2.90	2.95	3.00	3.05	3.10	3.15	3.20									
0.68 ~ 0.72	2.50	2.55	2.60	2.65	2.70	2.75	2.80	2.85	2.90	2.95	3.00	3.05	3.10	3.15	3.20										
0.73 ~ 0.77	2.55	2.60	2.65	2.70	2.75	2.80	2.85	2.90	2.95	3.00	3.05	3.10	3.15	3.20											
0.78 ~ 0.82	2.60	2.65	2.70	2.75	2.80	2.85	2.90	2.95	3.00	3.05	3.10	3.15	3.20												
0.83 ~ 0.87	2.65	2.70	2.75	2.80	2.85	2.90	2.95	3.00	3.05	3.10	3.15	3.20													
0.88 ~ 0.92	2.70	2.75	2.80	2.85	2.90	2.95	3.00	3.05	3.10	3.15	3.20														
0.93 ~ 0.97	2.75	2.80	2.85	2.90	2.95	3.00	3.05	3.10	3.15	3.20															
0.98 ~ 1.02	2.80	2.85	2.90	2.95	3.00	3.05	3.10	3.15	3.20																
1.03 ~ 1.07	2.85	2.90	2.95	3.00	3.05	3.10	3.15	3.20																	
1.08 ~ 1.12	2.90	2.95	3.00	3.05	3.10	3.15	3.20																		
1.13 ~ 1.17	2.95	3.00	3.05	3.10	3.15	3.20																			
1.18 ~ 1.22	3.00	3.05	3.10	3.15	3.20																				
1.23 ~ 1.27	3.05	3.10	3.15	3.20																					
1.28 ~ 1.32	3.10	3.15	3.20																						
1.33 ~ 1.37	3.15	3.20																							
1.38 ~ 1.45	3.20																								

position on the valve while the follower and camshaft are installed.

15 Lubricate the follower with molybdenum disulphide grease and install it onto the valve. Repeat the process for any other valves which required attention, then install the camshafts (see Chapter 2).

16 Rotate the crankshaft several turns to seat the new shim(s), then re-check the clearances.

17 Install all disturbed components following the reverse of the removal sequence. Apply a smear of sealant to the crankcase joints on the pulse generator assembly cover mating surface **(see illustration)**. Install the pulse generator assembly cover using a new gasket and tighten its bolts to the torque setting specified at the beginning of this Chapter **(see illustration)**.

19 Idle speed - check and adjustment (ZR750 D)

1 The procedure for checking and adjusting the idle speed is the same as for the other models (see Section 5).

20 Carburettors - synchronisation (ZR750 D)

1 The procedure for synchronising the carburettors is the same as for the other models (see Section 6).

21 Air filter - cleaning

1 Remove the fuel tank and the tank bracket (see Chapter 3).

2 Unscrew the two screws securing the air filter cover to the filter housing **(see illustration)**. Remove the cover and withdraw the filter from the housing **(see illustrations)**.

3 Tap the filter on a hard surface to dislodge any dirt. Soak the element in a high flash-point solvent until it is clean, then if compressed air is available, use it to dry the element, directing the air from the inside out **(see illustration)**. Otherwise dry it by shaking it or leaving it in the open air for a while.

18.17a Apply a smear of sealant to the areas shown (arrowed) . . .

18.17b . . . then install the cover using a new gasket

21.2a Remove the two screws (arrowed) securing the cover to the air filter housing (550 model shown)

21.2b Remove the cover . . .

21.2c . . . and withdraw the filter

21.3 Dry the element using compressed air directed from the inside outwards

4 Check the element and its cage for signs of damage. If the element is torn or cannot be cleaned, replace it with a new one.

5 Soak the element in SE or SF grade SAE 30 oil, then wrap it in a clean rag and squeeze it as dry as possible (see illustration). Install the filter by reversing the removal procedure. Press the front of the element against the

21.5 Apply oil to the element, then squeeze it out

housing as you fit the cover to ensure it seats correctly.

Caution: If the machine is continually ridden in dusty conditions, the filter should be cleaned more frequently.

22 Throttle and choke cable - check

Throttle cables

1 Make sure the throttle grip rotates easily from fully closed to fully open with the front wheel turned at various angles. The grip should return automatically from fully open to fully closed when released.

2 If the throttle sticks, this is probably due to a cable fault. Remove the cables (refer to Chapter 3) and lubricate them (Section 16). Install the cables, making sure they are correctly routed. If this fails to improve the operation of the throttle, the cables must be

replaced. Note that in very rare cases the fault could lie in the carburettors rather than the cables, necessitating the removal of the carburettors and inspection of the throttle linkage (see Chapter 3).

3 With the throttle operating smoothly, check the freeplay in the twistgrip and compare with the amount specified (see illustration). If the

22.3 Throttle cable freeplay is measured in terms of twistgrip rotation

22.4 Throttle accelerator cable adjuster locknut (A), adjuster (B)

22.8 Choke cable adjuster

amount of freeplay is incorrect, adjust the cables to correct it.

4 Freeplay adjustments can be made at the throttle end of the cables. Loosen the locknut on the accelerator cable where it leaves the handlebar **(see illustration)**. Turn the adjuster until the specified amount of freeplay is obtained (see this Chapter's Specifications), then retighten the locknut.

5 If the cable can't be adjusted to within specifications, screw the adjuster all the way in, then remove the fuel tank for access to the cable lower adjusters at the carburettor end. Adjust the in-line adjusters in the accelerator and decelerator cables using the same procedure. If the cables still can't be adjusted to within specifications, replace them (see Chapter 3).

> *Warning: Turn the handlebars all the way through their travel with the engine idling. Idle speed should not change. If it does, the cable may be routed incorrectly. Correct this condition before riding the bike.*

6 Check that the throttle twistgrip operates smoothly and snaps shut quickly when released.

Choke cable

7 If the choke does not operate smoothly this is probably due to a cable fault. Remove the cable (see Chapter 3) and lubricate it (see Section 16). Install the cable, routing it so it takes the smoothest route possible.

8 Check for a small amount of freeplay (see Specifications) in the cable before the plungers in the carburettors move. If adjustment is necessary, remove the fuel tank, then use the adjuster in the middle of the cable, using the method described in Step 4 above for the throttle cables **(see illustration)**. If this fails to improve the operation of the choke, the cable must be replaced. Note that in very rare cases the fault could lie in the carburettors rather than the cable,

necessitating the removal of the carburettors and inspection of the choke plungers (see Chapter 3).

23 Engine - oil and oil filter change

> *Warning: Be careful when draining the oil, as the exhaust pipes, the engine, and the oil itself can cause severe burns.*

1 Consistent routine oil and filter changes are the single most important maintenance procedure you can perform on a motorcycle. The oil not only lubricates the internal parts of the engine, transmission and clutch, but it also acts as a coolant, a cleaner, a sealant, and a protectant. Because of these demands, the oil takes a terrific amount of abuse and should be replaced often with new oil of the recommended grade and type. Saving a little money on the difference in cost between a good oil and a cheap oil won't pay off if the engine is damaged. The oil filter should be changed with every second oil change.

2 Before changing the oil, warm up the engine so the oil will drain easily.

3 Put the motorcycle on its centre stand (where fitted), or support it upright using an auxiliary stand, and position a clean drain tray below the engine. Unscrew the oil filler cap on the clutch cover to vent the crankcase and to act as a reminder that there is no oil in the engine **(see illustration 9.3)**.

4 Next, unscrew the oil drain plug from the bottom of the engine and allow the oil to flow into the drain tray **(see illustration 9.4)**. Discard the sealing washer on the drain plug as it should be replaced whenever the plug is removed.

5 When the oil has completely drained, fit a new sealing washer over the drain plug. Fit the plug to the sump and tighten it to the torque setting specified at the beginning of the Chapter **(see illustration 9.5)** - avoid overtightening, as damage to the sump will result.

6 Now place the drain tray below the oil filter. Unscrew the oil filter cover bolt and drop the filter assembly out of the engine **(see illustrations)**. Twist the filter out of its seat and off its bolt, then remove the washer and spring **(see illustration)**. If the washer is not on top of the spring, it will be stuck to the underside of the filter. Make sure you retrieve it before discarding the filter. Withdraw the

23.6a Unscrew the oil filter cover bolt (arrowed) . . .

23.6b . . . and withdraw the filter assembly

23.6c Remove the washer and spring from the bolt

23.6d Check the cover and cover bolt O-rings (arrowed) and replace them if necessary

bolt from the cover and check the condition of its O-ring. Also check the cover O-ring, and replace them if they are damaged or deteriorated **(see illustration)**.

7 Install the filter bolt through the cover and the filter seat, then fit the spring and the washer onto the bolt, then install the new filter using a twisting motion, making sure the rubber grommets in the filter remain in place **(see illustration)**. Install the filter assembly into the engine and tighten the bolt to the specified torque setting **(see illustration)**.

8 Refill the crankcase to the proper level using the recommended type and amount of oil (see *Daily (pre-ride) checks*). With the motorcycle held vertical, the oil level should lie between the upper and lower marks (550 models) or H and L lines (750 models) on the inspection window in the clutch cover (see *Daily (pre-ride) checks*). Install the filler cap. Start the engine and let it run for two or three minutes (make sure that the oil pressure light

extinguishes after a few seconds). Shut it off, wait a few minutes, then check the oil level. If necessary, add more oil to bring the level up to the high level line on the inspection window. Check around the drain plug and the oil filter cover for leaks.

9 The old oil drained from the engine cannot be re-used and should be disposed of properly. Check with your local refuse disposal company, disposal facility or environmental agency to see whether they will accept the used oil for recycling. Don't pour used oil into drains or onto the ground.

24 Fuel system - check

⚠ *Warning: Petrol (gasoline) is extremely flammable, so make sure you take extra precautions when you work on any part of*

the fuel system. Don't smoke or allow open flames or bare light bulbs near the work area, and don't work in a garage where a natural gas-type appliance is present. If you spill any fuel on your skin, rinse it off immediately with soap and water. When you perform any kind of work on the fuel system, it is advisable to wear safety glasses and to have a fire extinguisher suitable for a Class B type fire (flammable liquids) on hand.

Check

1 Remove the fuel tank (see Chapter 3) and check the tank, the fuel tap, and the fuel hoses for signs of leakage, deterioration or damage; in particular check that there is no leakage from the fuel hoses. Replace any hoses which are cracked or deteriorated.

2 If the fuel tap is leaking, remove the tap and tighten the assembly screws on the back of the tap (see Chapter 3). If leakage persists

23.7a Assemble the components as shown . . .

23.7b . . . then install the assembly and tighten the bolt to the specified torque setting

remove the screws and disassemble the tap, noting how the components fit. Inspect all components for wear or damage. If any of the components are worn or damaged, check if they can be purchased separately - in certain cases, it may be necessary to purchase a new tap.

3 If the carburettor gaskets are leaking, the carburettors should be disassembled and rebuilt using new gaskets and seals (see Chapter 3).

Filter cleaning

4 Cleaning or replacement of the fuel filter is advised after a particularly high mileage has been covered. It is also necessary if fuel starvation is suspected.

5 The fuel filter is mounted in the tank and is integral with the fuel tap. Remove the fuel tank and the fuel tap (see Chapter 3). Clean the gauze filter to remove all traces of dirt and fuel sediment. Check the gauze for holes. If any are found, a new filter should be fitted (check for availability - it may be necessary to replace the whole tap). Check the condition of the O-ring and replace it if it is in any way damaged or deteriorated.

25 Cylinder head nuts -
tightness check
(ZR550 B and ZR750 C)

1 Kawasaki recommend that the cylinder head nuts are checked to ensure they are tightened to their correct torque settings. The engine must be completely cool for these maintenance procedures, so let the machine sit overnight before beginning.

2 Remove the valve cover (see Chapter 2).

3 On 550 models, the cylinder head is secured by twelve 8 mm domed nuts with plain washers and five 6 mm bolts, and the cylinder block by three 6 mm nuts. First slacken the bolts and nuts on the front and back of the cylinder head and block **(see illustrations)**. The twelve domed nuts are numbered for identification **(see illustration)**. Slacken the nuts evenly and a little at a time in a **reverse** of their numerical sequence until they are all slack. Using a torque wrench, now tighten the domed nuts evenly and a little at a time in numerical sequence to the torque setting specified at the beginning of the Chapter. When the nuts are correctly torqued,

tighten the bolts at the front and back of the cylinder head and the nuts at the front and back of the cylinder block to the specified torque setting.

4 On 750 models, the cylinder head is secured by twelve 10 mm domed nuts with plain washers and two 8 mm bolts, which are located inside the cam chain tunnel, one at the front and one at the back. The nuts and bolts are numbered for identification **(see illustration)**. Slacken them evenly and a little at a time in a **reverse** of their numerical sequence until they are all slack. Using a torque wrench, now tighten the nuts evenly and a little at a time in numerical sequence to the torque settings specified at the beginning of the Chapter, noting that the 8 mm bolts have a lower setting than the 10 mm nuts.

5 Install the valve cover (see Chapter 2).

26 Suspension - checks

1 The suspension components must be maintained in top operating condition to

25.3a Remove the cylinder head front bolts (A) and cylinder block nut (B) . . .

25.3b . . . and the cylinder head rear bolts (A) and cylinder block nuts (B)

25.3c Cylinder head tightening sequence - 550 models

25.4 Cylinder head tightening sequence - 750 models

ensure rider safety. Loose, worn or damaged suspension parts decrease the motorcycle's stability and control.

Front suspension

2 While standing alongside the motorcycle, apply the front brake and push on the handlebars to compress the forks several times. See if they move up-and-down smoothly without binding. If binding is felt, the forks should be disassembled and inspected (see Chapter 5).

3 Inspect the area above the dust seal for signs of oil leakage, then carefully lever up the dust seal using a flat-bladed screwdriver and inspect the area around the fork seal **(see illustrations)**. If leakage is evident, the seal must be replaced (see Chapter 5).

4 Check the tightness of all suspension nuts and bolts to be sure none have worked loose.

Rear suspension

5 Inspect the rear shocks for fluid leakage and tightness of their mountings. If leakage is found, the shock should be replaced (see Chapter 5).

6 With the aid of an assistant to support the bike, compress the rear suspension several times. It should move up and down freely without binding. If any binding is felt, the worn or faulty component must be identified and replaced. The problem could be due to either the shock absorber or the swingarm components.

7 Position the motorcycle on its centre stand (where fitted), or support it using an auxiliary stand so that the rear wheel is off the ground. Grab the swingarm and rock it from side to side - there should be no discernible movement at the rear **(see illustration)**. If there's a little movement or a slight clicking can be heard, inspect the tightness of all the rear suspension mounting bolts and nuts, referring to the torque settings specified at the beginning of the Chapter, and re-check for movement. Next, grasp the top of the rear wheel and pull it upwards - there should be no discernible freeplay before the shock absorber begins to compress **(see illustration)**. Any freeplay felt in either check indicates worn bearings in the swingarm, or worn shock absorber mountings. The worn components must be replaced (see Chapter 5).

8 To make an accurate assessment of the swingarm bearings, remove the rear wheel (see Chapter 6) and the shock absorbers (see Chapter 5). Grasp the rear of the swingarm with one hand and place your other hand at the junction of the swingarm and the frame. Try to move the rear of the swingarm from side-to-side. Any wear (play) in the bearings should be felt as movement between the swingarm and the frame at the front. If there is any play the swingarm will be felt to move forward and backward at the front (not from side-to-side). Next, move the swingarm up and down through its full travel. It should move freely, without any binding or rough spots. If any play in the swingarm is noted or if the swingarm does not move freely, the bearings must be removed for inspection or replacement (see Chapter 5).

26.3a Lever up the dust seal . . .

26.3b . . . and check for signs of oil leakage

26.7a Checking for play . . .

26.7b . . . in the rear suspension

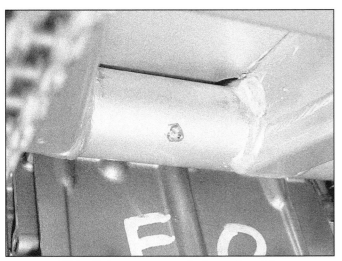

27.1a Swingarm grease nipple - 750 models

27.1b Applying grease to the 550 swingarm using a grease gun

27 Swingarm pivot and bearing - lubrication

1 The swingarm is equipped with a grease nipple **(see illustration)**. Using a suitable grease gun filled with molybdenum disulphide grease, fit the gun onto the nipple and pump it until a small amount of grease seeps past the seals on each end of the pivot shaft **(see illustration)**.

28 Nuts and bolts - tightness check

1 Since vibration of the machine tends to loosen fasteners, all nuts, bolts, screws, etc. should be periodically checked for proper tightness.
2 Pay particular attention to the following:

> Spark plugs
> Engine oil drain plug and oil filter bolt
> Gearshift pedal bolt
> Footrest and stand bolts
> Engine mounting bolts

> Shock absorber mounting bolts
> Handlebar bolts
> Front axle and axle clamp bolts
> Front fork clamp bolts -
> (top and bottom yoke)
> Rear axle nut
> Swingarm pivot nut
> Brake caliper mounting bolts
> Brake hose banjo bolts and caliper bleed valves
> Brake disc bolts and rear sprocket nuts
> Exhaust system bolts/nuts

3 If a torque wrench is available, use it along with the torque specifications at the beginning of this, or other, Chapters.

Every 12 000 miles (20 000 km) or 2 years - ZR550 B & ZR750 C

Every 15 000 miles (24 000 km) or 2 years - ZR750 D

29 Air filter - replacement

1 Remove the old air filter as described in Section 21 and install a new one.

30 Brake fluid - change

1 The brake fluid should be replaced at the prescribed interval or whenever a master cylinder or caliper overhaul is carried out. Refer to the brake bleeding section in Chapter 6, noting that all old fluid must be pumped from the fluid reservoir and hydraulic line before filling with new fluid.

  HAYNES HiNT *Old brake fluid is invariably much darker in colour than new fluid, making it easy to see when all old fluid has been expelled from the system.*

31 Steering head bearings - lubrication

1 Disassemble the steering head for re-greasing of the bearings. Refer to Chapter 5 for details.

32 Front forks - oil change (ZR750 D)

1 Fork oil degrades over a period of time, and will lose its damping qualities. The forks fitted to these machines are equipped with drain plugs, so that they do not have to be removed from the yokes to effect an oil change. Place the machine on its centre stand (if fitted) or else support it in an upright position using an auxiliary stand. Raise the front wheel off the ground using a jack and a block of wood under the engine. To be on the safe side, it is advisable to remove the fuel tank (see Chapter 3) to prevent the possibility of damage should a tool slip.

32.2a Slacken the fork clamp bolt (arrowed)

32.2b With the handlebars displaced, unscrew the fork top bolt

32.3 Remove the fork drain screw and allow all the oil to drain

32.5a Withdraw the spacer . . .

32.5b . . . the spring seat and the spring from the fork

32.6a Pour in the specified amount and type of oil . . .

32.6b . . . then measure the level of oil in the fork

2 Slacken, but do not remove, the fork clamp bolts in the top yoke **(see illustration)**. Displace the handlebars for access to the fork top bolts (see Chapter 5), then remove the top bolts **(see illustration)**.

 HAYNES HiNT *Slackening the fork clamp bolts in the top yoke before slackening the fork top bolts releases pressure on the top bolt. This makes it much easier to remove and helps to preserve the threads.*

3 Place a suitable container under the drain screw of the fork being drained, then remove the screw and allow all the oil to drain **(see illustration)**. Pump the forks up and down to help expel all the oil; bear in mind that it could squirt out forcibly. Discard the drain screw sealing washer - a new one must be used.
4 When all the oil has drained, clean the drain screw threads and apply a suitable non-permanent thread locking compound to them. Install the screw using a new sealing washer and tighten it to the torque setting specified at the beginning of the Chapter.

5 Withdraw the spacer, spring seat and the spring from the tube, noting which way up they fit **(see illustrations)**. Compress the forks if necessary to access the components.
6 Slowly pour in the specified quantity of the specified grade of fork oil and pump the fork to distribute it evenly **(see illustration)**; the oil level should also be measured and adjustment made by adding or subtracting oil. Fully compress the fork and measure the fork oil level from the top of the tube **(see illustration)**. Add or subtract fork oil until the oil is at the level given in the Specifications.

32.8a Fit a new O-ring onto the top bolt . . .

32.8b . . . and tighten it to the specified torque setting

7 Install the spring, followed by the spring seat and the spacer **(see illustrations 32.5b and a)**.

8 Fit a new O-ring to the fork top bolt and thread the bolt into the top of the fork tube **(see illustration)**. Screw the top bolt carefully into the fork tube making sure it is not cross-threaded, and tighten it to the specified torque setting **(see illustration)**. Also tighten the fork clamp bolts in the top yoke to the specified torque setting.

Warning: It will be necessary to compress the spring by pressing down on the spacer using the top bolt to engage the threads of the bolt with the fork tube. This is a potentially dangerous operation and should be performed with care, using an assistant if necessary. Wipe off any excess oil before starting to prevent the possibility of slipping.

9 Install the handlebars (see Chapter 5) and the fuel tank (see Chapter 3).

TOOL TiP *Use a ratchet-type tool when installing the fork top bolt. This makes it unnecessary to remove the tool from the bolt whilst threading it in making it easier to maintain a downward pressure on the spring.*

Every 18 000 miles (30 000 km) or two years - ZR550 B & ZR750 C

33 Front forks - oil change (ZR750 B and ZR750 C)

1 The procedure for changing the front fork oil is the same as for the other models (see Section 32).

Every two or four years - see schedule

34 Brake calipers and master cylinders - seal replacement

This task must be carried out every two years on ZR550 B and ZR750 C models, and every four years on ZR750 D models.
1 Refer to Chapter 6 and dismantle the components for seal replacement.

35 Brake hoses - replacement

This task must be carried out every four years.
1 The hoses should be replaced regardless of their condition.
2 Refer to Chapter 6 and disconnect the brake hoses from the master cylinders and calipers. Always replace the banjo union sealing washers with new ones.

36 Fuel hose - replacement

This task must be carried out every four years.

Warning: Petrol (gasoline) is extremely flammable, so take extra precautions when you work on any part of the fuel system. Don't smoke or allow open flames or bare light bulbs near the work area, and

don't work in a garage where a natural gas-type appliance is present. If you spill any fuel on your skin, rinse it off immediately with soap and water. When you perform any kind of work on the fuel system, it is advisable to wear safety glasses and have a fire extinguisher *suitable for a Class B type fire (flammable liquids) on hand.*

1 The hoses should be replaced regardless of their condition.
2 Remove the fuel tank (see Chapter 3). Disconnect the fuel hoses from the fuel tap and from the carburettors, noting the routing of each hose and where it connects (see Chapter 3 if required). It is advisable to make a sketch of the various hoses before removing them to ensure they are correctly installed.
3 Secure each new hose to its unions using new clamps. Run the engine and check for leaks before taking the bike out on the road.

Non-scheduled maintenance

37 Headlight aim - check and adjustment

Note: *An improperly adjusted headlight may cause problems for oncoming traffic or provide poor, unsafe illumination of the road ahead. Before adjusting the headlight aim, be sure to consult with local traffic laws and regulations - for UK models refer to MOT Test Checks in the Reference section.*
1 The headlight beam can adjusted both horizontally and vertically. Before making any adjustment, check that the tyre pressures are correct and the suspension is adjusted as required. Make any adjustments to the headlight aim with the machine on level ground, with the fuel tank half full and with an assistant sitting on the seat. If the bike is usually ridden with a passenger on the back, have a second assistant to do this.
2 Horizontal adjustment is made by turning the adjuster screw in the right-hand side of the headlight rim **(see illustration)**. Turn it clockwise to move the beam to the right, and anti-clockwise to move it to the left.
3 Vertical adjustment is made by turning the adjuster screw in the base of the headlight **(see illustration)**. Turn it clockwise to move the beam up, and anti-clockwise to move it down.

38 Wheel bearings - check

1 Place the motorcycle on its centre stand (where fitted) or support it upright using an auxiliary stand. Check for any play in the bearings by pushing and pulling the wheel against the hub. Also rotate the wheel and check that it rotates smoothly. If any play is detectable in the hub, or if the wheel does not rotate smoothly (and this is not due to brake or transmission drag), the wheel bearings must be removed and inspected for wear or damage (see Chapter 6).

39 Engine - cylinder compression check

1 Among other things, poor engine performance may be caused by leaking valves, incorrect valve clearances, a leaking head gasket, or worn pistons, rings and/or cylinder walls. A cylinder compression check will help pinpoint these conditions and can also indicate the presence of excessive carbon deposits in the cylinder heads.
2 The only tools required are a compression gauge and a spark plug wrench. A compression gauge with a threaded end for the spark plug hole is preferable to the type which requires hand pressure to maintain a tight seal. Depending on the outcome of the initial test, a squirt-type oil can may also be needed.
3 Make sure the valve clearances are correctly set (see Section 18) and that the cylinder head nuts are tightened to the correct torque setting (see Section 25).
4 Refer to *Fault Finding Equipment* in the Reference section for details of the compression test.

40 Engine - oil pressure check

1 To check the oil pressure, a suitable gauge and adapter piece (which screws into the crankcase) will be needed. Kawasaki provide a kit (part nos. 57001-164 and 57001-1278) for this purpose.
2 Warm the engine up to normal operating temperature then stop it.
3 Unscrew the oil gallery plug below the pulse generator assembly cover and swiftly screw the adapter into the crankcase threads **(see illustration)**. Connect the gauge to the adapter.
4 Start the engine and increase the engine speed to 4000 rpm whilst watching the gauge reading. The oil pressure should be similar to that given in the Specifications at the start of this Chapter.
5 If the pressure is significantly lower than the standard, either the pressure regulator is stuck open, the oil pump is faulty, the oil strainer or filter is blocked, or there is other engine damage. Begin diagnosis by checking the oil filter, strainer and regulator, then the oil pump (see Chapter 2). If those items check out okay, chances are the bearing oil clearances are excessive and the engine needs to be overhauled.
6 If the pressure is too high, either an oil passage is clogged, the regulator is stuck closed or the wrong grade of oil is being used.
7 Stop the engine and unscrew the gauge and adapter from the crankcase.
8 Install the oil gallery plug, and tighten it to the torque setting specified at the beginning of the Chapter. Check the oil level (see *Daily (pre-ride) checks*).

37.2 Headlight beam horizontal adjuster screw (arrowed)

37.3 Headlight beam vertical adjuster screw (arrowed)

40.3 Remove the oil gallery plug (arrowed) and install the pressure gauge

Chapter 2
Engine, clutch and transmission

Contents

Degrees of difficulty

Easy, suitable for novice with little experience	Fairly easy, suitable for beginner with some experience	Fairly difficult, suitable for competent DIY mechanic	Difficult, suitable for experienced DIY mechanic	Very difficult, suitable for expert DIY or professional 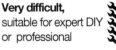

Specifications

ZR550 models

General

Type	Four-stroke DOHC in-line four
Capacity	553 cc
Bore	58.0 mm
Stroke	52.4 mm
Compression ratio	9.5 to 1
Clutch	Wet multi-plate
Transmission	Six-speed constant mesh
Final drive	Chain and sprockets

Cylinder head

Warpage (max)	0.05 mm

Cylinder block

Bore	
Standard	58.000 to 58.012 mm
Wear limit (max)	58.10 mm
Cylinder compression	see Chapter 1

ZR550 models (continued)

Camshafts

	Standard	Service limit
Intake camshaft lobe height	36.23 to 36.37 mm	36.1 mm (min)
Exhaust camshaft lobe height	36.23 to 36.37 mm	36.1 mm (min)
Journal diameter	21.900 to 21.922 mm	21.87 mm (min)
Journal holder diameter	22.000 to 22.021 mm	22.08 mm (max)
Journal oil clearance	0.078 to 0.121 mm	0.21 mm (max)
Runout (max)	0.10 mm	
Camchain 21 pin length (see text)	127.0 to 127.4 mm	128.9 mm

Valves, guides and springs

	Standard	Service limit
Valve clearances	see Chapter 1	
Intake valve	**Standard**	**Service limit**
Stem diameter	5.475 to 5.490 mm	5.46 mm (min)
Guide bore diameter	5.500 to 5.512 mm	5.58 mm (max)
Stem-to-guide clearance	0.010 to 0.037 mm	0.12 mm (max)
Stem deflection (see text)	0.02 to 0.09 mm	0.24 mm (max)
Face thickness	0.85 to 1.15 mm	0.6 mm (min)
Seat width	0.5 to 1.0 mm	
Seat diameter	26.9 to 27.1 mm	
Stem runout	0.05 mm (max)	
Exhaust valve		
Stem diameter	5.455 to 5.470 mm	5.44 mm (min)
Guide bore diameter	5.500 to 5.512 mm	5.58 mm (max)
Stem-to-guide clearance	0.030 to 0.057 mm	0.14 mm (max)
Stem deflection (see text)	0.07 to 0.13 mm	0.28 mm (max)
Face thickness	0.85 to 1.15 mm	0.7 mm (min)
Seat width	0.5 to 1.0 mm	
Seat diameter	22.9 to 23.1 mm	
Stem runout (max)	0.05 mm	
Valve springs free length (intake and exhaust)		
Original parts		
Inner spring	36.7 mm	35.1 mm (min)
Outer spring	38.7 mm	37.1 mm (min)
Replacement parts		
Inner spring	37.25 mm	35.8 mm (min)
Outer spring	41.85 mm	40.2 mm (min)

Pistons

Piston diameter (measured 5.0 mm up from skirt, at 90° to piston pin axis)

Standard	57.965 to 57.980 mm	
Service limit (min)	57.82 mm	
Piston-to-bore clearance	0.020 to 0.047 mm	
1st oversize	+ 0.5 mm	
2nd oversize	+ 1.0 mm	

Piston rings

	Standard	Service limit
End gap (installed)		
Top ring and 2nd ring	0.15 to 0.30 mm	0.60 mm (max)
Oil ring	0.20 to 0.70 mm	1.0 mm (max)
Piston ring thickness - top ring and 2nd ring	1.175 to 1.190 mm	1.1 mm (min)
Piston ring groove width		
Top ring	1.21 to 1.23 mm	1.31 mm (max)
2nd ring	1.23 to 1.25 mm	1.33 mm (max)
Ring-to-groove clearance		
Top ring	0.020 to 0.055 mm	0.16 mm (max)
2nd ring	0.040 to 0.075 mm	0.18 mm (max)
1st oversize	+ 0.5 mm	
2nd oversize	+ 1.0 mm	

Clutch

Friction plate		
Quantity	7	
Thickness		
Standard	2.9 to 3.1 mm	
Service limit (min)	2.8 mm	
Warpage (max)	0.3 mm	
Plain plate		
Quantity	6	
Warpage (max)	0.3 mm	

ZR550 models (continued)

Clutch (continued)

Spring free length
    Standard . . . .   32.6 mm
    Service limit (min) . . . .   31.7 mm

Transmission

Gear ratios (No. of teeth)
    Primary reduction . . . .   2.934 to 1 (27/23T x 65/26T)
    Final reduction
        UK models . . . .   2.375 to 1 (38/16T)
        US models . . . .   2.562 to 1 (41/16T)
    1st gear . . . .   2.571 to 1 (36/14T)
    2nd gear . . . .   1.777 to 1 (32/18T)
    3rd gear . . . .   1.380 to 1 (29/21T)
    4th gear . . . .   1.125 to 1 (27/24T)
    5th gear . . . .   0.961 to 1 (25/26T)
    6th gear . . . .   0.851 to 1 (23/27T)

Selector drum and forks

	Standard	Service limit
Selector fork-to-groove clearance	0.05 to 0.25 mm	0.45 mm (max)
Selector fork end thickness	4.9 to 5.0 mm	4.8 mm (min)
Selector fork groove width	5.05 to 5.15 mm	5.25 mm (max)
Selector fork guide pin diameter		
Input shaft	7.985 to 8.000 mm	7.9 mm (min)
Output shaft	7.9 to 8.0 mm	7.8 mm (min)
Selector drum groove width	8.05 to 8.20 mm	8.3 mm (max)

Crankshaft and bearings

	Standard	Service limit
Journal diameter	31.984 to 32.000 mm	31.96 mm (min)
Main bearing oil clearance	0.014 to 0.038 mm	0.08 mm
Runout (max)	0.05 mm (max)	
Side clearance	0.05 to 0.20 mm	0.40 mm
Primary chain slack	0 to 5 mm	25 mm

Connecting rods

	Standard	Service limit
Big-end side clearance	0.13 to 0.33 mm	0.5 mm (max)
Crankpin diameter	32.984 to 33.000 mm	32.97 mm (min)
Big-end oil clearance	0.035 to 0.059 mm	0.10 mm (max)

Lubrication system

Oil pressure . . . .   see Chapter 1

Torque settings

Engine mounting bolts and nuts . . . .   39 Nm
Engine mounting bracket bolts . . . .   23 Nm
Pulse generator assembly cover bolts . . . .   10 Nm
Oil cooler hose union nuts . . . .   22 Nm
Oil cooler hose union bolts . . . .   8.8 Nm
Valve cover bolts . . . .   12 Nm
Cam chain tensioner mounting bolts . . . .   12 Nm
Cam chain tensioner cap bolt . . . .   5 Nm
Cam chain tensioner blade pivot bracket bolts . . . .   12 Nm
Camshaft cap bolts . . . .   12 Nm
Camshaft sprocket bolts . . . .   15 Nm
Cylinder head 8 mm nuts . . . .   25 Nm
Cylinder head 6 mm bolts . . . .   12 Nm
Cylinder block 6 mm nuts . . . .   9.8 Nm
Clutch nut . . . .   130 Nm
Clutch pressure plate bolts . . . .   8.8 Nm
Gearchange shaft centralising spring locating pin . . . .   20 Nm
Gearchange mechanism cover bolts . . . .   10 Nm
Starter clutch Allen bolts . . . .   34 Nm
Secondary shaft nut . . . .   59 Nm
Oil pressure regulator . . . .   15 Nm
Oil sump bolts . . . .   10 Nm
Crankcase 6 mm bolts . . . .   12 Nm
Crankcase 8 mm bolts . . . .   29 Nm
Connecting rod cap nuts . . . .   24 Nm

ZR750 models

General

Type	Four-stroke DOHC in-line four
Capacity	738 cc
Bore	66.0 mm
Stroke	54.0 mm
Compression ratio	9.5 to 1
Clutch	Wet multi-plate
Transmission	Five-speed constant mesh
Final drive	Chain and sprockets

Camshafts

	Standard	Service limit
Intake camshaft lobe height	36.245 to 36.353 mm	36.15 mm (min)
Exhaust camshaft lobe height	36.245 to 36.353 mm	36.15 mm (min)
Journal diameter	21.940 to 22.040 mm	21.91 mm (min)
Journal holder diameter	22.060 to 22.081 mm	22.14 mm (max)
Journal oil clearance	0.100 to 0.141 mm	0.23 mm (max)
Runout (max)	0.10 mm	
Camchain 21 pin length (see text)	127.0 to 127.36 mm	128.9 mm

Cylinder head

Warpage (max)	0.05 mm

Valves, guides and springs

	Standard	Service limit
Valve clearances	see Chapter 1	
Intake valve		
Stem diameter	6.95 to 6.97 mm	6.94 mm (min)
Guide bore diameter	7.000 to 7.015 mm	7.08 mm (max)
Stem-to-guide clearance	0.030 to 0.065 mm	0.14 mm (max)
Stem deflection (see text)	0.07 to 0.15 mm	0.30 mm (max)
Head thickness	0.80 to 1.20 mm	0.5 mm (min)
Seat width	0.5 to 1.0 mm	
Seat diameter	32.9 to 33.1 mm	
Stem runout (max)	0.05 mm	
Exhaust valve		
Stem diameter	6.95 to 6.97 mm	6.94 mm (min)
Guide bore diameter	7.000 to 7.015 mm	7.08 mm (max)
Stem-to-guide clearance	0.030 to 0.065 mm	0.14 mm (max)
Stem deflection (see text)	0.06 to 0.14 mm	0.28 mm (max)
Head thickness	0.80 to 1.20 mm	0.7 mm (min)
Seat width	0.5 to 1.0 mm	
Seat diameter	28.9 to 29.1 mm	
Stem runout (max)	0.05 mm	
Valve springs free length (intake and exhaust)		
Inner spring	37.25 mm	35.9 mm (min)
Outer spring	41.85 mm	40.3 mm (min)

Cylinder block

Bore	
Standard	66.005 to 66.017 mm
Wear limit (max)	66.10 mm
Cylinder compression	see Chapter 1

Pistons

Piston diameter (measured 5.0 mm up from skirt, at 90° to piston pin axis)	
Standard	65.951 to 65.966 mm
Service limit (min)	65.81 mm
Piston-to-bore clearance	0.039 to 0.066 mm
1st oversize	+ 0.5 mm
2nd oversize	+ 1.0 mm

Piston rings

	Standard	Service limit
End gap (installed)		
Top ring and 2nd ring	0.20 to 0.40 mm	0.70 mm (max)
Piston ring thickness		
Top ring	0.970 to 0.990 mm	0.90 mm (min)
2nd ring	1.170 to 1.190 mm	1.10 mm (min)

ZR750 models (continued)

Piston rings (continued)	Standard	Service limit
Piston ring groove width		
Top ring	1.02 to 1.04 mm	1.12 mm (max)
2nd ring	1.21 to 1.23 mm	1.31 mm (max)
Ring-to-groove clearance		
Top ring	0.030 to 0.070 mm	0.17 mm (max)
2nd ring	0.020 to 0.060 mm	0.16 mm (max)
1st oversize	+ 0.5 mm	
2nd oversize	+ 1.0 mm	

Clutch

Friction plate - C1, C2, C3 and C4 models		
Quantity	7	
Thickness		
Standard	2.65 to 2.95 mm	
Service limit (min)	2.5 mm	
Warpage (max)	0.3 mm	
Friction plate - C5 and D1 models		
Type A plate		
Quantity	2	
Thickness	not available	
Warpage (max)	0.3 mm	
Type B plate		
Quantity	5	
Thickness	not available	
Warpage (max)	0.3 mm	
Plain plate		
Quantity	6	
Warpage (max)	0.3 mm	
Spring free length		
Standard	33.6 mm	
Service limit (min)	32.6 mm	

Transmission

Gear ratios (No. of teeth)	
Primary reduction	2.550 to 1 (27/23T x 63/29T)
Final reduction	2.600 to 1 (39/15T)
1st gear	2.333 to 1 (35/15T)
2nd gear	1.631 to 1 (31/19T)
3rd gear	1.272 to 1 (28/22T)
4th gear	1.040 to 1 (26/25T)
5th gear	0.875 to 1 (21/24T)

Selector drum and forks

	Standard	Service limit
Selector fork-to-groove clearance	0.05 to 0.25 mm	0.45 mm (max)
Selector fork end thickness	4.9 to 5.0 mm	4.8 mm (min)
Selector fork groove width	5.05 to 5.15 mm	5.25 mm (max)
Selector fork guide pin diameter		
Input shaft fork	7.985 to 8.000 mm	7.9 mm (min)
Output shaft forks	7.9 to 8.0 mm	7.8 mm (min)
Selector drum groove width	8.05 to 8.20 mm	8.3 mm (max)

Crankshaft and bearings

	Standard	Service limit
Journal diameter	35.984 to 36.000 mm	35.96 mm (min)
Main bearing oil clearance	0.020 to 0.044 mm	0.08 mm (max)
Runout (max)	0.05 mm	
Side clearance	0.05 to 0.15 mm	0.35 mm
Primary chain slack	0 to 5 mm	25 mm

Connecting rods

	Standard	Service limit
Big-end side clearance	0.15 to 0.30 mm	0.48 mm (max)
Crankpin diameter	34.984 to 35.000 mm	34.97 mm (min)
Big-end oil clearance	0.036 to 0.066 mm	0.10 mm (max)

Lubrication system

Oil pressure	see Chapter 1

ZR750 models (continued)

Torque settings

Engine mounting bolts and nuts . . . . 39 Nm
Engine mounting bracket bolts . . . . 23 Nm
Pulse generator assembly cover bolts . . . . 10 Nm
Oil cooler hose union nuts . . . . 22 Nm
Oil cooler hose union bolts . . . . 8.8 Nm
Valve cover bolts . . . . 12 Nm
Cam chain tensioner plunger bolt . . . . 10 Nm
Cam chain tensioner mounting bolts . . . . 10 Nm
Cam chain tensioner cap bolt . . . . 26 Nm
Camshaft cap bolts . . . . 12 Nm
Camshaft sprocket bolts . . . . 15 Nm
Cylinder head 10 mm nuts . . . . 39 Nm
Cylinder head 8 mm bolts . . . . 29 Nm
Clutch nut . . . . 130 Nm
Clutch pressure plate bolts . . . . 8.8 Nm
Gearchange shaft centralising spring locating pin . . . . 20 Nm
Gearchange mechanism cover bolts . . . . 10 Nm
Starter clutch Allen bolts . . . . 34 Nm
Secondary shaft nut . . . . 59 Nm
Oil pressure regulator . . . . 15 Nm
Oil sump bolts . . . . 10 Nm
Crankcase 6 mm bolts . . . . 12 Nm
Crankcase 8 mm bolts . . . . 29 Nm
Connecting rod cap nuts . . . . 36 Nm
Selector drum cam plunger bolt . . . . 25 Nm
Selector drum guide bolt . . . . 25 Nm

1 General information

The engine/transmission unit is an air-cooled in-line four. The valves (two per cylinder) are operated by double overhead camshafts which are chain driven off the crankshaft. The engine/transmission assembly is constructed from aluminium alloy. The crankcase is divided horizontally.

The crankcase incorporates a wet sump, pressure-fed lubrication system which uses a gear-driven, dual-rotor oil pump, an oil filter and by-pass valve assembly, a relief valve and an oil pressure switch.

Power from the crankshaft is transmitted via a Hy-Vo primary chain to the secondary shaft which runs behind the crankshaft. The secondary shaft carries the starter clutch assembly and provides gear drive to the clutch, which is of the wet, multi-plate type. From the clutch, power is transmitted directly to the input shaft of the transmission, which is a six-speed (550 models) or five-speed (750 models) constant-mesh unit.

2 Operations possible with the engine in the frame

The components and assemblies listed below can be removed without having to remove the engine/transmission assembly from the frame. If however, a number of areas require attention at the same time, removal of the engine is recommended.

Valve cover
Cam chain tensioner & cam chain guides
Camshafts
Cylinder head
Cylinder block, pistons and piston rings
Ignition rotor and pulse generator coil
Clutch
Gearchange mechanism (external parts)
Alternator
Starter clutch and idle gear
Engine sprocket
Oil sump, oil pump, oil strainer and oil pressure relief valve
Starter clutch
Starter motor

3 Operations requiring engine removal

It is necessary to remove the engine/transmission assembly from the frame and separate the crankcase halves to gain access to the following components:

Transmission shafts
Selector drum and forks
Crankshaft and bearings
Connecting rod big-ends and bearings
Cam chain
Primary chain

4 Major engine repair - general note

1 It is not always easy to determine when or if an engine should be completely overhauled, as there are a number of factors to be considered.

2 High mileage is not necessarily an indication that an overhaul is needed, while low mileage, on the other hand, does not preclude the need for an overhaul. Frequency of servicing is probably the single most important factor. An engine that has regular and frequent oil and filter changes, and other required maintenance, will most likely give many miles of reliable service. Conversely, a neglected engine, or one which has not been run in properly, may require an overhaul very early in its life.

3 Exhaust smoke and excessive oil consumption are both indications that piston rings and/or valve guides are in need of attention, although make sure that the fault is not due to oil leakage.

4 If the engine is making obvious knocking or rumbling noises, the connecting rod and/or main bearings are probably at fault.

5 Loss of power, rough running, excessive valve train noise and high fuel consumption rates may also point to the need for an overhaul, especially if they are all present at the same time. If a complete tune-up does not remedy the situation, major mechanical work is the only solution.

6 An engine overhaul generally involves restoring the internal parts to the specifications of a new engine. The piston rings and main and connecting rod bearings are usually replaced and the cylinder walls honed or, if necessary, re-bored during a major overhaul. Generally the valve seats are re-ground, since they are usually in less than perfect condition at this point. The end result should be a like new engine that will give as many trouble-free miles as the original.

5.5 Disconnect the negative lead wire at the connector

5.10 Make alignment marks then remove the bolt (arrowed) and slide the arm off the shaft

7 Before starting the engine overhaul, read through the related procedures to familiarise yourself with the scope and requirements of the job. Overhauling an engine is not all that difficult, but it is time consuming. Plan on the bike being tied up for a minimum of two weeks. Check on the availability of parts and make sure that any necessary special tools, equipment and supplies are obtained in advance.

8 Most work can be done with typical workshop hand tools, although some precision measuring tools are required for inspecting parts to determine if they must be replaced. Often a dealer will handle the inspection of parts and offer advice on reconditioning and replacement. As a general rule, time is the primary cost of an overhaul so it does not pay to install worn or substandard parts.

9 As a final note, to ensure maximum life and minimum trouble from a rebuilt engine, everything must be assembled with care in a spotlessly clean environment.

5 Engine - removal and installation

Note: *The engine is very heavy. Engine removal and installation should be carried out with the aid of at least one assistant; personal injury or damage could occur if the engine falls or is dropped. A hydraulic or mechanical floor jack should be used to support and lower or raise the engine if possible.*

Removal

1 Position the bike on its centre stand or support it securely in an upright position using an auxiliary stand. Work can be made easier by raising the machine to a suitable working height on a hydraulic ramp or a suitable platform.

2 If the engine is dirty, particularly around its mountings, wash it thoroughly before starting

any major dismantling work. This will make work much easier and rule out the possibility of caked on lumps of dirt falling into some vital component.

3 Drain the engine oil and, if required, remove the oil filter (see Chapter 1).

4 Remove the seat and the side panels (see Chapter 7).

5 Disconnect the battery negative (-) lead (see Chapter 8). Trace the black/yellow wire connected to the battery negative lead and disconnect it at its connector **(see illustration)**. Feed the lead through to the engine and coil it on the crankcase, noting its routing.

6 Remove the fuel tank (see Chapter 3).

7 Remove the carburettors (see Chapter 3). Plug the engine intake manifolds with clean rag.

8 Disconnect all the spark plug leads from the plugs and secure them clear of the engine. If the leads are not already marked, make a note of the cylinder number for each lead.

9 On US models, release the air suction valve hose clamps and detach the hoses from their unions. Remove the valve with the hoses attached, noting the routing of each hose.

10 Unscrew the gearchange lever linkage arm pinch bolt and remove the arm from the shaft, noting any alignment marks **(see illustration)**. If no marks are visible, make

your own before removing the arm so that it can be correctly aligned with the shaft on installation.

11 Remove the front sprocket cover and the front sprocket (see Chapter 5).

12 Remove the clutch cable (see Section 19).

13 On 550 models, unscrew the two bolts securing the starter motor top cover and lift off the cover **(see illustration)**. Slacken the starter motor upper mounting bolt, then remove the lower cover **(see illustration)**.

14 Pull back the rubber cover on the starter motor terminal and disconnect the lead **(see illustration)**.

5.13a On 550 models, remove the starter motor top cover . . .

5.13b . . . and the starter motor lower cover

5.14 Pull back the rubber cover and disconnect the starter motor lead

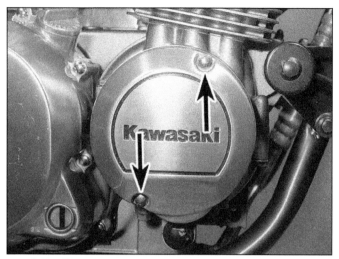

5.15a The pulse generator cover assembly is secured by two bolts (arrowed)

5.15b The pulse generator wiring connector is behind the right-hand side panel on 750 models

5.15c Oil pressure switch wiring connector (arrowed) - 550 models

5.16 Alternator wire connectors (A) - 550 models (750 models have a single block connector), sidestand switch wire connector (B), neutral switch wire connector (C)

15 Remove the ignition pulse generator coil assembly cover **(see illustration)**, then, on 750 models, disconnect the oil pressure switch wiring. Trace the ignition pulse generator wiring back and disconnect it at the ignition control unit (550 models - remove the unit for access to the connectors (refer to Chapter 4) or at the connector behind the right-hand side panel (750 models) **(see illustration)**. Release the wiring from any clips or ties, noting its routing, and coil it on top of the crankcase so that it does not impede engine removal. On 550 models, disconnect the oil pressure switch wiring from the switch on the left-hand side of the sump **(see illustration)**.
16 Trace the alternator wiring back from the alternator cover and disconnect it at the connector(s) **(see illustration)**. Release the wiring from any clips or ties, noting its routing. Also disconnect the sidestand switch wiring at

the connector and pull the neutral switch wiring connector off the switch.
17 Remove the ignition HT coils (refer to Chapter 4).
18 Remove the exhaust system (refer to Chapter 3).
19 Remove the oil cooler and hoses (see Section 7). Also remove the horn if required for improved clearance and access when removing the engine (see Chapter 8).
20 At this point, position an hydraulic or mechanical jack under the engine with a block of wood between the jack head and sump. Make sure that the jack is centrally positioned so that the engine will not topple in any direction when the last mounting bolt is removed. Take the weight of the engine on the jack.
21 Remove the engine front mounting nuts and bolts, then remove the nuts and bolts securing the right-hand front engine mounting

bracket to the frame downtube and remove the bracket, noting how it fits **(see illustrations)**.
22 Make sure that the engine is properly supported on the jack, and have an assistant

5.21a Engine front mounting bolt (A), mounting bracket bolts (B)

5.21b The bolts are secured by nuts on the inside

5.22b Rear mounting bracket bolts (arrowed) - 550 models

5.22a Engine rear mounting bolts (arrowed)

5.22c Rear mounting bracket bolts (arrowed) - 750 models

support it as well. Remove the nuts on the left-hand end of the lower and upper rear engine mounting bolts, then withdraw the bolts **(see illustration)**. Remove the bolts securing the right-hand rear engine mounting bracket to the frame and remove the bracket, noting how it fits **(see illustrations)**.

23 The engine can now be removed from the frame. Check that all wiring, cables and hoses are well clear, then manoeuvre the engine out of the right-hand side of the frame.

24 Check the condition of the front mounting bracket rubber dampers and replace them if they are damaged or deteriorated. Lubricate the new dampers with a soapy solution to aid installation.

Installation

25 Installation is the reverse of removal, noting the following points:

a) *Make sure no wires, cables or hoses become trapped between the engine and the frame when installing the engine.*

b) *The engine mounting bolts are of different lengths. Make sure the correct bolt is installed in its correct location.*

c) *Install the rear engine mounting bolts from the right-hand side. The longer bolt is for the upper rear mounting, and the shorter for the lower rear mounting.*

d) *Do not fully tighten any of the bolts until they have all been installed. Make sure the brackets are correctly positioned.*

e) *Tighten the engine mounting bolt nuts, the mounting bracket bolt nuts and any other bolts and nuts to the torque settings specified at the beginning of the Chapter.*

f) *Use new gaskets on the exhaust pipe connections.*

g) *Align the marks made on the gearchange lever linkage arm and shaft when installing the arm onto the shaft, and tighten the pinch bolt securely.*

h) *Make sure all wires, cables and hoses are correctly routed and connected, and secured by any clips or ties.*

i) *Refill the engine with oil (see Chapter 1).*

j) *Adjust the drive chain freeplay (see Chapter 1).*

k) *Adjust the throttle cable freeplay, the clutch freeplay and the idle speed (see Chapter 1).*

6 Engine disassembly and reassembly - general information

Disassembly

1 Before disassembling the engine, the external surfaces of the unit should be thoroughly cleaned and degreased. This will prevent contamination of the engine internals, and will also make working a lot easier and cleaner. A high flash-point solvent, such as paraffin (kerosene) can be used, or better still, a proprietary engine degreaser. Use old paintbrushes and toothbrushes to work the solvent into the various recesses of the engine casings. Take care to exclude solvent or water from the electrical components and intake and exhaust ports.

> **Warning: The use of petrol (gasoline) as a cleaning agent should be avoided because of the risk of fire.**

2 When clean and dry, arrange the unit on the workbench, leaving suitable clear area for working. Gather a selection of small containers and plastic bags so that parts can be grouped together in an easily identifiable manner. Some paper and a pen should be on hand to permit notes to be made and labels attached where necessary. A supply of clean rag is also required.

3 Before commencing work, read through the appropriate section so that some idea of the necessary procedure can be gained. When removing various engine components it should be noted that great force is seldom required, unless specified. In many cases, a component's reluctance to be removed is indicative of an incorrect approach or removal method. If in any doubt, re-check with the text.

4 An engine support stand made from short lengths of 2 x 4 bolted together into a rectangle will help support the engine **(see illustration)**. The perimeter of the mount should be just big enough to accommodate the sump within it so that the engine rests on its crankcase.

5 When disassembling the engine, keep "mated" parts together (including gears, cylinders, pistons, connecting rods, valves, etc. that have been in contact with each other during engine operation). These "mated" parts must be reused or replaced as an assembly.

6 Engine/transmission disassembly should be done in the following general order with reference to the appropriate Sections.

> *Remove the valve cover*
> *Remove the cam chain tensioner and cam chain guide blades*
> *Remove the camshafts*
> *Remove the cylinder head*
> *Remove the cylinder block*
> *Remove the pistons*
> *Remove the ignition rotor and pulse generator coil assembly (see Chapter 4)*
> *Remove the clutch*
> *Remove the gearchange mechanism external components*
> *Remove the starter clutch and idle gear*
> *Remove the alternator (see Chapter 8)*
> *Remove the starter motor (see Chapter 8)*

6.4 An engine support made from pieces of 2 x 4 inch wood

7.2a Each union is secured to the sump by two bolts (arrowed)

7.2b Separate the hose from the cooler by unscrewing the nut (arrowed)

7.3 The cooler is secured by three bolts (arrowed)

8.6 Note the locations of the different valve cover bolts as you remove them

Remove the oil sump
Remove the oil pump
Separate the crankcase halves
Remove the crankshaft and connecting rods
Remove the transmission shafts/gears
Remove the selector drum and forks

Reassembly

7 Reassembly is accomplished by reversing the general disassembly sequence.

7 Oil cooler and hoses -
removal and installation

Note: *The oil cooler and its hoses can be removed with the engine in the frame.*

Removal

1 Drain the engine oil (see Chapter 1).
2 Unscrew the bolts securing each oil cooler hose union to the oil sump **(see illustration)**. Discard the O-rings as new ones must be used. If required, unscrew the nut securing each hose union to the bottom of the cooler and detach the hoses **(see illustration)**. Discard the O-rings as new ones must be used.
3 Unscrew the three bolts securing the cooler to the frame, then carefully remove the cooler **(see illustration)**.

Installation

4 Installation is the reverse of removal. Always use new O-rings when installing the hoses. Tighten the hose union nuts and bolts to the torque settings specified at the beginning of the Chapter.

8 Valve cover -
removal and installation

Note: *The valve cover can be removed with the engine in the frame. If the engine has been removed, ignore the steps which do not apply.*

Removal

1 Remove the seat and the side panels (see Chapter 7) and disconnect the battery negative (-) lead.
2 Remove the fuel tank (see Chapter 3).
3 On US models, release the air suction valve hose clamps and detach the hoses from their unions. Remove the valve with the hoses attached, noting the routing of each hose.
4 Disconnect the spark plug leads from the plugs and secure them clear of the engine. If the leads are not already marked, label each lead with its cylinder number.
5 Remove the ignition HT coils (Chapter 4). On 750 models, remove the horn (Chapter 8).
6 Unscrew the valve cover bolts and remove them, noting the positions of the different types of bolt **(see illustration)**.
7 Lift the valve cover off the cylinder head. If it is stuck, do not try to lever it off with a screwdriver; tap it gently around the sides with a rubber hammer or block of wood to dislodge it. Remove the gasket and the camshaft end plugs.

8.9a Apply a sealant to the cut-outs . . .

8.9b . . . then fit the end plugs

8.10 Lay a new gasket onto the cylinder head . . .

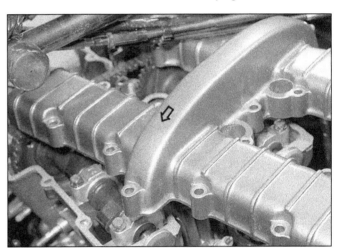

8.11 . . . then install the valve cover with the arrow facing forward

Installation

8 Examine the valve cover gasket and camshaft end plugs for signs of damage or deterioration and replace them if necessary. On 750 models, Kawasaki recommend that they are replaced as a matter of course.

9 Clean the mating surfaces of the cylinder head and the valve cover with lacquer thinner, acetone or brake system cleaner. Apply a silicone sealant to the cut-outs where the camshaft end plugs fit, then install the plugs with the flattened inner section facing up **(see illustrations)**.

10 Lay the gasket onto the cylinder head, making sure all the bolt holes align **(see illustration)**. On 750 models the tab on the gasket must be on the left-hand front portion of the cylinder head.

11 Position the valve cover on the cylinder head with the arrow on its raised centre section facing forward, making sure the gasket stays in place and the cover locates correctly **(see illustration)**. Install the cover bolts and tighten them to the specified torque.

12 Install the remaining components in the reverse order of removal.

9 Cam chain tensioner - removal, inspection and installation

Note: *The cam chain tensioner can be removed with the engine in the frame. If the engine has been removed, ignore the steps that don't apply.*

ZR550 B1 and B2 to frame no. 064686

Caution: Once you start to remove the tensioner bolts, you must remove the tensioner all the way and reset it before tightening the bolts. The tensioner extends itself and locks in place, so if you loosen the bolts partway and then retighten them, the tensioner or cam chain will be damaged. Do not rotate the crankshaft once the tensioner has been removed.

Removal

1 Remove the carburettors (see Chapter 3).

2 Slacken the tensioner cap bolt, then unscrew the two tensioner mounting bolts

and withdraw the tensioner from the back of the cylinder block.

3 Remove the O-ring from the base of the tensioner or from the cylinder block and discard it as a new one must be used.

Inspection

4 Examine the tensioner components for signs of wear or damage.

5 Remove the tensioner cap bolt. Discard the O-ring as a new one must be used. Using a flat-bladed screwdriver, turn the slotted end of the tensioner clockwise to release the tension and allow the plunger to retract into the tensioner body. Remove the screwdriver and check that the tensioner plunger springs back out of the tensioner body.

6 If the tensioner is worn or damaged, or if the plunger is seized in the body or the spring mechanism broken, the tensioner must be replaced. The internal components of the tensioner are not available individually.

Installation

7 Fit a new O-ring onto the tensioner body.

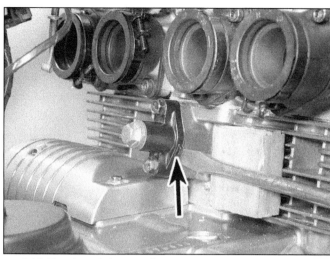

9.13 Tensioner spring cap bolt (A), tensioner mounting bolts (B)

9.14 Use the tab (arrowed) as a leverage point if necessary

8 If not already done, remove the tensioner cap bolt. Discard the O-ring as a new one must be used. Using a flat-bladed screwdriver, turn the slotted end of the tensioner clockwise to release the tension and allow the plunger to retract fully into the tensioner body. Keep the screwdriver located in the slotted end of the tensioner to prevent the plunger springing back out.

9 With the screwdriver still located, fit the tensioner into the cylinder block and install the tensioner mounting bolts. Tighten the bolts to the torque setting specified at the beginning of the Chapter.

10 Remove the screwdriver from the end of the tensioner. As the slotted end turns itself back, the tensioner automatically sets itself to the correct tension against the cam chain. It is advisable to remove the valve cover (see Section 8) and check that the cam chain is tensioned. If this is not the case, remove the pulse generator assembly cover and turn the crankshaft clockwise using a 17 mm socket on the timing rotor hex **(see illustrations 11.2a and b).**

Caution: DO NOT use the timing rotor bolt to turn the crankshaft - it may snap or strip out. Also be sure to turn the engine in its normal direction of rotation.

Set the rotor so that the T mark aligns with the static timing mark on the crankcase. If this does not cure the problem, remove the tensioner and check that it has been correctly installed. Also check that the valve timing marks are all correctly aligned (refer to Section 11).

11 Fit a new O-ring onto the tensioner cap bolt and tighten it to the specified torque.

12 Apply a smear of sealant to the crankcase joints on the pulse generator assembly cover mating surface **(see illustration 9.24a).** Install the pulse generator assembly cover using a new gasket and tighten its bolts to the specified torque setting **(see illustration 9.24b).** If removed, install the valve cover (see Section 8).

ZR550 B2 from frame no. 064687, B3, B4, B5 and B6

Caution: Once you start to remove the tensioner bolts, you must remove the tensioner all the way and reset it before tightening the bolts. The tensioner extends itself and locks in place, so if you loosen the bolts partway and then retighten them, the tensioner or cam chain will be damaged.

Removal

13 Unscrew the tensioner spring cap bolt and withdraw the spring from the tensioner body **(see illustration).**

14 Unscrew the two tensioner mounting bolts and withdraw the tensioner from the back of the cylinder block **(see illustration 9.13).** If it is difficult to remove, there is a little tab on the right-hand side of the tensioner which can be used as a leverage point **(see illustration).**

15 Remove the gasket from the base of the tensioner or from the cylinder block and discard it as a new one must be used.

Inspection

16 Examine the tensioner components for signs of wear or damage.

17 Release the ratchet mechanism from the tensioner plunger and check that the plunger

moves freely in and out of the tensioner body **(see illustrations 9.20a and b).**

18 If the tensioner or any of its components are worn or damaged, or if the plunger is seized in the body, the tensioner assembly must be replaced. Individual components are not available.

Installation

19 Unscrew the bolts securing the pulse generator assembly cover to the right-hand side of the engine **(see illustration 11.2a).** Turn the crankshaft in a clockwise direction with a 17 mm socket on the timing rotor hex **(see illustration 11.2b).** Alternatively, place the motorcycle on its centre stand (where fitted) or support it using an auxiliary stand so that the rear wheel is off the ground, then select a high gear and rotate the rear wheel by hand in its normal direction of rotation. This removes all the slack between the crankshaft and the camshaft in the front run of the chain and transfers it to the back run where it will be taken up by the tensioner.

Caution: DO NOT use the timing rotor bolt to turn the crankshaft - it may snap or strip out. Also be sure to turn the engine in its normal direction of rotation.

20 Release the ratchet mechanism and press the tensioner plunger all the way into the tensioner body **(see illustrations).**

9.20a Release the ratchet (arrowed) . . .

9.20b . . . and press the plunger into the tensioner

9.21a Fit a new gasket on the tensioner . . .

9.21b . . . then install it with the arrow pointing up

9.22 Install the spring into the tensioner and tighten the cap bolt
to the specified torque setting

9.24a Apply sealant to the areas shown (arrowed) . . .

21 Place a new gasket on the tensioner body, then install it in the engine, making sure the arrow on the left-hand side of the tensioner faces up **(see illustrations)**. Tighten the mounting bolts to the torque setting specified at the beginning of the Chapter.

22 Install a new sealing washer on the spring cap bolt. Install the spring and cap bolt and tighten the bolt to the specified torque setting **(see illustration)**.

23 It is advisable to remove the valve cover (see Section 8) and check that the cam chain is tensioned. If it is slack, the tensioner piston did not release.

24 Apply a smear of sealant to the crankcase joints on the pulse generator assembly cover mating surface **(see illustration)**. Install the pulse generator assembly cover using a new gasket and tighten its bolts to the specified torque setting **(see illustration)**. If removed, install the valve cover (see Section 8).

ZR750

Caution: Once you start to remove the tensioner bolts, you must remove the

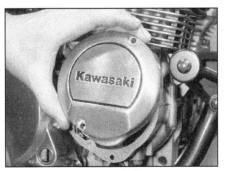

9.24b . . . then fit the cover
using a new gasket

tensioner all the way and reset it before tightening the bolts. The tensioner extends itself and locks in place, so if you loosen the bolts partway and then retighten them, the tensioner or cam chain will be damaged. Do not rotate the crankshaft once the tensioner has been removed.

Removal

25 Remove the starter motor (see Chapter 8).

9.26 Unscrew the cap bolt and withdraw
the spring and stopper

26 Unscrew the tensioner cap bolt from the side of the tensioner body and withdraw the stopper spring and stopper **(see illustration)**.

27 Unscrew the two tensioner mounting bolts and withdraw the tensioner from the back of the cylinder block **(see illustration 9.33)**.

28 Remove the gasket from the base of the tensioner or from the cylinder block and discard it as a new one must be used.

Inspection

29 Keeping your thumb on the plunger to prevent it from springing out, unscrew the plunger bolt from the side of the tensioner body **(see illustration)**. Remove the bolt and release the plunger, then remove it along with the plunger spring. Check that the plunger moves freely in and out of the tensioner body. If it does not, clean all components with solvent and apply molybdenum disulphide grease to all moving parts.

30 Examine the tensioner components for signs of wear or damage **(see illustration)**.

31 If the tensioner or any of its components are worn or damaged, or if the plunger is seized in the body, they must be replaced. Individual components are available.

Installation

32 Install the plunger spring and plunger into the tensioner, aligning the slot in the plunger with the plunger bolt hole **(see illustration)**. Press the plunger into the tensioner and install

the plunger bolt and its washer, making sure the bolt end locates in the slot in the plunger **(see illustration 9.29)**. Tighten the bolt to the torque setting specified at the beginning of the Chapter.

33 Place a new gasket on the tensioner body, then install the tensioner, making sure the longer bolt is installed uppermost and with its aluminium washer **(see illustration)**. Tighten the mounting bolts gradually and evenly to the torque setting specified at the beginning of the Chapter.

34 Install the stopper into the tensioner with its tapered face up, making sure it fits against the tapered face of the plunger **(see illustration 9.26)**. The end of the stopper should protrude about 10 mm from the tensioner. If the stopper sticks out too far the tension has not been taken up by the plunger. If this is the case, remove the pulse generator assembly cover and turn the crankshaft clockwise using a 17 mm socket on the timing rotor hex **(see illustration 11.2a and b)**.

Caution: DO NOT use the timing rotor bolt to turn the crankshaft - it may snap or strip out. Also be sure to turn the engine in its normal direction of rotation.

Set the rotor so that the T mark aligns with the static timing mark on the crankcase. If this does not cure the problem, remove the tensioner and check that it has been correctly assembled. With the stopper correctly installed, install the spring and cap bolt with its washer **(see illustration 9.26)**. Tighten the cap bolt to the specified torque setting.

35 It is advisable to remove the valve cover (see Section 8) and check that the cam chain is tensioned and that the valve timing marks are all correctly aligned (see Section 11).

36 Apply a smear of sealant to the crankcase joints on the pulse generator assembly cover mating surface **(see illustration 9.24a)**. Install the pulse generator assembly cover using a new gasket and tighten its bolts to the specified torque **(see illustration 9.24b)**. If removed, install the valve cover (Section 8).

9.29 Remove the plunger bolt and release the plunger

9.30 Tensioner components - 750 models

9.32 Align the slot in the plunger with the bolt hole (arrowed)

9.33 Install the tensioner with the longer bolt and aluminium washer uppermost

10.3 Measure the cam chain as shown to determine stretch

10.9 Fit the guide blade into the tunnel sideways and twist it round

10 Cam chain and blades - removal, inspection and installation

Note: *To remove the cam chain the engine must be removed from the frame and the crankcases separated. The tensioner blade and guide blade can be removed with the engine in the frame.*

Cam chain

Removal

1 Separate the crankcase halves (Section 24) and remove the crankshaft (see Section 27).
2 Slip the cam chain off the crankshaft.

Inspection

3 Pull the chain tight to remove any slack, then measure the length of 21 pins (from the centre of the 1st pin to the centre of the 21st pin) and compare the result with the service limit specified at the beginning of the Chapter **(see illustration)**. Take several measurements at different places in case the chain has worn unevenly. If any measurement exceeds the service limit, the chain must be replaced. If the chain is replaced, also replace the camshaft sprockets (see Section 11). The sprocket on the crankshaft should also be checked (see Section 27).

Installation

4 Slip the cam chain onto its sprocket on the crankshaft, making sure it is properly engaged.
5 Install the crankshaft (see Section 27).

Cam chain guide blade

Removal

6 Remove the cylinder head (see Section 12).
7 Lift the blade out of the front of the cam chain tunnel in the cylinder block, noting which way round it fits and how it locates.

Inspection

8 Examine the sliding surface of the guide for signs of wear or damage, and replace it if necessary.

Installation

9 Install the blade into the front of the cam chain tunnel in the cylinder block, making sure

the sliding surface faces inwards and that it seats correctly in the cut-outs. On 550 models, install the blade sideways into the block and twist it round when it is in position **(see illustration)**.
10 Install the cylinder head (see Section 12).

Cam chain tensioner blade

Removal

11 Remove the cylinder block (Section 15).
12 On 550 models, remove the two bolts securing the tensioner blade pivot bracket to the crankcase and remove the blade, noting which way round it fits. If required, push out the pivot pin and separate the blade and the bracket.
13 On 750 models, lift the cam chain tensioner blade out of its cut-outs in the crankcase, noting which way round it fits **(see illustration 10.16)**. Take care not to lose the rubber dampers and pivot shaft which fits into the end of the blade.

Inspection

14 Examine the sliding surface of the tensioner blade for signs of wear or damage, and replace it if necessary. Check the condition of the pivot hardware and replace any components that are damaged or deteriorated.

Installation

15 On 550 models, if removed, install the bracket onto the end of the blade and slide the pin through to secure it. Install the blade onto the crankcase, making sure the sliding surface faces inwards, and tighten the bolts to

10.16 Fit the tensioner blade into the crankcase as shown

the torque setting specified at the beginning of the Chapter.
16 On 750 models, if removed, install the pivot shaft into the blade so that the flat ends face up. Fit the rubber dampers with the UP mark facing up onto the flat ends and secure them with some adhesive. Install the blade into the crankcase, making sure the sliding surface faces inwards and the shaft ends locate in their cut-outs **(see illustration)**.
17 Install the cylinder block (see Section 15).

11 Camshafts and followers - removal, inspection and installation

Note: *The camshafts and followers can be removed with the engine in the frame.*

Removal

1 Remove the valve cover (see Section 8).
2 Unscrew the bolts securing the pulse generator coil cover to the right-hand side of the engine **(see illustration)**. The engine can be rotated by using a 17 mm socket on the timing rotor hex and turning it in a clockwise direction only **(see illustration)**.
Caution: DO NOT use the timing rotor bolt to turn the crankshaft - it may snap or strip out. Also be sure to turn the engine in its normal direction of rotation.
Alternatively, place the motorcycle on its centre stand (where fitted) or support it using an auxiliary stand so that the rear wheel is off the ground, then select a high gear and rotate the rear wheel by hand in its normal

11.2a The pulse generator assembly cover is secured by two bolts (arrowed)

11.2b Rotate the engine using a 17 mm socket on the timing rotor hex

11.2c Align the mark next to the T with the index mark (arrowed)

direction of rotation. Rotate the engine until the T mark on the rotor is aligned with the static timing mark on the crankcase **(see illustration)**, and so that the Z5EX mark (550 models) or Z7EX mark (750 models) on the exhaust camshaft sprocket points at the valve cover gasket mating surface on the front of the cylinder head **(see illustrations 11.24a and b)**. Check the positions of all the marks on the exhaust and intake sprockets. This is how they should be positioned for installation later. On 550 models, as the camshafts are identical, make an EX mark on the exhaust camshaft and an IN mark on the intake camshaft (or use tags or labels) so they can be readily identified for installation. On 750 models, the exhaust camshaft has a raised section to the right of the sprocket mounting flange. It is essential the shafts do not get mixed up.

3 Remove the cam chain tensioner (see Section 9).

4 Before disturbing the camshaft caps, check for the identification number on each cap which corresponds to the number marked close to it on the cylinder head **(see illustration)**. Also note the arrow on each cap which points to the front of the engine. These markings ensure that the caps can be matched up to their original journals on installation. If no markings are visible, mark your own using a suitable felt pen. If necessary, make a sketch of the layout as an aid for installation.

5 Unscrew the cap bolts for one of the camshafts, evenly and a little at a time and in a reverse of the tightening sequence **(see illustration 11.26b)**, until they are all loose, then unscrew the cap bolts for the other camshaft. Remove the bolts and lift off the camshaft caps. Retrieve the dowels from either the cap or the cylinder head if they are loose **(see illustration 11.26a)**.

Caution: If the bearing cap bolts aren't loosened evenly, the camshaft may bind.

6 Pull up on the cam chain and carefully guide one camshaft out. With the chain still held taut, remove the other camshaft.

7 While the camshafts are out, don't allow the chain to go slack - the chain may drop down and bind between the crankshaft and case, which could damage these components. Wire the chain to another component to prevent it from dropping. Also, cover the top of the cylinder head with a rag to prevent foreign objects from falling into the engine.

8 Obtain a container which is divided into eight compartments, and label each compartment with the location of its corresponding valve in the cylinder head and whether it belongs with an intake or an exhaust valve. Pick each follower and shim out of the cylinder head and store them in the corresponding compartment in the container **(see illustrations)**.

Inspection

9 Inspect the bearing surfaces of the head and the bearing caps and the corresponding journals on the camshaft. Look for score marks, deep scratches or for any evidence of spalling (a pitted appearance) **(see illustration)**.

11.4 Note the number on each cap (A) and the corresponding number on the cylinder head (B). Arrow on each cap faces forward

11.8a Remove the follower . . .

11.8b . . . and the shim from each valve

11.9 Check the journal surfaces of the camshaft for scratches or wear

11.10a Check the lobes of the camshaft for wear - here's an example of damage requiring camshaft repair or renewal

11.10b Measure the height of the camshaft lobes with a micrometer

10 Check the camshaft lobes for heat discoloration (blue appearance), score marks, chipped areas, flat spots and spalling **(see illustration)**. Measure the height of each lobe with a micrometer **(see illustration)** and compare the results to the minimum lobe height listed in this Chapter's Specifications. If damage is noted or wear is excessive, the camshaft must be replaced.

11 The sprocket must be removed before camshaft runout can be checked. Check the sprocket markings in relation to the sprocket holding bolts before removing the bolts and separating the sprocket from the camshaft **(see illustration 11.21a or b)**. Support each end of the camshaft on V-blocks, and measure any runout using a dial gauge positioned with its tip against the sprocket mounting shoulder **(see illustration)**. If the runout exceeds the specified limit the camshaft must be replaced. Install the sprocket on the camshaft as described in Step 21.

12 Next, check the camshaft bearing oil clearances. Clean the camshafts, the bearing surfaces in the cylinder head and the bearing caps with a clean, lint-free cloth, then lay the camshafts in their correct place in the cylinder head, with the sprocket bolt heads facing the right-hand side of the engine and with the marks correctly aligned **(see illustration 11.24a and b)**. Make sure the exhaust camshaft is on the exhaust side of the engine, and the intake camshaft is on the intake side of the engine. Engage the cam chain with the sprockets as you position the camshafts, so they don't turn as the bearing caps are tightened.

13 Cut eight strips of Plastigauge and lay one piece on each bearing journal, parallel with the camshaft centreline **(see illustration)**.

14 Make sure the camshaft cap dowels are installed **(see illustration 11.26a)**. Install the caps in their correct numbered positions and with the arrow on each cap pointing to the front of the engine **(see illustration 11.4)** and install the bolts. Tighten the bolts evenly and a little at a time in the sequence shown, to the torque listed in this Chapter's Specifications **(see illustration 11.26b)**. While doing this, DO NOT let the camshafts rotate!

15 Now unscrew the bolts, a little at a time, and carefully lift off the caps.

16 To determine the oil clearance, compare the crushed Plastigauge (at its widest point) on each journal to the scale printed on the Plastigauge container **(see illustration)**. Compare the results to this Chapter's Specifications. If the oil clearance is greater than specified, measure the diameter of the cam bearing journal with a micrometer **(see illustration)**. If the journal diameter is less

11.11 Camshaft runout measurement

11.13 Place a strip of Plastigauge on each bearing journal

11.16a Compare the width of the crushed Plastigauge to the scale provided with it to obtain the clearance

11.16b Measure the cam bearing journal with a micrometer

than the specified limit, replace the camshaft with a new one and recheck the clearance. If the clearance is still too great, or if the journal diameter was within limits, replace the cylinder head and camshaft caps with new parts.

 Before replacing camshafts or the cylinder head and caps because of damage, check with local machine shops specialising in motorcycle engine work. In the case of the camshafts, it may be possible for cam lobes to be welded, re-ground and hardened, at a cost far lower than that of a new camshaft. If the bearing surfaces in the cylinder head are damaged, it may be possible for them to be bored out to accept bearing inserts. Due to the cost of a new cylinder head it is recommended that all options be explored before condemning it as trash!

17 Except in cases of oil starvation, the cam chain wears very little. If the chain has stretched beyond its limit (see Section 10), which makes it difficult to maintain proper tension, replace it with a new one.
18 Check the sprockets for wear, cracks and other damage, replacing them if necessary. If the sprockets are worn, the chain is also worn, and also the sprocket on the crankshaft (which can only be remedied by replacing the crankshaft). If wear this severe is apparent, the entire engine should be disassembled for inspection.
19 Inspect the outer surfaces of the cam followers for evidence of scoring or other damage. If a follower is in poor condition, it is probable that the bore in which it works is also damaged. Check for clearance between the followers and their bores. Whilst no specifications are given, if slack is excessive, replace the followers. If the bores are seriously out-of-round or tapered, the cylinder head and the followers must be replaced.

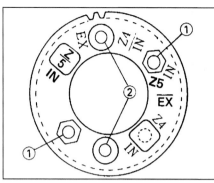

11.21a Sprocket details - 550 models

1 Bolt holes for intake camshaft
2 Bolt holes for exhaust camshaft

Installation

20 Lubricate each shim and its follower with engine oil and install them in the cylinder head, noting that the shim must be installed with its size marking downwards **(see illustrations 11.8b and a)**. **Note:** *It is most important that the shims and followers are returned to their original valves otherwise the valve clearances will be inaccurate.*
21 If removed, install each sprocket onto its camshaft. The sprockets are identical and can be interchanged, but are installed using different mounting holes **(see illustrations)**. Be sure to correctly identify each camshaft (see Step 2), then install the sprockets accordingly. Make sure they are installed correctly and with the marked side of each sprocket facing out otherwise the timing marks will not align. Apply a smear of a suitable non-permanent thread locking compound to the sprocket bolts, then install them and tighten them to the torque setting specified at the beginning of the Chapter.
22 Make sure the bearing surfaces in the cylinder head and the camshaft caps are clean, then apply a light coat of engine assembly lube or moly-based grease to each of them. Apply a coat of moly-based grease to the camshaft lobes.

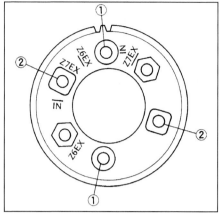

11.21b Sprocket details - 750 models

1 Bolt holes for intake camshaft
2 Bolt holes for exhaust camshaft

23 Check that the cam chain is engaged around the lower sprocket teeth on the crankshaft and that the crankshaft is positioned as described in Step 2. Next identify which is the exhaust camshaft and which is the intake (see Step 2). Install the exhaust camshaft through the cam chain. Position it so that the Z5EX mark (550 models) or Z7EX mark (750 models) on the sprocket points forwards and is flush with the top of the cylinder head mating surface **(see illustrations 11.24a and b)**. Keeping the front run of the chain taut engage the chain on the sprocket teeth.
24 Starting with the cam chain pin that is directly opposite the Z5EX mark (550 models) and slightly above the Z7EX mark (750 models) on the exhaust camshaft sprocket, count the specified number of pins along the chain towards the intake side **(see illustrations)**. Install the intake camshaft through the cam chain and engage the sprocket with the chain so that the Z5IN mark (550 models) or IN mark (750 models) on the sprocket aligns with the specified pins as shown.
25 Before proceeding further, check that everything aligns as described in Steps 2, 23

11.24a Camshaft timing details - 550 models

1 Z5IN mark
2 Sprocket bolts (intake)
3 Intake camshaft sprocket
4 Cam chain
5 Cylinder head gasket surface
6 Exhaust camshaft sprocket
7 Sprocket bolts (exhaust)
8 Z5EX mark
9 Pull this side of the chain taut

FRONT

11.24b Camshaft timing details - 750 models

1 IN mark
2 Sprocket bolts (intake)
3 Intake camshaft sprocket
4 Cam chain
5 Cylinder head gasket surface
6 Exhaust camshaft sprocket
7 Sprocket bolts (exhaust)
8 Z7EX mark
9 Pull this side of the chain taut

11.26a Check that the camshaft cap dowels are installed

11.26b Camshaft cap bolt tightening sequence

11.26c Tighten the bolts to the specified torque setting

and 24. If it doesn't, the valve timing will be inaccurate and the valves will contact the pistons when the engine is turned over.

26 Oil the camshaft caps. Ensure the camshaft cap dowels are installed **(see illustration)**, then fit the caps, making sure they are in their proper positions as noted on removal (Step 4) **(see illustration 11.4)**. Tighten the cap bolts on one camshaft evenly and a little at a time in the sequence shown, until the specified torque setting is reached **(see illustrations)**. Repeat for the other camshaft. **Note:** *The cap bolts are of the high tensile type - don't use any other type of bolt..*
27 With all caps tightened down, check that the valve timing marks still align (see Steps 2, 23 and 24). Check that each camshaft is not pinched by turning the crankshaft a few degrees in each direction with a 17 mm socket on the timing rotor hex **(see illustration 11.2b)**.
Caution: If the marks are not aligned exactly as described, the valve timing will be incorrect and the valves may strike the pistons, causing extensive damage to the engine.
28 Install the cam chain tensioner (see Section 9).
29 Check the valve clearances (see Chapter 1).
30 The remainder of installation is the reverse of removal Apply a smear of sealant to the crankcase joints on the pulse generator assembly cover mating surface **(see illustration 9.24a)**. Install the pulse generator assembly cover using a new gasket and

tighten its bolts to the specified torque setting **(see illustration 9.24b)**. Install the valve cover (see Section 8).

12 Cylinder head - removal and installation

Caution: The engine must be completely cool before beginning this procedure or the cylinder head may become warped.
Note: *The cylinder head can be removed with the engine in the frame. If the engine has already been removed, ignore the steps which don't apply.*

Removal

1 Remove the carburettors (see Chapter 3).

12.5a Remove the cylinder head front bolts (A) and cylinder block nut (B) . . .

2 Remove the exhaust system (see Chapter 3).
3 Remove the spark plugs (see Chapter 1).
4 Remove the camshafts (see Section 11).
5 On 550 models, the cylinder head is secured by twelve 8 mm domed nuts with plain washers and five 6 mm bolts, and the cylinder block by three 6 mm nuts. Unscrew the bolts and nuts on the front and back of the cylinder head and block **(see illustrations)**. The twelve domed nuts are numbered for identification **(see illustration)**. Slacken the nuts evenly and a little at a time in a **reverse** of their numerical sequence until they are all slack. Remove all the nuts and their washers, taking great care not to drop any of them into the crankcase.
6 On 750 models, the cylinder head is secured by twelve 10 mm domed nuts with plain washers and two 8 mm bolts, which are

12.5b . . . and the cylinder head rear bolts (A) and cylinder block nuts (B)

12.5c Cylinder head nut TIGHTENING sequence - 550 models

12.6 Cylinder head nut TIGHTENING sequence - 750 models

located inside the cam chain tunnel. The nuts and bolts are numbered for identification (see illustration). Slacken them evenly and a little at a time in a reverse of their numerical sequence until they are all slack. Remove all the nuts and their washers, and the bolts, taking great care not to drop any of them into the crankcase.

7 Pull the cylinder head up off the studs. If it is stuck, tap around the joint faces of the cylinder head with a soft-faced mallet to free the head. Do not attempt to free the head by inserting a screwdriver between the head and cylinder block - you'll damage the sealing surfaces.

8 Lift the head off the block, passing the cam chain down through the tunnel as you do. Do not let the chain fall into the block - secure it with a piece of wire or metal bar to prevent it from doing so. Remove the old cylinder head gasket and the two oil nozzles and the O-rings which fit around them on each end of the block. Stuff a clean rag into the cam chain tunnel to prevent any debris falling into the engine. Discard the gasket and O-rings as new ones must be used.

9 If they are loose, remove the dowels from around the front outer studs (see illustration). If either appears to be missing it is probably stuck in the underside of the cylinder head.

10 Check the cylinder head gasket and the mating surfaces on the cylinder head and block for signs of leakage, which could indicate warpage. Refer to Section 14 and check the flatness of the cylinder head.

11 Clean all traces of old gasket material from the cylinder head and block. If a scraper is used, take care not to scratch or gouge the soft aluminium. Be careful not to let any of the gasket material fall into the crankcase, the cylinder bores or the oil passages.

Installation

12 If removed, install the two dowels onto the front outer studs on the cylinder block (see illustration 12.9). Lubricate the cylinder bores with engine oil.

13 Make sure the oil nozzles are clean and not blocked, then install them into each end of the cylinder block (see illustration). Fit new O-rings around them (see illustration). Make sure they are pressed into their recesses and are properly seated.

14 Ensure both cylinder head and block mating surfaces are clean, then lay the new head gasket in place on the cylinder block, making sure all the holes are correctly aligned and that the UP or HEAD letters on the gasket face up. Never re-use the old gasket.

15 Carefully lower the cylinder head over the studs and onto the block (see illustration). It is helpful to have an assistant to pass the cam chain up through the tunnel and slip a piece of wire through it to prevent it falling back into the engine. Keep the chain taut to prevent it becoming disengaged from the crankshaft sprocket.

16 On 550 models, install the twelve 10 mm domed nuts with their plain washers and tighten them finger-tight. Now tighten the nuts evenly and a little at a time in their numerical sequence (see illustration 12.5c) to the torque setting specified at the beginning of the Chapter (see illustration). When the nuts are correctly torqued, tighten the bolts at the front and back of the cylinder head and the nuts at the front and back of the cylinder block to the specified torque setting (see illustration 12.5a and b).

12.9 Remove the dowel (arrowed) from each front outer stud if it is loose

12.13a Press each oil nozzle into its hole . . .

12.13b . . . and fit a new O-ring around it

12.15 Keep the cam chain taut when fitting the cylinder head

12.16 Tighten the cylinder head nuts in the correct sequence to the specified torque

17 On 750 models, install the twelve 10 mm domed nuts with their plain washers, and the two 8 mm bolts and tighten them finger-tight. Now tighten the nuts and bolts evenly and a little at a time in their numerical sequence **(see illustration 12.6)** to the torque settings specified at the beginning of the Chapter **(see illustration 12.16)**.
18 Install the camshafts (see Section 11) and the valve cover (see Section 8).
19 Install the spark plugs (see Chapter 1).
20 Install the exhaust system (see Chapter 3).
21 Install the carburettors (see Chapter 3).

13 Valves/valve seats/valve guides - servicing

1 Because of the complex nature of this job and the special tools and equipment required, most owners leave servicing of the valves, valve seats and valve guides to a professional.
2 The home mechanic can, however, remove the valves from the cylinder head, clean and check the components for wear and assess the extent of the work needed, and, unless a valve service is required, grind in the valves (see Section 14).
3 The dealer service department will remove the valves and springs, recondition or replace the valves and valve seats, replace the valve guides, check and replace the valve springs, spring retainers and collets/keepers (as necessary), replace the valve seals with new ones and reassemble the valve components.
4 After the valve service has been performed, the head will be in like-new condition. When the head is returned, be sure to clean it again very thoroughly before installation on the engine to remove any metal particles or abrasive grit that may still be present from the valve service operations. Use compressed air, if available, to blow out all the holes and passages.

14 Cylinder head and valves - disassembly, inspection and reassembly

1 As mentioned in the previous section, valve servicing, valve seat re-cutting and valve

guide replacement should be left to a Kawasaki dealer. However, disassembly, cleaning and inspection of the valves and related components can be done (if the necessary special tools are available) by the home mechanic. This way no expense is incurred if the inspection reveals that overhaul is not required at this time.
2 To disassemble the valve components without the risk of damaging them, a valve spring compressor is absolutely necessary. This special tool can usually be rented, but if it's not available, have a dealer service department or motorcycle repair shop handle the entire process of disassembly, inspection, service or repair (if required) and reassembly of the valves.

Disassembly

3 Before proceeding, arrange to label and store the valves along with their related components in such a way that they can be returned to their original locations without getting mixed up **(see illustration)**. An excellent way to do this is to make up a container which is divided into eight compartments, and then to label each with the identity of the valve and components which will be stored in it (ie the number of the cylinder, and intake or exhaust valve).

Alternatively, labelled plastic bags will do just as well.
4 If not already done, clean all traces of old gasket material from the cylinder head. If a scraper is used, take care not to scratch or gouge the soft aluminium. Gasket removing solvents, which work very well, are available at most motorcycle shops and auto parts stores. Carefully scrape all carbon deposits out of the combustion chamber area. A hand held wire brush or a piece of fine emery cloth can be used once the majority of deposits have been scraped away. Do not use a wire brush mounted in a drill motor, or one with extremely stiff bristles, as the head material is soft and may be eroded away or scratched by the wire brush.
5 Compress the valve spring on the first valve with a spring compressor, making sure it is correctly located onto each end of the valve assembly **(see illustration)**. Do not compress the springs any more than is absolutely necessary. Remove the collets, using either needle-nose pliers, tweezers, a magnet or a screwdriver with a dab of grease on it **(see illustration)**. Carefully release the valve spring compressor and remove the spring retainer, noting which way up it fits, the springs and the valve from the head **(see illustrations 14.27c, b and a)**. If the valve binds in the guide (won't

14.3 Valve components

1	Follower	6	Inner spring
2	Shim	7	Stem seal
3	Collets (keepers)	8	Spring seat
4	Spring retainer	9	Exhaust valve
5	Outer spring	10	Intake valve

14.5a Compressing the valve springs with a valve spring compressor

14.5b Remove the collets with needle-nose pliers, tweezers, a magnet or a screwdriver with a dab of grease on it

14.5c If the valve stem won't pull through the guide, deburr the area above the collet groove

14.13 Measure the valve seat width with a ruler (or for greater precision use a vernier caliper)

pull through), push it back into the head and deburr the area around the collet groove with a very fine file or whetstone (see illustration).

6 Repeat the procedure for the remaining valves. Remember to keep the parts for each valve together and in order so they can be reinstalled in the same location.

7 Once the valves have been removed and labelled, pull the valve stem seals off the top of the valve guides with pliers and discard them (the old seals should never be reused), then remove the spring seats, noting which way up they fit (see illustrations 14.26b and a).

8 Next, clean the cylinder head with solvent and dry it thoroughly. Compressed air will speed the drying process and ensure that all holes and recessed areas are clean.

9 Clean all of the valve springs, collets, retainers and spring seats with solvent and dry them thoroughly. Do the parts from one valve at a time so that no mixing of parts between valves occurs.

10 Scrape off any deposits that may have formed on the valve, then use a motorised wire brush to remove deposits from the valve heads and stems. Again, make sure the valves do not get mixed up.

Inspection

11 Inspect the head very carefully for cracks and other damage. If cracks are found, a new head will be required. Check the cam bearing surfaces for wear and evidence of seizure. Check the camshafts and followers for wear as well (see Section 11).

12 Using a precision straight-edge and a feeler gauge set to the warpage limit listed in the specifications at the beginning of the Chapter, check the head gasket mating surface for warpage. Refer to *Tools and Workshop Tips* in the Reference section for details of how to check for use a straight-edge. If the head is warped, it must either be machined or, if warpage is excessive, replaced with a new one.

13 Examine the valve seats in the combustion chamber. If they are pitted, cracked or burned, the head will require work beyond the scope of the home mechanic. Measure the valve seat

width and compare it to this Chapter's Specifications (see illustration). If it exceeds the service limit, or if it varies around its circumference, valve overhaul is required. If available, use Prussian blue to determine the extent of valve seat wear. Uniformly coat the seat with the Prussian blue, then install the valve and rotate it back and forth using a lapping tool. Remove the valve and check whether the ring of blue on the valve is uniform and continuous around the valve, and of the correct width as specified.

14 Clean the valve guides to remove any carbon build-up, then install the valve in its guide so that its face is 10 mm above the seat. Mount a dial gauge against the side of the valve as close to the cylinder head surface as possible and measure the amount of side clearance (wobble) between the valve stem and its guide in two perpendicular directions (see illustration). If the clearance exceeds the limit specified, remove the valve and measure the valve stem diameter (see illustration). Also measure the inside diameter of the guide

14.14a Measuring valve stem-to-guide clearance (wobble method)
1 Valve   2 Guide   3 Wobble

14.14b Measure the valve stem diameter with a micrometer

14.14c Insert a small hole gauge into the valve guide and expand it so there's a slight drag when it's pulled out

14.14d Measure the small hole gauge with a micrometer

14.15 Measure the valve face thickness as shown

14.16 Check the valve face (A), stem (B) and collet groove (C) for signs of wear and damage

(at both ends and the centre of the guide) with a small hole gauge and micrometer (see illustrations). The guides are measured at the ends and at the centre to determine if they are worn in a bell-mouth pattern (more wear at the ends). If the valve stem or guide is worn beyond its limit, it must be replaced.

15 Carefully inspect each valve face for cracks, pits and burned spots. Measure the valve face thickness and compare it to this Chapter's Specifications (see illustration). If it exceeds the service limit, or if it varies around its circumference, valve overhaul is required.

16 Check the valve stem and the collet groove area for cracks (see illustration). Rotate the valve and check for any obvious indication that it is bent. Check the end of the stem for pitting and excessive wear. The presence of any of the above conditions indicates the need for valve servicing.

17 Using V-blocks and a dial gauge, measure the valve stem runout and compare the results to the specifications (see illustration). If the measurement exceeds the service limit specified, the valve must be replaced.

18 Check the end of each valve spring for wear and pitting. Measure the spring free length and compare it to that listed in the specifications (see illustration). If any spring is shorter than specified it has sagged and must be replaced. Also place the spring upright on a flat surface and check it for bend

14.17 Measure the valve stem runout using V-blocks and a dial gauge as shown

14.18a Measure the free length of the valve springs

14.18b Check the valve springs for squareness

14.22 Apply the lapping compound very sparingly, in small dabs, to the valve face only

by placing a ruler against it **(see illustration)**. If the bend in any spring is excessive, it must be replaced.

19 Check the spring retainers and collets for obvious wear and cracks. Any questionable parts should not be reused, as extensive damage will occur in the event of failure during engine operation.

20 If the inspection indicates that no overhaul work is required, the valve components can be reinstalled in the head.

Reassembly

21 Unless a valve service has been performed, before installing the valves in the head they should be ground in (lapped) to ensure a positive seal between the valves and seats. This procedure requires coarse and fine valve grinding compound and a valve grinding tool. If a grinding tool is not available, a piece of rubber or plastic hose can be slipped over the valve stem (after the valve has been installed in the guide) and used to turn the valve.

22 Apply a small amount of coarse grinding compound to the valve face, then slip the valve into the guide **(see illustration)**. **Note:** *Make sure each valve is installed in its correct guide and be careful not to get any grinding compound on the valve stem.*

23 Attach the grinding tool (or hose) to the valve and rotate the tool between the palms of your hands. Use a back-and-forth motion (as though rubbing your hands together) rather than a circular motion (ie so that the valve rotates alternately clockwise and anti-clockwise rather than in one direction only) **(see illustration)**. Lift the valve off the seat and turn it at regular intervals to distribute the grinding compound properly. Continue the grinding procedure until the valve face and seat contact area is of uniform width and unbroken around the entire circumference of the valve face and seat **(see illustration)**.

24 Carefully remove the valve from the guide and wipe off all traces of grinding compound. Use solvent to clean the valve and wipe the seat area thoroughly with a solvent soaked cloth.

25 Repeat the procedure with fine valve grinding compound, then repeat the entire procedure for the remaining valves.

26 Lay the spring seats for all the valves in place in the cylinder head with their shouldered side facing up so that they fit into the base of the springs (the spring seat can be identified from the spring retainer by its larger internal diameter - be sure not to mix up the two), then install new valve stem seals on each of the guides **(see illustrations)**. Use an appropriate size deep socket to push the seals over the end of the valve guide until they are felt to clip into place. Don't twist or cock them, or they will not seal properly against the valve stems. Also, don't remove them again or they will be damaged.

14.23a Rotate the valve grinding tool back and forth between the palms of your hands

14.23b The face and seat should be the specified width and with a smooth, unbroken appearance (arrowed)

14.26a Install the spring seat, not confusing the spring seat with the spring retainer which goes on top of the springs

14.26b Fit the oil seal over the valve stem

14.27a Coat the valve stem with molybdenum disulphide grease and install the valve in its guide

14.27b Install the inner and outer springs with their closer wound coils at the bottom next to the head

14.27c Make sure the spring retainer is the correct way round

14.28 A small dab of grease will help to keep the collets in place on the valve while the spring is released

27 Coat the valve stems with molybdenum disulphide grease, then install one of them into its guide, rotating it slowly to avoid damaging the seal **(see illustration)**. Check that the valve moves up and down freely in the guide. Next, install the inner and outer springs, with their closer wound coils facing down into the cylinder head, followed by the spring retainer, with its larger shouldered side which fits into the top of the springs facing down, and with the shim cut-out facing up **(see illustrations)**.
28 Apply a small amount of grease to the collets to help hold them in place as the pressure is released from the springs **(see illustration)**. Compress the springs with the valve spring compressor and install the collets **(see illustration 14.5b)**. When compressing the springs, depress them only as far as is absolutely necessary to slip the collets into place. Make certain that the collets are securely locked in their retaining grooves.
29 Support the cylinder head on blocks so the valves can't contact the workbench top, then very gently tap each of the valve stems with a soft-faced hammer. This will help seat the collets in their grooves.

 HAYNES HiNT *Check for proper sealing of the valves by pouring a little solvent into each of the valve ports. If the solvent leaks past any valve into the combustion chamber area the valve grinding operation on that valve should be repeated.*

15 Cylinder block - removal, inspection and installation

Note: *The cylinder block can be removed with the engine in the frame.*

Removal

1 Remove the cylinder head (see Section 12). On 550 models, don't forget to remove the three 6 mm nuts which retain the block to the crankcase studs.
2 Hold the cam chain up and lift the cylinder block up to remove it from the studs, then pass the cam chain down through the tunnel. Do not let the chain fall into the crankcase - secure it with a piece of wire or metal bar to prevent it from doing so. If the block is stuck, tap around the joint faces of the block with a soft-faced mallet to free it from the crankcase, taking great care not to damage any of the cooling fins. Don't attempt to free the block by inserting a screwdriver between it and the crankcase - you'll damage the sealing surfaces. When the block is removed, stuff clean rags around the pistons to prevent anything falling into the crankcase.
3 Note the location of the oil nozzle on each end of the block mating surface on the crankcase. Remove the nozzles and their O-rings **(see illustration)**; discard the O-rings as new ones must be used.
4 Remove the gasket and, where a paper-based gasket has been used, clean all traces of old gasket material from the cylinder block

and crankcase mating surfaces. If a scraper is used, take care not to scratch or gouge the soft aluminium. Be careful not to let any of the gasket material fall into the crankcase or the oil passages.

Inspection

5 Do not attempt to separate the cylinder liners from the cylinder block.
6 Check the cylinder walls carefully for scratches and score marks. A rebore will be necessary to remove any deep scores.
7 No figure is given for block gasket face warpage, but a check can be performed as described for the cylinder head in Section 12. If warpage seems excessive, seek the advice of a bike engineering specialist.
8 Using telescoping gauges and a micrometer (see *Tools and Workshop Tips*), check the dimensions of each cylinder to assess the

15.3 Remove each oil nozzle and its O-ring *O-ring not fitted to 750 C5 and D1 models*

15.8 Measure the cylinder bore in the directions shown with a telescoping gauge, then measure the gauge with a micrometer

15.16 The cut-out in the gasket (arrowed) must be on the left-hand side - 550 models

amount of wear, taper and ovality. Measure near the top (but below the level of the top piston ring at TDC - about 10 mm below the top of the cylinder), centre and bottom (but above the level of the oil ring at BDC - about 20 mm above the bottom of the cylinder) of the bore, both parallel to and across the crankshaft axis **(see illustration)**. Calculate any differences between the measurements taken to determine any taper and ovality in the bore. Compare the results to the specifications at the beginning of the Chapter. If the cylinders are tapered, oval, or worn beyond the service limits, or badly scratched, scuffed or scored, have them rebored and honed by a Kawasaki dealer or bike engineering specialist. If the cylinders are rebored, they will require oversize pistons and rings.

9 If the precision measuring tools are not available, take the block to a Kawasaki dealer or specialist motorcycle repair shop for assessment and advice.

10 If the block and cylinders are in good condition and the piston-to-bore clearance is within specifications (see Section 16), the cylinders should be honed (de-glazed). To perform this operation you will need the proper size flexible hone with fine, or a bottle-brush type hone, plenty of light oil or honing oil, some clean rags and an electric drill motor.

11 Hold the block sideways (so that the bores are horizontal rather than vertical) in a vice with soft jaws or cushioned with wooden blocks. Mount the hone in the drill motor, compress the stones and insert the hone into the cylinder. Thoroughly lubricate the cylinder, then turn on the drill and move the hone up and down in the cylinder at a pace which produces a fine cross-hatch pattern on the cylinder wall with the lines intersecting at an angle of approximately 60°. Be sure to use plenty of lubricant and do not take off any more material than is necessary to produce the desired effect. Do not withdraw the hone

from the cylinder while it is still turning. Switch off the drill and continue to move it up and down in the cylinder until it has stopped turning, then compress the stones and withdraw the hone. Wipe the oil from the cylinder and repeat the procedure on the other cylinder. Remember, do not take too much material from the cylinder wall.

12 Wash the cylinders thoroughly with warm soapy water to remove all traces of the abrasive grit produced during the honing operation. Be sure to run a brush through the bolt holes and flush them with running water. After rinsing, dry the cylinders thoroughly and apply a thin coat of light, rust-preventative oil to all machined surfaces.

13 If you do not have the equipment or desire to perform the honing operation, take the block to a Kawasaki dealer or specialist motorcycle repair shop.

14 Check that all the cylinder head studs are tight in the crankcase. If any are loose, remove them, noting which fits where as they are of different lengths, then clean their threads. Apply a suitable non-permanent thread locking compound and tighten them securely.

Installation

15 Check that the mating surfaces of the cylinder block and crankcase are free from oil or pieces of old gasket.

16 Remove the rags from around the pistons, and lay the new base gasket in place on the crankcase making sure all the holes are correctly aligned and that the cut-out in one end of the gasket is on the left-hand side of the engine (550 models) **(see illustration)** or the UP letters on the gasket face up (750 models). Never re-use the old gasket. **Note:** *The gasket material on 750 C1 to C4 models was changed from paper-based to aluminium. If working on one of these models, always ensure that the aluminium gasket is fitted.*

17 Make sure the oil nozzles are clean and not

15.17 Oil nozzle installation

1	Cylinder block	4	O-ring -
2	Oil nozzle		all 550 models,
3	Gasket		and 750 C1 to C4

blocked, then install them into their holes in the crankcase making sure they are the correct way up **(see illustration)**. On all 550 models and 750 C1 to C4 models, fit a new O-ring around each oil nozzle.

18 If required, install piston ring clamps onto the pistons to ease their entry into the bores as the block is lowered. This is not essential as each cylinder has a good lead-in enabling the piston rings to be hand-fed into the bore. If possible, have an assistant to support the block while this is done.

 HAYNES HiNT *Rotate the crankshaft until the inner pistons are uppermost and feed them into the block first. This makes access to the lower pistons easier when compressing the rings and feeding them into the bores as they are on the outside.*

15.19 Make sure the pistons enter their bores squarely

15.20 Pass the cam chain up through the block

19 Lubricate the cylinder bores, pistons and piston rings, and the connecting rod big and small-ends, with clean engine oil, then install the block down over the studs until the uppermost piston crowns fit into the bores **(see illustration)**. At this stage feed the cam chain up through the block and secure it in place with a piece of wire to prevent it from falling back down.
20 Gently push down on the cylinder block, making sure the pistons enter the bore squarely and do not get cocked sideways **(see illustration)**. If piston ring clamps are not being used, carefully compress and feed each ring into the bore as the block is lowered. If necessary, use a soft mallet to gently tap the block down, but do not use force if the block appears to be stuck as the pistons and/or rings will be damaged. If clamps are used, remove them once the pistons are in the bore.
21 When the pistons are correctly installed in the cylinders, press the block down onto the base gasket.
22 Install the cylinder head (see Section 11).

16 Pistons - removal, inspection and installation

Note: *The pistons can be removed with the engine in the frame.*

Removal

1 Remove the cylinder block (see Section 15).
2 Before removing the piston from the connecting rod, stuff a clean rag into the hole around the rod to prevent the circlips or anything else from falling into the crankcase. Use a sharp scribe or felt marker pen to write the cylinder identity on the crown of each piston (or on the skirt if the piston is dirty and going to be cleaned). Each piston should also have an arrow marked on its crown which should face forwards **(see illustration 16.3b)**. If this is not visible, mark the piston accordingly so that it can be installed the correct way round.
3 Carefully prise out the circlip on one side of

the piston using needle-nose pliers or a small flat-bladed screwdriver inserted into the notch **(see illustration)**. Push the piston pin out from the other side to free the piston from the connecting rod **(see illustration)**. Remove the other circlip and discard them as new ones

 To prevent the circlip from pinging away or from dropping into the crankcase, pass a rod or screwdriver, whose diameter is greater than the gap between the circlip ends, through the piston pin - this will trap the circlip if it springs out.

 If a piston pin is a tight fit in the piston bosses, soak a rag in boiling water then wring it out and wrap it around the piston - this will expand the alloy piston sufficiently to release its grip on the pin.

16.3a Remove the circlip using a pair of pliers or screwdriver inserted in the notch . . .

16.3b . . . then push the pin out from the other side and withdraw it from the piston. Note the arrow stamped into each piston crown which must face forward

16.5 Removing the piston rings using a ring removal and installation tool

16.11 Measure the piston ring-to-groove clearance with a feeler gauge

must be used. When the piston has been removed, install its pin back into its bore so that related parts do not get mixed up. Rotate the crankshaft so that the best access is obtained for each piston.

Inspection

4 Before the inspection process can be carried out, the pistons must be cleaned and the old piston rings removed. Note that if the cylinders are being rebored, piston inspection can be overlooked as new ones will be fitted.

5 Using your thumbs or a piston ring removal and installation tool, carefully remove the rings from the pistons **(see illustration)**. Do not nick or gouge the pistons in the process. Carefully note in which groove each ring fits as they must be installed in their original positions if being re-used. The top ring is unmarked and can be installed either way up. The upper surface of the second (middle) ring is marked with a letter at one end; on 550 models, the ring is identified by the letter T, and on 750 models by the letter N **(see illustration 17.11a)**. The top and middle rings can also be identified by their different cross-section shape **(see illustration 17.11b)**.

6 Scrape all traces of carbon from the tops of the pistons. A hand-held wire brush or a piece of fine emery cloth can be used once most of the deposits have been scraped away. Do not, under any circumstances, use a wire brush mounted in a drill motor to remove deposits from the pistons; the piston material is soft and will be eroded away by the wire brush.

7 Use a piston ring groove cleaning tool to remove any carbon deposits from the ring grooves. If a tool is not available, a piece broken off an old ring will do the job. Be very careful to remove only the carbon deposits. Do not remove any metal and do not nick or gouge the sides of the ring grooves.

8 Once the deposits have been removed, clean the pistons with solvent and dry them thoroughly. If the identification previously

marked on the piston is cleaned off, be sure to re-mark it with the correct identity. Make sure the oil return holes below the oil ring groove are clear.

9 Carefully inspect each piston for cracks around the skirt, at the pin bosses and at the ring lands. Normal piston wear appears as even, vertical wear on the thrust surfaces of the piston and slight looseness of the top ring in its groove. If the skirt is scored or scuffed, the engine may have been suffering from overheating and/or abnormal combustion, which caused excessively high operating temperatures. The oil pump should be checked thoroughly. Also check that the circlip grooves are not damaged.

10 A hole in the piston crown, an extreme to be sure, is an indication that abnormal combustion (pre-ignition) was occurring. Burned areas at the edge of the piston crown are usually evidence of spark knock (detonation). If any of the above problems exist, the causes must be corrected or the damage will occur again.

11 Measure the piston ring-to-groove clearance by laying each piston ring in its groove and slipping a feeler gauge in beside it **(see illustration)**. Make sure you have the correct ring for the groove (see Step 5). Check the clearance at three or four locations around

the groove. If the clearance is greater than specified, replace both the piston and rings as a set. If new rings are being used, measure the clearance using the new rings. If the clearance is greater than that specified, the piston is worn and must be replaced.

12 Check the piston-to-bore clearance by measuring the bore (see Section 15) and the piston diameter. Make sure each piston is matched to its correct cylinder. Measure the piston 5.0 mm up from the bottom of the skirt and at 90° to the piston pin axis **(see illustration)**. Subtract the piston diameter from the bore diameter to obtain the clearance. If it is greater than the specified figure, the piston must be replaced (assuming the bore itself is within limits, otherwise a rebore is necessary).

13 Apply clean engine oil to the piston pin, insert it into the piston and check for any freeplay between the two **(see illustration)**.

14 If the pistons are to be replaced, ensure the correct size of piston is ordered. Kawasaki produce two oversize pistons as well as the standard piston. The oversize pistons available are: +0.5 mm and +1.00 mm. **Note:** *Oversize pistons usually have their relevant size stamped on top of the piston crown, eg a 0.50 mm oversize piston will be marked 0.50. Be sure to obtain the correct oversize rings for the pistons.*

16.12 Measure the piston diameter with a micrometer at the specified distance from the bottom of the skirt

16.13 Slip the pin (A) into the piston (B) and try to rock it back and forth. If it's loose, replace the piston and pin

16.17 Install the circlip, making sure it is properly seated in its groove, with the open end away from the notch

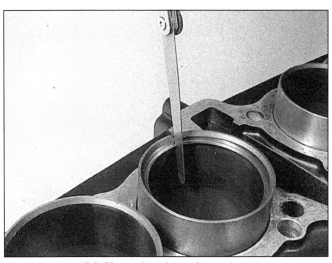

17.3 Measuring piston ring end gap

Installation

15 Inspect and install the piston rings (see Section 17).

16 Lubricate the piston pin, the piston pin bore and the connecting rod small-end bore with clean engine oil.

17 Install a new circlip in one side of the piston (do not re-use old circlips) **(see illustration)**. Line up the piston on its correct connecting rod, making sure the arrow on the piston crown faces forwards, and insert the piston pin from the other side **(see illustration 16.3b)**. Secure the pin with the other new circlip. When installing the circlips, compress them only just enough to fit them in the piston, and make sure they are properly seated in their grooves with the open end away from the removal notch.

17 Piston rings -
inspection and installation

1 It is good practice to replace the piston rings when an engine is being overhauled. Before installing the new piston rings, the ring end gaps must be checked.

2 Lay out the pistons and the new ring sets so the rings will be matched with the same piston and cylinder during the end gap measurement procedure and engine assembly.

3 To measure the end gap, insert the top ring into the bottom of the first cylinder and square it up with the cylinder walls by pushing it in with the top of the piston. The ring should be close to the bottom edge of the cylinder. To measure the end gap, slip a feeler gauge between the ends of the ring and compare the measurement to the specifications at the beginning of the Chapter **(see illustration)**.

4 If the gap is larger or smaller than specified, double check to make sure that you have the correct rings before proceeding.

5 If the gap is too small, it must be enlarged or the ring ends may come in contact with each other during engine operation, which can cause serious damage. The end gap can be increased by filing the ring ends very carefully with a fine file. When performing this operation, file only from the outside in **(see illustration)**.

6 Excess end gap is not critical unless it is greater than 0.6 mm. Again, double check to make sure you have the correct rings for your engine and check that the bore is not worn.

7 Repeat the procedure for each ring that will be installed in the cylinders. Remember to keep the rings, pistons and cylinders matched up.

8 Once the ring end gaps have been checked/corrected, the rings can be installed on the pistons.

9 The oil control ring (lowest on the piston) is installed first. It is composed of three separate components, namely the expander and the upper and lower side rails. Slip the expander into the groove, then install the upper side rail. Do not use a piston ring installation tool on the oil ring side rails as they may be damaged. Instead, place one end of the side rail into the groove between the expander and the ring land. Hold it firmly in place and slide a finger around the piston while pushing the rail into the groove. Next, install the lower side rail in the same manner **(see illustrations)**. Make sure the ends of the expander do not overlap.

10 After the three oil ring components have been installed, check to make sure that both the upper and lower side rails can be turned smoothly in the ring groove.

11 The upper surface of each second (middle) ring is marked with a letter at one end, whilst the top rings are unmarked. On 550 models,

17.5 Ring end gap can be enlarged by clamping a file in a vice and filing the ring ends

17.9a Install the oil ring expander in its groove . . .

17.9b . . . and fit the side rails each side of it. The oil ring must be installed by hand

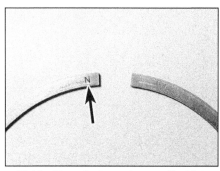

17.11a Note the letter (arrowed) which must face up

17.11b Compression ring cross-sections - 550 models

1 Top ring   2 Second ring

17.11c Compression ring cross-sections - 750 models

A Top ring   B Second ring   C "N" mark

17.13 When installing the rings, stagger their end gaps as shown

1 Top ring	*4 Oil ring expander*
2 Second ring	*5 Directional arrow*
3 Oil ring side rails	

the ring is identified by the letter T, and on 750 models by the letter N **(see illustration)**. The second and top rings can also be identified by their different cross-section shape **(see illustrations)**. Install the second (middle) ring next. Make sure that the identification letter near the end gap is facing up. Fit the ring into the middle groove in the piston. Do not expand the ring any more than is necessary to slide it into place. To avoid breaking the ring, use a piston ring installation tool.

12 Finally, install the top ring in the same manner into the top groove in the piston. The top ring can be installed either way up.

13 Once the rings are correctly installed, check they move freely without snagging and stagger their end gaps as shown **(see illustration)**.

18 Clutch - removal, inspection and installation

Note: *The clutch can be removed with the engine in the frame.*

Removal

1 Drain the engine oil (refer to Chapter 1).
2 Disconnect the clutch cable (Section 19, Step 1).

3 Free the pulse generator coil and oil pressure switch wiring from any clamps on the clutch cover bolts, noting its routing. Working in a criss-cross pattern, evenly slacken the clutch cover retaining bolts, noting which size bolt fits where **(see illustrations)**. Rotate the clutch release lever towards the back of the machine and lift the cover away from the engine, being prepared to catch any residual oil which may be released as the cover is removed. Remove the gasket and discard it. Remove the two dowels from either the cover or the crankcase, if they are loose.

4 Working in a criss-cross pattern, gradually and evenly slacken the clutch pressure plate bolts until spring pressure is released **(see illustration)**. Remove the bolts and springs, then withdraw the pressure plate **(see illustrations 18.21b and a)**. Remove the release rod, and on 750 models the thrust washer and release bearing, from either the back of the pressure plate or the end of the input shaft **(see illustration 18.20)**. On 550 models the release bearing is fitted into the pressure plate and remains there unless being replaced **(see illustration 18.13)**.

18.3a Clutch cover bolts (arrowed) - 550 models. Note the positions of the wiring clamps (A)

18.3b Clutch cover bolts (arrowed) - 750 models. Note the positions of the wiring clamps (A)

18.4 Clutch components

1 Inner thrust washer	6 Clutch centre	11 Release rod	14 Thrust washer - 750 models
2 Spacer	7 Friction plates	12 Release bearing (ball type) -	15 Pressure plate
3 Needle roller bearing	8 Plain plates	550 models	16 Spring
4 Clutch housing	9 Washer	13 Release bearing (needle type)	17 Pressure plate bolt
5 Thrust washer	10 Clutch nut	- 750 models	

5 Grasp the complete set of clutch plates and remove them as a pack. Unless the plates are being replaced with new ones, keep them in their original order. If the plates are being separated, note that on 550 models the innermost plain plate is thicker than the outer ones, and on 750 C5 and D1 models the innermost and outermost friction plates differ from the rest.

6 To remove the clutch nut the input shaft must be locked. This can be done in several ways. If the engine is in the frame, engage 1st gear and have an assistant hold the rear brake on hard with the rear tyre in firm contact with the ground. Alternatively, the Kawasaki service tool (Pt. No. 57001-1243), or a similar home-made tool made from two strips of steel bent at the ends and bolted together in the

middle **(see Tool tip)**, can be used to stop the clutch centre from turning whilst the nut is slackened **(see illustration)**. Unscrew the nut and remove the washer from the input shaft. Discard the nut as a new one must be used.
7 Remove the clutch centre from the shaft, followed by the thrust washer **(see illustrations 18.18b and a)**.
8 Slide the clutch housing off the shaft, along

A clutch centre holding tool can easily be made using two strips of steel bent over at the ends and bolted together in the middle

18.6 Use the holding tool as shown when slackening the clutch nut

18.9 Measure the thickness of the friction plates

18.10 Check the plain plates for warpage

with the needle roller bearing and spacer **(see illustrations 18.17c, b and a)**. Also remove the inner thrust washer, noting which way round it fits **(see illustration 18.16)**.

Inspection

9 After an extended period of service the clutch friction plates will wear and promote clutch slip. Measure the thickness of each friction plate using a vernier caliper **(see illustration)**. If any plate has worn to or beyond the service limits given in the Specifications at the beginning of the Chapter, the friction plates must be replaced as a set. Also, if any of the plates smell burnt or are glazed, they must be replaced as a set.

10 The plain plates should not show any signs of excess heating (bluing). Check for warpage using a flat surface and feeler gauges **(see illustration)**. If any plate exceeds the maximum permissible amount of warpage, or shows signs of bluing, all plain plates must be replaced as a set.

11 Measure the free length of each clutch spring using a vernier caliper **(see illustration)**. If any spring is below the service limit specified, replace all the springs as a set.

12 Inspect the clutch assembly for burrs and indentations on the edges of the protruding tangs of the friction plates and/or slots in the edge of the housing with which they engage. Similarly check for wear between the inner tongues of the plain plates and the slots in the clutch centre. Wear of this nature will cause clutch drag and slow disengagement during gear changes, since the plates will snag when the pressure plate is lifted. With care a small amount of wear can be corrected by dressing with a fine file, but if this is excessive the worn components should be replaced.

13 Check the pressure plate, release bearing, release rod and thrust washer (750 models) for signs of roughness, wear or damage, and replace any parts as necessary. On 550 models, the release bearing fits into a housing in the pressure plate **(see illustration)**.

14 Check the clutch release lever and shaft mechanism in the clutch cover for smooth operation and any signs of wear or damage. If the shaft oil seal shows signs of leakage, or if the shaft bearings feels rough, withdraw the lever and shaft from the cover and replace the bearings and seal. **Note:** *Removal of the release shaft from the cover will damage the oil seal - always make sure the oil seal is replaced with a new one if the shaft is disturbed.* If the release lever is removed from the shaft, install it so that the punch mark on the shaft aligns with the mark on the lever as shown **(see illustrations)**. Apply grease to the oil seal lips and clean engine oil to the shaft and bearings.

Installation

15 Remove all traces of old gasket from the crankcase and clutch cover surfaces.

16 Slide the inner thrust washer, with its flat surface facing out, onto the end of the input shaft **(see illustration)**.

18.11 Measure the free length of the clutch springs

18.13 The release bearing on 550 models fit into the pressure plate

18.14a Clutch release lever alignment marks (arrowed) - 550 models

18.14b Clutch release lever alignment marks (arrowed) - 750 models

18.16 Install the inner thrust washer with the chamfered side facing in, flat side facing out

18.17a Slide the spacer . . .

18.17b . . . the needle roller bearing . . .

18.17c . . . and the clutch housing onto the input shaft

18.18a Slide the thrust washer . . .

18.18b . . . and the clutch centre onto the shaft

18.18c Fit the washer and the clutch nut . . .

17 Lubricate the spacer and needle roller bearing with clean engine oil and slide them onto the shaft (see illustrations). Slide the clutch housing onto the shaft, making sure it engages correctly with the teeth on the primary drive gear (see illustration).

18 Slide the thrust washer onto the shaft, then install the clutch centre, making sure it locates correctly onto the shaft splines (see illustrations). Slide the clutch nut washer onto the shaft splines, then install a new clutch nut. Using the method employed on removal to prevent the input shaft turning, tighten the nut to the torque setting specified at the beginning of the Chapter (see illustrations). Note: Check that the clutch centre rotates freely after tightening.

19 Coat each clutch plate with clean engine oil, then build up the plates in the clutch

housing, starting with a friction plate, then a plain plate and alternating friction and plain plates until all are installed (see illustrations). On 550 models, note that one plain plate is

thicker than the rest and must be the first plain plate fitted. On 750 C5 and D1 models, note that two friction plates differ from the rest and must be the first and last fitted.

18.18d . . . and tighten the nut to the specified torque setting

18.19a Install a friction plate first . . .

18.19b . . . followed by a plain plate

18.20 Fit the release rod through the back of the pressure plate

18.21a Fit the pressure plate . . .

18.21b . . . then install the springs and bolts . . .

18.21c . . . and tighten them to the specified torque setting

18.22a Apply a smear of sealant to the areas arrowed

18.22b Fit the dowels (arrowed) if removed, and a new gasket

18.22c The cut-out (A) engages behind the head of the release rod (B)

18.22d Move the lever back when fitting the cover, then move it forwards to engage the release rod

20 Lubricate the release rod with molybdenum disulphide grease. On 750 models lubricate both sides of the release bearing and thrust washer with clean engine oil, then install them onto the release rod. Install the release rod into the back of the pressure plate so that the headed end protrudes from the front **(see illustration)**.

21 Install the pressure plate onto the clutch **(see illustration)**. Install the springs, then install the pressure plate bolts, and tighten them evenly in a criss-cross sequence to the specified torque setting **(see illustrations)**.

22 Apply a smear of silicone sealant to the area around the crankcase joints as shown **(see illustration)**. Check that the dowels are in place, then place a new gasket onto the crankcase **(see illustration)**. Install the clutch cover with the release lever pushed back, and tighten the cover bolts evenly in a criss-cross

sequence **(see illustrations)**. Move the release lever forward so that the cutout in the shaft end engages with the release rod. If the shaft is difficult to engage with the rod, pull up on the lever so that there is about 4 mm clearance between it and the clutch cover, and again move it forward to engage it. Make sure the pulse generator and oil pressure switch wiring is correctly routed and secured by its clamps **(see illustrations 18.3a and b)**.

23 Connect the clutch cable (see Section 19, Step 3).

24 Refill the engine with oil (see Chapter 1).

19 Clutch cable - removal and installation

1 Slide the rubber boot off the adjuster on the

lower end of the clutch cable **(see illustration)**. Fully slacken the upper nut and thread the lower nut off the end of the adjuster, then slide the adjuster down in the bracket to provide as much inner cable

19.1a Pull back the rubber boot . . .

19.1b . . . then slacken the upper nut and thread the nut off the adjuster

19.1c Slacken the lockwheel (A) and screw the adjuster (B) in

19.1d With the slots aligned, remove the outer cable from the adjuster . . .

19.1e . . . and detach the inner cable nipple from the lever

19.1f Withdraw the adjuster from its bracket . . .

19.1g . . . and remove the cable end nipple from the lever

freeplay as possible **(see illustration)**. Fully slacken the lockwheel on the freeplay adjuster at the handlebar end of the cable, then screw the adjuster fully in **(see illustration)**. Align the slots in the adjuster and lockwheel with that in the lever bracket, then pull the outer cable end from the socket in the adjuster and release the inner cable from the lever **(see illustrations)**. Now release the lower end adjuster from its bracket and the end of the inner cable from the release lever on the clutch cover **(see illustrations)**.
2 Remove the cable from the machine, noting its routing.

> **HAYNES HiNT** *Before removing the cable from the bike, tape the lower end of the new cable to the upper end of the old cable. Slowly pull the lower end of the old cable out, guiding the new cable down into position. Using this method will ensure the cable is routed correctly.*

3 Install the cable, making sure it is correctly routed. Apply grease to the ends of the inner cables. Fit the lower inner cable end into the release lever and the adjuster into the bracket on the clutch cover **(see illustrations 19.1g and f)**. Attach the upper end of the inner cable to the clutch lever, then align the slots in the adjuster and lockwheel with that in the lever bracket and fit the cable into the adjuster **(see illustrations 19.1e and d)**. Thread the nuts on the lower adjuster so that it is secure in the

bracket **(see illustrations 19.1b and a)**, then check and adjust the amount of clutch lever freeplay (see Chapter 1).

20 Gearchange mechanism (external parts) - removal, inspection and installation

Note: *The gearchange mechanism external component parts can be removed with the engine in the frame.*

Removal

1 Remove the engine (front) sprocket (see Chapter 5).
2 Remove the sidestand switch (Chapter 8). Also disconnect the neutral switch wiring connector from the gearchange mechanism cover.

20.3 The gearchange mechanism cover is secured by seven screws (550 models) or bolts (750 models)

3 Remove the screws (550 models) or bolts (750 models) securing the gearchange mechanism cover to the crankcase and remove the cover, noting which length screws or bolts fit where **(see illustration)**. Be prepared to catch any residue oil. Discard the gasket as a new one must be used. Remove the two dowels from either the cover or the crankcase if they are loose.
4 Note how the gearchange shaft centralising spring ends fit on each side of the locating pin in the crankcase, and how the selector arm and stopper arm engage with the pins in the end of the selector drum **(see illustration 20.10)**. Lift the selector arm and stopper arm off the selector drum, then withdraw the gearchange shaft from the crankcase.
5 If necessary, remove the screw securing the pin holder plate to the end of the selector drum, then remove the plate, noting which hole locates over the longer pin in the selector drum, and which hole in the drum the longer pin fits into. Mark the holes with a felt pen to ensure correct installation, otherwise the neutral light will not work correctly. Take care not to lose any of the pins.

Inspection

6 Inspect the shaft centralising spring for fatigue, wear or damage. If any is found, it must be replaced. Also check that the spring locating pin in the crankcase is securely tightened. If it is loose, remove it and apply a non-permanent thread locking compound to its threads, then tighten it to the torque setting specified at the beginning of the Chapter.

20.7 Replace the cover oil seals if necessary

20.10 The installed mechanism should be as shown

7 Check the gearchange shaft for straightness and damage to the splines. If the shaft is bent you can attempt to straighten it, but if the splines are damaged the shaft must be replaced. Also check the condition of the shaft oil seal in the cover. If it is damaged, deteriorated or shows signs of leakage it must be replaced with a new one. Lever out the old seal and drive the new one squarely into place, with its lip facing inward, using a seal driver or suitable socket. Similarly check the condition of the transmission output shaft oil seal **(see illustration)**.
8 Check the selector arm and stopper arm pawls, and the pins in the selector drum for wear and damage. Also check the arm return spring, and make sure it is correctly installed. Replace any components that are worn or damaged.

Installation

9 If removed, install the pins into the end of the selector drum, making sure the longer pin is fitted into the hole noted on removal. Install the holder onto the pins, then apply a non-permanent thread locking compound to the holder screw and tighten it securely.

10 If removed, slide the centralising spring onto the gearchange shaft and locate the spring ends either side of the pin on the arm. Smear clean engine oil over the shaft then guide it into place, lifting the selector arm and stopper arm onto the pins as you do, and making sure the centralising spring ends locate correctly on each side of the pins on the shaft arm and the crankcase **(see illustration)**.
11 Apply a smear of silicone sealant to the area where the cover fits over the crankcase joints. Also apply high-temperature grease to the lips of the gearchange shaft oil seal and the transmission output shaft oil seal in the cover.
12 If removed, install the gearchange mechanism cover dowels into the crankcase. Install the cover using a new gasket **(see illustration)**. On 750 models, apply a non-permanent thread locking compound to the longer cover bolts only, and tighten all bolts to the specified torque setting.
13 Temporarily install the gearchange lever onto the end of the shaft and check that the mechanism works correctly between neutral and first gear. Due to the positive neutral selector mechanism, which allows only

neutral to be selected from first gear unless the output shaft is rotating (ie the machine is moving), it is not possible to select each gear in turn.
14 Install the sidestand switch (see Chapter 8) and connect the neutral switch wiring connector.
15 Install the sprocket (see Chapter 5).

21 Starter clutch and idle/ reduction gear - removal, inspection and installation

Note: *The starter clutch and idle gear assembly can be removed with the engine in the frame.*

Removal

1 Remove the clutch (see Section 18).
2 Remove the oil pump (see Section 23).
3 Before the secondary shaft is removed, check the primary chain slack by measuring the amount of up and down movement in the chain mid-way between the crankshaft and secondary shaft sprockets **(see illustration)**. If it exceeds the service limit specified, the

20.12 Fit the cover using a new gasket

21.3 Primary chain wear measurement
1 Crankshaft   2 Secondary shaft   3 Primary chain slack

21.4 Unscrew the pinch bolt (arrowed) and slide the arm off the shaft

21.5a Engine sprocket cover bolts (arrowed) - 550 models

21.5b Engine sprocket cover bolts (arrowed) - 750 models

21.6 Remove the shaft bearing cap and discard its O-ring

21.8 On 750 models, remove the remaining screw securing the retainer plate and remove the plate

chain must be replaced. Rotate the crankshaft and repeat the measurement at various points along the chain. If chain slack is excessive, remove the chain as described in Section 27 and replace it with a new one.

4 Unscrew the gearchange linkage arm pinch bolt and remove the arm from the shaft, noting any alignment marks **(see illustration)**. If no marks are visible, make your own before removing the arm so that it can be correctly aligned with the shaft on installation.

5 Unscrew the bolts securing the engine sprocket cover to the crankcase and remove the cover **(see illustrations)**.

6 Remove the two screws securing the secondary shaft bearing cap and remove the cap **(see illustration)**. Discard the O-ring as a new one must be used. On 750 models, do not lose the wiring clamps.

7 To remove the secondary shaft nut it is necessary to stop the engine from turning. If the engine is in the frame, engage 1st gear and have an assistant hold the rear brake on hard with the rear tyre in firm contact with the ground. Alternatively, unscrew the bolts securing the alternator cover to the left-hand side of the engine and remove the cover. Discard the gasket as a new one must be

used. Using the Kawasaki service tool (Pt. No. 09920-34810), or a similar commercially available rotor holder to hold the alternator rotor, unscrew the secondary shaft nut.

8 On 750 models, working on the right-hand end of the secondary shaft, remove the remaining screw (the others secured the oil pump) securing the shaft bearing retainer plate and remove the plate **(see illustration)**.

9 Tap the left-hand end of the shaft with a hammer until the right-hand end bearing is

displaced from the crankcase, then withdraw the shaft from the right, supporting the starter clutch and damper assembly via the bottom of the crankcase as you do **(see illustrations)**. Note the sleeve fitted between the shaft and the left-hand bearing, and the thrust washer fitted between the starter clutch and the shaft's integral pinion. 750 models also have a needle roller bearing between the shaft and the starter driven gear hub, which might come out with the shaft but could stay inside the starter

21.9a Tap the left-hand end of the shaft . . .

21.9b . . . and withdraw it from the right (750 model with needle roller bearing shown)

21.9c Disengage the primary chain and remove the starter clutch assembly

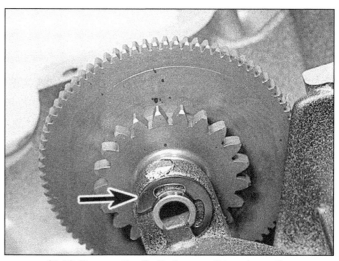

21.10 Remove the E-clip (arrowed) to release the idle/reduction gear shaft

21.11 Secondary shaft and starter clutch components

1 Secondary shaft
2 Bearing
3 Thrust washer
4 Primary drive gear
5 Circlip
6 Thrust washer
7 Needle roller bearing (750 models)
8 Starter driven gear
9 Idle/reduction gear
10 Idle/reduction gear shaft
11 E-clip
12 Allen bolt
13 Starter clutch
14 Roller
15 Plunger
16 Spring
17 Damper hub
18 Damper rubbers
19 Primary chain
20 Bearing sleeve
21 Shaft nut
22 Bearing
23 Damper assembly sprocket

clutch. With the shaft removed, disengage the starter clutch assembly from the primary chain and remove it **(see illustration)**.

10 Remove the E-clip from the end of the idle/reduction gear shaft, then withdraw the shaft and remove the gear, noting which way round it fits **(see illustration)**.

Inspection

11 Install the starter driven gear into the starter clutch (if removed) and, with the clutch face down on a workbench, check that the gear rotates freely in an anti-clockwise direction and locks against the rotor in a clockwise direction **(see illustration)**. If it doesn't, replace the starter clutch.

12 Remove the needle bearing from the centre of the starter driven gear if it didn't come out with the secondary shaft (750 models only). Withdraw the starter driven

gear from the starter clutch. If it appears stuck, rotate it anti-clockwise as you withdraw it to free it from the starter clutch. Note the thrust washer fitted between the driven gear and the damper assembly.

13 Check the bearing surface of the starter driven gear hub and the condition of the rollers inside the clutch body **(see illustration)**. If the bearing surface shows signs of excessive wear or the rollers are

21.13 Check the rollers and the hub of the gear they run on

21.14 Replace the springs and plungers if worn or damaged

21.16a Remove the circlip securing the
damper assembly sprocket . . .

21.16b . . . and check the damper components

damaged, marked or flattened at any point, they should be replaced.

14 Remove the rollers and check the plungers and springs for signs of deformation or damage (see illustration). Make sure the plungers move freely in their sockets.

15 Check that the three Allen bolts securing the starter clutch to the damper assembly hub are tight (see illustration 21.13). If any are loose, unscrew all the bolts, then apply a suitable non-permanent thread locking compound to their threads and tighten them to the specified torque. Lubricate the starter clutch rollers with new engine oil.

16 Remove the circlip from the back of the damper assembly sprocket and withdraw the damper hub (see illustration). Check the rubber damper segments for wear, damage and deterioration and replace them if necessary (see illustration).

17 Examine the teeth of the starter idle/reduction gear and the corresponding teeth of the starter driven gear and starter motor drive shaft. Replace the gears and/or starter motor if worn or chipped teeth are discovered on related gears. Also check the idle/reduction gear shaft for damage, and check that the gear is not a loose fit on the shaft. Replace the shaft if necessary.

18 Examine the secondary shaft bearings and replace them if necessary. The right-hand bearing will have been displaced with the secondary shaft and can be separated from the shaft by removing the circlip, primary drive gear and washer from the shaft end; draw the bearing off the shaft using a puller if necessary. Install the bearing on the secondary shaft using a drift or bearing driver which bears on the bearing's inner race only. The left-hand bearing can be driven out of the crankcase using a drift or bearing driver which bears on its outer race only. When installing the bearing make sure that it is positioned to the precise depth in its housing (see illustration); use a drift or bearing driver which bears on the bearing's outer race only.

10.7 ~ 11.3 mm

21.18 Secondary shaft left-hand bearing
installed depth

1 Crankcase outer surface
2 Crankcase inner surface
3 Bearing

21.21a Slide the shaft into the case and through the starter clutch/damper assembly

21.21b Bearing sleeve fits between secondary shaft and bearing

Installation

19 Lubricate the idle/reduction gear shaft with clean engine oil, then install the idle/reduction gear followed by its shaft, making sure the smaller pinion on the idle/reduction gear faces the left-hand side of the engine. Secure the shaft with the E-clip **(see illustration 21.10)**.

20 Fit the thrust washer into the starter clutch. Lubricate the hub of the starter driven gear with clean engine oil, then install the starter driven gear into the clutch, rotating it anti-clockwise as you do so to spread the rollers and allow the hub of the gear to enter. On 750 models, lubricate the needle bearing and fit it into the starter driven gear.

21 Slide the thrust washer onto the left-hand end of the secondary shaft. Manoeuvre the starter clutch assembly into the crankcase so that the starter driven gear faces the right-hand side of the engine and engage the sprocket with the primary chain **(see illustration 21.9c)**. Supporting the assembly, install the secondary shaft into the right-hand side of the crankcase and slide it through the starter clutch assembly and into the bearing in the left-hand side **(see illustration)**. Tap the right-hand end of the shaft with a hammer until the right-hand bearing is fully seated in the crankcase. Slide the bearing sleeve onto the left-hand end of the shaft and drive it into place between the shaft and the bearing **(see illustration)**.

22 Fit the nut onto the left-hand end of the shaft and, using the method employed on removal to prevent the shaft turning, tighten the nut to the torque setting specified at the beginning of the Chapter **(see illustration)**.

23 Install the remaining components in a reverse order of removal. Use a new O-ring on the shaft bearing cap and smear it with grease, and on 750 models, make sure the wiring clamps are fitted with the screws.

22 Oil sump and oil pressure regulator - removal, inspection and installation

Note: *The oil sump and pressure regulator can be removed with the engine in the frame. If work is being carried out with the engine removed ignore the preliminary steps.*

Removal

1 Remove the exhaust system (see Chapter 3).
2 Drain the engine oil (see Chapter 1).

21.22 Tighten the secondary shaft nut to the specified torque setting

22.3b . . . and disconnect the oil pressure switch wiring (550 models)

3 Unscrew the bolts securing each oil cooler hose union to the oil sump **(see illustration)**. Discard the O-rings as new ones must be used. On 550 models (except the B4 model), disconnect the oil pressure switch wiring from the switch on the left-hand side of the sump **(see illustration)**.

4 Unscrew the sump bolts, slackening them evenly in a criss-cross sequence to prevent distortion. Remove the sump and its gasket **(see illustration)**. Discard the gasket as a new one must be used.

5 If required, unscrew the oil pressure

22.3a Remove the two bolts securing each hose union . . .

22.4 Unscrew the bolts and remove the sump

22.5 The oil pressure regulator threads into the sump

22.12a Fit the three small O-rings (arrowed) to the oil passages . . .

22.12b . . . and large O-ring (arrowed) around oil filter chamber

23.3 The oil pump is secured by two screws and a bolt (arrowed)

regulator from the sump and remove it **(see illustration)**.

6 Remove all traces of gasket from the sump and crankcase mating surfaces.

Inspection

7 Clean the sump, making sure all the oil passages are free of any debris.

8 Make sure the oil strainer is clean and remove any debris caught in the mesh. Inspect the strainer for any signs of wear or damage.

9 Clean the pressure regulator, and check that the plunger moves freely in the body. Inspect it for signs of wear or damage and replace it if necessary.

10 Remove the three oil passage O-rings and the oil filter chamber O-ring from the sump **(see illustrations 22.12a and b)**. Check their condition and replace them if they are in any way damaged or deteriorated. Install the new ones with the flat side facing the crankcase, and smear them with clean engine oil.

Installation

11 If removed, apply a small amount of non-permanent thread locking compound to the oil pressure regulator threads and tighten it to the torque setting specified at the beginning of the Chapter **(see illustration 22.5)**.

12 Lay a new gasket onto the sump (if the engine is in the frame) or onto the crankcase (if the engine has been removed and is positioned upside down on the work surface). Make sure the holes in the gasket align correctly with the bolt holes, and that all O-rings are installed **(see illustrations)**.

13 Position the sump onto the crankcase and install the sump bolts. Tighten the bolts evenly in a criss-cross pattern to the torque setting specified at the beginning of the Chapter.

14 Install the oil cooler hoses onto the sump using new O-rings smeared with oil, and tighten the bolts to the specified torque setting **(see illustration 22.3a)**. On 550 models, connect the oil pressure switch wiring **(see illustration 22.3b)**.

15 Install the exhaust system (see Chapter 3).

16 Fill the engine with the correct type and quantity of oil (see Chapter 1). Start the engine and check for leaks around the sump.

23 Oil pump - removal, inspection and installation

Note: *The oil pump can be removed with the engine in the frame. If work is being carried out with the engine removed ignore the preliminary steps.*

Removal

1 Remove the clutch (see Section 18).

2 Remove the oil sump (see Section 22).

3 The oil pump is secured by a bolt and two screws **(see illustration)**. The screws also secure the secondary shaft bearing retainer plate. Remove the bolt and the screws, noting how they are staked to the retainer plate, and remove the pump from below. On 550 models,

23.5a Remove the circlip and washer . . .

23.5b . . . and push the shaft through to expose the drive pin (arrowed)

23.5c The cover is secured by three screws (arrowed)

23.5d Withdraw the shaft and its second pin (arrowed) . . .

23.5e . . . then remove the rotors

23.6 Make sure the dowel (arrowed) is fitted, and use a new gasket

remove the retainer plate with the screws (on 750 models, the plate is secured by three screws and therefore remains in situ). Remove the two dowels from either the crankcase or the pump if they are loose.

Inspection

4 Inspect the pump body for any obvious damage such as cracks or distortion, and check that the shaft rotates freely and without any side-to-side play or excessive endfloat.
5 Whilst the pump can be disassembled for cleaning and inspection and individual components replaced if required, Kawasaki provide no service specifications for rotor clearance and endfloat. To disassemble the pump, remove the circlip and washer from the cover end of the pump shaft (see illustration). Push the shaft through the pump until the drive pin is clear of the driven gear, then remove the pin and slide the driven gear off the shaft (see illustration). Remove the

three screws securing the pump cover, then remove the cover (see illustration). Discard the gasket as a new one must be used, and remove the cover dowel if it is loose. Withdraw the drive shaft and its rotor pin (see illustration), then remove the inner and outer rotors from the pump body, noting how they fit (see illustration).
6 Inspect the rotors for scoring and wear. If any damage, scoring or uneven or excessive wear is evident, replace the components as required. Make sure all components are clean, then reassemble the pump applying clean oil to all components. Use a new cover gasket and make sure the cover dowel is fitted (see illustration). Check that the shaft rotates freely and without any side-to-side play or excessive endfloat.
7 Make sure the oil strainer is clean and remove any debris caught in the mesh. Inspect the strainer for any signs of wear or damage and replace it if necessary.

Installation

8 If removed, fit the dowels into their holes in the crankcase, making sure they are secure (see illustration).
9 Before installing the pump, prime it by pouring oil into the outlet and turning the shaft by hand. This ensures that oil is being pumped as soon as the engine is turned over.
10 Install the pump, making sure it is correctly located over the dowels (see illustration). On 550 models, install the bearing retainer plate (on 750 models it is still in situ, retained by a single screw). Apply a suitable non-permanent thread locking compound to the threads of the retainer plate/pump screws and bolt, then tighten them securely (see illustration 23.3). Using a centre punch, stake the screws against the retainer plate to lock them (see illustration).
11 Install the sump (see Section 22) and the clutch (see Section 18).

23.8 Fit the pump dowels (arrowed) into the crankcase if removed

23.10a Locate the pump onto the dowels

23.10b Stake the screws against the plate using a centre punch

24.3 Upper crankcase half 6 mm bolts (arrowed)

Tightening sequence for 8 mm bolts (B)

24.5 Lower crankcase half - 6 mm bolts (A), 8 mm bolts (B)

24 Crankcase -
separation and reassembly

Note: *When the engine is upside down (Steps 4 to 19), referrals to the right and left-hand ends or sides of the transmission shafts or components are made as though the engine is the correct way up. Therefore the right-hand end of a shaft or side of a crankcase will actually be on your left as you look down onto the underside of the crankcase assembly.*

Separation

1 To access the crankshaft, connecting rods, bearings and transmission components, the crankcase must be split into two parts.
2 To enable the crankcases to be separated, the engine must be removed from the frame (see Section 5). Before the crankcases can be separated, the cam chain tensioner, camshafts, cylinder head, cylinder block, ignition pulse generator coil assembly, clutch, gearchange mechanism (external components), alternator, starter motor, starter clutch and starter idle/reduction gear, oil sump and oil pump must be removed. See the relevant Sections or Chapters for details. **Note:** *If the crankcases are being separated to inspect or access the transmission components, or to inspect the crankshaft without removing it, the engine top-end components (cam chain tensioner, camshafts, cylinder head, cylinder block, pistons) can remain in situ. However, if removal of the crankshaft and connecting rod assemblies is intended, full disassembly of the top-end is necessary.*
3 Unscrew the thirteen 6 mm upper crankcase bolts **(see illustration)**. **Note:** *As*

each bolt is removed, store it in its relative position in a cardboard template of the crankcase halves. This will ensure all bolts are installed in the correct location on reassembly.
4 Turn the engine upside down so that it rests on the cylinder head studs and the back of the upper crankcase half.
5 Unscrew the seven 6 mm lower crankcase bolts as shown **(see illustration)**.
6 Working in a **reverse** of the tightening sequence shown **(see illustration 24.5)**, slacken the ten 8 mm lower crankcase bolts a little a time until they are all finger-tight, then remove the bolts. **Note:** *As each bolt is removed, store it in its relative position in a cardboard template of the crankcase halves. This will ensure all bolts are installed in the correct location on reassembly.*
7 Carefully lift the lower crankcase half off the upper half, using either a soft hammer to tap around the joint or a screwdriver inserted into one of the leverage points cast into the crankcase, to initially separate the halves if necessary **(see illustration)**. There are three leverage points, one on either side of the

engine near the ends of the crankshaft as shown, and one at the back of the engine. **Note:** *If the halves do not separate easily, make sure all fasteners have been removed. Do not try and separate the halves by levering against the crankcase mating surfaces as they are easily scored and will leak oil. Use only the two leverage points.* The lower crankcase half will come away with the selector drum and selector forks, leaving the crankshaft and transmission shafts in the upper crankcase half.
8 Remove the two locating dowels from the crankcase if they are loose (they could be in either crankcase half), noting their locations **(see illustration)**.
9 Refer to Sections 25 to 31 for the removal and installation of the components housed within the crankcases.

Reassembly

Note: *Kawasaki advise that the 8 mm bolts should be replaced with new ones if they have already been removed five times before.*
10 Remove all traces of sealant from the crankcase mating surfaces.

24.7 Use a screwdriver in one of the leverage points to separate the crankcase halves

24.8 Remove the two dowels (arrowed) if they are loose

24.12 Generously lubricate the crankshaft main bearings

11 Ensure that all components and their bearings are in place in the upper and lower crankcase halves. Check that the transmission bearing locating pins and half-ring retainers are all correctly located, and that the oil jets and the rubber oil passage plug in the transmission input shaft right-hand bearing (upper crankcase half) have been installed, if removed.

12 Generously lubricate the transmission shafts, selector drum and forks, and the crankshaft, particularly around the bearings, with clean engine oil, then use a rag soaked in high flash-point solvent to wipe over the gasket surfaces of both halves to remove all traces of oil **(see illustration)**.

13 Install the two locating dowels in the upper crankcase half **(see illustration 24.8)**. Make sure that the gear selector drum is in the neutral position.

14 Apply a small amount of suitable sealant (Kawasaki-Bond 92104-002 or equivalent) to the mating surfaces of the crankcase halves as shown **(see illustration)**.

Caution: Do not apply an excessive amount of sealant as it will ooze out when the case halves are assembled and may obstruct oil passages. Do not apply the sealant on or too close to any of the oil passages, bearing inserts or bearing surfaces.

15 Check again that all components are in position, particularly that the bearing shells are still correctly located in the lower crankcase half. Carefully install the lower crankcase half down onto the upper crankcase half, making sure that the gear selector forks locate correctly into their grooves in the gears **(see illustration)**. Make

24.15 Fit the lower half down onto the upper half

24.14 Apply sealant to the shaded areas

sure the dowels locate correctly into the lower crankcase half.

16 Check that the lower crankcase half is correctly seated. **Note:** *The crankcase halves should fit together without being forced. If the casings are not correctly seated, remove the lower crankcase half and investigate the problem. Do not attempt to pull them together using the crankcase bolts as the casing will crack and be ruined.*

17 Check that the transmission shafts rotate freely and independently in neutral. Due to the positive neutral selector mechanism, which allows only neutral to be selected from first gear unless the output shaft is rotating (ie the machine is moving), it is not possible to select each gear in turn and check the shafts.

18 Clean the threads of the ten 8 mm lower crankcase bolts and insert them in their original locations (see **Note** above). Secure all bolts finger-tight at first, then tighten the bolts a little at a time and in the numerical sequence shown to the torque setting specified at the beginning of the Chapter **(see illustrations 24.5)**.

19 Clean the threads of the seven 6 mm lower crankcase bolts and insert them in their original locations **(see illustration 24.5)**. Tighten all the bolts a little at a time to the specified torque setting.

20 Turn the engine over. Install the thirteen 6 mm upper crankcase bolts **(see illustration 24.3)**. Tighten all the bolts a little at a time to the specified torque setting.

21 With all crankcase fasteners tightened, check that the crankshaft and transmission shafts rotate smoothly and easily. If there are

any signs of undue stiffness, tight or rough spots, or of any other problem, the fault must be rectified before proceeding further.

22 Install all other removed assemblies in the reverse of the sequence given in Step 2.

25 Crankcase - inspection and servicing

1 After the crankcases have been separated, remove the crankshaft, bearings, oil pressure switch and transmission components, referring to the relevant Sections of this Chapter and to Chapter 8 for the oil pressure switch. If required, remove the oil jets from the passage adjacent to the middle big-end bearing cut-out and from the transmission output shaft right-hand bearing cut-out in the lower crankcase half. Note that the jet adjacent to the big-end bearing is staked in place and could easily be damaged, necessitating replacement **(see illustration)**. Also remove the rubber oil passage plug in the transmission input shaft right-hand bearing in the upper crankcase half if it is loose **(see illustration)**.

2 The crankcases should be cleaned thoroughly with new solvent and dried with compressed air. All oil passages and oil jets should be blown out with compressed air.

3 All traces of old gasket sealant should be removed from the mating surfaces. Minor damage to the surfaces can be cleaned up with a fine sharpening stone or grindstone.

Caution: Be very careful not to nick or gouge the crankcase mating surfaces, or

25.1a This oil nozzle is staked in place

25.1b Remove the rubber plug

oil leaks will result. Check both crankcase halves very carefully for cracks and other damage.

4 Small cracks or holes in aluminium castings may be repaired with an epoxy resin adhesive as a temporary measure. Permanent repairs can only be effected by argon-arc welding, and only a specialist in this process is in a position to advise on the economy or practical aspect of such a repair. If any damage is found that can't be repaired, replace the crankcase halves as a set.

5 Damaged threads can be economically reclaimed by using a diamond section wire insert, of the Helicoil type, which is easily fitted after drilling and re-tapping the affected thread.

 Refer to "Tools and Workshop Tips" in the Reference section for details of how to fit a thread insert, use screw and stud extractors and for gasket removal methods.

6 Sheared studs or screws can usually be removed with screw extractors, which consist of a tapered, left-thread screw of very hard steel. These are inserted into a pre-drilled hole in the stud, and usually succeed in dislodging the most stubborn stud or screw. If a problem arises which seems beyond your scope, it is worth consulting a professional engineering firm before condemning an otherwise sound casing. Many of these firms advertise regularly in the motorcycle press.

7 Check that all the cylinder head studs are tight in the crankcase halves. If any are loose, remove them, noting which fits where as they are of different lengths, then clean their threads. Apply a suitable non-permanent thread locking compound and tighten them securely.

8 If removed, install the jets into their correct locations and stake the jet adjacent to the big-end bearing in place, taking care not to deform the nozzle (see illustration 25.1a). Also install the rubber oil passage plug into the transmission input shaft right-hand bearing cut-out in the upper crankcase half if removed (see illustrations 25.1b). Install all other components and assemblies, referring to the relevant Sections of this Chapter and to Chapter 8, before reassembling the crankcase halves.

26 Main and connecting rod bearings - general information

1 Even though main and connecting rod bearings are generally replaced with new ones during the engine overhaul, the old bearings should be retained for close examination as they may reveal valuable information about the condition of the engine.

2 Bearing failure occurs mainly because of lack of lubrication, the presence of dirt or other foreign particles, overloading the engine and/or corrosion. Regardless of the cause of bearing failure, it must be corrected before the engine is reassembled to prevent it from happening again.

3 When examining the connecting rod bearings, remove them from the connecting rods and caps and lay them out on a clean surface in the same general position as their location on the crankshaft journals. This will enable you to match any noted bearing problems with the corresponding crankshaft journal.

4 Dirt and other foreign particles get into the engine in a variety of ways. It may be left in the engine during assembly or it may pass through filters or breathers. It may get into the oil and from there into the bearings. Metal chips from machining operations and normal engine wear are often present. Abrasives are sometimes left in engine components after reconditioning operations, especially when parts are not thoroughly cleaned using the proper cleaning methods. Whatever the source, these foreign objects often end up imbedded in the soft bearing material and are easily recognised. Large particles will not imbed in the bearing and will score or gouge the bearing and journal. The best prevention for this cause of bearing failure is to clean all parts thoroughly and keep everything spotlessly clean during engine reassembly. Frequent and regular oil and filter changes are also recommended.

5 Lack of lubrication or lubrication breakdown has a number of interrelated causes. Excessive heat (which thins the oil), overloading (which squeezes the oil from the bearing face) and oil leakage or throw off (from excessive bearing clearances, worn oil pump or high engine speeds) all contribute to lubrication breakdown. Blocked oil passages will also starve a bearing and destroy it. When lack of lubrication is the cause of bearing failure, the bearing material is wiped or extruded from the steel backing of the bearing. Temperatures may increase to the point where the steel backing and the journal turn blue from overheating.

 Refer to "Tools and Workshop Tips" for bearing fault finding and further information.

6 Riding habits can have a definite effect on bearing life. Full throttle low speed operation, or labouring the engine, puts very high loads on bearings, which tend to squeeze out the oil film. These loads cause the bearings to flex, which produces fine cracks in the bearing face (fatigue failure). Eventually the bearing material will loosen in pieces and tear away from the steel backing. Short trip riding leads to corrosion of bearings, as insufficient engine

heat is produced to drive off the condensed water and corrosive gases produced. These products collect in the engine oil, forming acid and sludge. As the oil is carried to the engine bearings, the acid attacks and corrodes the bearing material.

7 Incorrect bearing installation during engine assembly will lead to bearing failure as well. Tight fitting bearings which leave insufficient bearing oil clearances result in oil starvation. Dirt or foreign particles trapped behind a bearing insert result in high spots on the bearing which lead to failure.

8 To avoid bearing problems, clean all parts thoroughly before reassembly, double check all bearing clearance measurements and lubricate the new bearings with clean engine oil during installation.

27 Crankshaft - removal, inspection and installation

Note: *To remove the crankshaft the engine must be removed from the frame and the crankcases separated.*

Removal

1 Separate the crankcase halves (Section 24).

2 Before removing the crankshaft check the side clearance. Insert a feeler gauge between the crankshaft web and the no. 2 main bearing journal and record the clearance (see illustration). Compare the measurement with this Chapter's Specifications. If the clearance is excessive, replace the crankcase halves as a set.

3 Lift the crankshaft together with the connecting rods, cam chain and primary chain out of the upper crankcase half (see illustration). If the crankshaft appears stuck, tap it gently using a soft-faced mallet. Remove the oil seal from each end of the crankshaft and discard them as new ones must be used.

27.2 Crankshaft side clearance measurement

1 *Crankshaft*
2 *Side clearance measurement*
3 *No. 2 main bearing journal*

27.3 Lift the crankshaft out of the case

27.10a Crankshaft main bearing journal and crankpin journal size markings

☐ *Main bearing journal diameter mark - 1 mark or unmarked*
O *Crankpin diameter mark - O or unmarked*

4 The main bearing shells can be removed from their cutouts by pushing their centres to the side, then lifting them out. Keep the bearing shells in order.

5 If required, remove the connecting rods from the crankshaft (see Section 28), and disengage the cam chain and primary chain from their sprockets.

Inspection

6 Clean the crankshaft with solvent, using a rifle-cleaning brush to scrub out the oil passages. If available, blow the crank dry with compressed air, and also blow through the oil passages. Check the cam chain sprocket and primary chain sprocket for wear or damage. If any of the sprocket teeth are excessively worn, chipped or broken, the crankshaft must be replaced. Similarly check the primary drive gear on the end of the secondary shaft.

7 Refer to Section 26 and examine the main bearings. If they are scored, badly scuffed or appear to have been seized, new bearings must be installed. Always replace the main bearings as a set. If they are badly damaged, check the corresponding crankshaft journal. Evidence of extreme heat, such as discoloration, indicates that lubrication failure has occurred. Be sure to thoroughly check the oil pump and pressure regulator as well as all oil holes and passages before reassembling the engine.

8 The crankshaft journals should be given a close visual examination, paying particular attention where damaged bearings have been discovered. If the journals are scored or pitted in any way a new crankshaft will be required. Note that undersizes are not available, precluding the option of re-grinding the crankshaft.

9 Place the crankshaft on V-blocks and check the runout at the main bearing journals using a dial gauge. Compare the reading to the maximum specified at the beginning of the Chapter. If the runout exceeds the limit, the crankshaft must be replaced.

Main bearing shell selection

10 Replacement bearing shells for the main bearings are supplied on a selected fit basis. Marks stamped on various components are used to identify the correct replacement bearings. The crankshaft main bearing journal size marks (either a 1 or no mark) are stamped

27.10b Crankcase main bearing housing size markings (A) and their corresponding housings (arrowed)

on the outside of the crankshaft webs **(see illustration)**. The corresponding main bearing housing size marks (either a O or no mark) are stamped into the front of the upper crankcase half **(see illustration)**.

11 A range of bearing shells is available. To select the correct bearing for a particular journal, using the table below cross-refer the main bearing journal size mark (stamped on the crank web) with the main bearing housing size mark (stamped on the crankcase) to determine the colour code of the bearing required. For example, if the journal size is 1, and the housing size is unmarked, then the bearing required is Black. The colour is marked on the side of the shell **(see illustration)**.

Crankcase housing code	Crankshaft journal code	
	1	None
O	Brown	Black
None	Black	Blue

Oil clearance check

12 Whether new bearing shells are being fitted or the original ones are being re-used, the main bearing oil clearance should be checked before the engine is reassembled.

27.11 Bearing shell colour code location

13 Clean the backs of the bearing shells and the bearing housings in both crankcase halves.

14 Press the bearing shells into their cut-outs, ensuring that the tab on each shell engages in the notch in the crankcase **(see illustration)**. Make sure the bearings are fitted in the correct locations and take care not to touch any shell's bearing surface with your fingers.

15 Ensure the shells and crankshaft are clean and dry. Lay the crankshaft in position in the upper crankcase **(see illustration 27.3)**.

16 Cut several lengths of the appropriate size Plastigauge (they should be slightly shorter than the width of the crankshaft journal). Place a strand of Plastigauge on each (cleaned) journal **(see illustration)**. Make sure the crankshaft is not rotated.

27.14 Make sure the tab (A) locates in the notch (B)

27.16 Lay a strip of Plastigauge (arrowed) on each journal parallel to the crankshaft centreline

17 Carefully install the lower crankcase half on to the upper half. Make sure that the selector forks (if fitted) engage with their respective slots in the transmission gears as the halves are joined. Check that the lower crankcase half is correctly seated. **Note:** *Do not tighten the crankcase bolts if the casing is not correctly seated.* Install the lower crankcase 8 mm bolts **(see illustration 24.5)** in their original locations and tighten them a little at a time in the sequence shown to the torque setting specified at the beginning of the Chapter. Make sure that the crankshaft is not rotated as the bolts are tightened.

18 Slacken each bolt in reverse sequence starting at number 10 and working backwards to number 1. Slacken each bolt a little at a time until they are all finger-tight, then remove the bolts. Carefully lift off the lower crankcase half, making sure the Plastigauge is not disturbed.

19 Compare the width of the crushed Plastigauge on each crankshaft journal to the scale printed on the Plastigauge envelope to obtain the main bearing oil clearance **(see illustration)**. Compare the reading to the specifications at the beginning of the Chapter.

20 If the oil clearance falls into the specified range, no bearing shell replacement is required (provided they are in good shape). If the clearance is more than the standard range, but within the service limit, refer to the marks on the case and the marks on the crankshaft and select new bearing shells (see Steps 10 and 11). Install the new shells and check the oil clearance once again (the new shells may bring bearing clearance within the specified range). Always replace all of the shells at the same time.

21 On completion carefully scrape away all traces of the Plastigauge material from the crankshaft journal and bearing shells; use a fingernail or other object which is unlikely to score them.

22 If the clearance is greater than the service limit listed in this Chapter's Specifications (even with replacement shells), measure the diameter of the crankshaft journals with a micrometer and compare your findings with this Chapter's Specifications. By measuring the diameter at a number of points around each journal's circumference, you'll be able to determine whether or not the journal is out-of-round. Also take a measurement at each end of the journal, near the crank throws, as well as in the middle, to determine if the journal is tapered. Replace the crankshaft if it is worn, tapered or out-of-round.

Installation

23 If removed, install the connecting rods onto the crankshaft (see Section 28), and engage the cam chain and primary chain onto their sprockets.

24 Clean the backs of the bearing shells and the bearing cut-outs in both crankcase halves. If new shells are being fitted, ensure that all traces of the protective grease are cleaned off using paraffin (kerosene). Wipe dry the shells and crankcase halves with a lint-free cloth. Make sure all the oil passages and holes are clear, and blow them through with compressed air if it is available.

25 Lubricate each shell, preferably with molybdenum paste, or if not available then with clean engine oil. Press the bearing shells into their locations. Make sure the tab on each shell engages in the notch in the casing **(see illustration 27.14)**. Make sure the bearings are fitted in the correct locations and take care not to touch any shell's bearing surface with your fingers.

26 Apply high temperature grease to the inner lip and silicone sealant to the outer lip of each crankshaft oil seal. Fit the seals so that the arrow marked on one side faces out and points in the normal direction of rotation of the crankshaft (with the engine the correct way up, the right-hand end of the crankshaft rotates clockwise as you look at it, and the left-hand end anti-clockwise).

27 Lower the crankshaft into position in the upper crankcase, feeding the cam chain down through its tunnel **(see illustration 27.3)**.

28 Reassemble the crankcase halves (see Section 24).

28 Connecting rods - removal, inspection and installation

Note: *To remove the connecting rods the engine must be removed from the frame and the crankcases separated.*

Removal

1 Remove the crankshaft (see Section 27).

2 Before removing the rods from the crankshaft, measure the side clearance on each rod with a feeler gauge **(see illustration)**. If the clearance on any rod is greater than the service limit listed in this Chapter's Specifications, replace the rod and recheck the clearance. If it is still too great, replace the crankshaft as well.

3 Using paint or a felt marker pen, mark the relevant cylinder identity on each connecting

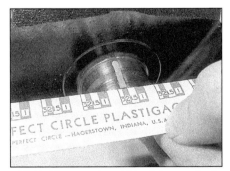

27.19 Measure the width of the crushed Plastigauge (be sure to use the correct scale - metric and imperial are included)

28.2 Measure the connecting rod side clearance using a feeler gauge

28.4 Unscrew the nuts and remove the cap

rod and bearing. Mark across the cap-to-connecting rod join and note which side of the rod faces the front of the engine to ensure that the cap and rod are fitted the correct way around on reassembly. Note that the letter already across the rod and cap indicates rod weight - each left-hand or right-hand pair of rods should have the same letter for proper balance **(see illustration 28.8)**.

4 Unscrew the big-end cap nuts and separate the connecting rod, cap and both bearing shells from the crankpin **(see illustration)**. Do not remove the bolts from the connecting rods. Keep the rod, cap, nuts and (if they are to be reused) the bearing shells together in their correct positions to ensure correct installation.

Inspection

5 Check the connecting rods for cracks, bend or twist and other obvious damage. Have the rods checked for twist and bend by a Kawasaki dealer if you are in doubt about their straightness.

6 If not already done (see Section 16), apply clean engine oil to the piston pin, insert it into the connecting rod small-end and check for freeplay between the two **(see illustration)**.

7 Refer to Section 26 and examine the connecting rod bearing shells. If they are scored, badly scuffed or appear to have seized, new shells must be installed. Always replace the shells in the connecting rods as a set. If they are badly damaged, check the corresponding crankpin. Evidence of extreme heat, such as discoloration, indicates that lubrication failure has occurred. Be sure to thoroughly check the oil pump and pressure regulator as well as all oil holes and passages before reassembling the engine.

Bearing shell selection

8 Replacement bearing shells for the big-end bearings are supplied on a selected fit basis. Marks stamped on various components are used to identify the correct replacement bearings. The crankpin journal size marks (either a O or no mark) are stamped on the crankshaft web **(see illustration 27.10a)**. The

connecting rod size mark (either a O or no mark) is marked around the weight letter on the flat face of the connecting rod and cap **(see illustration)**.

9 A range of bearing shells is available. To select the correct bearing for a particular big-end, using the table below cross-refer the crankpin journal size mark (stamped on the web) with the connecting rod size mark (stamped on the rod) to determine the colour code of the bearing required. For example, if the connecting rod size is O, and the crankpin is unmarked, then the bearing required is Blue. The colour is marked on the side of the shell **(see illustration 27.11)**.

| Connecting rod code | Crankpin code | |
	O	None
O	Black	Blue
None	Brown	Black

28.6 Slip the piston pin into the rod's small-end and rock it back and forth to check for looseness

28.8 Connecting rod weight group letter and size marking (O or no mark)

28.12 Make sure the tab (A) locates in the notch (B)

28.21 Tighten the cap nuts to the specified torque setting

Oil clearance check

10 Whether new bearing shells are being fitted or the original ones are being re-used, the connecting rod bearing oil clearance should be checked prior to reassembly.

11 Clean the backs of the bearing shells and the bearing locations in both the connecting rod and cap.

12 Press the bearing shells into their locations, ensuring that the tab on each shell engages the notch in the connecting rod/cap **(see illustration)**. Make sure the bearings are fitted in the correct locations and take care not to touch any shell's bearing surface with your fingers.

13 Cut a length of the appropriate size Plastigauge (it should be slightly shorter than the width of the crankpin) **(see illustration 27.16)**. Place a strand of Plastigauge on the (cleaned) crankpin journal and fit the (clean) connecting rod, shells and cap. Make sure the cap is fitted the correct way around so the previously made markings align, and that the rod is facing the right way, and tighten the bearing cap nuts to the torque setting specified at the beginning of the Chapter, whilst ensuring that the connecting rod does not rotate. Slacken the cap nuts and remove the connecting rod, again taking great care not to rotate the crankshaft.

14 Compare the width of the crushed Plastigauge on the crankpin to the scale printed on the Plastigauge envelope to obtain the connecting rod bearing oil clearance **(see illustration 27.19)**. Compare the reading to the specifications at the beginning of the Chapter.

15 If the clearance is within the range listed in this Chapter's Specifications and the bearings are in perfect condition, they can be reused. If the clearance is beyond the service limit, replace the bearing shells with new ones (see Steps 8 and 9). Check the oil clearance once again (the new shells may be thick enough to bring bearing clearance within the specified

range). Always replace all of the inserts at the same time.

16 If the clearance is still greater than the service limit listed in this Chapter's Specifications, measure the diameter of the crankpin journal with a micrometer and compare your findings with this Chapter's Specifications. Also, by measuring the diameter at a number of points around the journal's circumference, you'll be able to determine whether or not the journal is out-of-round. Also take a measurement at each end of the journal, near the crank throws, as well as in the middle, to determine if the journal is tapered.

17 If any journal has worn down past the service limit, replace the crankshaft.

18 Repeat the bearing selection procedure for the remaining connecting rods.

19 On completion carefully scrape away all traces of the Plastigauge material from the crankpin and bearing shells using a fingernail or other object which is unlikely to score the shells.

Installation

20 Install the bearing shells in the connecting rods and caps, aligning the notch in the bearing with the groove in the rod or cap **(see illustration 28.12)**. Lubricate the shells, preferably with molybdenum paste, or if not available with clean engine oil, and assemble each connecting rod on its correct crankpin so that the previously made matchmarks align and the rods face the right way **(see illustration 28.4)**. Tighten the nuts finger-tight at this stage. Check to make sure that all components have been returned to their original locations using the marks made on disassembly.

21 Tighten the bearing cap nuts to the torque setting specified at the beginning of the Chapter **(see illustration)**.

22 Check that the rods rotate smoothly and freely on the crankpin. If there are any signs of

roughness or tightness, remove the rods and re-check the bearing clearance. Sometimes tapping the bottom of the connecting rod cap will relieve tightness, but if in doubt, recheck the clearances.

23 Install the crankshaft (see Section 27).

29 Transmission shafts - removal and installation

Note: *To remove the transmission shafts the engine must be removed from the frame and the crankcases separated.*

Note: *Referrals to the right and left-hand ends of the transmission shafts are made as though the engine is the correct way up, even though throughout this procedure it is upside down. Therefore the right-hand end of a shaft will actually be on your left as you look down onto the underside of the upper crankcase assembly.*

Removal

1 Separate the crankcase halves (Section 24).

2 Lift the input shaft and output shaft out of the crankcase, noting their relative positions in the crankcase and how they fit together **(see illustration)**. If they are stuck, use a soft-

29.2 Lift the shafts out of the crankcase (550 six-speed transmission shown)

29.5a Install the caged ball bearing half-ring retainers . . .

29.5b . . . and the needle bearing dowel pins (arrowed)

29.6 Install the output shaft . . .

29.7 . . . and the input shaft (750 five-speed transmission shown)

faced hammer and gently tap on the ends of the shafts to free them.

3 Remove the caged-ball bearing half-ring retainers and the needle bearing dowel pins from the upper crankcase half, noting how they fit (see illustrations 29.5a and b). If they are not in their slots or holes in the crankcase, remove them from the bearings themselves on the shafts.

4 If necessary, the input shaft and output shaft can be disassembled and inspected for wear or damage (see Section 30).

Installation

5 Install the caged ball bearing half-ring retainers into their slots in the upper crankcase half, and install the needle bearing dowels into their holes (see illustrations).

6 Lower the output shaft into position in the crankcase half, making sure the hole in the needle bearing engages correctly with the dowel, and the groove in the caged-ball bearing engages correctly with the bearing half-ring retainer (see illustration). On 750 models,

check that the 1st gear pinion on the right-hand end of the shaft rotates freely without any drag (remove the input shaft before making this check). If drag is felt, remove the needle bearing outer race from the right-hand end of the shaft, then remove the circlip and needle bearing and replace the plain washer behind it with a thinner one. The standard washer is 1 mm thick. Replacements are available either 0.7 mm or 0.5 mm thick.

7 Lower the input shaft into position in the upper crankcase, making sure the hole in the needle bearing engages correctly with the dowel, and the groove in the caged-ball bearing engages correctly with the bearing half-ring retainer (see illustration). On 750 models, check that the shaft rotates freely without any drag. If drag is felt, remove the needle bearing outer race from the left-hand end of the shaft, then remove the circlip and needle bearing and replace the washer behind it with a thinner one. The standard washer is 1 mm thick. Replacements are available either 0.7 mm or 0.5 mm thick.

8 Make sure both transmission shafts are correctly seated and their related pinions are correctly engaged.

Caution: If the caged-ball bearing half-ring retainers or needle bearing dowel pins are not correctly engaged, the crankcase halves will not seat correctly.

9 Position the gears in the neutral position and check the shafts are free to rotate easily and independently (ie the input shaft can turn whilst the output shaft is held stationary) before proceeding further.

10 Reassembly the crankcase halves (see Section 24).

30 Transmission shafts -
disassembly, inspection and reassembly

Note: Referrals to the right and left-hand ends of the transmission shafts are made as though they are installed in the engine and the engine is the correct way up.

30.2 Six-speed transmission - input shaft components

1 Needle bearing outer race
2 Circlip
3 Needle bearing
4 Thick thrust washer
5 2nd gear pinion
6 Circlip
7 Splined washer
8 6th gear pinion
9 6th gear pinion bush
10 Splined washer
11 Circlip
12 3rd/4th gear pinion
13 Circlip
14 Splined washer
15 5th gear pinion bush (B4, B5 and B6 models only)
16 5th gear pinion
17 Input shaft with integral 1st gear pinion
18 Caged ball bearing

1 Remove the transmission shafts from the upper crankcase half (see Section 29). Always disassemble the transmission shafts separately to avoid mixing up the components.

ZR550 models - six-speed transmission

Input shaft disassembly

HAYNES HiNT *When disassembling the transmission shafts, place the parts on a long rod or thread a wire through them to keep them in order and facing the proper direction.*

2 Remove the needle bearing outer race from the left-hand end of the shaft, then remove the circlip and slide the needle bearing and thick thrust washer and the 2nd gear pinion off the shaft **(see illustration)**.
3 Remove the circlip securing the 6th gear pinion, then slide the splined washer, the 6th gear pinion and its bush, and the splined washer off the shaft.
4 Remove the circlip securing the combined 3rd/4th gear pinion, then slide the pinion off the shaft.
5 Remove the circlip securing the 5th gear pinion, then slide the splined washer and 5th gear pinion off the shaft, along with its bush (B4, B5 and B6 models only).
6 The 1st gear pinion is integral with the shaft.

Input shaft inspection

7 Wash all of the components in clean solvent and dry them off.

8 Check the gear teeth for cracking chipping, pitting and other obvious wear or damage. Any pinion that is damaged as such must be replaced.
9 Inspect the dogs and the dog holes in the gears for cracks, chips, and excessive wear especially in the form of rounded edges. Make sure mating gears engage properly. Replace the paired gears as a set if necessary.
10 Check for signs of scoring or bluing on the pinions, bushes and shaft. This could be caused by overheating due to inadequate lubrication. Check that all the oil holes and passages are clear. Replace any damaged pinions or bushes.
11 Check that each pinion moves freely on the shaft or bush but without undue freeplay. Check that each bush moves freely on the shaft but without undue freeplay.
12 The shaft is unlikely to sustain damage unless the engine has seized, placing an unusually high loading on the transmission, or the machine has covered a very high mileage. Check the surface of the shaft, especially where a pinion turns on it, and replace the shaft if it has scored or picked up, or if there are any cracks. Place the shaft on V-blocks and check the runout at the shaft centre using a dial gauge. Damage of any kind can only be cured by replacement.
13 Check the caged-ball bearing for play or roughness, and that it is a tight fit on the shaft. Replace the bearing if it is worn, loose or damaged, using a bearing puller to remove it **(see illustration)**. If one is not available, you could try carefully levering it off using a pair of tyre levers, though it is preferable to take the shaft to a Kawasaki dealer. Install the bearing using a press. Install the needle roller bearing

onto the shaft, and check it for play or roughness. Replace the bearing if it is worn or damaged.
14 Check the washers and replace any that are bent or appear weakened or worn. Discard all the circlips as new ones must be used.

Input shaft reassembly

15 During reassembly, apply molybdenum paste or engine oil to the mating surfaces of the shaft, pinions and bushes. Install the bushes with their oil hole aligned with the hole in the shaft. When installing the circlips, do not expand the ends any further than is necessary, and install them so that the chamfered side faces the pinion it secures and the open ends are in a gap between splines (see illustrations in Fasteners section of *Tools and Workshop Tips* in the Reference section of this manual).

30.13 Use a puller to remove the bearing

30.16a Slide the 5th gear pinion . . .

30.16b . . . and the splined washer onto the shaft . . .

30.16c . . . and secure them with the circlip

30.17a Slide the 3rd/4th gear pinion onto the shaft . . .

30.17b . . . and secure it with circlip (A), then slide the splined washer (B) . . .

30.18a . . . the 6th gear bushing . . .

30.18b . . . the 6th gear pinion . . .

30.18c . . . and the splined washer onto the shaft . . .

30.18d . . . and secure them with the circlip

16 Slide the 5th gear pinion and its bush (B4, B5 and B6 models only), with its dogs facing away from the integral 1st gear, onto the left-hand end of the shaft **(see illustration)**. Slide the splined washer onto the shaft, then install the circlip, making sure that it locates correctly in the groove in the shaft **(see illustrations)**.

17 Slide the combined 3rd/4th gear pinion onto the shaft, so that the smaller (3rd gear) pinion faces the 5th gear pinion dogs **(see illustration)**. Secure it in place with the circlip, making sure it is properly seated in its groove **(see illustration)**.

18 Slide the splined washer, the 6th gear bush and the 6th gear pinion onto the shaft, with the pinion dog holes facing the dogs on the 4th gear pinion **(see illustrations)**. Slide the other splined washer onto the shaft and secure the 6th gear pinion with the circlip,

30.19a Slide the 2nd gear pinion . . .

making sure it locates correctly in the groove in the shaft **(see illustrations)**.

19 Slide the 2nd gear pinion onto the shaft, followed by the thick thrust washer and the needle bearing **(see illustrations)**. Secure the

30.19b . . . the thick thrust washer . . .

bearing with the circlip, making sure it locates correctly in the groove, then fit the bearing outer race **(see illustrations)**.

20 Check that all components have been correctly installed.

30.19c . . . and the needle bearing onto the shaft . . .

30.19d . . . and secure them with the circlip . . .

30.19e . . . then slide the outer race over the bearing

30.21 Six-speed transmission - output shaft components

1 Caged ball bearing
2 Output shaft
3 Steel balls
4 2nd gear pinion
5 Splined washer
6 Circlip
7 6th gear pinion
8 Circlip
9 Splined washer
10 4th gear pinion
11 4th and 3rd gear bush
12 3rd gear pinion
13 Splined washer
14 Circlip
15 5th gear pinion
16 1st gear pinion
17 Thick thrust washer
18 Needle bearing
19 Circlip
20 Needle bearing outer race

Output shaft disassembly

21 Remove the needle bearing outer race from the right-hand end of the shaft, then remove the circlip and slide the needle bearing, the thick thrust washer and the 1st gear pinion off the shaft (see illustration).

22 To remove the 5th gear pinion it is necessary to displace the steel balls for the positive neutral system from the slots in the shaft and into the holes in the pinion using centrifugal force. Support the shaft vertically with the 5th gear pinion facing down and hold it above a soft container padded with rags into which the pinion and balls can drop when the shaft is rotated. Holding the shaft by any of the freely rotating pinions, spin the shaft as hard as possible while keeping it as vertical as possible (see illustration). When the balls are flung out of their slots and into the holes in the pinion, the pinion should drop off the shaft. Take care not to lose the balls.

23 Remove the circlip securing the 3rd gear pinion, then slide the splined washer, the 3rd gear pinion, the 4th gear pinion, the 3rd and 4th gear pinion bush and the splined washer off the shaft.

30.22 Hold the output shaft as shown and spin it hard to release the 5th gear pinion

24 Remove the circlip securing the 6th gear pinion, then slide the pinion off the shaft.

25 Remove the circlip securing the 2nd gear pinion, then slide the splined washer and the 2nd gear pinion off the shaft.

Output shaft inspection

26 Refer to Steps 7 to 14 above.

Output shaft reassembly

27 During reassembly, apply molybdenum paste or engine oil to the mating surfaces of the shaft, pinions and bush. Install the bush with its oil hole aligned with the hole in the shaft. When installing the circlips, do not expand the ends any further than is necessary, and install them so that the chamfered side faces the pinion it secures and the open ends are in a gap between (see illustrations in Fasteners section of *Tools and Workshop Tips* in the Reference section of this manual).

30.28a Slide the 2nd gear pinion . . .

30.28b . . . and the splined washer
onto the shaft . . .

30.28c . . . and secure them
with the circlip

30.29a Slide the 6th gear pinion
onto the shaft . . .

30.29b . . . secure it with the circlip, then
slide the splined washer onto the shaft

30.30a Slide the 4th/3rd gear bush onto
the shaft, then slide the 4th gear pinion . . .

30.30b . . . and the 3rd gear pinion
onto the bush . . .

30.30c . . . then slide on the
splined washer . . .

30.30d . . . and secure it with the circlip

28 Slide the 2nd gear pinion onto the shaft, followed by the splined washer, and secure them in place with the circlip, making sure it is properly seated in its groove (see illustrations).
29 Slide the 6th gear pinion onto the shaft with its selector fork groove facing away from the 2nd gear pinion, and secure it in place with the circlip, making sure it is properly seated in its groove (see illustrations).
30 Slide the spline washer, followed by the 4th and 3rd gear bushing onto the shaft, then slide the 4th gear pinion and the 3rd gear pinion onto the bushing, followed by the spline washer, and secure them with the circlip, making sure it is properly seated in its groove (see illustrations).
31 The 5th gear pinion has six drillings, three of which are narrower on the outside of the pinion (in the selector fork groove) (see illustration). Fit one of the positive neutral

30.31a Identify the three holes with the
narrower diameter (arrowed) . . .

system balls into each of the holes with the narrower outside diameter (see illustration). To stop them from continuously rolling out, squirt some clean engine oil into each of the

30.31b . . . and insert a steel ball
into each of them

drillings after the ball has been installed. Do not use grease as the balls will stick too much and the neutral system will not work. Holding the shaft vertical and the pinion flat, slide the

30.31c Align the holes with the balls (A) with the groove in the shaft (B) and fit the 5th gear pinion as shown

30.32a Slide the 1st gear pinion . . .

30.32b . . . the thick thrust washer . . .

30.32c . . . and the needle bearing onto the shaft . . .

30.32d . . . and secure them with the circlip . . .

30.32e . . . then slide the outer race over the bearing

pinion onto the shaft with the selector fork groove facing the 3rd gear pinion and so that the drillings with the balls align with the slots in the shaft (see illustration). Check that the balls have located themselves in the slot in the shaft, thereby locking the pinion, by trying to slide the pinion off the shaft again.

32 Slide the 1st gear pinion onto the shaft, followed by the thick thrust washer and the needle bearing (see illustrations). Secure the bearing with the circlip, making sure it locates correctly in the groove, then fit the bearing outer race (see illustrations).

33 Check that all components have been correctly installed.

ZR750 - five-speed transmission

Input shaft disassembly

 When disassembling the transmission shafts, place the parts on a long rod or thread a wire through them to keep them in order and facing the proper direction.

34 Remove the needle bearing outer race from the left-hand end of the shaft, then remove the circlip and slide the needle bearing, plain washer, the 2nd gear pinion, the 5th gear pinion and its bush, and the thrust washer off the shaft (see illustration).

35 Remove the circlip securing the 3rd gear pinion, then slide the pinion off the shaft.

36 Remove the circlip securing the 4th gear pinion, then slide the thrust washer and the pinion off the shaft.

37 The 1st gear pinion is integral with the shaft.

Input shaft inspection

38 Wash all of the components in clean solvent and dry them off.

39 Check the gear teeth for cracking chipping, pitting and other obvious wear or

30.34 Five-speed transmission - input shaft components

1 Needle bearing outer race
2 Circlip
3 Needle bearing
4 Thick thrust washer
5 2nd gear pinion
6 5th gear pinion
7 5th gear pinion bush
8 Thrust washer
9 Circlip
10 3rd gear pinion
11 Circlip
12 Thrust washer
13 4th gear pinion
14 Input shaft
15 Caged ball bearing

30.47a Slide the 4th gear pinion . . .

30.47b . . . and the thrust washer onto the shaft . . .

30.47c . . . and secure them with the circlip

30.48a Slide the 3rd gear pinion onto the shaft . . .

30.48b . . . and secure it with the circlip, then slide the thrust washer . . .

30.49a . . . the 5th gear bush . . .

damage. Any pinion that is damaged as such must be replaced.

40 Inspect the dogs and the dog holes in the gears for cracks, chips, and excessive wear especially in the form of rounded edges. Make sure mating gears engage properly. Replace the paired gears as a set if necessary.

41 Check for signs of scoring or bluing on the pinions, bush and shaft. This could be caused by overheating due to inadequate lubrication. Check that all the oil holes and passages are clear. Replace any damaged pinions or the bush.

42 Check that each pinion moves freely on the shaft or bush but without undue freeplay. Check that the bush moves freely on the shaft but without undue freeplay.

43 The shaft is unlikely to sustain damage unless the engine has seized, placing an unusually high loading on the transmission, or the machine has covered a very high mileage. Check the surface of the shaft, especially where a pinion turns on it, and replace the shaft if it has scored or picked up, or if there are any cracks. Place the shaft on V-blocks and check the runout at the shaft centre using a dial gauge. Damage of any kind can only be cured by replacement.

44 Check the caged-ball bearing for play or roughness, and that it is a tight fit on the shaft. Replace the bearing if it is worn, loose or damaged, using a bearing puller to remove it **(see illustration 30.13)**. If one is not available, you could try carefully levering it off using a pair of tyre levers, though it is preferable to take the shaft to a Kawasaki dealer. Install the

30.49b . . . the 5th gear pinion . . .

bearing using a press. Install the needle roller bearing onto the shaft, and check it for play or roughness. Replace the bearing if it is worn or damaged.

45 Check the washers and replace any that are bent or appear weakened or worn. Discard all the circlips as new ones must be used.

Input shaft reassembly

46 During reassembly, apply molybdenum paste or engine oil to the mating surfaces of the shaft, pinions and bush. Install the bush with its oil hole aligned with the hole in the shaft. When installing the circlips, do not expand the ends any further than is necessary, and install them so that the chamfered side faces the pinion it secures and the open ends are in a gap between splines (see illustrations in Fasteners section of *Tools and Workshop Tips* in the Reference section of this manual).

30.50a . . . the 2nd gear pinion . . .

47 Slide the 4th gear pinion, with its dogs facing away from the integral 1st gear, onto the left-hand end of the shaft, followed by the thrust washer **(see illustrations)**. Install the circlip, making sure that it locates correctly in the groove in the shaft **(see illustration)**.

48 Slide the 3rd gear pinion onto the shaft with its selector fork groove facing away from the 4th gear pinion **(see illustration)**. Secure it in place with the circlip, making sure it is properly seated in its groove **(see illustration)**.

49 Slide the thrust washer onto the shaft, followed by the 5th gear pinion and its bush, making sure the dog holes in the pinion face the dogs on the 3rd gear pinion, and the oil hole in the bush aligns with the hole in the shaft **(see illustrations)**.

50 Slide the 2nd gear pinion onto the shaft, followed by the plain washer and the needle bearing **(see illustrations)**. Secure the bearing with the circlip, making sure it locates

30.50b ... the thick thrust washer ...

30.50c ... and the needle bearing onto the shaft

30.50d Secure the needle bearing with the circlip ...

30.50e ... then slide the outer race over the bearing

correctly in the groove, then fit the bearing outer race **(see illustrations)**.
51 Check that all components have been correctly installed.

Output shaft disassembly

52 Remove the needle bearing outer race from the left-hand end of the shaft, then

remove the circlip and slide the needle bearing, thick thrust washer and the 1st gear pinion off the shaft **(see illustration)**.
53 To remove the 4th gear pinion it is necessary to displace the steel balls for the positive neutral system from the slots in the shaft and into the holes in the pinion using centrifugal force. Support the shaft vertically

with the 4th gear pinion facing down and hold it above a container padded with rags into which the pinion and balls can drop when the shaft is rotated. Holding the shaft by any of the freely rotating pinions, spin the shaft as hard as possible while keeping it as vertical as possible **(see illustration)**. When the balls are flung out of their slots and into the holes in the pinion, the pinion should drop off the shaft **(see illustration)**. Take care not to lose the balls.
54 Remove the circlip securing the 3rd gear pinion, then slide the splined washer, the pinion and the splined washer off the shaft.
55 Remove the circlip securing the 5th gear pinion, then slide the pinion off the shaft.
56 Remove the circlip securing the 2nd gear pinion, then slide the splined washer and the 2nd gear pinion off the shaft.

Output shaft inspection

57 Refer to Steps 38 to 45 above.

Output shaft reassembly

58 During reassembly, apply molybdenum paste or engine oil to the mating surfaces of the shaft, pinions and bushings. Install the bushings with their oil hole aligned with the hole in the shaft. When installing the circlips, do not expand the ends any further than is necessary, and install them so that the chamfered side faces the pinion it secures and the open ends are in a gap between splines **(see illustration 30.15)**.
59 Slide the 2nd gear pinion onto the shaft, followed by the splined washer, and secure

30.53a Hold the output shaft as shown and spin it hard ...

30.53b ... to release the 4th gear pinion

30.52 Five-speed transmission - output shaft components

1 Caged ball bearing
2 Output shaft
3 Steel balls
4 2nd gear pinion
5 Splined washer
6 Circlip
7 5th gear pinion
8 Circlip
9 Splined washer
10 3rd gear pinion
11 Splined washer
12 Circlip
13 4th gear pinion
14 1st gear pinion
15 Thick thrust washer
16 Needle bearing
17 Circlip
18 Needle bearing outer race

30.59a Slide the 2nd gear pinion . . .

30.59b . . . and the thrust washer onto the shaft, and secure them with the circlip

30.60a Slide the 5th gear pinion onto the shaft . . .

30.60b . . . and secure it with the circlip, then slide the splined washer . . .

30.61a . . . the 3rd gear pinion . . .

30.61b . . . and the splined washer onto the shaft, and secure them with the circlip

30.63a Slide the 1st gear pinion, thick thrust washer . . .

30.63b . . . and needle bearing onto the shaft, and secure them with the circlip . . .

30.63c . . . then fit the outer race over the bearing

them in place with the circlip, making sure it is properly seated in its groove **(see illustrations)**.
60 Slide the 5th gear pinion onto the shaft with its selector fork groove facing away from the 2nd gear pinion and secure it with the circlip, making sure it is properly seated in its groove **(see illustrations)**.
61 Slide the splined washer followed by the 3rd gear pinion onto the shaft, followed by the splined washer, and secure them in place with the circlip, making sure it is properly seated in its groove **(see illustrations)**.
62 The 4th gear pinion has six drillings, three of which are narrower on the outside of the pinion (in the selector fork groove) **(see illustration 30.31a)**. Fit one of the positive neutral system balls into each of the holes with the narrower outside diameter **(see illustration 30.31b)**. To stop them from continuously rolling out, squirt some clean

engine oil into each of the drillings after the ball has been installed. Do not use grease as the balls will stick too much and the neutral system will not work. Holding the shaft vertical and the pinion flat, slide the pinion onto the shaft with the selector fork groove facing the 3rd gear pinion and so that the drillings with the balls align with the slots in the shaft **(see illustration 30.31c)**. Check that the balls have located themselves in the slot in the shaft, thereby locking the pinion, by trying to slide the pinion off the shaft again.
63 Slide the 1st gear pinion onto the shaft, followed by the thick thrust washer and the needle bearing, and secure the bearing with the circlip, making sure it locates correctly in the groove **(see illustrations)**. Fit the outer race over the bearing **(see illustration)**.
64 Check that all components have been correctly installed.

31 Selector drum and forks - removal, inspection and installation

Note: *Access can be gained to the gearchange mechanism (external components) with the engine in the frame and the clutch removed (see Section 20). All other operations require the engine to be removed and the crankcases to be separated.*

Removal

1 Separate the crankcase halves (refer to Section 24). The selector drum and forks are housed inside the lower half.
2 Before removing the selector forks, note the position of each and which way round they fit as an aid to installation.

31.3a Withdraw the shaft (arrowed) . . .

31.3b . . . and remove the two forks

31.4a Remove the split pin (arrowed) . . .

31.4b . . . and withdraw the guide pin

31.5 Bend back the lockwasher tab (arrowed) and remove the bolt

31.6 Unscrew the cam plunger bolt and remove it with the spring and plunger

31.7 Remove the circlip securing the cam, then slide the cam (arrowed) off the drum

31.8 Withdraw the drum, sliding the fork off as you do, noting which way round it fits (550 models shown)

3 Supporting the selector forks on the fork shaft, withdraw the shaft from the left-hand side of the crankcase, then remove the forks **(see illustrations)**. Once removed from the crankcase, slide the forks back onto the shaft in their correct order and way round.

4 Remove the split pin from the top of the guide pin on the selector fork which fits around the selector drum **(see illustration)**. Discard the split pin as a new one must be used. Withdraw the guide pin **(see illustration)**.

5 Bend back the tab on the lockwasher securing the selector drum guide bolt, then

unscrew the bolt **(see illustration)**. Discard the lockwasher if the tab is weakened or damaged.

6 Unscrew the cam plunger bolt and remove it with its spring and plunger **(see illustration)**.

7 Remove the circlip securing the cam to the right-hand end of the drum **(see illustration)**. Remove the cam, noting how the pin in the drum locates in the slot in the cam **(see illustration 31.17b)**. Remove the pin for safekeeping if it is loose.

8 Withdraw the selector drum from the left-hand side of the crankcase, sliding the selector

fork off the drum as you do. On 550 models, the longer side of the fork boss faces the left-hand end of the drum **(see illustration)**. On 750 models, the longer side of the fork boss faces the right-hand end of the drum **(see illustration 31.16)**.

Inspection

9 Inspect the selector forks for any signs of wear or damage, especially around the fork ends where they engage with the groove in the pinion. Check that each fork fits correctly in its pinion groove. Check closely to see if the

31.10a Measure the fork-to groove clearance using a feeler gauge

31.10b Measure the thickness of the fork end . . .

31.10c . . . and the width of the groove

31.14 Check the needle bearing in the crankcase

31.16 Ensure the fork is fitted the correct way round for your model (see text)

31.17a Fit the pin into the drum (arrowed) . . .

forks are bent. If the forks are in any way damaged they must be replaced.

10 With the fork engaged with its pinion groove, measure the fork-to-groove clearance using a feeler gauge, and compare the result to the specifications at the beginning of the Chapter **(see illustration)**. If the clearance exceeds the service limit specified, measure the thickness of the fork ends and the width of the groove and compare the readings to the specifications **(see illustrations)**. Replace whichever components are worn beyond their specifications.

11 Check that the forks fit correctly on their shaft. They should move freely with a light fit but no appreciable freeplay. Check that the fork shaft holes in the crankcases are not worn or damaged.

12 The selector fork shaft can be checked for trueness by rolling it along a flat surface. A bent rod will cause difficulty in selecting gears and make the gearchange action heavy. Replace the shaft if it is bent.

13 Inspect the selector drum grooves and selector fork guide pins for signs of wear or damage. Measure the width of each groove and the diameter of the corresponding fork guide pin and compare the results to the specifications. If any component is worn beyond its service limit or is damaged, it must be replaced.

14 Check that the selector drum needle bearing rotates freely and has no sign of freeplay between it and the crankcase **(see illustration)**. Replace the bearing if necessary. Drift it out of the crankcase, noting

31.17b . . . then locate the slot in the cam over the pin

that once it has been removed it cannot be re-used. Draw or drive the new bearing onto place, making sure it enters squarely.

15 Make sure the cam plunger moves freely in the plunger bolt, and that the spring is not worn or damaged.

Installation

16 Slide the drum halfway into the crankcase, then fit the input shaft selector fork over the drum. On 550 models, the fork must be fitted so that the longer side of the fork boss faces the left-hand end of the drum **(see illustration 31.8)**. On 750 models, the fork must be fitted so that the longer side of the fork boss faces the right-hand end of the drum **(see illustration)**. Slide the drum all the way home, then fit the fork guide pin into the fork, making sure it enters the middle groove

31.18 Align the drum so the plunger fits into the neutral detent (arrowed)

in the drum, and secure it with a new split pin **(see illustrations 31.4b and a)**.

17 If removed, fit the cam locating pin into the hole in the drum **(see illustration)**. Slide the cam onto the right-hand end of the drum, making sure the slot in the cam locates over the pin **(see illustration)**. Secure the cam with the circlip, making sure it is properly seated in its groove **(see illustration 31.7)**.

18 Fit the spring and plunger into the cam plunger bolt, then fit the bolt into the bottom of the crankcase and tighten it securely **(see illustration 31.6)**. On 750 models, a torque setting is specified (see the beginning of the Chapter). Align the selector drum so that the neutral detent in the cam faces down and the plunger locates in it **(see illustration)**.

19 Install the selector drum guide bolt and its lockwasher into the bottom of the crankcase, making sure the bolt end fits into the guide

31.19 Fit the guide bolt with its tab washer

groove in the drum **(see illustration)**. Tighten the bolt securely, then bend up the tab on the washer to secure it **(see illustration 31.5)**. On 750 models, a torque setting is specified (see the beginning of the Chapter).
20 Lubricate the selector fork shaft with clean engine oil and slide it into its bore in the crankcase, making sure the E-clip is fitted to the left-hand end **(see illustration 31.3a)**. As the shaft is installed, fit each output shaft selector fork in turn, making sure the longer side of each fork boss faces the left-hand side, and that the guide pins locate in the outer tracks in the selector drum **(see illustration 31.3b)**.
21 Reassemble the crankcase halves (see Section 24).

32 Initial start-up after overhaul

1 Make sure the engine oil level is correct (see *Daily (pre-ride) checks*).

2 Pull the plug caps off the spark plugs and insert a spare spark plug into each cap. Position the spare plugs so that their bodies are earthed (grounded) against the engine. Turn the ignition switch ON and make sure the kill switch is in the RUN position, then crank the engine over with the starter until the oil pressure light goes off (which indicates that oil pressure exists). Turn off the ignition. Remove the spare spark plugs and reconnect the plug caps.
3 Make sure there is fuel in the tank, then turn the fuel tap to the ON position and operate the choke.
4 Start the engine and allow it to run at a moderately fast idle until it reaches operating temperature.

 Warning: If the oil pressure light doesn't go off, or it comes on while the engine is running, stop the engine immediately.

5 Check carefully for oil leaks and make sure the transmission and controls, especially the brakes, function properly before road testing the machine. Refer to Section 33 for the recommended running-in procedure.
6 Upon completion of the road test, and after the engine has cooled down completely, recheck the valve clearances (see Chapter 1) and check the engine oil level (see *Daily (pre-ride) checks*).

33 Recommended running-in procedure

1 Treat the machine gently for the first few miles to make sure oil has circulated throughout the engine and any new parts installed have started to seat.
2 Even greater care is necessary if the engine has been rebored or a new crankshaft has been installed. In the case of a rebore, the bike will have to be run in as when new. This means greater use of the transmission and a restraining hand on the throttle until at least 500 miles (800 km) have been covered. There's no point in keeping to any set speed limit - the main idea is to keep from labouring the engine and to gradually increase performance up to the 500 mile (800 km) mark. These recommendations can be lessened to an extent when only a new crankshaft is installed. Experience is the best guide, since it's easy to tell when an engine is running freely. The following maximum engine speed limitations, which Kawasaki provide for new motorcycles, can be used as a guide.
3 If a lubrication failure is suspected, stop the engine immediately and try to find the cause. If an engine is run without oil, even for a short period of time, severe damage will occur.

Running-in recommendations

Up to 500 miles (800 km)	4000 rpm max	Vary throttle position/speed
500 to 1000 miles (800 to 1600 km)	6000 rpm max	Vary throttle position/speed. Use full throttle for short bursts
Over 1000 miles (1600 km)	10 000 rpm max	Do not exceed tachometer red line

Chapter 3
Fuel and exhaust systems

Contents

Degrees of difficulty

Easy, suitable for novice with little experience		**Fairly easy,** suitable for beginner with some experience		**Fairly difficult,** suitable for competent DIY mechanic		**Difficult,** suitable for experienced DIY mechanic		**Very difficult,** suitable for expert DIY or professional	

Specifications

Fuel
Grade . . . . Unleaded, minimum 91 RON (Research Octane Number)
Fuel tank capacity (inc. reserve)
    550 models . . . . 15 litres
    750 models . . . . 17 litres
Fuel tank reserve capacity
    550 models . . . . 3.2 litres
    750 models . . . . 3.0 litres

Carburettors
550 models
    Type . . . . Keihin CVK30
    Bore . . . . 30 mm
750 models
    Type . . . . Keihin CVK32
    Bore . . . . 32 mm

Carburettor adjustments
Pilot screw setting (turns out)
    550 (UK) . . . . 1 3/4 to 2 1/4 turns out
    750 C1, C2, C3 and C4 models (UK) . . . . 1 5/8 turns out
    750 C5 and D1 models (UK) . . . . 1 1/2 turns out
    All US models . . . . Pre-set
Float height . . . . 15.0 to 17.0 mm
Fuel level . . . . 0.5 mm below to 1.5 mm above float bowl mating surface
Idle speed . . . . see Chapter 1
Synchronisation vacuum . . . . see Chapter 1

Jet sizes - 550 models

Pilot jet	35
Pilot air jet	160
Needle jet	6
Jet needle	N67J
Main jet	
Cylinders 1 and 4	108
Cylinders 2 and 3	110
Main air jet	100
Starter jet	52

Jet sizes - 750 models

Pilot jet	35
Pilot air jet	not available
Needle jet	not available
Jet needle	
C1, C2, C3 and C4 models	N52S
C5 and D1 models	
Cylinders 1 and 4	N1GK
Cylinders 2 and 3	N2NZ
Main jet	
C1, C2, C3 and C4 models	
Cylinders 1 and 4	88
Cylinders 2 and 3	92
C5 and D1 models	
Cylinders 1 and 4	82
Cylinders 2 and 3	85
Main air jet	100
Starter jet	not available

Torque setting

Cylinder head intake adapter bolts	12 Nm

1 General information and precautions

General information

The fuel system consists of the fuel tank, the fuel tap and filter, the carburettors, fuel hoses and control cables.

The fuel tap incorporates a filter which sits inside the tank.

The carburettors used on all models are CV types. For cold starting, a choke lever mounted on the left-handlebar and connected by a cable controls an enrichment circuit in the carburettor.

All except US ZR550 B1 and B2 models have a fuel gauge operated by a level sensor inside the tank.

UK ZR550 B4, B5 and B6 models, and UK ZR750 C3, C4, C5 and D1 models are fitted as standard with a carburettor heating system; this may have been subsequently fitted on earlier models.

Air is drawn into the carburettors via an air filter which is housed under the fuel tank.

The exhaust system on 550 models is a one piece four-into-one design, and on 750 models a three piece four-into-two.

Many of the fuel system service procedures are considered routine maintenance items and for that reason are included in Chapter 1.

Precautions

 Warning: Petrol (gasoline) is extremely flammable, so take extra precautions when you work on any part of the fuel system. Don't smoke or allow open flames or bare light bulbs near the work area, and don't work in a garage where a natural gas-type appliance is present. If you spill any fuel on your skin, rinse it off immediately with soap and water. When you perform any kind of work on the fuel system, wear safety glasses and have a fire extinguisher suitable for a class B type fire (flammable liquids) on hand.

Always perform service procedures in a well-ventilated area to prevent a build-up of fumes.

Never work in a building containing a gas appliance with a pilot light, or any other form of naked flame. Ensure there are no naked light bulbs or any sources of flame or sparks nearby.

Do not smoke (or allow anyone else to smoke) while in the vicinity of petrol (gasoline) or of components containing it. Remember the possible presence of vapour from these sources and move well clear before smoking.

Check all electrical equipment belonging to the house, garage or workshop where work is being undertaken (see the Safety first! section of this manual). Remember that certain electrical appliances such as drills, cutters etc. create sparks in the normal course of operation and must not be used near petrol

(gasoline) or any component containing it. Again, remember the possible presence of fumes before using electrical equipment.

Always mop up any spilt fuel and safely dispose of the rag used.

Any stored fuel that is drained off during servicing work must be kept in sealed containers that are suitable for holding petrol (gasoline), and clearly marked as such; the containers themselves should be kept in a safe place. Note that this last point applies equally to the fuel tank if it is removed from the machine; also remember to keep its cap closed at all times.

Read the Safety first! section of this manual carefully before starting work.

Owners of machines used in the US, particularly California, should note that their machines must comply at all times with Federal or State legislation governing the permissible levels of noise and of pollutants such as unburnt hydrocarbons, carbon monoxide etc. that can be emitted by those machines. All vehicles offered for sale must comply with legislation in force at the date of manufacture and must not subsequently be altered in any way which will affect their emission of noise or of pollutants.

In practice, this means that adjustments may not be made to any part of the fuel, ignition or exhaust systems by anyone who is not authorised or mechanically qualified to do so, or who does not have the tools, equipment

2.3 The tank is secured to the bracket by two bolts

2.4a Raise the tank and detach the fuel hose (A) and the vacuum hose (B) from the tap . . .

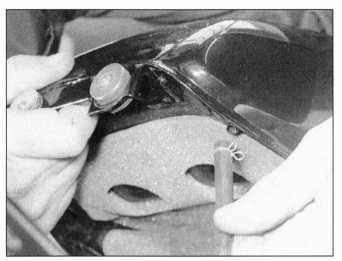

2.4b . . . and the water drain hose from its union

2.4c Detach the fuel level sensor overflow hose (arrowed) . . .

and data necessary to properly carry out the task. Also if any part of these systems is to be replaced it must be replaced with only genuine Kawasaki components or by components which are approved under the relevant legislation. The machine must never be used with any part of these systems removed, modified or damaged.

2 Fuel tank and fuel tap - removal and installation

 Warning: *Refer to the precautions given in Section 1 before starting work.*

Fuel tank

Removal

1 Make sure the fuel tap is turned to the ON position and the fuel cap is secure.

2 Remove the seat and the side panels (see Chapter 7), then disconnect the battery, negative (-) terminal first.
3 Unscrew the bolts securing the rear of the tank to the tank bracket on the frame **(see illustration)**.
4 Draw the tank back slightly and raise it up at the rear, then release the clamps securing the fuel hose and the vacuum hose to the tap and detach the hoses **(see illustration)**. Also detach the water drain hose from its union on the underside of the tank **(see illustration)**. On models with a fuel gauge, also detach the sensor overflow drain hose and disconnect the sensor wiring at the connector **(see illustrations)**. On California models, detach the EVAP system hoses. Plug the fuel return hose (red) to prevent fuel flowing into the canister. Label the hoses to prevent confusion on installation.
5 Remove the tank by carefully drawing it back and away from the bike. Take care not to

lose the mounting rubbers from the front of the tank and from between the sides of the tank and the frame, noting how they fit.
6 Inspect the tank mounting rubbers for signs of damage or deterioration and replace them if necessary. Also inspect the rubbers on the fuel tank mounting bracket. If necessary,

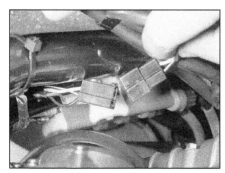

2.4d . . . and disconnect the sensor wiring

2.6 The tank bracket is secured by two bolts (arrowed)

2.7 Carefully manoeuvre the tank into position

unscrew the two bolts securing the bracket to the frame and remove the bracket **(see illustration)**. Replace the rubbers if necessary.

Installation

7 If removed, install the tank mounting bracket and tighten the bracket bolts securely **(see illustration 2.6)**. Check that the front and side tank rubbers are fitted, then carefully lower the fuel tank into position, making sure the rubbers remain in place **(see illustration)**.

8 With the tank raised at the rear, attach the water drain hose, the fuel hose and the vacuum hose to their unions **(see illustrations 2.4b and a)**. On models with a fuel gauge, attach the sensor overflow drain hose and connect the sensor wiring connector **(see illustrations 2.4c and d)**. On California models, attach the EVAP system hoses. Make sure all hoses are fitted fully onto their unions and secured by their clamps. Lower the tank and check that it is properly seated and is not pinching any control cables or wires. Check that there is no sign of fuel leakage.

9 Install the tank mounting bolts and tighten them securely **(see illustration)**.

10 Connect the battery, fitting the negative (-) terminal last. Start the engine and check that there is no sign of fuel leakage, then shut if off.

11 Install the seat and the side panels (see Chapter 7).

Fuel tap

Removal

12 The tap should not be removed unnecessarily due to the possibility of damaging the O-ring or the filter, and the tap should not be dismantled.

13 Remove the fuel tank as described above. Connect a drain hose to the fuel hose union and insert its end in a container suitable and large enough for storing the petrol (gasoline).

Turn the fuel tap to the PRI position, and allow the tank to fully drain.

14 Unscrew the two bolts securing the tap to the tank and withdraw the tap assembly **(see illustrations)**. Check the condition of the O-ring **(see illustration)**. If it is in good condition it can be re-used. If it is in any way deteriorated or damaged it must be replaced.

15 Clean the gauze filters using a high flash-point solvent to remove all traces of dirt and fuel sediment. Check the gauze for holes. If any are found, a new tap should be fitted as the filters are not available individually. Flush high flash-point solvent through the tap with

2.9 Tighten the tank mounting bolts securely

2.14b ... and remove the tap

the lever in all positions, then blow it through with compressed air.

16 If the fuel tap is leaking, tightening the assembly screws on the front and back of the tap may help **(see illustrations)**. If leakage persists, remove the screws and disassemble the tap, noting how the components fit. Clean all components using a high flash-point solvent and inspect them for wear or damage. Replace the O-rings and gasket, whatever their condition. If any of the other components are worn or damaged, or if the tap is still leaking with new O-rings and gasket, a new tap must be fitted.

2.14a Unscrew the bolts ...

2.14c Check the condition of the O-ring and replace it if necessary

2.16a Tighten the front . . .

2.16b . . . and rear assembly screws (arrowed)

Installation

17 Check the condition of the tap mounting bolt nylon washers and replace them if damaged or deteriorated. Do not use steel washers.
18 Install the fuel tap into the tank, using a new O-ring if necessary, and tighten its bolts securely **(see illustrations 2.14c, b and a)**.
19 Install the fuel tank (see above).

3 Fuel tank -
cleaning and repair

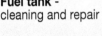

1 All repairs to the fuel tank should be carried out by a professional who has experience in this critical and potentially dangerous work. Even after cleaning and flushing of the fuel system, explosive fumes can remain and ignite during repair of the tank.
2 If the fuel tank is removed from the bike, it should not be placed in an area where sparks or open flames could ignite the fumes coming out of the tank. Be especially careful inside garages where a natural gas-type appliance is located, because the pilot light could cause an explosion.
3 Flush and clean the tank using a high flash-point solvent. Make sure none of the hose unions are blocked.

4 Idle fuel/air mixture
adjustment -
general information

1 Due to the increased emphasis on controlling motorcycle exhaust emissions, certain governmental regulations have been formulated which directly affect the carburation of this machine. In order to comply with the regulations, the carburettors on US models are sealed so they can't be tampered with. The pilot screws on other models are accessible, but the use of an exhaust gas analyser is the only accurate way to adjust the idle fuel/air mixture and be sure the machine doesn't exceed the emissions regulations.
2 The pilot screws are set to their correct position by the manufacturer and should not be adjusted unless it is necessary to do so for a carburettor overhaul. If the screws are adjusted they should be reset to the settings specified at the beginning of the Chapter.
3 If the engine runs extremely rough at idle or continually stalls, and if a carburettor overhaul does not cure the problem, take the motorcycle to a Kawasaki dealer equipped with an exhaust gas analyser. They will be able to properly adjust the idle fuel/air mixture to achieve a smooth idle and restore low speed performance.

5 Carburettor overhaul -
general information

1 Poor engine performance, hesitation, hard starting, stalling, flooding and backfiring are all signs that major carburettor maintenance may be required.
2 Keep in mind that many so-called carburettor problems are really not carburettor problems at all, but mechanical problems within the engine or ignition system malfunctions. Try to establish for certain that the carburettors are in need of maintenance before beginning a major overhaul.
3 Check the fuel filter, the fuel hoses, the intake manifold joint clamps, the air filter, the ignition system, the spark plugs and carburettor synchronisation before assuming that a carburettor overhaul is required.
4 Most carburettor problems are caused by dirt particles, varnish and other deposits which build up in and block the fuel and air passages. Also, in time, gaskets and O-rings shrink or deteriorate and cause fuel and air leaks which lead to poor performance.
5 When overhauling the carburettors, disassemble them completely and clean the parts thoroughly with a carburettor cleaning solvent and dry them with filtered, unlubricated compressed air. Blow through the fuel and air passages with compressed air to force out any dirt that may have been loosened but not removed by the solvent. Once the cleaning process is complete, reassemble the carburettor using new gaskets and O-rings.
6 Before disassembling the carburettors, make sure you have a carburettor rebuild kit (which will include all necessary O-rings and other parts), some carburettor cleaner, a supply of clean rags, some means of blowing out the carburettor passages and a clean place to work. It is recommended that only one carburettor be overhauled at a time to avoid mixing up parts.

6 Carburettors -
removal and installation

 Warning: Refer to the precautions given in Section 1 before starting work.

Removal

1 Remove the fuel tank and its bracket (see Section 2).
2 On 550 models, carefully pull each air filter housing end cover away from the housing **(see illustration)**.

6.2 Remove the air filter housing end covers

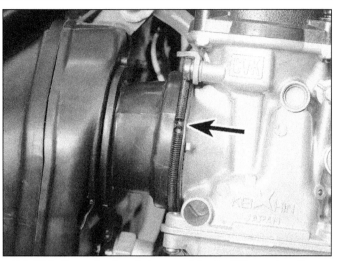

6.3 Remove the screw (arrowed) and lift out the rear section of the housing

6.4 Slide the spring bands (arrowed) back off the carburettors

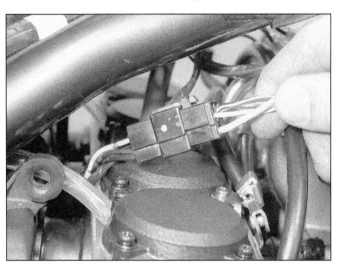

6.5 Disconnect the carburettor heater system wiring connector

6.6a Slacken each clamp screw (arrowed) to release the carburettors . . .

3 Remove the screw securing the rear section of the air filter housing to the front section, then lift the rear section out **(see illustration)**.
4 Slide back the spring bands securing the air filter housing rubbers to the carburettor intakes **(see illustration)**. Manoeuvre the air filter housing backwards so that the rubbers detach from the carburettor intakes and provide clearance for the carburettors to be removed.
5 On UK ZR550 B4, B5 and B6 models and UK ZR750 C3, C4, C5 and D1 models, trace the carburettor heater wiring and disconnect it at the connector **(see illustration)**.
6 Slacken the clamps securing the carburettors to the cylinder head intake adapters and ease the carburettors off the adapters, noting how they fit **(see illustration)**. Manoeuvre the carburettors out of the frame, noting the routing of the various hoses, and support them on the frame or engine for removal of the cables **(see illustration)**.

Note: *Keep the carburettors upright to prevent fuel spillage from the float chambers and the possibility of the piston diaphragms being damaged.*
7 Detach the throttle cables from carburettors (see Section 10).

6.6b . . . and ease them off the adapters and out of the frame

8 Detach the choke cable from the carburettors (see Section 11).
9 Place a suitable container below the float chambers then slacken the drain screws and drain all the fuel from the carburettors. Once all the fuel has been drained, tighten the drain screws securely.
10 If necessary, unscrew the screws securing the intake adapters to the cylinder head and remove the adapters and O-rings, noting how they fit. Discard the O-rings as new ones must be used. Note that the cylinder number for each adapter is marked at the top of the intake duct - they are not interchangeable and must be installed correctly.

Installation

11 Installation is the reverse of removal, noting the following.
   a) *Check for cracks or splits in the cylinder head intake adapters and air filter housing rubbers, and replace them if necessary.*

7.2a Remove the screws (arrowed) and lift off the top cover . . .

7.2b . . . then remove the spring

7.3 Carefully remove the diaphragm and piston assembly

7.4 Push the jet needle up from the bottom and remove it along with the spring seat if not already removed

b) *If removed, make sure the intake adapters are installed correctly using new O-rings (see Step 10). Apply a non-permanent thread locking compound to the bolt threads and tighten to the specified torque.*

c) *Make sure the air filter housing and the cylinder head intake adapters are fully engaged with the carburettors and their retaining springs or clamps are secure.*

d) *Make sure all hoses are correctly routed and secured, and not trapped or kinked.*

e) *On UK ZR550 B4, B5 and B6 models and UK ZR750 C3, C4, C5 and D1 models, do not forget to connect the carburettor heater wiring connectors.*

f) *Check the operation of the choke and throttle cables and adjust them as necessary (see Chapter 1).*

g) *Check idle speed and carburettor synchronisation and adjust as necessary (see Chapter 1).*

7 Carburettors - disassembly, cleaning and inspection

⚠ **Warning: Refer to the precautions given in Section 1 before starting work.**

Disassembly

1 Remove the carburettors from the machine as described in the previous Section. **Note:** *Do not separate the carburettors unless this is absolutely necessary; each carburettor can be dismantled sufficiently for all normal cleaning and adjustments while still in place on the mounting brackets. Dismantle the carburettors separately to avoid interchanging parts, or else store the parts from each in marked containers.*

2 Unscrew and remove the top cover retaining screws **(see illustration)**. Lift off the cover and remove the spring from inside the piston **(see illustration)**. The spring seat may come out with the spring - if not, it will come out with the jet needle (Step 4).

3 Carefully peel the diaphragm away from its sealing groove in the carburettor and withdraw the diaphragm and piston assembly, noting which way round it fits **(see illustration)**. *Caution: Do not use a sharp instrument to displace the diaphragm as it is easily damaged.*

4 Push the jet needle up from the bottom of the piston and withdraw it from the top **(see illustration)**. Take care not to lose the spring seat, if not already removed.

5 Where fitted, remove the screw securing the carburettor heater bracket and pull the heater out of the carburettor body **(see illustration)**.

6 Remove the screws securing the float chamber to the base of the carburettor and

7.5 Remove the heater bracket screw and pull out the heater

7.6a The float chamber is secured by four screws (arrowed)

7.6b Note the throttle stop screw bracket secured to the float chamber on the no. 1 carburettor on 550 models

7.7 Withdraw the float pivot pin and remove the float assembly

remove the float chamber, noting how it fits **(see illustration)**. Remove the rubber gasket and discard it as a new one must be used. On 550 models, note that two of the float chamber screws on the no. 1 carburettor also secure the throttle stop screw bracket **(see illustration)**.

7 Using a pair of thin-nose pliers, carefully withdraw the float pivot pin **(see illustration)**. If necessary, carefully displace the pin using a suitable small punch or a nail. Remove the float assembly, noting how it fits **(see illustration 9.6b)**. Unhook the needle valve from the tab on the float, noting how it fits **(see illustration 9.6a)**.

8 Unscrew and remove the main jet from the base of the needle jet holder **(see illustration)**.

9 Unscrew and remove the needle jet holder **(see illustration)**. With the holder removed the needle jet may come out if it is loose - if it does, note which way round it fits **(see illustration 9.4a)**.

10 Unscrew and remove the pilot jet **(see illustration)**.

7.8 Unscrew and remove the main jet (arrowed)

7.9 Unscrew and remove the needle jet holder (arrowed)

7.10 Unscrew and remove the pilot jet (arrowed)

7.11 Unscrew and remove the pilot screw (arrowed)

7.12 Detach the vacuum hose (A) and remove the caps (B).
Unhook the spring (C), then remove the three linkage
bar screws (D) and lift off the bar

11 On UK models, the pilot screw can be removed from the carburettor, but note that its setting will be disturbed (see *Haynes Hint*). Unscrew and remove the pilot screw along with its spring, washer and O-ring **(see illustration)**. Discard the O-ring as a new one must be used.

 To record the pilot screw's current setting, turn the screw in until it seats lightly, counting the number of turns necessary to achieve this, then fully unscrew it. On installation, the screw is simply backed out the number of turns you've recorded.

12 Detach the vacuum hose and remove the vacuum blanking caps, then unhook the choke linkage bar return spring from the vacuum take-off adapter **(see illustration)**. Remove the three screws securing the linkage bar to the carburettors, then remove the outer plastic washers **(see illustration 9.1d)**. Lift off the bar, noting how it fits, and remove the inner plastic washers **(see illustrations 9.1c, b and a)**.

13 Unscrew the choke plunger nut and withdraw the plunger and spring from the carburettor body, noting how they fit. Take care not to lose the spring when removing the nut.

Cleaning

Caution: Use only a petroleum based solvent for carburettor cleaning. Don't use caustic cleaners.

14 Submerge the metal components in the solvent for approximately thirty minutes (or longer, if the directions recommend it).

15 After the carburettor has soaked long enough for the cleaner to loosen and dissolve most of the varnish and other deposits, use a nylon-bristled brush to remove the stubborn deposits. Rinse it again, then dry it with compressed air.

16 Use a jet of compressed air to blow out all of the fuel and air passages in the main and upper body, not forgetting the air jets in the carburettor intake **(see illustration)**.

Caution: Never clean the jets or passages with a piece of wire or a drill bit, as they will be enlarged, causing the fuel and air metering rates to be upset.

Inspection

17 Check the operation of the choke plunger. If it doesn't move smoothly, inspect the needle on the end of the choke plunger, the spring and the plunger linkage bar. Replace any component that is worn, damaged or bent.

18 If removed from the carburettor, check the tapered portion of the pilot screw and the spring and O-ring for wear or damage. Replace them if necessary.

19 Check the carburettor body, float chamber and top cover for cracks, distorted sealing surfaces and other damage. If any defects are found, replace the faulty component, although replacement of the entire carburettor will probably be necessary

7.16 Do not forget the air passages
in the intakes (arrowed)

(check with a Kawasaki dealer on the availability of separate components).

20 Check the piston diaphragm for splits, holes and general deterioration. Holding it up to a light will help to reveal problems of this nature.

21 Insert the piston in the carburettor body and check that it moves up-and-down smoothly. Check the surface of the piston for wear. If it's worn excessively or doesn't move smoothly in the guide, replace the components as necessary.

22 Check the jet needle for straightness by rolling it on a flat surface such as a piece of glass. Replace it if it's bent or if the tip is worn.

23 Check the tip of the float needle valve and the valve seat. If either has grooves or scratches in it, or is in any way worn, they must be replaced as a set.

24 Operate the throttle shaft to make sure the throttle butterfly valve opens and closes smoothly. If it doesn't, cleaning the throttle linkage may help. Otherwise, replace the carburettor.

25 Check the floats for damage. This will usually be apparent by the presence of fuel inside one of the floats. If the floats are damaged, they must be replaced.

8 Carburettors - separation and joining

 Warning: Refer to the precautions given in Section 1 before proceeding

Separation

1 The carburettors do not need to be separated for normal overhaul. If you need to separate them (to replace a carburettor body, for example), refer to the following procedure.

8.4 Note the arrangement of the various linkage and synchronisation springs (arrowed) before separation

and joining pipes and vent hose T-pieces as they are separated. Discard their O-rings as new ones must be used.

Joining

7 Assembly is the reverse of the disassembly procedure, noting the following.

  a) Make sure the fuel hose T-pieces and joining pipes and the air vent hose T-pieces are correctly and securely installed with new O-rings.

  b) Install the synchronisation springs after the carburettors are joined together. Make sure they are correctly and squarely seated **(see illustration 8.4)**.

  c) Apply a suitable non-permanent thread-locking compound to the carburettor bracket screws and tighten them securely.

  d) Check the operation of both the choke and throttle linkages ensuring that both operate smoothly and return quickly under spring pressure before installing the carburettors on the machine.

  e) Install the carburettors (see Section 6) and check carburettor synchronisation and idle speed (see Chapter 1).

2 Remove the carburettors from the machine (see Section 6). Mark the body of each carburettor with its cylinder location to ensure that it is positioned correctly on reassembly.
3 Disconnect the fuel tap vacuum hose and remove the blanking caps or hoses (UK models), or EVAP and suction valve hoses or blanking caps as appropriate (US and California models) from the take-off stubs on the carburettors. Make a note of which hoses fit where. Unhook the choke linkage bar return spring **(see illustration 7.12 and 9.1e)**. Remove the three screws securing the linkage bar to the carburettors, then remove the outer plastic washers **(see illustration 9.1d)**. Lift off the bar, noting how it fits, and remove the inner plastic washers **(see illustrations 9.1c, b and a)**.
4 Make a note of how the throttle return

springs, linkage assembly and carburettor synchronisation springs are arranged to ensure that they are fitted correctly on reassembly **(see illustration)**. Also note the arrangement of the various hoses and their unions. On 550 models, depending on which carburettors are being separated, remove the two screws on the no. 1 carburettor float chamber securing the throttle stop screw bracket **(see illustration 7.6b)**.
5 Remove the screws securing the carburettors to the two mounting brackets and remove the brackets **(see illustrations)**. The carburettors are assembled using a thread-locking compound which may make the bracket screws difficult to remove.
6 Carefully separate the carburettors. Retrieve the synchronisation springs and note the fitting of the various fuel hose T-pieces

9 Carburettors -
reassembly, float height and fuel level check

> ⚠️ **Warning: Refer to the precautions given in Section 1 before proceeding.**

Reassembly and float height check

Note: When reassembling the carburettors, be sure to use all new O-rings and seals. Do not overtighten the carburettor jets and screws as they are easily damaged.
1 Install the choke plunger and spring into the carburettor body and tighten the nut to

8.5a Unscrew the upper mounting bracket screws (arrowed) . . .

8.5b . . . and the lower mounting bracket screws (arrowed) (600 type shown)

9.1a Fit the inner plastic washers . . .

9.1b . . . and the linkage bar . . .

9.1c . . . making sure it locates correctly onto each plunger

9.1d Install the screws with the outer plastic washers

9.1e Hook the spring around the take-off adapter . . .

9.1f . . . then fit the caps and the vacuum hose

secure it. Install the choke linkage bar inner plastic washers, then fit the bar onto the plungers, making sure the slots locate correctly behind the nipple on the end of each choke plunger (see illustrations). Install the outer plastic washers and secure the linkage bar in place with the screws (see illustration). Hook the return spring to the vacuum take-off adapter, then fit the cap (see illustration).

2 Install the pilot screw (if removed) along with its spring, washer and O-ring, turning it in until it seats lightly (see illustration 7.11). Now, turn the screw out the number of turns previously recorded, or as specified at the beginning of the Chapter.

3 Install the pilot jet (see illustration).

4 If removed, fit the needle jet into the carburettor with its tapered (smaller) end first (see illustration). Screw the needle jet holder into the carburettor (see illustration).

5 Install the main jet into the needle jet holder (see illustration).

6 Hook the float needle valve onto the tab on the float assembly, then position the float assembly in the carburettor and install the pin, making sure it is secure (see illustrations).

7 To check the float height, hold the carburettor so the float hangs down, then tilt it back until the needle valve is just seated, but not so far that the needle's spring-loaded tip is compressed. Measure the height of the bottom of the float above the gasket face (with the gasket removed) with an accurate ruler (see illustration). The correct setting should be as given in the Specifications at the beginning of the Chapter. If it is incorrect, adjust the float height by carefully bending the float tab a little at a time until the correct height is obtained. Repeat the procedure for both carburettors.

9.3 Install the pilot jet . . .

9.4a . . . the needle jet (if removed) . . .

9.4b . . . the needle jet holder . . .

9.5 . . . and the main jet

9.6a Fit the needle valve onto its tab on the float . . .

9.6b . . . making sure the needle valve fits into the seat (arrowed) . . .

9.6c . . . then install the float and fit the pivot pin

9.7 Float height measurement

1	Carburettor	3	Float
	body gasket face	4	Float height
2	Needle valve tip	5	Needle valve

9.8 Install the float chamber using a new gasket

9.11 Install the diaphragm assembly with the indent in the piston facing the air intake side

8 With the float height checked, fit a new gasket to the float chamber, making sure it is seated properly in its groove, then install the chamber on the carburettor and tighten its screws securely **(see illustration)**.

9 Where fitted, fit the carburettor heater into the carburettor body and mount the bracket on the float chamber **(see illustration 7.5)**.

10 Install the jet needle and spring seat into the diaphragm assembly **(see illustration 7.4)**.

11 Insert the diaphragm assembly into the piston guide with the indent on the piston facing the intake side of the carburettor **(see illustration)**. Lightly push the piston down, ensuring the needle is correctly aligned with the needle jet. Press the diaphragm outer edge into its groove, making sure it is correctly seated. Check the diaphragm is not creased, and that the piston moves smoothly up and down in the guide.

12 Install the spring into the diaphragm assembly, making sure it locates correctly onto the spring seat, then fit the top cover, making sure the top of the spring fits over the lug in the middle of the cover, and tighten its screws securely **(see illustration)**.

13 Checking the fuel level is advised before the carburettors are installed (see Step 15 on).

14 Install the carburettors (see Section 6).

Fuel level check

15 Lightly clamp the carburettor assembly in the jaws of a vice. Make sure the vice jaws are lined with wood. Set the fuel tank next to the vice, but at an elevation that is higher than the carburettors (resting on a box, for example). Connect a hose from the fuel tap to the fuel inlet fitting on the carburettor assembly - make sure the fuel tap is in the ON or RES position.

16 Attach Kawasaki service tool no. 57001-1017 to the drain fitting on the bottom of one of the carburettor float chambers (all four will be checked) **(see illustration)**. This is a clear plastic tube graduated in millimetres. An alternative is to use a length of clear plastic tubing and an accurate ruler. Hold the graduated tube (or the free end of the clear plastic tube) against the carburettor body, as

9.12 Install the top cover, making sure the spring is correctly located top and bottom

shown in the accompanying illustration. If the Kawasaki tool is being used, raise the zero mark to a point several millimetres above the bottom edge of the carburettor main body. If a piece of clear plastic tubing is being used, make a mark on the tubing at a point several millimetres above the bottom edge of the carburettor main body.

17 Unscrew the drain screw at the bottom of the float chamber a couple of turns, then turn

9.16 Fuel level measurement

1	Fuel level gauge	4	Bottom edge of
2	Gauge zero mark		carburettor body
3	Fuel level	5	Drain screw

the fuel tap to the PRI position - fuel will flow into the tube. Wait for the fuel level to stabilise, then slowly lower the tube until the zero mark is level with the bottom edge of the carburettor body. **Note:** *Don't lower the zero mark below the bottom edge of the carburettor then bring it back up - the reading won't be accurate.*

18 Measure the distance between the mark and top of the fuel level in the tube or gauge. This distance is the fuel level - write it down on a piece of paper, screw in the drain screw, turn the fuel tap to the On or Reserve position, then move on to the next carburettor and check it the same way.

19 Compare your fuel level readings to the value listed in this Chapter's Specifications. If the fuel level in any carburettor is not correct, remove the float chamber and bend the tang up or down (see Step 7), as necessary, then recheck the fuel level. **Note:** *Bending the tang up increases the float height and lowers the fuel level - bending it down decreases the float height and raises the fuel level.*

20 After the fuel level for each carburettor has been adjusted, install the carburettor assembly (see Section 6).

10 Throttle cables - removal and installation

> ⚠ **Warning: Refer to the precautions given in Section 1 before proceeding.**

Removal

1 Remove the carburettors (see Section 6, Steps 1 to 6).

2 Lift the lower end of the cable out of its mounting bracket and detach the inner cable from the throttle cam **(see illustration)**. Repeat for the other cable. Keep the carburettors upright to prevent fuel spillage.

3 Remove the handlebar switch/throttle pulley housing screws and separate the

halves **(see illustrations)**. Remove the cable elbows from the housing, noting how they fit and hook the cable ends out of the pulley **(see illustration)**. Mark each cable to ensure it is connected correctly on installation.

4 Remove the cables from the machine noting the correct routing of each cable.

Installation

5 Install the cables making sure they are correctly routed. The cables must not interfere with any other component and should not be kinked or bent sharply.

6 Lubricate the end of each inner cable with multi-purpose grease and attach them to the pulley **(see illustration 10.3c)**. Install the cables into the throttle pulley housing, making sure the accelerator cable is at the front and the decelerator is at the back. Assemble the housing, aligning its locating pin with the hole in the front of the handlebar **(see illustration 10.3b)**. Install the retaining screws, and tighten them securely.

10.2 Lift the outer cable out of its bracket and detach the inner cable nipple from the cam

10.3a The switch housing is secured by two screws (arrowed)

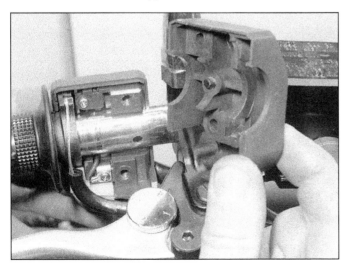

10.3b Separate switch halves and displace the cable elbows . . .

10.3c . . . then detach the cable ends from the pulley

10.8 Cables should be correctly located in the throttle cam and bracket

11.2a Pull the outer cable out of its bracket . . .

11.2b . . . and detach the inner cable nipple

11.3a Separate the switch halves . . .

11.3b . . . and remove the cable and lever

7 Lubricate the lower end of each inner cable with multi-purpose grease and attach them to the carburettor throttle cam **(see illustration 10.2)**.

8 Make sure the cables are correctly connected and locate the outer cables in the mounting brackets **(see illustration)**.

9 Install the carburettors (see Section 6).

10 Adjust the cables as described in Chapter 1. Turn the handlebars back and forth to make sure the cables don't cause the steering to bind.

11 Install the fuel tank (see Section 2).

12 Start the engine and check that the idle speed does not rise as the handlebars are turned. If it does, correct the problem before riding the motorcycle.

11 Choke cable - removal and installation

Removal

1 Remove the fuel tank (see Section 2).

2 Free the choke outer cable from its bracket on the carburettor and detach the inner cable from the choke linkage bar **(see illustrations)**.

3 Unscrew the two left-hand side handlebar switch/choke lever housing screws and separate the two halves, noting how the lever fits into the housing **(see illustration)**. Withdraw the cable and lever from the housing and detach the cable nipple from the choke lever **(see illustration)**.

4 Remove the cable from the machine noting its correct routing.

Installation

5 Install the cable making sure it is correctly routed. The cable must not interfere with any other component and should not be kinked or bent sharply.

6 Lubricate the upper cable nipple with multi-purpose grease. Attach the nipple to the choke lever **(see illustration 11.3b)**, then install the lever and cable in the switch/choke lever housing, making sure the cable elbow is correctly fitted **(see illustration)**. Fit the two halves of the housing onto the handlebar, making sure the lever fits correctly, and the pin in the front half locates in the hole in the front of the handlebar **(see illustration 11.3a)**. Install the screws and tighten them securely.

7 Lubricate the lower cable nipple with multi-purpose grease and attach it to the choke linkage bar on the carburettor **(see illustration 11.2b)**. Fit the outer cable into its bracket **(see illustration 11.2a)**.

8 Check the operation and adjustment of the choke cable (see Chapter 1).

9 Install the fuel tank (see Section 2).

12 Air filter housing - removal and installation

Removal

1 Remove the fuel tank (see Section 2).

2 Remove the carburettors (see Section 6).

3 On UK models with a carburettor heater system, disconnect the atmospheric

11.6 Check that the cable elbow is correctly fitted in the switch housing

12.3 Disconnect the atmospheric temperature sensor wiring connector

12.4 Detach the air filter drain hose (A) from the housing and the breather hose (B) from the breather cover

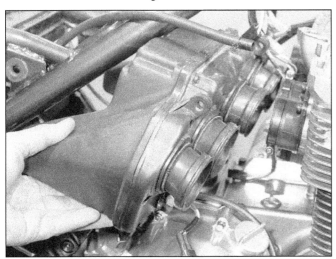

12.5 Manoeuvre the housing out of the frame

13.1 Remove the silencer mounting bolt and nut

temperature sensor wiring connector **(see illustration)**.

4 Release the clamp securing the air filter drain hose to the bottom of the front of the air filter housing, then detach the hose from its union **(see illustration)**. Also release the clamp securing the engine breather hose to the breather on the top of the crankcase and detach the hose.

5 Manoeuvre the air filter housing forwards and out of the frame **(see illustration)**.

Installation

6 Installation is the reverse of removal.

13 Exhaust system -
removal and installation

Warning: If the engine has been running the exhaust system will be very hot. Let the system cool before carrying out any work.

550 models

Removal

1 Unscrew and remove the silencer mounting nut and bolt **(see illustration)**.

2 Support the system, unscrew the downpipe clamp nuts from the cylinder head, then remove the system **(see illustrations)**. Note

13.2a Unscrew the downpipe clamp nuts (arrowed) . . .

how the half-ring retainers locate against the head of each pipe and are taped in place **(see illustration)**. Remove the gasket from each port in the cylinder head and discard them; new ones must be used **(see illustration 13.4)**.

3 Check the rubber dampers in the silencer mounting points; if damaged or deteriorated replace them with new ones.

13.2b . . . and remove the system

13.2c Note how the half-ring retainers fit

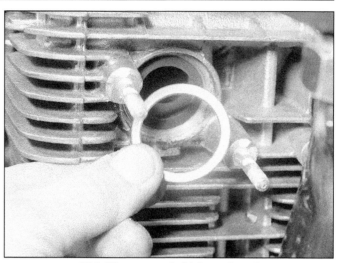

13.4 Fit a new gasket into each port

13.5 Butt the clamps against the half-ring retainers

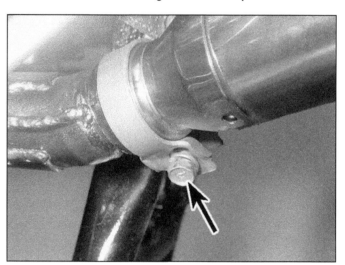

13.7 Slacken the clamp bolt (arrowed) . . .

Installation

4 Fit a new gasket into each of the cylinder head ports (see illustration). Apply a smear of grease to the gaskets to keep them in place whilst fitting the downpipe if necessary.

5 Manoeuvre the system into position so that the head of each downpipe is located in its port in the cylinder head (see illustration 13.2b). Fit the clamps onto the studs, making sure the half-ring retainers are installed and the clamps butt up against them, then install the clamp nuts finger-tight to hold the system in place (see illustration). Supporting the system, align the silencer mounting bracket at the rear and install the bolt with its washer but do not yet tighten the nut (see illustration 13.1). Now tighten the flange nuts securely, then tighten the silencer nut.

6 Run the engine until it is warmed up and check the system for leaks. Allow the engine to cool then retighten all the clamp nuts and the silencer nut.

750 models

Silencers

7 Slacken the clamp on the joint between the silencer and the downpipe (see illustration).

8 Unscrew and remove the silencer mounting nut and bolt, then release the silencer from the exhaust downpipe assembly using a twisting motion (see illustration).

13.8 . . . and remove mounting nut and bolt

9 Inspect the bushes for signs of damage and replace them if necessary. Remove the sealing ring from either the end of the silencer or inside the downpipe assembly and check it for damage. Replace it if necessary.

10 Install the silencer into the downpipe assembly, using a new sealing ring if required, and making sure it is pushed fully home (see illustration). Align the silencer mounting

13.10 Use a new sealing ring if required

bracket at the rear then install the bolt from the inside. Tighten the clamp bolt and the silencer nut securely **(see illustrations 13.7 and 13.8)**.

11 Run the engine until it is warmed up and check the system for leaks. Allow the engine to cool then retighten the clamp bolts and silencer nuts.

Downpipe assembly

12 Remove the silencers (see above).

13 Supporting the assembly, unscrew the downpipe clamp nuts from the cylinder head, then remove the assembly from the machine **(see illustration 13.2a)**. Note how the half-ring retainers locate against the head of each pipe and are taped in place **(see illustration 13.2c)**.

14 Remove the gasket from each port in the cylinder head and check them for damage. Replace them if necessary.

15 Fit the gasket into each of the cylinder head ports **(see illustration 13.4)**. Apply a thin smear of grease to the gaskets to keep them in place whilst fitting the downpipe if necessary.

16 Manoeuvre the system into position so that the head of each downpipe is located in its port in the cylinder head **(see illustration 13.2b)**. Fit the clamps onto the studs with the notch in the clamp facing down, making sure the half-ring retainers are installed and the clamps butt up against them, then install the clamp nuts and tighten them securely **(see illustration 13.5)**.

17 Install the silencers (see above).

18 Run the engine until it is warmed up and check the system for leaks. Allow the engine to cool then retighten all the clamp bolts and silencer nuts.

Complete system

19 Unscrew and remove the silencer mounting nuts and bolts **(see illustration 13.8)**.

20 Supporting the system, unscrew the downpipe clamp nuts from the cylinder head then remove the system from the machine **(see illustration 13.2a)**. Note how the half-ring retainers locate against the head of each pipe and are taped in place **(see illustration 13.2c)**.

21 Remove the gasket from each port in the cylinder head and check them for damage. Replace them if necessary.

22 Fit a new gasket into each of the cylinder head ports **(see illustration 13.4)**. Apply a smear of grease to the gaskets to keep them in place whilst fitting the downpipe if necessary.

23 Manoeuvre the system into position so that the head of each downpipe is located in its port in the cylinder head **(see illustration 13.2b)**. Fit the clamps onto the studs with the notch in the clamp facing down, making sure the half-ring retainers are installed and the clamps butt up against them, then install the clamp nuts finger-tight to hold the system in place **(see illustration 13.5)**. Supporting the system, align the silencer mounting brackets at the rear and install the bolts with their

washers but do not yet tighten the nut **(see illustration 13.8)**. Now tighten the flange nuts securely, then tighten the silencer nut.

24 Run the engine until it is warmed up and check the system for leaks. Allow the engine to cool then retighten all the clamp nuts and the silencer nuts.

14 Evaporative emission control (EVAP) system (California models) - general information

1 The EVAP system prevents the escape of fuel vapours into the atmosphere and functions as follows **(see illustration)**.

2 Whilst the engine is stopped, vapour emitted by the evaporation of fuel in the tank passes through a vent hose to the top of the separator where some of it condenses and passes through the separator into the pump unit, but the majority passes into the canister. Vapour emitted from the carburettor float chambers passes through a vent hose directly to the canister. From there it can only escape to the atmosphere by passing through the activated charcoal which traps the vapour completely.

3 When the engine is started all vapour stored in the canister is purged via the purge hose into the air filter housing where it passes into the engine for burning in the normal way. At the same time a simple pump, operated by

the vacuum from no. 3 carburettor intake stub, returns all liquid fuel in the separator to the fuel tank via the return hose.

4 The fuel tank filler cap has a one way valve which allows air into the tank as the volume of fuel decreases, but prevents any fuel vapour from escaping.

5 The system is not adjustable and can be tested only by a Kawasaki dealer. Checks which can be performed by the owner are given in Chapter 1.

15 Air suction valves (US models) - general information

1 The US models incorporate an air injection system designed to enhance the burning of hydrocarbons in the exhaust gases, thus reducing toxic emissions. The system employs a modified cylinder head and valve cover, in which air is drawn through a reed valve arrangement into the exhaust ports.

2 The system is automatic in operation and except for the reed valve check described in Chapter 1, should not require attention. The most likely fault is that unfiltered air may be drawn into the system through a damaged air filter element or leaking hose, making tickover unstable and reducing engine power. Backfiring or other unusual noises may be apparent.

14.1 EVAP system - California models only (750 model shown, 550 similar)

1	Fuel return hose (red)	5	Vacuum hose (white)
2	Vent hose (blue)	6	Vent hose (yellow)
3	Vent hose (blue)	7	Vapour separator
4	Purge hose (green)	8	Canister

Chapter 4
Ignition system

Contents

Degrees of difficulty

| Easy, suitable for novice with little experience | | Fairly easy, suitable for beginner with some experience | | Fairly difficult, suitable for competent DIY mechanic | | Difficult, suitable for experienced DIY mechanic | | Very difficult, suitable for expert DIY or professional | |

Specifications

General information

Cylinder identification	1 - 2 - 3 - 4, from left to right
Firing order	1 - 2 - 4 - 3
Spark plugs	see Chapter 1

Ignition timing

550 models
UK models	12.5° BTDC @ 1200 rpm to 35° BTDC @ 7000 rpm
US models	13° BTDC @ 1200 rpm to 36° BTDC @ 7000 rpm

750 models
UK models	12.5° BTDC @ 1100 rpm to 35° BTDC @ 7000 rpm
US models	12.5° BTDC @ 1300 rpm to 35° BTDC @ 7000 rpm

Pulse generator coil

Resistance
550 models	380 to 560 ohms
750 models	350 to 540 ohms

Air gap
550 models	0.4 to 0.6 mm
750 models	not available

Ignition HT coils

Primary winding resistance
550 models	2.30 to 3.50 ohms
750 models	2.61 to 3.19 ohms

Secondary winding resistance (with plug cap removed)
550 models	12.0 to 18.0 K ohms
750 models	13.5 to 16.5 K ohms

Arcing distance
550 models	min 6 mm
750 models	min 7 mm

Torque settings

Pulse generator coil mounting plate screws	2.9 Nm
Timing rotor bolt	25 Nm
Pulse generator assembly cover bolts	10 Nm

1 General information

All models are fitted with a fully transistorised electronic ignition system, which due to its lack of mechanical parts is totally maintenance-free. The system comprises a rotor, pulse generator coil, ignition control unit and ignition HT coils (refer to the wiring diagrams at the end of Chapter 8 for details).

The triggers on the rotor, which is fitted to the right-hand end of the crankshaft, magnetically operate the pulse generator coil as the crankshaft rotates. The pulse generator coil sends a signal to the ignition control unit which then supplies the ignition HT coils with the power necessary to produce a spark at the plugs.

The system uses two HT coils mounted on the frame tubes under the fuel tank. The left-hand coil supplies nos. 1 and 4 cylinder spark plugs and the right-hand coil supplies nos. 2 and 3 cylinder plugs.

The system incorporates an electronic advance system controlled by signals generated by the rotor and the pulse generator coil.

The system incorporates a safety interlock circuit which will cut the ignition if the sidestand is lowered whilst the engine is running and in gear, or if a gear is selected whilst the engine is running and the sidestand is down.

Because of their nature, the individual ignition system components can be checked but not repaired. If ignition system troubles occur, and the faulty component can be isolated, the only cure for the problem is to replace the part with a new one. Keep in mind that most electrical parts, once purchased, cannot be returned. To avoid unnecessary expense, make very sure the faulty component has been positively identified before buying a replacement part.

2 Ignition system - check

Caution: The energy levels in electronic systems can be very high. On no account should the ignition be switched on whilst the plugs or plug caps are being held. Shocks from the HT circuit can be most unpleasant. Secondly, it is vital that the engine is not turned over or run with any of the plug caps removed, and that the plugs are soundly earthed (grounded) when the system is checked for sparking. The ignition system components can be seriously damaged if the HT circuit becomes isolated.

1 As no means of adjustment is available, any failure of the system can be traced to failure of a system component or a simple wiring fault.

Of the two possibilities, the latter is by far the most likely. In the event of failure, check the system in a logical fashion, as described below.

2 Disconnect the HT leads from the spark plugs. Connect each lead to a spare spark plug and lay each plug on the engine with the threads contacting the engine. If necessary, hold each spark plug with an insulated tool.

⚠️ *Warning: Do not remove any of the spark plugs from the engine to perform this check - atomised fuel being pumped out of an open spark plug hole could ignite, causing severe injury!*

3 Having observed the above precautions, check that the kill switch is in the RUN position, turn the ignition switch ON and turn the engine over on the starter motor. If the system is in good condition a regular, fat blue spark should be evident at each plug electrode. If the spark appears thin or yellowish, or is non-existent, further investigation will be necessary. Before proceeding further, turn the ignition off and remove the key as a safety measure.

4 The ignition system must be able to produce a spark which is capable of jumping a particular size gap. Kawasaki specify that a healthy system should produce a spark capable of jumping 6 mm (550 models) or 7 mm (750 models). A simple testing tool can be made to test the minimum gap across which the spark will jump (see Tool Tip).

5 Connect one of the spark plug HT leads from one coil to the protruding electrode on the test tool, and clip the tool to a good earth (ground) on the engine or frame. Check that the kill switch is in the RUN position, turn the ignition switch ON and turn the engine over on the starter motor. If the system is in good condition a regular, fat blue spark should be seen to jump the gap between the nail ends. Repeat the test for the other coil. If the test results are good the entire ignition system can

A simple spark gap testing tool can be made from a block of wood, a large alligator clip and two nails, one of which is fashioned so that a spark plug cap or bare HT lead end can be connected to its end. Make sure the gap between the two nail ends is the same as specified.

be considered good. If the spark appears thin or yellowish, or is non-existent, further investigation will be necessary.

6 Ignition faults can be divided into two categories, namely those where the ignition system has failed completely, and those which are due to a partial failure. The likely faults are listed below, starting with the most probable source of failure. Work through the list systematically, referring to the subsequent sections for full details of the necessary checks and tests. *Note: Before checking the following items ensure that the battery is fully charged and that all fuses are in good condition.*

a) *Loose, corroded or damaged wiring connections, broken or shorted wiring between any of the component parts of the ignition system (see Chapter 8).*
b) *Faulty HT lead or spark plug cap, faulty spark plug, dirty, worn or corroded plug electrodes, or incorrect gap between electrodes.*
c) *Faulty ignition switch or engine kill switch (see Chapter 8).*
d) *Faulty neutral or sidestand switch (see Chapter 8).*
e) *Faulty pulse generator coil or damaged rotor.*
f) *Faulty ignition HT coil(s).*
g) *Faulty ignition control unit.*

7 If the above checks don't reveal the cause of the problem, have the ignition system tested by a Kawasaki dealer. Kawasaki produce special testers which can perform a complete diagnostic analysis of the ignition system.

3 Ignition HT coils - check, removal and installation

Check

1 In order to determine conclusively that the ignition coils are defective, they should be tested by a Kawasaki dealer equipped with the special diagnostic tester.

2 However, the coils can be checked visually (for cracks and other damage) and the primary and secondary coil resistance can be measured with a multimeter. If the coils are undamaged, and if the resistance readings are as specified at the beginning of the Chapter, they are probably capable of proper operation.

3 Remove the seat (see Chapter 7) and disconnect the battery negative (-) lead. To gain access to the coils, remove the fuel tank (see Chapter 3). The coils are mounted on the frame tubes (see illustration 3.10).

4 Disconnect the primary circuit electrical connectors from the coil being tested and the HT leads from the spark plugs (see illustration). Mark the locations of all wires and leads before disconnecting them.

5 Set the meter to the ohms x 1 scale and measure the resistance between the primary circuit terminals (see illustration). This will

3.4 Disconnect the primary circuit connectors

3.5 Ignition coil primary circuit test connections

give a resistance reading of the primary windings and should be consistent with the value given in the Specifications at the beginning of the Chapter.

6 To check the condition of the secondary windings, set the meter to the K ohm scale. Unscrew the spark plug caps from the ends of the HT leads **(see illustration)**. Connect one meter probe to one HT lead and the other probe to the other lead **(see illustration)**. If the reading obtained is not within the range shown in the Specifications, it is likely that the coil is defective.

7 Should either of the above checks not produce the expected result, have your findings confirmed on the diagnostic tester (see Step 1). If the coil is confirmed to be faulty, it must be replaced; the coil is a sealed unit and cannot therefore be repaired.

> **HAYNES HiNT** *An inaccurate secondary winding reading could be due to an HT lead breakdown or poor connection between the HT lead and coil. Unscrew the lead connection at the coil and make the secondary winding test across the HT lead terminals - the reading should be slightly less than the specified figure.*

Removal

8 Remove the seat (see Chapter 7) and disconnect the battery negative (-) lead, then remove the fuel tank (see Chapter 3).

9 The coils are mounted on the frame tubes **(see illustration 3.10)**. Disconnect the primary circuit electrical connectors from the coils **(see illustration 3.4)** and disconnect the HT leads from the spark plugs. Mark the locations of all wires and leads before disconnecting them.

10 Unscrew the two nuts securing each coil, noting the earth (ground) terminal secured by the front nut for the left-hand coil, and remove the coils **(see illustration)**. Note the routing of the HT leads.

Installation

11 Installation is the reverse of removal. Install the coils with the HT leads facing forward. Make sure the wiring connectors and HT leads are securely connected.

4 Pulse generator coil assembly - check, removal and installation

Check

1 Remove the seat (see Chapter 7) and disconnect the battery negative (-) lead. On

750 models, also remove the right-hand side panel (see Chapter 7).

2 Trace the ignition pulse generator wiring back and disconnect it at the ignition control unit (550 models - remove the unit for access to the connectors - see Section 5) or at the connector behind the right-hand side panel (750 models) **(see illustration)**. Using a multimeter set to the ohms x 100 scale, measure the resistance between the black and yellow terminals on the coil side of the connector.

3 Compare the reading obtained with that given in the Specifications at the beginning of this Chapter. The pulse generator coil must be replaced if the reading obtained differs greatly

3.6a Unscrew the cap from the lead

3.6b Ignition coil secondary circuit test

3.10 Each coil is secured by two nuts (arrowed). Note the earth terminal secured by one of the nuts (A)

4.2 On 750 models the wiring connector is behind the right-hand side panel

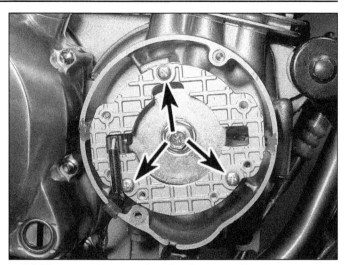

4.7 The pulse generator assembly cover is secured by two bolts (arrowed)

4.9 The assembly mounting plate is secured by three screws (arrowed)

from that given, particularly if the meter indicates a short circuit (no measurable resistance) or an open circuit (infinite, or very high resistance).

4 If the pulse generator coil is thought to be faulty, first check that this is not due to a damaged or broken wire from the coil to the connector; pinched or broken wires can usually be repaired. Note that the pulse generator coil is not available individually but comes as an assembly along with the mounting plate and wiring.

Removal

5 Remove the seat (see Chapter 7) and disconnect the battery negative (-) lead. On 750 models, also remove the right-hand side panel (see Chapter 7).

6 Trace the ignition pulse generator wiring back and disconnect it at the ignition control unit (550 models - remove the unit for access to the connectors - see Section 5) or at the connector behind the right-hand side panel

(750 models) **(see illustration 4.2)**. Free the wiring from any clips or ties and feed it through to the coil.

7 Unscrew the bolts securing the pulse generator assembly cover to the right-hand side of the crankcase **(see illustration)**. Remove the cover. Discard the gasket as a new one must be used.

8 On 750 models, remove the screw securing the wire to the terminal on the oil pressure switch and detach the wire.

9 Remove the three screws securing the pulse generator coil assembly mounting plate to the crankcase **(see illustration)**. Remove the rubber wiring grommet from its recess in the crankcase cover, then remove the coil assembly, noting how it fits.

10 Examine the rotor for signs of damage and replace it if necessary. To remove the rotor, use a 17 mm spanner on the rotor hex to counter-hold it, and unscrew the bolt in the centre of the rotor which secures it to the end of the crankcase **(see illustration)**. Remove

the rotor, noting how the pin in the end of the crankshaft locates in the slot in the rotor.

Installation

11 If removed, install the timing rotor onto the end of the crankshaft, making sure the slot in the rotor locates correctly over the pin in the end of the crankshaft. Using a 17 mm spanner to counter-hold the rotor, install the rotor bolt and tighten it to the torque setting specified at the beginning of the Chapter **(see illustration)**.

12 Apply a smear of sealant to the rubber wiring seal and fit it into its recess in the crankcase, then mount the pulse generator coil assembly and tighten the mounting screws to the specified torque setting **(see illustrations)**.

13 On 750 models, connect the oil pressure switch wire to its terminal on the switch and tighten the screw securely.

14 Apply a smear of sealant to the crankcase joints on the pulse generator assembly cover

4.10 Counter-hold the outer hex on the rotor and unscrew the centre bolt

4.11 Tighten the rotor bolt to the specified torque setting

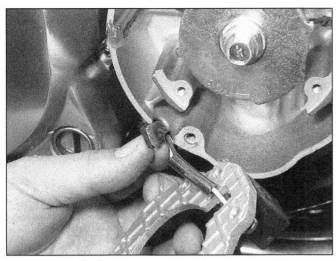

4.12a Fit the grommet into its cut-out . . .

4.12b . . . and secure the assembly with its screws

4.14a Apply a smear of sealant to the areas shown (arrowed)

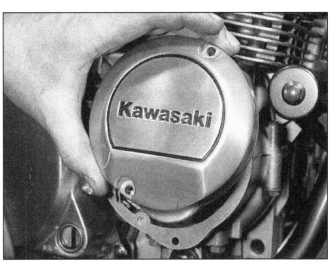

4.14b Install the cover using a new gasket

mating surface **(see illustration)**. Install the pulse generator assembly cover using a new gasket and tighten its bolts to the specified torque setting **(see illustration)**.

15 Route the wiring up to the connector and reconnect it **(see illustration 4.2)**. Secure the wiring in its clips or ties.

16 Reconnect the battery negative (-) lead and install the seat and side panel (750 models) (see Chapter 7).

5 Ignition control unit - check, removal and installation

Check

1 If the tests shown in the preceding Sections have failed to isolate the cause of an ignition fault, it is likely that the ignition control unit itself is faulty. No test details are available with which the unit can be tested on home workshop equipment. Take the machine to a Kawasaki dealer for testing.

Removal

2 Remove the seat (see Chapter 7) and the battery (see Chapter 8).

3 The ignition control unit is mounted behind the battery **(see illustration)**.

4 Remove the ignition control unit from its rubber sleeve, or lift the sleeve and unit together off the sleeve's mounting lugs.

5.3 The control unit is mounted behind the battery

Disconnect the two wiring connectors from the ignition control unit remove the unit **(see illustration)**.

Installation

5 Installation is the reverse of removal. Make sure the wiring connectors are correctly and securely connected.

5.4 Disconnect the two wiring connectors (arrowed) and remove the unit

6 Ignition timing - general information and check

General information

1 Since no provision exists for adjusting the ignition timing and since no component is subject to mechanical wear, there is no need for regular checks; only if investigating a fault such as a loss of power or a misfire, should the ignition timing be checked.

2 The ignition timing is checked dynamically (engine running) using a stroboscopic lamp. The inexpensive neon lamps should be adequate in theory, but in practice may produce a pulse of such low intensity that the timing mark remains indistinct. If possible, one of the more precise xenon tube lamps should be used, powered by an external source of the appropriate voltage. **Note:** *Do not use the machine's own battery as an incorrect reading may result from stray impulses within the machine's electrical system.*

Check

3 Warm the engine up to normal operating temperature then stop it.

4 Unscrew the bolts securing the pulse generator assembly cover to the right-hand side crankcase cover **(see illustration 4.7)**. Discard the gasket as a new one must be used.

5 The timing mark on the rotor is the line next to the letter F which indicates the firing point at idle speed for cylinder nos. 1 and 4 **(see illustration)**. The static timing mark with which this should align is the protrusion on the case.

 The rotor timing mark can be highlighted with white paint to make it more visible under the stroboscope light.

6 Connect the timing light to the no. 1 cylinder HT lead as described in the manufacturer's instructions.

7 Start the engine and aim the light at the static timing mark.

8 With the machine idling at the specified speed, the timing mark F should align with the static timing mark.

9 Slowly increase the engine speed whilst observing the timing mark. The timing mark should move anti-clockwise, increasing in relation to the engine speed until it reaches full advance (no identification mark).

6.5 Ignition rotor timing mark (A) and static mark (B)

10 As already stated, there is no means of adjustment of the ignition timing on these machines. If the ignition timing is incorrect, or suspected of being incorrect, one of the ignition system components is at fault, and the system must be tested as described in the preceding Sections of this Chapter.

11 When the check is complete, apply a smear of sealant to the crankcase joints on the pulse generator assembly cover mating surface **(see illustration 4.14a)**. Install the pulse generator assembly cover using a new gasket and tighten its bolts to the specified torque setting **(see illustration 4.14b)**.

Chapter 5
Frame, suspension and final drive

Contents

Degrees of difficulty

Easy, suitable for novice with little experience	**Fairly easy,** suitable for beginner with some experience	**Fairly difficult,** suitable for competent DIY mechanic	**Difficult,** suitable for experienced DIY mechanic	**Very difficult,** suitable for expert DIY or professional

Specifications

Front forks

Fork oil type	SAE 10W20 fork oil
Fork oil capacity	
550 models	
Oil change	350 cc
Following fork overhaul (completely dry)	408 to 416 cc
750 models	
C1 and C2 models	
Oil change	400 cc
Following fork overhaul (completely dry)	466 to 474 cc
C3, C4 and C5 models	
Oil change	417 cc
Following fork overhaul (completely dry)	490 cc
D1 model	
Oil change	400 cc
Following fork overhaul (completely dry)	463 to 471 cc
Fork oil level*	
550 models	96 to 100 mm*
750 models	
C1 and C2 models	108 to 112 mm*
C3, C4 and C5 models	88 to 92 mm*
D1 model	111 to 115 mm*

*Oil level is measured from the top of the tube with the fork spring removed and the tube fully compressed in the slider.

Front forks (continued)

Fork spring free length (min)
    550 models
        Standard . . . . 395.5 mm
        Service limit (min) . . . . 387 mm
    750 models
        C1 and C2 models
            Standard . . . . 402.5 mm
            Service limit . . . . 394 mm
        C3, C4 and C5 models
            Standard . . . . 396.5 mm
            Service limit . . . . 389 mm
        D1 model
            Standard . . . . 391.5 mm
            Service limit . . . . 384 mm

Final drive

Chain freeplay and wear limit . . . . see Chapter 1
Chain size, no. of links
    550 UK models . . . . 520 O-ring type, 106 links
    550 US and Canada models . . . . 520 O-ring type, 108 links
    750 models . . . . 525 O-ring type, 106 links
Front sprocket diameter - 750 models
    Standard . . . . 65.58 to 65.78 mm
    Service limit . . . . 64.9 mm
Rear sprocket diameter - 750 models
    Standard . . . . 187.02 to 187.52 mm
    Service limit . . . . 186.7 mm
Rear sprocket warpage - all models
    Standard . . . . less than 0.4 mm
    Service limit . . . . 0.5 mm

Torque settings

Brake pedal pivot bolt
    550 models . . . . 10 Nm
    750 models . . . . 9 Nm
Gearchange lever pivot bolt . . . . 23 Nm
Handlebar clamp bolts . . . . 23 Nm
Fork clamp bolts
    550 models . . . . 21 Nm
    750 models . . . . 20 Nm
Fork top bolt . . . . 23 Nm
Damper rod Allen bolt
    550 models . . . . 29 Nm
    750 models . . . . 61 Nm
Steering stem bolt . . . . 39 Nm
Rear shock absorber lower mounting bolt and nut . . . . 39 Nm
Swingarm pivot bolt nut
    550 models . . . . 93 Nm
    750 models . . . . 109 Nm
Brake torque arm nuts
    550 models . . . . 32 Nm
    750 models . . . . 34 Nm
Front sprocket bolts - 550 models . . . . 10 Nm
Front sprocket nut - 750 models . . . . 125 Nm
Rear sprocket nuts . . . . 74 Nm

1 General information

All models use a full cradle twin spar steel frame.

Front suspension is by a pair of conventional oil-damped telescopic forks which are non-adjustable.

At the rear, a box-section aluminium swingarm acts on twin shock absorbers with remote reservoirs. The shock absorbers are adjustable for pre-load and both compression and rebound damping.

The drive to the rear wheel is by chain. A rubber damper system (often called a 'cush drive') is fitted between the rear wheel coupling and the wheel.

2 Frame - inspection and repair

1 The frame should not require attention unless accident damage has occurred. In most cases, frame replacement is the only satisfactory remedy for such damage. A few frame specialists have the jigs and other equipment necessary for straightening the frame to the required standard of accuracy, but even then there is no simple way of assessing to what extent the frame may have been over stressed.

2 After the machine has accumulated a lot of miles, the frame should be examined closely for signs of cracking or splitting at the welded joints. Loose engine mount bolts can cause ovaling or fracturing of the mounting tabs. Minor damage can often be repaired by welding, depending on the extent and nature of the damage.

3 Remember that a frame which is out of alignment will cause handling problems. If misalignment is suspected as the result of an accident, it will be necessary to strip the machine completely so the frame can be thoroughly checked.

3 Footrests, brake pedal and gearchange lever - removal and installation

Footrests

Removal

1 Remove the E-clip from the bottom of the footrest pivot pin, then withdraw the pivot pin and remove the footrest **(see illustrations)**. On the front footrests, note the fitting of the return spring. On the rear footrests, note the fitting of the two interlocking plates and the spring **(see illustration)**.

Installation

2 Installation is the reverse of removal.

Brake pedal

Removal

3 Unhook the brake pedal return spring and the brake light switch spring from the brake pedal **(see illustration)**.

4 Remove the split pin from the clevis pin securing the brake pedal to the master cylinder pushrod **(see illustration)**. Remove the clevis pin and separate the pedal from the pushrod.

5 Unscrew the pivot bolt securing the brake pedal to the footrest bracket and remove the pedal **(see illustration)**. On 550 models, note how the brake light switch lever fits.

Installation

6 Installation is the reverse of removal. Check the operation of the rear brake light switch and the height of the brake pedal (see Chapter 1).

Gearchange lever

Removal

7 Unscrew the gearchange lever linkage arm pinch bolt and remove the arm from the shaft, noting any alignment marks **(see illustration)**. If no marks are visible, make your own before removing the arm so that it can be correctly aligned with the shaft on installation.

3.1a Remove the E-clip (A) and withdraw the pivot pin (B). Note how the spring ends (C) locate

3.1b Rear footrest assembly

3.3 Unhook the brake pedal return spring (A) and the brake light switch spring (B) - 550 model shown

3.4 Remove the split pin and withdraw the clevis pin (arrowed)

3.5 Remove the pivot bolt, detach the pushrod and slide the pedal off

3.7 Remove the pinch bolt (arrowed) and slide the arm off the shaft

3.8 Remove the pivot bolt (arrowed) and remove the lever and linkage

3.10a Align the previously made marks and install the pinch bolt

3.10b Slacken the locknuts (A) and turn the rod (B) to adjust lever height

8 Unscrew the pivot bolt securing the gearchange lever to the footrest bracket and remove the lever and linkage assembly **(see illustration)**.

9 If required, slacken the linkage rod locknuts and thread the lever off the rod. Note the how far the rod is threaded into the lever as this determines the height of the lever relative to the footrest.

Installation

10 Installation is the reverse of removal. Align the marks made on the gearchange lever linkage arm and shaft when installing the arm onto the shaft, and tighten the pinch bolt securely **(see illustration)**. Adjust the gear lever height as required by slackening the rod locknuts and screwing the rod in or out of the lever and linkage arm **(see illustration)**. Tighten the locknuts securely on completion.

4 Stands - removal and installation

Centre stand (750 models only)

1 The centre stand is secured in the frame by two pivot bolts. Support the bike on its

sidestand and unhook the centre stand spring, then unscrew the nuts, withdraw the bolts and remove the stand **(see illustration)**.

2 Inspect the stand and pivot bolts for signs of wear and replace them if necessary. Apply a smear of grease to the bolts and fit the stand back on the bike, tightening the bolts securely. Reconnect the return spring.

3 Make sure the spring is in good condition and capable of holding the stand up when not in use. A broken or weak spring is an obvious safety hazard.

Sidestand

4 The sidestand is attached to a bracket on the frame. A spring anchored to the bracket ensures that the stand is held in the retracted or extended position.

5 Support the bike on its centre stand if fitted, or support it using an auxiliary stand.

6 Unhook the stand spring and unscrew the nut from the pivot bolt **(see illustration)**. Withdraw the pivot bolt to free the stand from its bracket.

7 On installation apply grease to the pivot bolt shank and tighten the bolt securely. Reconnect the sidestand spring and check that the return spring holds the stand securely up when not in use - an accident is almost

certain to occur if the stand extends while the machine is in motion.

8 For check and replacement of the side stand switch see Chapter 8.

5 Handlebars and levers - removal and installation

Handlebars

Removal

Note: *If required, the handlebars can be displaced for access to the fork top bolts or the steering stem nut without removing the switch housings and the front brake master cylinder assembly and the clutch lever assembly.*

1 Remove the screws securing both the left- and right-hand switch housings to the handlebar, noting how the top mating surfaces of the switch housings align with the top mating surfaces of the brake master cylinder and clutch lever assembly clamps, then separate the switch halves. Detach the throttle cables from the throttle pulley and note how the choke lever fits (see Chapter 3 if required), then remove the housings from the

4.1 Unhook the stand spring, then unscrew the nuts and withdraw the bolts

4.6 Unhook the spring, then unscrew the nut (A) and withdraw the bolt (B)

5.3 Disconnect the clutch switch wiring connector (A) and unscrew the clamp bolts (B)

5.4a The handlebar clamp is secured by four bolts (arrowed)

5.4b The pin in the base of the lower clamp locates in the hole in the yoke, and the flat end of the clamp faces forward

5.6a Align the punch mark (arrowed) with the clamp mating surfaces

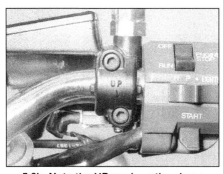

5.6b Note the UP mark on the clamp which points upwards

5.7 Lever main pivot bolt (A), span adjuster pivot bolt (B)

handlebar, noting how they fit (see Chapter 8 if required). There is no need to disconnect the switch housing wiring at its connector blocks.

2 Disconnect the brake light switch wiring connectors from the underside of the master cylinder. Unscrew the two clamp bolts securing the front brake master cylinder assembly to the handlebar and lift the assembly away (see Chapter 6 if required). There is no need to disconnect the hose from the master cylinder. Support the assembly in an upright position and so that no strain is placed on the hose.

3 Disconnect the clutch switch connector from the underside of the lever bracket **(see illustration)**. Unscrew the two clamp bolts securing the clutch lever assembly to the handlebar and lift the assembly away.

4 Unscrew the bolts securing the handlebar clamp and remove the clamp top and the handlebars **(see illustration)**. Note the punch mark on the back of the handlebar which aligns with the rear mating surfaces of the clamp. Remove the clamp bottoms, noting which way round they fit and how they locate **(see illustration)**.

5 If necessary, unscrew the handlebar end-weight retaining screws, then remove the weights from the end of the handlebars. If replacing the grips, it may be necessary to slit them using a sharp knife as they are adhered to the throttle twist (right-hand) and the handlebar (left-hand).

Installation

6 Installation is the reverse of removal, noting the following.

a) *Align the handlebars so that the punch mark on the rear of the handlebar aligns with the rear mating surfaces of the clamp (see illustration). Tighten the front handlebar clamp bolts to the torque setting specified at the beginning of the Chapter, then tighten the rear bolts to the specified torque. There should be a gap between the rear clamp mating surfaces.*

b) *Make sure the front brake master cylinder clamp is installed with the UP mark facing up, and so that the top clamp mating surfaces align with the top mating surfaces of the switch housings (see illustration). Tighten the upper clamp bolt first, then the lower bolt, to the torque setting specified at the beginning of the Chapter. There should be a gap between the lower clamp mating surfaces.*

c) *If removed, apply a suitable non-permanent thread-locking compound to the handlebar end-weight retaining screws. If new grips are being fitted, secure them using a suitable adhesive.*

Levers

Removal

7 To remove the complete front brake lever or clutch lever assembly from the master

cylinder, unscrew the main pivot bolt locknut, then withdraw the bolt and remove the lever assembly **(see illustration)**. If working on the clutch lever, slip the cable end out of the lever as it is withdrawn.

8 To remove the lever blade from the pivot assembly, unscrew the span adjuster pivot bolt locknut, then withdraw the bolt and remove the lever blade **(see illustration 5.7)**.

Installation

9 Installation is the reverse of removal. Apply grease to the pivot bolt shafts and to the contact areas between the lever and its bracket. Grease the clutch cable end and fit it into the lever before installing the lever in its bracket. If necessary, back off clutch cable adjustment to allow the cable to be reconnected (see Chapter 1).

6 Forks - removal and installation

Removal

1 Remove the front wheel (see Chapter 6).

2 Remove the front mudguard as described in Chapter 7.

3 On 750 models, unscrew the bolts securing the brake hose clamps and speedometer cable guide to the forks **(see illustration)**.

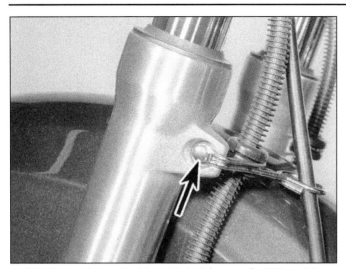

6.3 Hose guide and cable guide bolt (arrowed) - 750 models

6.4 Top yoke fork clamp bolt (arrowed). Note the alignment of the fork with the top yoke as an aid to installation

4 Slacken, but do not remove, the fork clamp bolts in the top yoke **(see illustration)**. If the forks are to be disassembled, it is advisable to slacken the fork top bolts at this stage. Displace the handlebars if required for improved access to the top bolts (Section 5).

 Slackening the fork clamp bolts in the top yoke before slackening the fork top bolts releases pressure on the top bolt. This makes it much easier to remove and helps to preserve the threads.

5 Note the position of the top of the fork tubes relative to the top yoke so that they are installed in the same position **(see illustration 6.4)**. Slacken but do not remove the fork clamp bolts in the bottom yoke, and remove the forks by twisting them and pulling them downwards **(see illustration)**.

 If the fork legs are seized in the yokes, spray the area with penetrating oil and allow time for it to soak in before trying again.

Installation

6 Remove all traces of corrosion from the fork tubes and the yokes and slide the forks up through the bottom yoke and the top yoke so that they align with the top yoke as noted on removal **(see illustration 6.4)**.

7 Tighten the fork clamp bolts in the bottom yoke to the torque setting specified at the beginning of the Chapter **(see illustration 6.5)**. If the fork legs have been dismantled or if the fork oil has been changed, the fork top bolts should now be tightened to the specified torque setting. Now tighten the fork clamp bolts in the top yoke to the specified torque setting. Install the handlebars if displaced.

8 If the forks were disassembled, install the axle nut into the bottom of the left-hand fork **(see illustration)**, but do not tighten the axle nut clamp bolt until the wheel has been installed and the axle has been tightened to the correct torque. Install the front mudguard (see Chapter 7) and the front wheel (see Chapter 6). On 750 models, install the brake hose clamps onto the forks and tighten their bolts securely.

9 Check the operation of the front forks and brakes before taking the machine out on the road.

7 Forks - disassembly, inspection and reassembly

Disassembly

1 Always dismantle the fork legs separately to avoid interchanging parts and thus causing an

6.5 Bottom yoke fork clamp bolts (arrowed)

6.8 Fit the axle nut into the bottom of the left-hand fork

7.1 Front fork components

1	Top bolt	6	Damper rod	11	Bottom bush	16	Top bush
2	O-ring	7	Piston ring	12	Dust seal	17	Fork slider
3	Spacer	8	Rebound spring	13	Retaining clip	18	Sealing washer
4	Spring seat	9	Damper rod seat	14	Oil seal	19	Damper rod bolt
5	Spring	10	Fork tube	15	Washer	20	Oil drain screw

accelerated rate of wear. Store all components in separate, clearly-marked containers **(see illustration)**.

2 Before dismantling the fork, it is advised that the damper rod bolt be slackened at this stage. To access the left-hand fork damper

bolt, slacken the axle nut clamp bolt in the base of the fork slider and remove the axle nut **(see illustration 6.8)**. Compress the fork tube in the slider so that the spring exerts maximum pressure on the damper rod head, then have an assistant slacken the damper rod bolt in the base of the fork slider.

3 If the fork top bolt was not slackened with the fork in situ, carefully clamp the fork tube in a vice, taking care not to overtighten or score its surface, and slacken the top bolt.

4 Unscrew the fork top bolt from the top of the fork tube.

⚠ **Warning: The fork spring is pressing on the fork top bolt with considerable pressure. Unscrew the bolt very carefully, keeping a downward pressure on it and release it slowly as it is likely to spring clear. It is advisable to wear some form of eye and face protection when carrying out this operation.**

5 Slide the fork tube down into the slider and withdraw the spacer, spring seat and the spring from the tube, noting which way up they fit **(see illustrations 7.26c, b and a)**.

6 Invert the fork leg over a suitable container and pump the fork vigorously to expel as much fork oil as possible.

7 Remove the slackened damper rod bolt and its copper sealing washer from the bottom of the slider. Discard the sealing washer as a new one must be used on reassembly. If the damper rod bolt was not slackened before dismantling the fork, it may be necessary to re-install the spring, spring seat, spacer and top bolt to prevent the damper rod from turning. Alternatively, a length of wooden doweling pressed hard into the damper rod head quite often suffices. **Note**: *A damper rod holding tool can be purchased from Kawasaki dealers (see Step 20)*.

8 Invert the fork and withdraw the damper rod from inside the fork tube. Remove the rebound spring from the damper rod **(see illustration)**.

9 Carefully prise out the dust seal from the top of the slider to gain access to the oil seal retaining clip **(see illustration)**. Discard the dust seal as a new one must be used.

10 Carefully remove the retaining clip, taking care not to scratch the surface of the tube **(see illustration)**.

7.8 Withdraw the damper rod and rebound spring from the tube

7.9 Prise out the dust seal using a flat-bladed screwdriver

7.10 Prise out the retaining clip using a flat-bladed screwdriver

7.11 To separate the fork tube and slider, pull apart firmly several times - the slide hammer effect will pull the tubes apart

7.12 The oil seal (1), washer (2), top bush (3) and bottom bush (4) will come out with the fork tube

7.15 Check the fork tube for runout using V-blocks and a dial gauge

7.17 Ease the bottom bush ends apart using a flat-bladed screwdriver

7.18 Replace the damper rod piston ring if it is worn or damaged

7.19a Slide the rebound spring onto the damper rod

11 To separate the tube from the slider it will be necessary to displace the top bush and oil seal. The bottom bush should not pass through the top bush, and this can be used to good effect. Push the tube gently inwards until it stops against the damper rod seat. Take care not to do this forcibly or the seat may be damaged. Then pull the tube sharply outwards until the bottom bush strikes the top bush. Repeat this operation until the top bush and seal are tapped out of the slider **(see illustration)**.

12 With the tube removed, slide off the oil seal and its washer, followed by the top bush, noting which way up they fit **(see illustration)**. Discard the oil seal as a new one must be used.

Caution: Do not remove the bottom bush from the tube unless it is to be replaced.

13 Tip the damper rod seat out of the slider, noting which way up it fits.

Inspection

14 Clean all parts in solvent and blow them dry with compressed air, if available. Check the fork tube for score marks, scratches, flaking of the chrome finish and excessive or abnormal wear. Look for dents in the tube and replace the tube in both forks if any are found. Check the fork seal seat for nicks, gouges and scratches. If damage is evident, leaks will occur.

15 Check the fork tube for runout using V-blocks and a dial gauge **(see illustration)**. No

7.19b Fit the seat to the bottom of the rod

service limit is given by Kawasaki, but if runout is excessive seek the advice of a Kawasaki dealer or suspension specialist.

⚠️ *Warning: If it is bent, it should not be straightened; replace it with a new one.*

16 Check the spring for cracks and other damage. Measure the spring free length using a steel rule and compare the measurement to the specifications at the beginning of the Chapter. If it is defective or sagged below the service limit, replace the springs in both forks with new ones. Never replace only one spring. Also check the rebound spring.

17 Examine the working surfaces of the two bushes; if worn or scuffed they must be replaced. To remove the bottom bush from the fork tube, prise it apart at the slit using a screwdriver and slide it off **(see illustration)**. Make sure the new one seats properly.

7.20a Slide the tube into the slider

18 Check the damper rod and its piston ring for damage and wear, and replace them if necessary **(see illustration)**.

Reassembly

19 If removed, install the piston ring into the groove in the damper rod head, then slide the rebound spring onto the rod **(see illustration)**. Insert the damper rod into the fork tube and slide it into place so that it projects fully from the bottom of the tube, then install the seat on the bottom of the damper rod **(see illustration)**.

20 Oil the fork tube and bottom bush with the specified fork oil and insert the assembly into the slider **(see illustration)**. Fit a new copper sealing washer to the damper rod bolt and apply a few drops of a suitable non-permanent thread-locking compound, then

7.20b Apply a thread-locking compound to the damper rod bolt and use a new sealing washer

7.21a Install the top bush . . .

7.21b . . . followed by the washer

7.22 Make sure the oil seal is the correct way up

7.23 Install the retaining clip . . .

7.24 . . . followed by the dust seal

7.25a Pour the oil into the top of the tube

7.25b Measure the oil level with the fork held vertical

install the bolt into the bottom of the slider **(see illustration)**. Tighten the bolt to the specified torque setting. If the damper rod rotates inside the tube, temporarily install the fork spring and top bolt (see Steps 26 and 27) and compress the fork to hold the damper rod. Alternatively, a length of wood doweling pressed hard into the damper rod head quite often suffices. **Note:** *If neither method succeeds in holding the damper rod, obtain the Kawasaki service tool adapter (pt. no. 57001-1057) and handle (pt. no. 57001-183).*
21 Push the fork tube fully into the slider, then oil the top bush and slide it down over the tube **(see illustration)**. Press the bush squarely into its recess in the slider as far as possible, then install the oil seal washer **(see illustration)**. Either use the service tool (pt. no. 57001-1219) or a suitable piece of tubing

to tap the bush fully into place; the tubing must be slightly larger in diameter than the fork tube and slightly smaller in diameter than the bush recess in the slider. Take care not to scratch the fork tube during this operation; it is best to make sure that the fork tube is pushed fully into the slider so that any accidental scratching is confined to the area above the oil seal.
22 When the bush is seated fully and squarely in its recess in the slider, (remove the washer to check, wipe the recess clean, then reinstall the washer), install the new oil seal. Smear the seal's lips with fork oil and slide it over the tube so that its markings face upwards and drive the seal into place as described in Step 21 until the retaining clip groove is visible above the seal.**(see illustration)**.

23 Once the seal is correctly seated, fit the retaining clip, making sure it is correctly located in its groove **(see illustration)**.
24 Lubricate the lips of the new dust seal then slide it down the fork tube and press it into position **(see illustration)**.
25 Slowly pour in the specified quantity of the specified grade of fork oil and pump the fork to distribute it evenly **(see illustration)**; the oil level should also be measured and adjustment made by adding or subtracting oil. Fully compress the fork tube into the slider and measure the fork oil level from the top of the tube **(see illustration)**. Add or subtract fork oil until the oil is at the level specified in the Specifications Section of this Chapter.
26 Clamp the slider in a vice via the brake caliper mounting lugs, taking care not to overtighten and damage them. Pull the fork

7.26a Install the spring . . .

7.26b . . . followed by the spring seat . . .

7.26c . . . and the spacer

tube out of the slider as far as possible then install the spring with its closer-wound coils at the top, followed by the spring seat and the spacer **(see illustrations)**.

27 Fit a new O-ring onto the fork top bolt if the old one is in any way damaged or deteriorated. Thread the bolt into the top of the fork tube.

 Warning: It will be necessary to compress the spring by pressing it down using the top bolt in order to engage the threads of the top bolt with the fork tube. This is a potentially dangerous operation and should be performed with care, using an assistant if necessary. Wipe off any excess oil before starting to prevent the possibility of slipping.

28 Keep the fork tube fully extended whilst pressing on the spring. Screw the top bolt carefully into the fork tube making sure it is not cross-threaded. **Note:** *The top bolt can be tightened to the specified torque setting at this stage if the tube is held between the padded jaws of a vice, but do not risk distorting the tube by doing so. A better method is to tighten the top bolt when the fork has been installed in the bike and is securely held in the bottom yoke.*

29 Install the forks (see Section 6).

 TOOL TiP *Use a ratchet-type tool when installing the fork top bolt. This makes it unnecessary to remove the tool from the bolt whilst threading it in, thus making it easier to maintain a downward pressure on the spring.*

8 Steering stem - removal and installation

Removal

1 Remove the fuel tank (see Chapter 3)

2 Unscrew the bolts securing the brake hose union to the bottom yoke **(see illustration)**; there is no need to disconnect the hydraulic hoses.

3 Remove the headlight and its bracket (see Chapter 8).

4 Remove the handlebars (see Section 5).

5 Remove the instrument cluster (see Chapter 8).

6 Remove the front forks (see Section 6).

7 Remove the steering stem bolt and washer **(see illustration)**. Lift the top yoke off the steering stem.

8.2 The brake hose union is secured by two bolts

8.8b Displace the O-ring and discard it

8 Supporting the bottom yoke, unscrew the locknut and adjuster ring using a suitable C-spanner, then remove the bearing cover from the steering stem (the adjuster ring has a collar which fits into the bearing cover, so they will probably come away together) **(see illustration)**. Push up on the bottom yoke to displace the O-ring from between the stem and the bearing, then remove the O-ring and discard it as a new one must be used **(see illustration)**.

9 Gently lower the bottom yoke and steering stem out of the frame **(see illustration 8.12a)**.

10 Remove the upper bearing from the top of the steering head **(see illustration)**. Remove all traces of old grease from the bearings and races and check them for wear or damage as described in Section 9. **Note:** *Do not attempt to remove the races from the frame or the lower bearing from the steering stem unless they are to be replaced.*

8.7 Unscrew the steering stem bolt and remove the washer

8.10 Remove the upper bearing

8.8a Remove the locknut (A), adjuster ring (B) and the bearing cover (C)

8.11 Apply grease liberally to the bearings

8.12a Lift the steering stem up into the head

8.12b Fit the bearing cover . . .

8.12c . . . the adjuster ring . . .

8.12d . . . and the locknut

8.13 Fit the top yoke onto the steering stem

8.14 Tighten the steering stem bolt to the specified torque setting

Installation

11 Smear a liberal quantity of grease on the bearing races in the frame. Work grease well into both the upper and lower bearings **(see illustration)**.

12 Carefully lift the steering stem/bottom yoke up through the frame **(see illustration)**. Install the upper bearing in the top of the steering head, then fit the new O-ring **(see illustration 8.8b)**. Install the bearing cover and thread the adjuster ring, with its stepped side facing down, and locknut on the steering stem **(see illustrations)**. Tighten the adjuster ring as required until all freeplay in the forks is removed, yet the steering is able to move freely from side to side. The object is to set the adjuster ring so that the bearings are under a very light loading, just enough to remove any freeplay. Tighten the locknut against the adjuster ring finger-tight only. Turn the steering stem through its full lock five or six times, then recheck for freeplay. Check

and adjust the bearings as described in Chapter 1 after installation is complete.
Caution: Take great care not to apply excessive pressure because this will cause premature failure of the bearings.

13 Install the top yoke onto the steering stem **(see illustration)**. Install the steering stem bolt and its washer and tighten it finger-tight only at this stage **(see illustration 8.7)**. Temporarily install one of the forks to align the top and bottom yokes, and secure it by tightening the bottom yoke clamp bolts only.

14 Tighten the steering stem bolt to the specified torque setting **(see illustration)**.

15 Install the front forks (see Section 6).

16 Install the remaining components and assemblies in a reverse of the removal procedure, referring to the relevant Sections and Chapters.

17 Carry out a check of the steering head bearing freeplay as described in Chapter 1, and if necessary re-adjust.

9 Steering head bearings - inspection and replacement

Inspection

1 Remove the steering stem (see Section 8).

2 Remove all traces of old grease from the bearings and races and check them for wear or damage.

3 The races should be polished and free from indentations. Inspect the bearing rollers for signs of wear, damage or discoloration, and examine the bearing roller retainer cage for signs of cracks or splits. Spin the bearings by hand. They should spin freely and smoothly. If there are any signs of wear on any of the above components both upper and lower bearing assemblies must be replaced as a set. Only remove the races if they need to be replaced - do not re-use them once they have been removed.

Replacement

4 The races are an interference fit in the steering head and can be tapped from position with a suitable drift **(see illustration)**. Tap firmly and evenly around each race to ensure that it is driven out squarely. It may prove advantageous to curve the end of the drift slightly to improve access.

5 Alternatively, remove the races using a slide-hammer type bearing extractor; these can often be hired from tool shops.

9.4 Drive the bearing races out with a brass drift as shown

9.6 Drawbolt arrangement for fitting steering stem bearing races

1 Long bolt or threaded bar
2 Thick washer
3 Guide for lower race

6 Press the new races into the head using a drawbolt arrangement **(see illustration)**, or by using a large diameter tubular drift. Ensure that the drawbolt washer or drift (as applicable) bears only on the outer edge of the race and does not contact the working surface. Alternatively, have the races installed by a Kawasaki dealer equipped with bearing race installing tools.

 HAYNES HiNT *Installation of new head bearing races is made much easier if the races are left overnight in the freezer. This causes them to contract slightly making them a looser fit.*

7 To remove the lower bearing from the steering stem, clamp the stem in a vice and use two flat-bladed screwdrivers placed on opposite sides of the race to work it free, using blocks of wood to protect the yoke **(see illustration)**. If the bearing is firmly in place it will be necessary to use a bearing puller, or in extreme circumstances to split the bearing's inner section **(see illustration)**.

9.8 Drive the new bearing on using a suitable bearing driver or a length of pipe that bears only against the inner race and not against the rollers or cage

9.7a Remove the lower bearing as shown . . .

8 Fit the new lower bearing onto the steering stem. A length of tubing with an internal diameter slightly larger than the steering stem will be needed to tap the new bearing into position **(see illustration)**. Ensure that the drift bears only on the inner edge of the bearing and does not contact the rollers, or better still fit a washer between the bearing and the tubing to protect the bearing.
9 Install the steering stem (see Section 8).

10 Rear shock absorbers - removal, inspection and installation

Removal

1 Place the machine on its centre stand or support it upright using an auxiliary stand. If both shock absorbers are to be removed at the same time, position a support under the rear wheel so that it does not drop when the

10.3a Right-hand shock absorber lower mounting

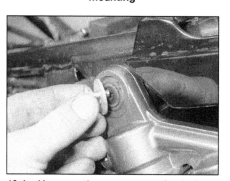

10.4a Unscrew the upper mounting bolt . . .

9.7b . . . or remove it using a bearing puller

second shock is removed, but also making sure that the weight of the machine is off the rear suspension so that the shocks are not compressed. Alternatively, remove only one shock at a time.
2 On 550 models, remove the exhaust system, and on 750 models, remove the silencer on the side which the shock is being removed from (remove both silencers if both shocks are being removed) (see Chapter 3).
3 Remove the shock absorber lower mounting bolt. The right-hand shock absorber bolt threads into a nut, whilst the left-hand shock bolt threads into the chain guard bracket **(see illustrations)**. When removing the right-hand shock, counter-hold the bolt and unscrew the nut. Swing the shock rearwards until the bottom clears the mounting bracket on the swingarm.
4 Supporting the shock absorber, unscrew and remove the upper mounting bolt and washer, then remove the shock **(see illustrations)**.

10.3b Left-hand shock absorber lower mounting

10.4b . . . and remove the shock absorber

10.6 Inspect the damper rod (arrowed) for pitting and leakage . . .

10.7 . . . and the bushes for wear and deterioration

10.10 Make sure the chain guard bracket is correctly aligned

11.1a Spring pre-load adjuster - 550 models

11.1b Spring pre-load adjuster - 750 models

Inspection

5 Inspect the shock absorber for obvious physical damage and the coil spring for looseness, cracks or signs of fatigue.
6 Inspect the damper rod for signs of bending, pitting and oil leakage **(see illustration)**.
7 Inspect the pivot hardware at the top and bottom of the shock for wear or damage **(see illustration)**.
8 If the shock absorber is in any way damaged or worn it must be replaced. Individual replacement components are not available.
9 Kawasaki specify releasing the nitrogen gas pressure before discarding the shock absorber. To do this, remove the cap from the base of the reservoir, then, using a screwdriver or other suitable tool, depress the valve until all the nitrogen is released. If in doubt, take the shocks to a dealer for disposal.

 Warning: Do not point the valve towards you when releasing the nitrogen - it is under considerable pressure, and an oil mist will also be released.

Installation

10 Installation is the reverse of removal, noting the following.
a) *Apply multi-purpose lithium grease to the pivot points.*
b) *Install the upper mounting bolt first, but do not tighten it until the lower mounting bolt is installed.*
c) *If the chain guard has been removed, make sure the chain guard bracket is correctly positioned* **(see illustration)**.
d) *Tighten the lower mounting bolt (left-hand side) and nut (right-hand side) to the torque setting specified at the beginning of the Chapter.*
e) *Adjust the suspension as required (see Section 11).*
f) *Check the operation of the suspension before taking the machine on the road.*

11 Rear shock absorbers - adjustment

Caution: Always ensure that both shock absorber settings are the same. Uneven settings will upset the handling of the machine and could cause it to become unstable.

Spring pre-load

1 Pre-load adjustment is made using a suitable slim bar (one of the Phillips screwdrivers provided in the toolkit will do) inserted into one of the holes in the pre-load adjuster ring on the bottom (550 models) or top (750 models) of the shock **(see illustrations)**. There are five positions, each indicated by a step in the adjuster ring. Align the step required with the adjustment stopper.
2 On 550 models, to increase the pre-load, turn the spring seat anti-clockwise (towards the front of the bike). To decrease the pre-load, turn the spring seat clockwise. Position 2 is the standard setting for a rider of average build, riding solo.
3 On 750 models, to increase the pre-load, turn the spring seat clockwise (towards the front of the bike). To decrease the pre-load, turn the spring seat anti-clockwise. Position 2 is the standard setting for a rider of average build, riding solo.

11.4 Compression damping adjuster

11.6 Rebound damping adjuster

Compression damping

4 Compression damping adjustment is made by turning the adjuster on the top of the shock absorber **(see illustration)**. There are four positions. Position 1 is the softest setting, position 4 the hardest.
5 Turn the adjuster until the number required aligns with the index mark on the shock. Do not set the adjuster in between any of the positions. Position 1 is the standard setting.

Rebound damping

6 Rebound damping adjustment is made by turning the adjuster on the bottom of the shock absorber **(see illustration)**. There are four positions, denoted by Roman numerals. Position I is the softest setting, position IIII the hardest.
7 Turn the adjuster until the number required is visible and clicks into position. Do not set the adjuster in between any of the positions. Position I is the standard setting.

12 Swingarm -
   removal and installation

Removal

Note: *Before removing the swingarm, it is advisable to perform the swingarm checks described in Chapter 1, Section 26.*
1 On 550 models, remove the exhaust system, and on 750 models, remove the silencers (see Chapter 3).
2 Remove the rear wheel (see Chapter 6).
3 Remove the nut and the bolt securing the brake torque arm to the swingarm and lift the torque arm off the swingarm **(see illustration)**. Support the brake caliper, caliper bracket and torque arm assembly so that it does not impede removal of the swingarm, making sure that no strain is placed on the hose.

4 Unhook the lower end of the brake light switch spring and position the spring out of the way.
5 Supporting the swingarm, remove the rear shock absorber lower mounting bolts (see Section 10). Also remove the chainguard if required (see Chapter 7).
6 Before removing the swingarm it is advisable to re-check for play in the bearings. Any problems which may have been overlooked with the checks made with the wheel and shock absorbers in place (see Chapter 1) are highlighted with these components removed.

12.3 Remove the brake torque arm bolt and lift the arm off

12.7b . . . then unscrew the nut . . .

7 Remove the swingarm end caps **(see illustration)**. Unscrew the nut on the left-hand end of the swingarm pivot bolt, and on 750 models remove the washer **(see illustration)**. With the aid of an assistant to support the swingarm if required, drift the pivot bolt out and withdraw it from the right-hand side of the frame **(see illustration)**. Note the positions of any breather and drain pipes and move them aside if necessary, then manoeuvre the swingarm out of the back of the machine.
8 Check the condition of the chain slider on the front of the swingarm and replace it if it is worn or damaged **(see illustration)**.

12.7a Remove the end cap . . .

12.7c . . . and withdraw the pivot bolt

12.8 Replace the chain slider if worn or damaged

9 Inspect all components for wear or damage (see Section 13).

Installation

10 Installation is the reverse of removal, noting the following.

 a) *Remove the grease seal from each bearing and withdraw the inner sleeve from the swingarm, then lubricate the bearings with molybdenum disulphide grease (see illustrations 13.4a and b and 13.5). Fit the sleeve and the seals back into the bearings. Also lubricate the pivot bolt and the shock absorber pivot bolt shanks with molybdenum disulphide grease.*

 b) *Loop the drive chain over the swingarm as it is offered up to the frame (see illustration). Make sure that the chain slider is fitted to the swingarm and that any breather and drain pipes are correctly positioned.*
 c) *Tighten the swingarm pivot bolt nut to the torque setting specified at the beginning of the Chapter (see illustration).*
 d) *Tighten the brake torque arm nut to the specified torque setting.*
 e) *Tighten the shock absorber bolts to the specified torque setting.*
 f) *Check the operation of the rear suspension before taking the machine on the road.*

13 Swingarm - inspection and bearing replacement

Inspection

1 Thoroughly clean all components, removing all traces of dirt, corrosion and grease.
2 Inspect all components closely, looking for obvious signs of wear such as heavy scoring, and cracks or distortion due to accident damage. Any damaged or worn component must be replaced.

3 Check the swingarm pivot bolt for straightness by rolling it on a flat surface such as a piece of plate glass (first wipe off all old grease and remove any corrosion using fine emery cloth). If the equipment is available, place the bolt in V-blocks and measure the runout using a dial indicator. If the bolt is bent or the runout is excessive, replace it.

Bearing replacement

4 Remove the grease seal from each bearing and withdraw the inner sleeve from the swingarm **(see illustrations)**. Inspect them and the bearings for signs of wear or damage and replace them if necessary.
5 Worn bearings can be drifted out of their bores, but note that removal will destroy them; new bearings should be obtained before work commences. The new bearings should be pressed or drawn into their bores rather than driven into position. Fit the bearings with the marked side facing out, and apply plenty of molybdenum disulphide grease **(see illustration)**.

> **HAYNES HiNT** *Refer to "Tools and Workshop Tips" in the Reference section for details of how to make up a bearing drawbolt.*

12.10a Do not forget to loop the chain around the swingarm

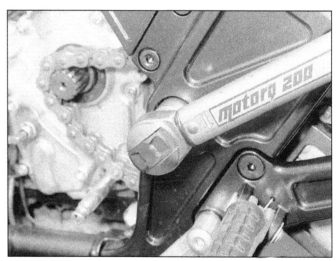

12.10b Tighten the swingarm nut to the specified torque setting

13.4a Remove the grease seals . . .

13.4b . . . and withdraw the inner sleeve

13.5 Liberally grease the bearings

14.2a Unscrew the pinch bolt (arrowed) and slide the arm off the shaft

14.2b Engine sprocket cover bolts (arrowed) - 550 models

14.2c Engine sprocket cover bolts (arrowed) - 750 models

14.2d The chain guard is secured by three bolts (arrowed)

14 Drive chain - removal, cleaning and installation

Removal

Note: *The original equipment drive chain fitted to all models is an endless chain. Removal requires the removal of the swingarm as detailed below, or if the necessary chain breaking and joining tool is available, the chain can be separated and rejoined (see Tools and Workshop Tips in the Reference section).*

⚠ **Warning: NEVER install a drive chain which uses a clip-type master (split) link.**

1 Remove the swingarm (see Section 12).
2 Unscrew the gearchange linkage arm pinch bolt and remove the arm from the shaft, noting any alignment marks **(see illustration)**.

If no marks are visible, make your own before removing the arm so that it can be correctly aligned with the shaft on installation. Unscrew the bolts securing the engine sprocket cover to the crankcase and remove it **(see illustrations)**. On 550 models, unscrew the three bolts securing the front sprocket chain guide and remove the guide **(see illustration)**.
3 Slip the chain off the front sprocket and remove it from the bike.

Cleaning

4 Soak the chain in paraffin (kerosene) for approximately five or six minutes.
Caution: Don't use gasoline (petrol), solvent, cleaning fluids, or high-pressure water. Remove the chain, wipe it off, then blow dry it with compressed air immediately. The entire process shouldn't take longer than ten minutes - if it does, the O-rings in the chain rollers could be damaged.

Installation

5 Installation is the reverse of removal. On completion adjust and lubricate the chain following the procedures described in Chapter 1.
Caution: Use only the recommended lubricant.

15 Sprockets - check and replacement

Check

1 Unscrew the gearchange linkage arm pinch bolt and remove the arm from the shaft, noting any alignment marks **(see illustration 14.2a)**. If no marks are visible, make your own before removing the arm so that it can be correctly aligned with the shaft on installation. Unscrew the bolts securing the engine sprocket cover to the crankcase and remove the cover **(see illustrations 14.2b and c)**.
2 Check the wear pattern on both sprockets **(see illustration)**. If the sprocket teeth are worn excessively, replace the chain and both sprockets as a set. Whenever the sprockets are inspected, the drive chain should be inspected also (see Chapter 1). If you are replacing the chain, replace the sprockets as well.
3 Place the machine on its centre stand, or support it using an auxiliary stand so that the rear wheel is off the ground. Check the amount of sprocket warpage using a dial gauge mounted against the outside of the sprocket next to the chain **(see illustration)**. Spin the wheel and record the amount of warpage indicated. If the amount exceeds the service limit specified, replace the sprocket.
4 On 750 models, use a vernier caliper to measure the diameter of each sprocket from the base of the sprocket teeth (you may need to remove the wheel to carry out this check successfully). If the diameter is less than the service limits specified, replace the sprocket.
5 Adjust and lubricate the chain following the procedures described in Chapter 1.
Caution: Use only the recommended lubricant.

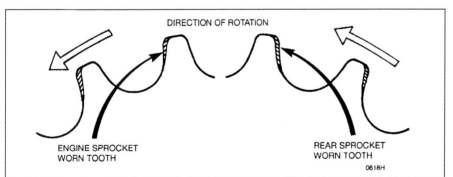

DIRECTION OF ROTATION

ENGINE SPROCKET WORN TOOTH

REAR SPROCKET WORN TOOTH

0618H

15.2 Check the sprocket teeth for wear

15.3 Measuring sprocket warpage with a dial gauge

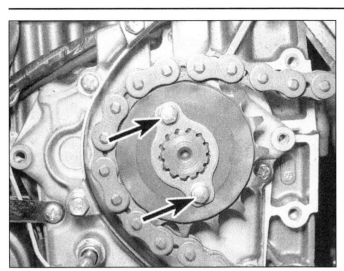

15.8 On 550 models, the sprocket is secured by two bolts (arrowed)

15.9 On 750 models, bend back the lockwasher tab (arrowed) and unscrew the nut

Replacement

Front sprocket

6 Unscrew the gearchange linkage arm pinch bolt and remove the arm from the shaft, noting any alignment marks **(see illustration 14.2a)**. If no marks are visible, make your own before removing the arm so that it can be correctly aligned with the shaft on installation. Unscrew the bolts securing the engine sprocket cover to the crankcase and remove the cover **(see illustration 14.2b and c)**.

7 Install the gearchange linkage arm onto the shaft and shift the transmission into gear, then have an assistant sit on the seat and apply the rear brake. This will lock the transmission and enable you to slacken and remove the engine sprocket bolts or nut.

8 On 550 models, unscrew the bolts, then turn the sprocket plate slightly anti-clockwise until the splines in the plate align with those on the shaft and remove the plate **(see illustration)**.

9 On 750 models, bend back the tab on the sprocket nut lockwasher, then unscrew the sprocket nut and remove it with the lockwasher. Check the condition of the lockwasher and renew it if weakened or damaged.

10 Slide the sprocket and chain off the shaft, then slip the sprocket out of the chain **(see illustration)**. If the chain is too tight to allow the sprocket to be slid off the shaft, slacken the chain adjusters to provide some freeplay (see Chapter 1), or, if the rear sprocket is being replaced as well, remove the rear wheel.

11 Engage the new sprocket with the chain and slide it on the shaft. On 550 models, fit the sprocket with the stepped inner circle facing in.

12 On 550 models install the sprocket plate on the shaft until it is in its slot, then turn it slightly clockwise until its holes align with

those in the sprocket **(see illustrations)**. Install the sprocket bolts and, using the method employed on removal to prevent the transmission from turning, tighten them to the torque setting specified at the beginning of the Chapter **(see illustration)**.

13 On 750 models, install the sprocket nut with its lockwasher and, using the method employed on removal to prevent the transmission from turning, tighten it to the torque setting specified at the beginning of the Chapter. Bend up the tabs on the lockwasher to secure the nut **(see illustration)**.

15.10 Slide the sprocket off the shaft and out of the chain

15.12a Slide the sprocket plate onto the shaft . . .

15.12b . . . then turn it to align the bolt holes

15.12c Tighten the sprocket bolts to the specified torque setting

15.13 Bend up a lockwasher tab to lock the nut

15.16 The sprocket is secured by six nuts (arrowed)

16.2 Lift the sprocket coupling out of the wheel . . .

14 Install the sprocket cover and the gearchange linkage arm, aligning the marks **(see illustrations 14.2c, b and a)**. Adjust and lubricate the chain following the procedures described in Chapter 1.

Rear sprocket

15 Remove the rear wheel (see Chapter 6).
16 Unscrew the nuts securing the sprocket to the wheel coupling, then remove the sprocket, noting which way round it fits **(see illustration)**.
17 Before installing the new rear sprocket, check the wheel coupling and damper assembly components (see Section 16).
18 Install the sprocket onto the coupling with the stamped mark facing out, then tighten the sprocket nuts to the torque setting specified at the beginning of the Chapter.
19 Install the rear wheel (see Chapter 6).
20 Adjust and lubricate the chain following the procedures described in Chapter 1.

16 Rear wheel coupling/ rubber dampers - check and replacement

1 Remove the rear wheel (see Chapter 6).
Caution: Do not lay the wheel down on the disc as it could become warped. Lay the wheel on wooden blocks so that the disc is off the ground.
2 Lift the sprocket coupling away from the wheel leaving the rubber dampers in position in the wheel **(see illustration)**. Note the spacer inside the coupling. Check the coupling for cracks or any obvious signs of damage. Also check the sprocket studs for wear or damage.
3 Lift the rubber damper segments from the wheel and check them for cracks, hardening and general deterioration **(see illustration)**. Replace the rubber dampers as a set if necessary.

16.3 . . . and check the damper segments for wear and deterioration

4 Checking and replacement procedures for the sprocket coupling bearing are described in Chapter 6.
5 Installation is the reverse of removal. Make sure the spacer is correctly installed in the coupling.
6 Install the rear wheel (see Chapter 6).

Chapter 6
Brakes, wheels and tyres

Contents

Degrees of difficulty

Easy, suitable for novice with little experience	**Fairly easy,** suitable for beginner with some experience	**Fairly difficult,** suitable for competent DIY mechanic	**Difficult,** suitable for experienced DIY mechanic
		Very difficult, suitable for expert DIY or professional	

Specifications

Brakes

Brake fluid type	DOT 4
Brake pad friction material thickness	
550 models	
Front	
Standard	4.35 mm
Service limit	1.0 mm
Rear	
Standard	4.3 mm
Service limit	1.0 mm
750 models - front and rear	
Standard	4.5 mm
Service limit	1.0 mm
Disc minimum thickness	
Front	
Standard	4.3 to 4.6 mm
Service limit	4.0 mm
Rear	
550 models	
Standard	4.8 to 5.1 mm
Service limit	4.5 mm
750 models	
Standard	5.8 to 6.1 mm
Service limit	5.0 mm
Disc maximum runout (front and rear, all models)	
Standard	less than 0.2 mm
Service limit	0.3 mm

Wheels

Maximum wheel runout (front and rear)	
Axial (side-to-side)	0.5 mm
Radial (out-of-round)	0.8 mm
Axle runout (front and rear)	
Standard	less than 0.05 mm
Service limit	0.2 mm

Tyres

Tyre pressures and tread depth . . . . see *Daily (pre-ride) checks*
Tyre sizes - 550 models
    Front . . . . 110/80 - 17
    Rear . . . . 140/70 - 18
Tyre sizes - 750 models
    Front . . . . 120/70 - 17
    Rear . . . . 150/70 - 17
*Refer to the owners handbook, the tyre information label, or a Kawasaki dealer for approved tyre brands and speed rating.

Torque settings

Front brake caliper mounting bolts
    550 models . . . . 32 Nm
    750 models . . . . 34 Nm
Front brake master cylinder clamp bolts
    550 models . . . . 11 Nm
    750 models . . . . 8.8 Nm
Brake hose banjo bolts . . . . 25 Nm
Brake disc bolts . . . . 23 Nm
Rear brake caliper mounting bolts
    550 models . . . . 25 Nm
    750 models . . . . 34 Nm
Brake torque arm nuts
    550 models . . . . 32 Nm
    750 models . . . . 34 Nm
Rear brake master cylinder bolts . . . . 23 Nm
Front axle . . . . 88 Nm
Front axle clamp bolts
    550 models . . . . 20 Nm
    750 models . . . . 34 Nm
Rear axle nut . . . . 88 Nm
Chain adjuster clamp bolts . . . . 39 Nm

1 General information

All models covered in this manual are fitted with cast alloy wheels, except the ZR750 D model, which has spoked wheels. Tubeless tyres are used on the cast wheels, and tubed tyres on spoked wheels.

Both front and rear brakes are hydraulically operated disc brakes. On 550 models, the front has dual sliding calipers with twin pistons, the rear on B1, B2 and B3 models has a single sliding caliper with twin pistons, and the rear on B4, B5 and B6 models has a single sliding caliper with single piston. On 750 models, the front has dual sliding calipers with twin pistons, and the rear has a single sliding caliper with twin pistons.

Caution: Disc brake components rarely require disassembly. Do not disassemble components unless absolutely necessary. If a hydraulic brake line is loosened, the entire system must be disassembled, drained, cleaned and then properly filled and bled upon reassembly. Do not use solvents on internal brake components. Solvents will cause the seals to swell and distort. Use only clean brake fluid or denatured alcohol for cleaning. Use care when working with brake fluid as it can injure your eyes and it will damage painted surfaces and plastic parts.

2 Front brake pads - replacement

⚠️ *Warning: The dust created by the brake system may contain asbestos, which is harmful to your health. Never blow it out with compressed air and don't inhale any of it. An approved filtering mask should be worn when working on the brakes.*

1 On all except ZR750 D models, unscrew the brake caliper mounting bolts and slide the caliper off the disc **(see illustration 3.2a)**. Remove the outer pad from the caliper body, noting how the protrusion on each end of the pad locates against the guide **(see illustration)**.

Slide the caliper in on its sliders until the inner pad can be lifted off its guide pins on the caliper mounting bracket **(see illustration)**. Also note how the pad spring is fitted and remove it if required.

2 On ZR750 D models, unscrew the brake caliper mounting bolts and slide the caliper off the disc. Remove the R-pin from the end of the pad retaining pin, then withdraw the pad pin. Remove the outer pad from the caliper body, noting how the protrusion on the end of the pad locates against the guide. Lift the inner pad off its guide pin on the caliper mounting bracket, noting how it fits.

3 Inspect the surface of each pad for contamination and check that the friction material has not worn beyond its service limit. If either pad is worn down to, or beyond, the

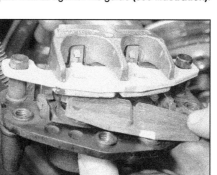

2.1a Remove the outer pad . . .

2.1b . . . then slide the caliper fully in until the inner pad can be lifted off the pins

2.3 Brake pad wear indicator step (arrowed)

2.9a Make sure the spring (A) and guides (B) are correctly positioned

2.9b Locate the outer pad ends as shown

service limit wear step, line or groove (ie they are no longer visible), fouled with oil or grease, or heavily scored or damaged by dirt and debris, both pads must be replaced as a set **(see illustration)**. If you are in doubt about the amount of friction material left, measure the thickness of the material. If it is 1 mm or less, the pads must be replaced. Note that it is not possible to degrease the friction material; if the pads are contaminated in any way they must be replaced.

4 If the pads are in good condition clean them carefully, using a fine wire brush which is completely free of oil and grease to remove all traces of road dirt and corrosion. Using a pointed instrument, clean out the grooves in the friction material and dig out any embedded particles of foreign matter. Any areas of glazing may be removed using emery cloth.

5 Check the brake disc condition (Section 4).

6 On ZR750 D models, remove all traces of corrosion from the pad pin. Inspect the pin for signs of damage and replace if necessary.

7 Push the pistons as far back into the caliper as possible using hand pressure only **(see illustration 7.11)**. Due to the increased friction material thickness of new pads, it may be necessary to remove the master cylinder reservoir cover and diaphragm and siphon out some fluid.

8 Smear the backs of the pads and the shank of the pad pin (ZR750 D models only) with copper-based grease, making sure that none gets on the front or sides of the pads.

9 On all except ZR750 D models, installation of the pads is the reverse of removal. Make sure the pad spring and guides are correctly positioned **(see illustration)**. Insert the pads into the caliper so that the friction material of each pad will be facing the disc. Make sure the protrusion on each end of the outer pad locates correctly against its guide **(see illustration)**.

10 On ZR750 D models, installation of the pads and pad pin is the reverse of removal. Make sure the pad spring and guide are correctly positioned. Insert the pads into the caliper so that the friction material of each pad will be facing the disc. Make sure the protrusion on the outer pad locates correctly against the guide. Make sure the pad pin passes through each pad and secure it with the R-pin.

11 Install the caliper on the brake disc making sure the pads sit squarely either side of the disc **(see illustration 3.13)**.

12 Install the caliper mounting bolts, and tighten them to the torque setting specified at the beginning of this Chapter **(see illustration 3.14)**.

13 Top up the master cylinder reservoir if necessary (see *Daily (pre-ride) checks*), and replace the reservoir cover and diaphragm if removed.

14 Operate the brake lever several times to bring the pads into contact with the disc. Check the master cylinder fluid level (see *Daily (pre-ride) checks*) and the operation of the brake before riding the motorcycle.

3 Front brake calipers - removal, overhaul and installation

⚠ *Warning: If a caliper indicates the need for an overhaul (usually due to leaking fluid or sticky operation), all old brake fluid should be flushed from the system. Also, the dust created by the brake system may contain asbestos, which is harmful to your health. Never blow it out with compressed air and don't inhale any of it. An approved filtering mask should be worn when working on the brakes. Do not, under any circumstances, use petroleum-based solvents to clean brake parts. Use clean brake fluid, brake cleaner or denatured alcohol only.*

Removal

1 Remove the brake hose banjo bolt, noting its position on the caliper and separate the hose from the caliper **(see illustration)**. Plug the hose end or wrap a plastic bag tightly around it to minimise fluid loss and prevent dirt entering the system. Discard the sealing washers as new ones must be used on installation. **Note:** *If you are overhauling the caliper and don't have a source of compressed air to blow out the pistons, just loosen the banjo bolt at this stage and retighten it lightly. The bike's hydraulic system can then be used to force the pistons out of the body once the pads have been removed. Disconnect the hose once the pistons have been sufficiently displaced.*

2 Unscrew the caliper mounting bolts, and slide the caliper away from the disc **(see illustration)**. Remove the brake pads. On all except ZR750 D models, remove the piston insulator pieces **(see illustration)**.

3.1 Note the brake hose alignment before unscrewing the banjo bolt (arrowed)

3.2a Brake caliper mounting bolts (arrowed)

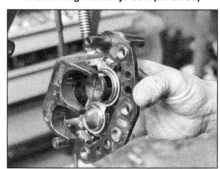

3.2b Remove the insulator piece from each piston

3.3a Front brake caliper components - all models except ZR750 D

1	Brake pads	4	Piston insulator	6	Dust seal
2	Pad spring		piece	7	Piston seal
3	Outer pad guides	5	Piston	8	Bleed valve
				9	Slider pin boot

3.3b Front brake caliper components - ZR750 D models

1	Brake pads	4	Piston seal	7	Pad spring
2	Pad pin	5	Dust seal	8	Slider pin boot
3	R-pin	6	Piston	9	Outer pad guide
				10	Bleed valve

Overhaul

3 Clean the exterior of the caliper with denatured alcohol or brake system cleaner **(see illustrations)**.

4 Remove the pistons from the caliper body, either by pumping them out by operating the front brake lever until the pistons are displaced, or by forcing them out using compressed air. Note that on all except 750 D1 models, two sizes of piston are used, and that different size seals are used accordingly. Mark each piston head and caliper body with a felt marker to ensure that the pistons can be matched to their original bores on reassembly. If the compressed air method is used, place a wad of rag between the pistons and the caliper to act as a cushion, then use compressed air directed into the fluid inlet to force the pistons out of the body. Use only low pressure to ease the pistons out and make sure both pistons are displaced at the same time. If the air pressure is too high and the pistons are forced out, the caliper and/or pistons may be damaged.

 Warning: Never place your fingers in front of the pistons in an attempt to catch or protect them when applying compressed air, as serious injury could result.

5 Using a wooden or plastic tool, remove the dust seals from the caliper bores and discard them **(see illustration)**. New seals must be used on installation. If a metal tool is being used, take great care not to damage the caliper bores.

6 Remove and discard the piston seals in the same way.

7 Clean the pistons and bores with denatured alcohol, clean brake fluid or brake system cleaner. If compressed air is available, use it to dry the parts thoroughly (make sure it's filtered and unlubricated).

Caution: Never use a petroleum-based solvent to clean brake parts.

8 Inspect the caliper bores and pistons for signs of corrosion, nicks and burrs and loss of plating. If surface defects are present, the caliper assembly must be replaced. Check that the caliper body is able to slide freely on the mounting bracket slider pins. If seized due to corrosion, separate the two components and clean off all traces of corrosion and hardened grease. Apply a smear of copper or silicone-based grease to the mounting bracket slider pins and reassemble the two components **(see illustration)**. Replace the rubber boots if they

are damaged or deteriorated **(see illustration)**. If the caliper is in bad shape the master cylinder should also be checked.

9 Lubricate the new piston seals with clean brake fluid and install them in their grooves in

3.5 Remove the dust seal with a plastic or wooden tool (a pencil works well) to avoid damage to the bore and seal groove

3.8a Apply a little of the specified grease to the slider pins on the caliper bracket

3.8b Replace the slider boots if necessary

3.13 Install the caliper . . .

3.14 . . . and tighten the bolts to the specified torque setting

the caliper bores. Note that on all except ZR750 D models, two sizes of bore and piston are used, and care must therefore be taken to ensure that the correct size seals are fitted to the correct bores. The same applies when fitting the new dust seals and pistons.

10 Lubricate the new dust seals with clean brake fluid and install them in their grooves in the caliper bores.

11 Lubricate the pistons with clean brake fluid and install them closed-end first into the caliper bores. Using your thumbs, push the pistons all the way in, making sure they enter the bore squarely **(see illustration 7.11)**.

Installation

12 On all except ZR750 D models, install the piston centre pieces **(see illustration 3.2b)**.Install the brake pads (see Section 2).

13 Install the caliper on the brake disc making sure the pads sit squarely either side of the disc **(see illustration)**.

14 Install the caliper mounting bolts, and tighten them to the torque setting specified at the beginning of this Chapter **(see illustration)**.

15 Connect the brake hose to the caliper, using new sealing washers on each side of the fitting. Position the hose so that it fits into its slot in the caliper **(see illustration 3.1)**.

Tighten the banjo bolt to the torque setting specified at the beginning of the Chapter.

16 Fill the fluid reservoir to the maximum level line with the specified brake fluid **(see illustration 5.24)** and bleed the hydraulic system as described in Section 11.

17 Check for leaks and thoroughly test the operation of the brake before riding the motorcycle.

4 Front brake disc - inspection, removal and installation

Inspection

1 Visually inspect the surface of the disc for score marks and other damage. Light scratches are normal after use and won't affect brake operation, but deep grooves and heavy score marks will reduce braking efficiency and accelerate pad wear. If a disc is badly grooved it must be machined or replaced.

2 To check disc runout, position the bike on its centre stand or an auxiliary stand, and support it so that the front wheel is raised off the ground. Turn the handlebars so that the steering is on full lock either way. Mount a dial

gauge to a fork leg, with the plunger on the gauge touching the surface of the disc about 10 mm (1/2 inch) from the outer edge **(see illustration)**. Rotate the wheel and watch the gauge needle, comparing the reading with the limit listed in the Specifications at the beginning of the Chapter. If the runout is greater than the service limit, check the wheel bearings for play (see Chapter 1). If the bearings are worn, replace them (Section 16) and repeat this check. If the disc runout is still excessive, it will have to be replaced, although machining by a competent engineering shop may be possible.

3 The disc must not be machined or allowed to wear down to a thickness less than the service limit as listed in this Chapter's Specifications and as marked on the disc itself **(see illustration)**. The thickness of the disc can be checked with a micrometer **(see illustration)**. If the thickness of the disc is less than the service limit, it must be replaced.

Removal

4 Remove the wheel (see Section 14).
Caution: Do not lay the wheel down and allow it to rest on the disc - the disc could become warped. Set the wheel on wood blocks so the disc doesn't support the weight of the wheel.

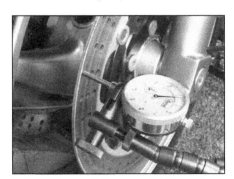

4.2 Set up a dial gauge with the probe contacting the brake disc, then rotate the wheel to check for runout

4.3a The minimum disc thickness is marked on the disc

4.3b Using a micrometer to measure disc thickness

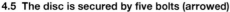

4.5 The disc is secured by five bolts (arrowed)

5.4 Slacken the reservoir cover screws (arrowed)

5 Mark the relationship of the disc to the wheel, so it can be installed in the same position. Unscrew the disc retaining bolts, loosening them a little at a time in a criss-cross pattern to avoid distorting the disc, then remove the disc from the wheel **(see illustration)**.

Installation

6 Install the disc on the wheel, aligning the previously applied matchmarks (if you're reinstalling the original disc). The arrow marked on the disc must be on the outside and point in the direction of normal wheel rotation **(see illustration 8.4)**.

7 Install the disc bolts and tighten them in a criss-cross pattern evenly and progressively to the torque setting specified at the beginning of the Chapter. Clean off all grease from the brake disc(s) using acetone or brake system cleaner. If a new brake disc has been installed, remove any protective coating from its working surfaces.

8 Install the front wheel (see Section 14).

9 Operate the brake lever several times to bring the pads into contact with the disc. Check the operation of the brakes carefully before riding the bike.

5 Front brake master cylinder - removal, overhaul and installation

1 If the master cylinder is leaking fluid, or if the lever does not produce a firm feel when the brake is applied, and bleeding the brakes does not help (see Section 11), and the hydraulic hoses are all in good condition, then master cylinder overhaul is recommended.

2 Before disassembling the master cylinder, read through the entire procedure and make sure that you have the correct rebuild kit. Also, you will need some new, clean brake fluid of the recommended type, some clean rags and internal circlip pliers. **Note:** *To*

prevent damage to the paint from spilled brake fluid, always cover the fuel tank when working on the master cylinder.

Caution: Disassembly, overhaul and reassembly of the brake master cylinder must be done in a spotlessly clean work area to avoid contamination and possible failure of the brake hydraulic system components.

Removal

3 Remove the rear view mirror (Chapter 7).

4 Loosen, but do not remove, the screws holding the reservoir cover in place **(see illustration)**.

5 Disconnect the electrical connectors from the brake light switch **(see illustration)**.

6 Remove the front brake lever (Chapter 5).

7 Pull back the rubber cover on the brake hose banjo bolt, then unscrew the bolt and separate the hose from the master cylinder, noting its alignment **(see illustration)**. Discard the two sealing washers as they must be

5.5 Disconnect the brake light switch electrical connectors (arrowed)

5.7 Peel back the rubber boot to expose the brake hose banjo bolt. Note the alignment of the hose

5.8 Front brake master cylinder clamp bolts (arrowed)

replaced with new ones. Wrap the end of the hose in a clean rag and suspend it in an upright position or bend it down carefully and place the open end in a clean container. The objective is to prevent excessive loss of brake fluid, fluid spills and system contamination.

8 Unscrew the master cylinder clamp bolts, then lift the master cylinder and reservoir away from the handlebar, noting how the top mating surfaces of the clamp align with the top mating surfaces of the switch housing **(see illustration)**.
Caution: Do not tip the master cylinder upside down or brake fluid will run out.

Overhaul

9 Remove the reservoir cover retaining screws and lift off the cover, the diaphragm plate and the rubber diaphragm **(see illustration)**. Drain the brake fluid from the reservoir into a suitable container. Wipe any remaining fluid out of the reservoir with a clean rag.
10 Unscrew the screw securing the brake light switch to the bottom of the master cylinder and remove the switch **(see illustration)**.
11 Carefully remove the dust boot from the end of the piston **(see illustration)**.
12 Using circlip pliers, remove the circlip and slide out the piston assembly and the spring, noting how they fit **(see illustration)**. Lay the parts out in the proper order to prevent confusion during reassembly **(see illustration)**.
13 Clean all parts with clean brake fluid or denatured alcohol. If compressed air is available, use it to dry the parts thoroughly (make sure it's filtered and unlubricated).
Caution: Do not, under any circumstances, use a petroleum-based solvent to clean brake parts.
14 Check the master cylinder bore for corrosion, scratches, nicks and score marks. If damage or wear is evident, the master cylinder must be replaced with a new one. If the master cylinder is in poor condition, then the calipers should be checked as well. Check that the fluid inlet and outlet ports in the master cylinder are clear.
15 The piston assembly and spring are included in the rebuild kit. Use all of the new parts, regardless of the apparent condition of the old ones.

5.9 Front brake master cylinder components

1 Rubber boot	5 Reservoir cover and
2 Brake hose banjo bolt	diaphragm plate
3 Sealing washers	6 Rubber diaphragm
4 Brake hose	7 Reservoir

8 Rubber dust boot
9 Circlip
10 Piston assembly & spring
11 Brake light switch

16 Install the spring in the master cylinder with its wider end first so that its tapered end faces the piston.
17 Lubricate the components with clean brake fluid and install the assembly into the master cylinder, ensuring all the components are the correct way round **(see illustration)**.

Make sure the lips on the cup seals do not turn inside out when they are slipped into the bore. Depress the piston and install the new circlip, ensuring it locates in the master cylinder groove **(see illustration)**.
18 Install the rubber dust boot, making sure the lip is seated correctly in the piston groove.

5.10 The brake light switch is secured by a single screw (arrowed)

5.11 Remove the rubber boot from the end of the master cylinder piston . . .

5.12a . . . then depress the piston and remove the circlip using a pair of internal circlip pliers

5.12b Lay out the internal parts as shown, even if new parts are being used, to avoid confusion on reassembly

5.17a Make sure the lips of the cups (arrowed) and all other components face in the right direction

5.17b Make sure the circlip is securely seated in its groove

5.24 Fill the reservoir to the maximum line (arrowed) with the specified fluid

5.25 Fit the diaphragm, plate and cover

19 Install the brake light switch.
20 Inspect the reservoir cover rubber diaphragm and replace if damaged or deteriorated.

Installation

21 Attach the master cylinder to the handlebar and fit the clamp with its UP mark facing up **(see illustration 5.8)**. Align the top mating surfaces of the clamp with the top mating surfaces of the switch housing, then tighten the upper bolt first then the lower bolt to the torque setting specified at the beginning of the Chapter. There should be a gap between the lower clamp mating surfaces.
22 Connect the brake hose to the master cylinder, using new sealing washers on each side of the union, and aligning the hose as noted on removal **(see illustration 5.7)**. Tighten the banjo bolt to the torque setting specified at the beginning of this Chapter.
23 Install the brake lever (see Chapter 5).
24 Fill the fluid reservoir to the maximum level line with the specified brake fluid **(see illustration)**. Refer to Section 11 of this Chapter and bleed the air from the system.
25 Fit the rubber diaphragm, making sure it is correctly seated, the diaphragm plate and the cover onto the master cylinder reservoir, and tighten the screws securely **(see illustration)**.
26 Connect the brake light switch wiring **(see illustration 5.5)** and install the rear view mirror (see Chapter 7).

6 Rear brake pads - replacement

⚠️ **Warning: The dust created by the brake system may contain asbestos, which is harmful to your health. Never blow it out with compressed air and don't inhale any of it. An approved filtering mask should be worn when working on the brakes.**
1 On ZR550 B1, B2 and B3 and all 750 models, unscrew the brake caliper mounting bolts and slide the caliper off the disc **(see illustration 7.2b)**. Remove the outer pad from the caliper body, noting how the protrusion on each end of the pad locates against the guide **(see illustration 2.1a)**. Slide the caliper in on its sliders until the inner pad can be lifted off its guide pins on the caliper mounting bracket **(see illustration 2.1b)**. Also take note of how

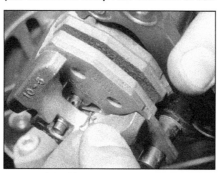

6.2a Remove the R-pin . . .

6.2c Lift the inner pad and slide it off the pin . . .

the pad spring is fitted and remove if required.
2 On ZR550 B4, B5 and B6 models, unscrew the brake caliper mounting bolts and slide the caliper off the disc **(see illustration 7.2a)**. Remove the R-pin from the end of the pad retaining pin, then withdraw the pad pin **(see illustrations)**. Lift the inner pad and slide it off its guide pin on the caliper mounting bracket, noting how it fits **(see illustration)**. Remove the outer pad from the caliper body, noting how the pad locates against the guide and the bracket **(see illustration)**. On B4 models to frame no. 024010, remove the shim from the back of the inner pad, noting which way round it fits.
3 Inspect the surface of each pad for contamination and check that the friction material has not worn beyond its service limit. If either pad is worn down to, or beyond, the service limit wear step, line or groove (ie they are no longer visible), fouled with oil or grease, or heavily scored or damaged by dirt and debris, both pads must be replaced. If you are

6.2b . . . and withdraw the pad pin

6.2d . . . then remove the outer pad, noting how its protrusions (arrowed) locate

6.10a Make sure the pad spring (arrowed) . . .

6.10b . . . and guide (arrowed) are correctly positioned

in doubt about the amount of friction material left, measure the thickness of the material. If it is 1 mm or less, the pads must be replaced. Note that it is not possible to degrease the friction material; if the pads are contaminated in any way they must be replaced.

4 If the pads are in good condition clean them carefully, using a fine wire brush which is completely free of oil and grease to remove all traces of road dirt and corrosion. Using a pointed instrument, clean out the grooves in the friction material and dig out any embedded particles of foreign matter. Any areas of glazing may be removed using emery cloth.

5 Check the brake disc condition (Section 4).

6 On ZR550 B4, B5 and B6 models, remove all traces of corrosion from the pad pin. Inspect the pin for signs of damage and replace if necessary.

7 Push the piston(s) as far back into the caliper as possible using hand pressure only (see illustration 7.11). Due to the increased friction material thickness of new pads, it may be necessary to remove the master cylinder reservoir cover and diaphragm and siphon out some fluid.

8 Smear the backs of the pads and the shank of the pad pin (ZR550 B4, B5 and B6 models only) with copper-based grease, making sure none gets on the front or sides of the pads.

9 On ZR550 B1, B2 and B3 and all 750 models, installation of the pads is the reverse of removal. Make sure the pad spring and guides are correctly positioned (see illustration 2.9a). Insert the pads into the caliper so that the friction material of each pad will be facing the disc. Make sure the protrusion on each end of the outer pad locates correctly against its guide (see illustration 2.9b).

10 On 550 B4, B5 and B6 models, installation of the pads and pad pin is the reverse of removal. Make sure the pad spring and guide are correctly positioned (see illustrations). Make sure the outer pad locates correctly against the guide and the bracket (see illustration 6.2d). Insert the pads into the caliper so that the friction material of each pad will be facing the disc (see illustration 6.2c). On B4 models to frame no. 024010, fit the shim onto the back of the inner pad with the open end facing back. Make sure the pad

pin passes through each pad and secure it with the R-pin (see illustrations 6.2b and a).

11 Install the caliper on the brake disc making sure the pads sit squarely either side of the disc (see illustration 7.13).

12 Install the caliper mounting bolts, and tighten them to the specified torque (see illustration 7.14b).

13 Top up the master cylinder reservoir if necessary (see Daily (pre-ride) checks), and replace the reservoir cover and diaphragm if removed.

14 Operate the brake lever several times to bring the pads into contact with the disc. Check the master cylinder fluid level (see Daily (pre-ride) checks) and the operation of the brake before riding the motorcycle.

7 Rear brake caliper - removal, overhaul and installation

⚠ **Warning: If a caliper needs an overhaul (usually due to leaking fluid or sticky operation), all old brake fluid should be flushed from the system. Also, the dust created by the brake system may contain asbestos, which is harmful to your health. Never blow it out with compressed air and don't inhale any of it. An approved filtering mask should be worn when working on the brakes. Do not, under any circumstances, use petroleum-based solvents to clean brake parts. Use clean brake fluid, brake cleaner or denatured alcohol only.**

7.2a Rear brake caliper mounting bolts (arrowed) - ZR550 B4, B5 and B6 models

Removal

1 Remove the brake hose banjo bolt, noting its position on the caliper and separate the hose from the caliper (see illustration). Plug the hose end or wrap a plastic bag tightly around it to minimise fluid loss and prevent dirt entering the system. Discard the sealing washers as new ones must be used on installation. **Note:** If you are planning to overhaul the caliper and don't have a source of compressed air to blow out the pistons, just loosen the banjo bolt at this stage and retighten it lightly. The bike's hydraulic system can then be used to force the pistons out of the body once the pads have been removed. Disconnect the hose once the pistons have been sufficiently displaced.

2 Unscrew the caliper mounting bolts, and slide the caliper away from the disc (see illustrations). Remove the brake pads (see Section 6), and the piston insulator piece(s) (see illustration 3.2b).

Overhaul

3 Clean the exterior of the caliper with denatured alcohol or brake system cleaner (see illustrations).

4 Remove the pistons from the caliper body, either by pumping them out by operating the front brake lever until the pistons are displaced, or by forcing them out using compressed air. Note that on 750 models, two sizes of piston are used, and that different size seals are used accordingly. Mark each piston head and caliper body with a felt marker to ensure that the pistons can be

7.1 Unscrew the brake hose banjo bolt (A), noting its alignment with the lug (B) - ZR550 B4, B5 and B6 type shown

7.2b Rear brake caliper mounting bolts (arrowed) - 750 models

7.3a Rear brake caliper components - ZR550 B1, B2 and B3 models

1 Inner pad
2 Outer pad
3 Caliper bracket
4 Slider pin boot
5 Slider pin boot
6 Caliper body
7 Bleed valve
8 Pad spring
9 Dust seal
10 Piston insulator piece
11 Piston
12 Piston seal

7.3b Rear brake caliper components - ZR550 B4, B5 & B6 models

1 R-pin	6 Slider pin boot	11 Pad spring
2 Pad pin	7 Slider pin boot	12 Piston
3 Inner pad	8 Caliper body	13 Dust seal
4 Outer pad	9 Bleed valve	14 Piston seal
5 Caliper bracket	10 Pad guide	

matched to their original bores on reassembly. If the compressed air method is used, place a wad of rag between the pistons and the caliper to act as a cushion, then use compressed air directed into the fluid inlet to force the pistons out of the body. Use only low pressure to ease the pistons out and make sure both pistons are displaced at the same time. If the air pressure is too high and the pistons are forced out, the caliper and/or pistons may be damaged.

⚠️ **Warning: Never place your fingers in front of the pistons in an attempt to catch or protect them when applying compressed air, as serious injury could result.**

5 Using a wooden or plastic tool, remove the dust seals from the caliper bores and discard them (see illustration 3.5). New seals must be used on installation. If a metal tool is being used, take great care not to damage the caliper bores.

6 Remove and discard the piston seals in the same way.

7 Clean the pistons and bores with denatured alcohol, clean brake fluid or brake system cleaner. If compressed air is available, use it to dry the parts thoroughly (make sure it's filtered and unlubricated).

Caution: Do not, under any circumstances, use a petroleum-based solvent to clean brake parts.

8 Inspect the caliper bores and pistons for signs of corrosion, nicks and burrs and loss of plating. If surface defects are present, the caliper assembly must be replaced. Check that the caliper body is able to slide freely on the mounting bracket slider pins. If seized due to corrosion, separate the two components and clean off all traces of corrosion and hardened grease. Apply a smear of copper or silicone-based grease to the mounting bracket slider pins and reassemble the two components (see illustration 3.8a). Replace the rubber boots if they are damaged or deteriorated (see illustration 3.8b). If the caliper is in bad shape the master cylinder should also be checked.

9 Lubricate the new piston seals with clean brake fluid and install them in their grooves in the caliper bores. Note that on 750 models, two sizes of bore and piston are used, and care must therefore be taken to ensure that the correct size seals are fitted to the correct bores. The same applies when fitting the new dust seals and pistons.

10 Lubricate the new dust seals with clean brake fluid and install them in their grooves in the caliper bores.

11 Lubricate the pistons with clean brake fluid and install them closed-end first into the caliper bores. Using your thumbs, push the

7.3c Rear brake caliper components - 750 models

1 Pad spring
2 Inner pad
3 Outer pad
4 Caliper bracket
5 Pad guides
6 Slider pin boot
7 Slider pin boot
8 Caliper body
9 Bleed valve
10 Bleed valve cap
11 Dust seal
12 Piston insulator piece
13 Piston
14 Piston seal

7.11 Push the piston squarely into the bore

7.14a ... then install the bolts ...

7.13 Mount the caliper onto the disc ...

7.14b ... and tighten them to the specified torque setting

8 Rear brake disc - inspection, removal and installation

Inspection

1 Refer to Section 4 of this Chapter, noting that the dial gauge should be attached to the swingarm.

Removal

2 Remove the rear wheel with reference to Section 15.
3 Mark the relationship of the disc to the wheel so it can be installed in the same position. Unscrew the disc retaining bolts, loosening them a little at a time in a criss-cross pattern to avoid distorting the disc, and remove the disc **(see illustration)**.

Installation

4 Position the disc on the wheel, aligning the previously applied matchmarks (if you're reinstalling the original disc). The arrow marked on the disc must be on the outside and point in the direction of normal wheel rotation **(see illustration)**.
5 Install the disc bolts and tighten them in a criss-cross pattern evenly and progressively to the torque setting specified at the beginning of this Chapter. Clean off all grease from the brake disc using acetone or brake system cleaner. If a new brake disc has been installed, remove any protective coating from its working surfaces.
6 Install the rear wheel with reference to Section 15.
7 Operate the brake pedal several times to bring the pads into contact with the disc. Check the operation of the brake, preferably before taking the machine out on the road.

pistons all the way in, making sure they enter the bore squarely **(see illustration)**.

Installation

12 On all except ZR550 B4, B5 and B6 models, install the piston insulator pieces **(see illustration 3.2b)**. Install the brake pads (see Section 6).
13 Install the caliper on the brake disc making sure the pads sit squarely either side of the disc **(see illustration)**.
14 Install the caliper mounting bolts, and tighten them to the specified torque **(see illustrations)**.

15 Connect the brake hose to the caliper, using new sealing washers on each side of the fitting. Position the hose as noted on removal **(see illustrations 7.1 and 7.2b)**. Tighten the banjo bolt to the torque setting specified at the beginning of the Chapter.
16 Fill the fluid reservoir to the upper level line with the specified brake fluid **(see illustration 5.24)** and bleed the hydraulic system as described in Section 11.
17 Check very carefully for leaks and thoroughly test the operation of the brake, preferably before taking the machine out on the road.

8.3 The disc is secured by four bolts (arrowed)

8.4 The arrow must point in the direction of normal rotation

9.4a Rear master cylinder banjo bolt (arrowed) - 550 models.
Note the alignment of the hose

9.4b Rear master cylinder banjo bolt (arrowed) - 750 models.
Note the alignment of the hose

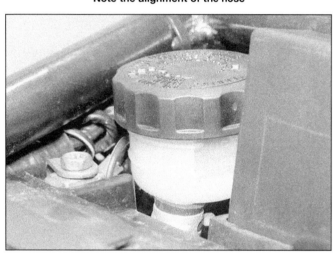

9.5 Rear master cylinder reservoir

9.6 Remove the split pin (A), withdraw the clevis pin (B),
and separate the pushrod from the pedal

9 Rear brake master cylinder - removal, overhaul and installation

1 If the master cylinder is leaking fluid, or if the lever does not produce a firm feel when the brake is applied, and bleeding the brakes does not help (see Section 11), and the hydraulic hoses are all in good condition, then master cylinder overhaul is recommended.
2 Before disassembling the master cylinder, read through the entire procedure and make sure that you have the correct rebuild kit. Also, you will need some new, clean brake fluid of the recommended type, some clean rags and internal circlip pliers. **Note:** *To prevent damage to the paint from spilled brake fluid, always cover surrounding painted surfaces when working on the master cylinder.* *Caution: Disassembly, overhaul and reassembly of the brake master cylinder must be done in a spotlessly clean work area to avoid contamination and possible*

failure of the brake hydraulic system components.

Removal

3 Remove the seat and the right-hand side panel (see Chapter 7).
4 Unscrew the brake hose banjo bolt and separate the brake hose from the master cylinder, noting its alignment **(see illustrations)**. Discard the two sealing washers as they must be replaced with new ones. Wrap the end of the hose in a clean rag and suspend the hose in an upright position or bend it down carefully and place the open end in a clean container. The objective is to prevent excessive loss of brake fluid, fluid spills and system contamination.
5 Unscrew the master cylinder fluid reservoir cap and remove the diaphragm plate and diaphragm **(see illustration)**. Separate the fluid reservoir hose from the elbow on the master cylinder by releasing the hose clamp, and allow the fluid to drain from the reservoir into a suitable container.

6 Remove the split pin from the clevis pin securing the brake pedal to the master cylinder pushrod **(see illustration)**. Withdraw the clevis pin and separate the pedal from the pushrod. Discard the split pin as a new one must be used.
7 Unscrew the two bolts securing the master cylinder to the bracket **(see illustration)**.

9.7 The master cylinder is secured by
two bolts (arrowed)

9.9 Hold the clevis with a pair of pliers and slacken the locknut

8 If required, unscrew the nut and remove the bolt securing the reservoir to the frame, then remove the reservoir with its hose.

Overhaul

9 If necessary, slacken the clevis locknut, then unscrew the clevis with its nut and locknut and remove them from the pushrod **(see illustration)**.

10 Dislodge the rubber dust boot from the base of the master cylinder to reveal the pushrod retaining circlip **(see illustrations)**.

11 Depress the pushrod and, using internal circlip pliers, remove the circlip **(see illustration)**. Slide out the piston assembly and spring. If they are difficult to remove, apply low pressure compressed air to the fluid outlet. Lay the parts out in the proper order to prevent confusion during reassembly.

12 Clean all of the parts with clean brake fluid or denatured alcohol.

Caution: Do not, under any circumstances, use a petroleum-based solvent to clean brake parts. If compressed air is available, use it to dry the parts thoroughly (make sure it's filtered and unlubricated).

13 Check the master cylinder bore for corrosion, scratches, nicks and score marks. If damage is evident, the master cylinder must be replaced with a new one. If the master cylinder is in poor condition, then the caliper should be checked as well.

14 If required, remove the fluid reservoir hose elbow circlip and detach the elbow from the master cylinder **(see illustration)**. Discard the

9.10a Rear brake master cylinder components

1 Split pin
2 Clevis pin
3 Master cylinder mounting bolt
4 Master cylinder
5 Circlip
6 Reservoir hose elbow
7 O-ring
8 Pushrod
9 Rubber dust boot
10 Circlip
11 Piston assembly
12 Spring
13 Hose clamp
14 Reservoir hose
15 Reservoir cap
16 Diaphragm plate
17 Rubber diaphragm
18 Reservoir
19 Reservoir mounting bolt
20 Banjo bolt
21 Sealing washer
22 Brake hose

O-ring as a new one must be used. Inspect the reservoir hose for cracks or splits and replace if necessary.

15 The piston assembly and spring are included in the rebuild kit. Use all of the new parts, regardless of the apparent condition of the old ones.

16 Install the spring in the master cylinder with its wider end first so that its tapered end faces the piston.

17 Lubricate the piston components with clean brake fluid and install the assembly into the master cylinder, ensuring all components are the correct way round **(see illustration)**. Ensure the cup seal lips do not turn inside out when they are slipped into the bore.

9.10b Remove the dust boot from the pushrod

9.11 Depress the pushrod and remove the circlip from the cylinder bore

9.14 Remove the circlip securing the reservoir hose elbow

9.17 Make sure the piston assembly is installed with the inner end (A) facing in, and the outer end (B) facing out

9.20 Use a new O-ring for the reservoir hose elbow

18 Install and depress the pushrod, then install a new circlip, making sure it is properly seated in the groove **(see illustration 9.11)**.

19 Install the rubber dust boot, making sure the lip is seated properly in the groove **(see illustration 9.10b)**.

20 If removed, fit a new O-ring into the fluid reservoir hose elbow socket **(see illustration)**, then install the elbow into the master cylinder and secure it with its circlip **(see illustration 9.14)**.

Installation

21 If removed, install the clevis locknut, the clevis and its nut onto the master cylinder pushrod end, but do not yet tighten the locknut.

22 Install the master cylinder onto the footrest bracket and tighten its mounting bolts to the torque setting specified at the beginning of the Chapter **(see illustration 9.7)**.

23 If removed, secure the fluid reservoir to the frame with its retaining bolt. Ensure that the hose is correctly routed, then connect it to

the elbow on the master cylinder and secure it with the clamp. Check that the hose is secure and clamped at the reservoir end as well. If the clamps have weakened, use new ones.

24 Connect the brake hose banjo bolt to the master cylinder, using a new sealing washer on each side of the banjo union. Ensure that the hose is positioned as noted on removal **(see illustrations 9.4a and b)** and tighten the banjo bolt to the specified torque setting.

25 Align the brake pedal with the master cylinder pushrod clevis, then slide in the clevis pin and secure it using a new split pin **(see illustration 9.6)**. If the clevis position on the pushrod was disturbed during overhaul, re-set the brake pedal to its specified height (see Chapter 1, Section 13).

26 Tighten the clevis locknut securely.

27 Fill the fluid reservoir to the upper level line with the specified brake fluid **(see illustration 9.5)** and bleed the system following the procedure in Section 11.

28 Check the operation of the brake carefully before riding the motorcycle.

10 Brake hoses and unions - inspection and replacement

Inspection

1 Brake hose condition should be checked regularly and the hoses replaced at the specified interval (see Chapter 1).

2 Twist and flex the rubber hoses while looking for cracks, bulges and seeping fluid **(see illustration)**. Check extra carefully around the areas where the hoses connect with the banjo fittings, as these are common areas for hose failure.

3 Inspect the metal banjo union fittings connected to the brake hoses. If the fittings are rusted, scratched or cracked, replace them.

Replacement

4 The brake hoses have banjo union fittings on each end **(see illustration)**. Cover the surrounding area with plenty of rags and

10.2 Flex the brake hoses and check for cracks, bulges and leaking fluid

10.4 Remove the banjo bolt and separate the hose from the caliper; there is a sealing washer on each side of the fitting

11.6a Brake caliper bleed valve

11.6b To bleed the brakes, you need a spanner, a short section of clear tubing, and a clear container half-filled with brake fluid

unscrew the banjo bolt on each end of the hose, noting its alignment. Free the hose from any clips or guides and remove the hose. Discard the sealing washers.

5 Position the new hose, making sure it isn't twisted or otherwise strained and that it is passed through any clips or guides, and abut the tab on the hose union with the lug on the component casting, where present. Otherwise align the hose as noted on removal. Install the banjo bolts, using new sealing washers on both sides of the unions, and tighten them to the torque setting specified at the beginning of this Chapter. Make sure they are correctly aligned and routed clear of all moving components.

6 Flush the old brake fluid from the system, refill with the recommended fluid (see *Daily (pre-ride) checks*) and bleed the air from the system (see Section 11). Check the operation of the brakes carefully before riding the motorcycle.

11 Brake system bleeding

1 Bleeding the brakes is simply the process of removing all the air bubbles from the brake fluid reservoirs, the hoses and the brake calipers. Bleeding is necessary whenever a brake system hydraulic connection is loosened, when a component or hose is replaced, or when the master cylinder or caliper is overhauled. Leaks in the system may also allow air to enter, but leaking brake fluid will reveal their presence and warn you of the need for repair.

2 To bleed the brakes, you will need some new, clean DOT 4 brake fluid, a length of clear vinyl or plastic tubing, a small container partially filled with clean brake fluid, some rags and a spanner to fit the brake caliper bleed valves.

3 Cover the fuel tank and other painted components to prevent damage in the event that brake fluid is spilled.

4 If bleeding the rear brake, remove the right-hand side panel for access to the fluid reservoir.

5 Remove the reservoir cap/cover, diaphragm plate and diaphragm and slowly pump the brake lever or pedal a few times, until no air bubbles can be seen floating up from the holes in the bottom of the reservoir. Doing this bleeds the air from the master cylinder end of the line. Loosely refit the reservoir cap/cover.

6 Pull the dust cap off the bleed valve **(see illustration)**. Attach one end of the clear vinyl or plastic tubing to the bleed valve and submerge the other end in the brake fluid in the container **(see illustration)**.

7 Remove the reservoir cap/cover and check the fluid level. Do not allow the fluid level to drop below the lower mark during the bleeding process.

8 Carefully pump the brake lever or pedal three or four times and hold it in (front) or down (rear) while opening the caliper bleed valve. When the valve is opened, brake fluid will flow out of the caliper into the clear tubing and the lever will move toward the handlebar or the pedal will move down.

9 Retighten the bleed valve, then release the brake lever or pedal gradually. Repeat the process until no air bubbles are visible in the brake fluid leaving the caliper and the lever or pedal is firm when applied. On completion, disconnect the bleeding equipment, then tighten the bleed valve to the torque setting specified at the beginning of the chapter and install the dust cap. In the case of the front brakes, always go on to bleed the other

> **HAYNES HiNT** *If it's not possible to produce a firm feel to the lever or pedal the fluid my be aerated. Let the brake fluid in the system stabilise for a few hours and then repeat the procedure when the tiny bubbles in the system have settled out.*

caliper, and on the 750 rear caliper, also bleed the system via the other bleed valve on the caliper.

10 Install the diaphragm and cap/cover assembly, wipe up any spilled brake fluid and check the entire system for leaks.

12 Wheels - inspection and repair

1 In order to carry out a proper inspection of the wheels, it is necessary to support the bike upright so that the wheel being inspected is raised off the ground. Position the motorcycle on its centre stand or an auxiliary stand. Clean the wheels thoroughly to remove mud and dirt that may interfere with the inspection procedure or mask defects. Make a general check of the wheels and tyres as described in Chapter 1.

2 Attach a dial gauge to the fork slider or the swingarm and position its stem against the side of the rim **(see illustration)**. Spin the

12.2 Check the wheel for radial (out-of-round) runout (A) and axial (side-to-side) runout (B)

wheel slowly and check the axial (side-to-side) runout of the rim. In order to accurately check radial (out of round) runout with the dial gauge, the wheel would have to be removed from the machine, and the tyre from the wheel. With the axle clamped in a vice and the dial gauge positioned on the top of the rim, the wheel can be rotated to check the runout.

3 An easier, though slightly less accurate, method is to attach a stiff wire pointer to the fork slider or the swingarm and position the end a fraction of an inch from the wheel (where the wheel and tyre join). If the wheel is true, the distance from the pointer to the rim will be constant as the wheel is rotated. **Note:** *If wheel runout is excessive, check the wheel bearings very carefully before replacing the wheel.*

4 The wheels should also be visually inspected for cracks, flat spots on the rim and other damage. On all cast alloy wheels, look very closely for dents in the area where the tyre bead contacts the rim. Dents in this area may prevent complete sealing of the tyre against the rim, which leads to deflation of the tyre over a period of time. If damage is evident, or if runout in either direction is excessive, the wheel will have to be replaced with a new one. Never attempt to repair a damaged cast alloy wheel.

5 On spoke wheel models, check for loose or broken spokes. Tapping the spokes with a screwdriver is the best guide to their tension. A loose spoke will make a dull flat note compared to a tight one. Loose spokes must be tightened by turning the nipple at the spoke end in an anti-clockwise direction. Always check for runout after altering the tension in any of the spokes. Small irregularities can be corrected by adjusting the spokes in the affected area, although a certain amount of practice is necessary to prevent over-correction. If the wheel runout continues to be excessive, take the wheel to a professional wheel builder for inspection and adjustment.

13 Wheels - alignment check

1 Misalignment of the wheels, which may be due to a cocked rear wheel or a bent frame or fork yokes, can cause strange and possibly serious handling problems. If the frame or yokes are at fault, repair by a frame specialist or replacement with new parts are the only alternatives.

2 To check the alignment you will need an assistant, a length of string or a perfectly straight piece of wood and a ruler. A plumb bob or other suitable weight will also be required.

3 In order to make a proper check of the wheels it is necessary to support the bike in an upright position, either on its centre stand or on an auxiliary stand. Measure the width of both tyres at their widest points. Subtract the smaller measurement from the larger measurement, then divide the difference by two. The result is the amount of offset that should exist between the front and rear tyres on both sides.

4 If a string is used, have your assistant hold one end of it about halfway between the floor and the rear axle, touching the rear sidewall of the tyre.

5 Run the other end of the string forward and pull it tight so that it is roughly parallel to the floor. Slowly bring the string into contact with the front sidewall of the rear tyre, then turn the front wheel until it is parallel with the string. Measure the distance from the front tyre sidewall to the string.

6 Repeat the procedure on the other side of the motorcycle. The distance from the front tyre sidewall to the string should be equal on both sides.

7 As was previously pointed out, a perfectly straight length of wood may be substituted for the string. The procedure is the same.

8 If the distance between the string and tyre is greater on one side, or if the rear wheel appears to be cocked, check that the drive chain adjuster alignment marks are the same on each side of the swingarm (see Chapter 1)..

9 If the front-to-back alignment is correct, the wheels still may be out of alignment vertically.

10 Using the plumb bob, or other suitable weight, and a length of string, check the rear wheel to make sure it is vertical. To do this, hold the string against the tyre upper sidewall and allow the weight to settle just off the floor. When the string touches both the upper and lower tyre sidewalls and is perfectly straight, the wheel is vertical. If it is not, place thin spacers under one leg of the stand.

11 Once the rear wheel is vertical, check the front wheel in the same manner. If both wheels are not perfectly vertical, the frame and/or major suspension components are bent.

14 Front wheel - removal and installation

Removal

1 Unscrew the knurled ring securing the speedometer cable to its drive housing on the left-hand side of the wheel hub, and detach the cable **(see illustration)**.

2 Remove the left-hand brake caliper mounting bolts and slide the caliper off the disc **(see illustration 3.2a)**. Support the caliper with a piece of wire or a bungee cord so that no strain is placed on its hydraulic hose. There is no need to disconnect the hose from the caliper.

3 Slacken the axle clamp bolt on the bottom of the right-hand side fork, then slacken the axle itself (right-hand end), while counter-holding the axle nut on the left-hand end **(see illustration)**.

14.1 Unscrew the knurled ring (arrowed) and detach the cable

14.3 Axle clamp bolt (A), axle (B)

14.5 Support the wheel and withdraw the axle

14.6a Remove the spacer . . .

14.6b . . . and the speedometer drive housing

14.13 Tighten the axle . . .

14.14 . . . and the axle clamp bolt to the specified torque setting

4 Position the motorcycle on its centre stand or on an auxiliary stand and support it under the crankcase so that the front wheel is off the ground. Always make sure the motorcycle is properly supported.

5 Support the wheel, then fully unscrew the axle and withdraw it from the right-hand side and carefully lower the wheel (see illustration).

6 Remove the wheel spacer from the right-hand side of the wheel, noting which way round it fits, and the speedometer drive housing from the left (see illustrations). Note: *Do not operate the front brake lever with the wheel removed.*

Caution: Don't lay the wheel down and allow it to rest on the disc - the disc could become warped. Set the wheel on wood blocks so the disc doesn't support the weight of the wheel.

7 Check the axle for straightness by rolling it on a flat surface such as a piece of plate glass (first wipe off all old grease and remove any corrosion using fine emery cloth). If the equipment is available, place the axle in V-blocks and measure the runout using a dial gauge. If the axle is bent or the runout exceeds the limit specified, replace it.

8 Check the condition of the wheel bearings and bearing seals (see Section 16).

Installation

9 Clean the speedometer drive components and apply grease to the drive gears. Fit the speedometer drive housing to the wheel's left-hand side, aligning its driven gear tabs with the slots in the drive unit in the hub (see illustration 14.6b).

10 Apply a smear of grease to the inside and ends of the wheel spacer and to the lips of the bearing seal in the hub, then fit the spacer into the wheel (see illustration 14.6a).

11 Manoeuvre the wheel into position. Apply a thin coat of grease to the axle.

12 Lift the wheel, making sure the spacer remains in place, and slide the axle into position from the right-hand side (see illustration 14.5). Align the speedometer drive housing so that its lug fits into the slot on the inside of the fork slider.

13 Counter-holding the axle nut on the left-hand end of the axle, tighten the axle to the torque setting specified at the beginning of the Chapter (see illustration).

14 Tighten the axle clamp bolt on the right-hand side fork to the specified torque setting (see illustration). If the axle nut clamp bolt was slackened, also tighten that to the specified torque setting.

15 Install the brake caliper, making sure the pads sit squarely on either side of the disc. Tighten the caliper mounting bolts to the torque setting specified at the beginning of the Chapter (see illustrations 3.13 and 3.14).

16 Pass the speedometer cable through its guides (if withdrawn), then connect the cable to the drive housing and securely tighten its knurled ring (see illustration).

17 Apply the front brake a few times to bring the pads back into contact with the discs. Move the motorcycle off its stand, apply the front brake and pump the front forks a few times to settle all components in position.

18 Check for correct operation of the front brake before riding the motorcycle.

15 Rear wheel -
removal and installation

Removal

1 Position the motorcycle on its centre stand or an auxiliary stand. Remove the chain guard (see Chapter 7).

14.16 Fit the speedometer cable into the drive housing

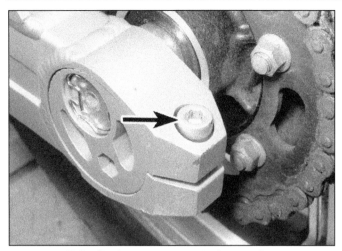

15.2a Slacken the clamp bolts (arrowed) . . .

15.2b . . . and turn the adjuster using an Allen key

15.3a Remove the retaining clip . . .

15.3b . . . and unscrew the axle nut

2 Slacken each chain adjuster clamp bolt, then rotate each adjuster using a 12 mm Allen key to provide the maximum amount of slack in the drive chain **(see illustrations)**. You will probably find that as you turn one adjuster the other adjuster turns as well. Make sure that each adjuster is in the same position relative to the cutout in each side of the swingarm, then retighten the clamp bolts.

3 Remove the retaining clip from the axle nut on the right-hand end of the axle **(see illustration)**. Unscrew the axle nut and remove the washer **(see illustration)**.

4 Remove the retaining clip from the left-hand end of the axle. Support the wheel then withdraw the axle from the left-hand side, then lower the wheel to the ground **(see illustration)**. Note how the axle passes through the spacer in the caliper mounting bracket. The brake torque arm should support the caliper assembly in position. If it doesn't, check that the torque arm nuts are tightened to the specified torque setting. Otherwise, support the assembly so that no strain is placed on the hose.

5 Disengage the chain from the sprocket and remove the wheel from the swingarm. Remove the spacers from both sides of the wheel, noting which way round they fit **(see illustrations)**. If required for safekeeping, also

15.4 Support the wheel and withdraw the axle

15.5a Remove the left-hand spacer . . .

15.5b . . . and the right-hand spacer from the wheel

15.9 Fit the spacer into the caliper bracket if removed

15.10a Engage the chain around the sprocket

15.10b Make sure the disc fits correctly between the brake pads

15.11 Tighten the axle nut to the specified torque setting

remove the spacer from the caliper bracket **(see illustration 15.9)**.
Caution: Do not lay the wheel down and allow it to rest on the disc or the sprocket - they could become warped. Set the wheel on wood blocks so the disc or the sprocket doesn't support the weight of the wheel. Do not operate the brake pedal with the wheel removed.
6 Check the axle for straightness by rolling it on a flat surface such as a piece of plate glass (if the axle is corroded, first remove the corrosion with fine emery cloth). If the equipment is available, place the axle in V-blocks and measure the runout using a dial gauge. If the axle is bent or the runout exceeds the limit specified at the beginning of the Chapter, replace it.
7 Check the condition of the wheel bearings and bearing seals (see Section 16).

Installation

8 Apply a thin coat of grease to the lips of each bearing seal, and also to the spacers.

Using a 12 mm Allen key in each of the chain adjusters, rotate them so that the axle hole is well forward in the swingarm (about 9 o'clock); ensure that the same adjuster mark aligns with the cutout on each side of the swingarm, then tighten the adjuster clamp bolts to the specified torque setting.
9 Install the spacers into the wheel **(see illustrations 15.5a and b)**. If removed, also fit the spacer into the brake caliper bracket **(see illustration)**. Manoeuvre the wheel so that it is in between the ends of the swingarm and apply a thin coat of grease to the axle.
10 Engage the drive chain with the sprocket and lift the wheel into position **(see illustration)**. Make sure the spacers remain correctly in place, and that the brake disc fits squarely into the caliper with the pads positioned correctly each side of the disc **(see illustration)**.
11 Install the axle from the left **(see illustration 15.4)**. Check that everything is correctly aligned, then fit the axle nut **(see**

illustration 15.3b) and tighten it to the specified torque setting, counter-holding the axle head on the other side of the wheel **(see illustration)**. Fit the retaining clips onto each end of the axle, making sure they fit correctly into their grooves **(see illustration 15.3a)**.
12 Adjust the chain slack as described in Chapter 1.
13 Operate the brake pedal several times to bring the pads into contact with the disc. Check the operation of the rear brake carefully before riding the bike.

16 Wheel bearings - removal, inspection and installation

Front wheel bearings

Note: *Always replace the wheel bearings in pairs. Never replace the bearings individually. Avoid using a high pressure cleaner on the wheel bearing area.*

16.1 Front wheel components

1	Axle nut	3	Circlip	5	Bearing	8	Spacer
2	Speedometer	4	Speedometer	6	Bearing spacer	9	Axle
	drive gear housing		drive	7	Grease seal		

1 Remove the wheel (see Section 14) **(see illustration)**.

2 Set the wheel on blocks so as not to allow the weight of the wheel to rest on the brake disc.

3 Using a flat-bladed screwdriver, remove the grease seal from the right-hand side of the wheel **(see illustration)**. Discard the seal if it is in any way damaged or deteriorated as a new one should be used. Kawasaki recommend using new ones as a matter of course. Using a pair of internal circlip pliers, remove the circlip securing the wheel bearing in the hub **(see illustration)**. Turn the wheel over and remove the circlip from the other side, then remove the speedometer drive **(see illustration)**.

4 Using a metal rod (preferably a brass drift punch) inserted through the centre of the left-hand bearing, tap evenly around the inner race of the right-hand bearing to drive it from the hub **(see illustrations)**. The bearing spacer will also come out.

5 Lay the wheel on its other side so that the remaining bearing faces down. Drive the bearing out of the wheel using the same technique as above.

 HAYNES HiNT *Refer to Tools and Workshop Tips in the Reference section for more information about bearings.*

6 If the bearings are of the unsealed type or are only sealed on one side, clean them with a high flash-point solvent (one which won't

16.3a Lever out the grease seal using a flat-bladed screwdriver . . .

16.3b . . . then remove the circlip on each side of the wheel . . .

16.3c . . . and remove the speedometer drive (arrowed)

16.4a Using a drift to knock out the bearings

16.4b Locate the drift as shown when driving out the bearing

16.9a Using a socket to drive in the bearings

16.9b Press in the grease seal

16.10a The tabs (A) on the speedometer drive locate
in the slots (B) in the wheel

16.10b Make sure the circlip is properly seated

leave any residue) and blow them dry with compressed air (don't let the bearings spin as you dry them). Apply a few drops of oil to the bearing. **Note:** *If the bearing is sealed on both sides don't attempt to clean it.*

7 Hold the outer race of the bearing and rotate the inner race - if the bearing doesn't turn smoothly, has rough spots or is noisy, replace it with a new one.

8 If the bearing is good and can be re-used, wash it in solvent once again and dry it, then pack the bearing with high melting-point grease. Kawasaki recommend that the bearings and circlips should be renewed if they are removed.

9 Thoroughly clean the hub area of the wheel. First install the right-hand bearing into its recess in the hub, with the marked or sealed side facing outwards. Using the old bearing (if new ones are being fitted), a bearing driver or a socket large enough to contact the outer race of the bearing, drive it in until it's completely seated **(see illustration)**. Fit the

circlip, making sure it is correctly seated in its groove **(see illustration 16.3b)**. Apply a smear of grease to the lips of the bearing seal, and press it into the right-hand side of the wheel using your fingers, a seal or bearing driver, a suitable socket or a flat piece of wood **(see illustration)**.

10 Turn the wheel over and install the bearing spacer. Drive the left-hand bearing into place as described above. Fit the speedometer drive into the hub, making sure the tabs on the drive locate in the slots in the hub, then fit the circlip, making sure it is correctly seated in its groove **(see illustrations)**.

11 Clean off all grease from the brake discs using acetone or brake system cleaner then install the wheel (see Section 14).

Rear wheel bearings

12 Remove the rear wheel (see Section 15). Lift the rear sprocket and sprocket coupling assembly out of the wheel, noting how it fits **(see illustrations)**.

13 Set the wheel on blocks so as not to allow the weight of the wheel to rest on the brake disc.

14 Using a flat-bladed screwdriver, prise out the grease seal from the right-hand side of the wheel **(see illustration 16.3a)**. Discard the seal if it is in any way damaged or deteriorated as a new one should be used. Kawasaki recommend using new ones as a matter of course. Using a pair of internal circlip pliers, remove the circlip securing the wheel bearing in the hub **(see illustration 16.3b)**.

15 Using a metal rod (preferably a brass drift punch) inserted through the centre of the right-hand bearing, tap evenly around the inner race of the left-hand bearing to drive it from the hub **(see illustrations 16.4a and b)**. The bearing spacer will also come out.

16 Lay the wheel on its other side so that the remaining bearing faces down. Drive the bearing out of the wheel using the same technique as above.

17 If the bearings are of the unsealed type or

16.12a Rear wheel
components

1 Retaining ring
2 Axle
3 Spacer (left)
4 Damper segments
5 Bearing
6 Bearing spacer
7 Circlip
8 Grease seal
9 Spacer (right)
10 Brake caliper
   bracket spacer
11 Washer
12 Axle nut

16.12b Lift the sprocket coupling out of
the wheel

Sprocket coupling bearing

23 Remove the rear wheel (see Section 15). Lift the sprocket and sprocket coupling assembly out of the wheel, noting how it fits **(see illustration 16.12b)**.
24 Remove the spacer from the inside of the coupling bearing, noting which way round it fits **(see illustrations)**. Using a flat-bladed screwdriver, prise out the grease seal from the outside of the coupling **(see illustration)**. If the seal appears stuck, make sure the tip of the screwdriver is not catching under the circlip. Discard the seal if it is in any way damaged or deteriorated as a new one should be used. Kawasaki recommend using new ones as a matter of course. Using a pair of internal circlip pliers, remove the circlip securing the wheel bearing in the hub **(see illustration)**.
25 Support the coupling on blocks of wood and drive the bearing out from the inside

are only sealed on one side, clean them with a high flash-point solvent (one which won't leave any residue) and blow them dry with compressed air (don't let the bearings spin as you dry them). Apply a few drops of oil to the bearing. **Note:** *If the bearing is sealed on both sides don't attempt to clean it.*
18 Hold the outer race of the bearing and rotate the inner race - if the bearing doesn't turn smoothly, has rough spots or is noisy, replace it with a new one.
19 If the bearing is good and can be re-used, wash it in solvent once again and dry it, then pack the bearing with high melting-point grease. Kawasaki recommend that the bearings and circlip should be renewed if they are removed.
20 Thoroughly clean the hub area of the wheel. First install the right-hand side bearing into its recess in the hub, with the marked or sealed side facing outwards. Using the old bearing (if new ones are being fitted), a bearing driver or a socket large enough to contact the outer race of the bearing, drive it in squarely until it's completely seated **(see illustration 16.9a)**. Fit the circlip, making sure it is correctly seated in its groove **(see illustration 16.3b)**. Apply a smear of grease to the lips of the bearing seal, and press it into the right-hand side of the wheel using your fingers, a seal or bearing driver, a suitable socket or a flat piece of wood **(see illustration 16.9b)**.
21 Turn the wheel over and install the bearing spacer. Drive the left-hand side bearing into place as described above.

22 Clean off all grease from the brake disc using acetone or brake system cleaner. Install the rear sprocket and sprocket coupling assembly onto the wheel, then install the wheel (see Section 15).

16.24a Sprocket coupling components

1 Grease seal   3 Bearing
2 Circlip   4 Spacer

16.24c Lever out the grease seal using a
flat-bladed screwdriver . . .

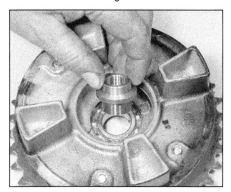

16.24b Remove the spacer from
inside the coupling

16.24d . . . then remove the circlip

16.25 Drive the bearing out from the inside

16.29a Drive the bearing in until seated

16.29b Install the circlip, then press in the grease seal

using a socket located on the bearing inner race **(see illustration)**. Do not remove the bearing unless a new one is being installed.

26 If the bearing is of the unsealed type or is only sealed on one side, clean it with a high flash-point solvent (one which won't leave any residue) and blow it dry with compressed air (don't let the bearing spin as you dry it). Apply a few drops of oil to the bearing. **Note:** *If the bearing is sealed on both sides don't attempt to clean it.*

27 Hold the outer race of the bearing and rotate the inner race - if the bearing doesn't turn smoothly, has rough spots or is noisy, replace it with a new one.

28 If the bearing is good and can be re-used, wash it in solvent once again and dry it, then pack the bearing with high melting-point grease. Kawasaki recommend that the bearing and circlip should be renewed if they are removed.

29 Thoroughly clean the bearing recess then install the bearing into the recess in the coupling, with the marked or sealed side facing out. Using the old bearing (if a new one is being fitted), a bearing driver or a socket large enough to contact the outer race of the bearing, drive it in until it is completely seated **(see illustration)**. Fit the circlip, making sure it is correctly seated in its groove **(see illustration 16.24d)**. Apply a smear of grease to the lips of the bearing seal, and press it into the right-hand side of the wheel using your fingers, a seal or bearing driver, a suitable socket or a flat piece of wood **(see illustration)**.

30 Install the spacer into the inside of the coupling, making sure it is the correct way round **(see illustration 16.24b)**. Install the sprocket coupling assembly onto the wheel **(see illustration 16.12b)**, then install the wheel (see Section 15).

17 Tyres - general information and fitting

General information

1 The cast wheels fitted to ZR550 and ZR750 C models are designed to take tubeless tyres only. The spoked wheels fitted to ZR750 D models use tubed tyres only.

2 Refer to the *Daily (pre-ride) checks* at the beginning of this manual for tyre maintenance.

Fitting new tyres

3 When selecting new tyres, refer to the tyre information label and the tyre options listed in the owners handbook. Ensure that front and rear tyre types are compatible, the correct size and correct speed rating; if necessary seek advice from a Kawasaki dealer or tyre fitting specialist **(see illustration)**.

17.3 Common tyre sidewall markings

4 It is recommended that tyres are only ever fitted by a motorcycle tyre specialist rather than attempted in the home workshop. This is particularly relevant in the case of tubeless tyres because the force required to break the seal between the wheel rim and tyre bead is substantial, and is usually beyond the capabilities of an individual working with normal tyre levers. Additionally, the specialist will be able to balance the wheels after tyre fitting.

5 In the case of tubeless tyres, note that punctured tyres can in some cases be repaired, but again, this should not be attempted in the home workshop. Kawasaki also recommend that a repaired tyre should not be used at speeds above 60 mph (100 kmh) for the first 24 hrs after the repair, and thereafter not above 110 mph (180 kmh). If a puncture occurs on a tubed tyre it is advisable to have a new inner tube fitted.

Chapter 7
Bodywork

Contents

Degrees of difficulty

Easy, suitable for novice with little experience		Fairly easy, suitable for beginner with some experience		Fairly difficult, suitable for competent DIY mechanic		Difficult, suitable for experienced DIY mechanic		Very difficult, suitable for expert DIY or professional	

---

1 General information

This Chapter covers the procedures necessary to remove and install the body parts. Since many service and repair operations on these motorcycles require the removal of the body parts, the procedures are grouped here and referred to from other Chapters.

In the case of damage to the body parts, it is usually necessary to remove the broken component and replace it with a new (or used) one. The material that the body panels are composed of doesn't lend itself to conventional repair techniques. There are however some shops that specialise in "plastic welding", so it may be worthwhile seeking the advice of one of these specialists before consigning an expensive component to the bin.

When attempting to remove any body panel, first study it closely, noting any fasteners and associated fittings, to be sure of returning everything to its correct place on installation. In some cases the aid of an assistant will be required when removing panels, to help avoid the risk of damage to paintwork. Once the evident fasteners have been removed, try to withdraw the panel as described but DO NOT FORCE IT - if it will not release, check that all fasteners have been removed and try again. Where a panel engages another by means of tabs, be careful not to break the tab or its mating slot or to damage the paintwork. Remember that a few moments of patience at this stage will save you a lot of money in replacing broken panels!

When installing a body panel, first study it closely, noting any fasteners and associated fittings removed with it, to be sure of returning everything to its correct place. Check that all fasteners are in good condition, including all trim nuts or clips and damping/rubber mounts; any of these must be replaced if faulty before the panel is reassembled. Check also that all mounting brackets are straight and repair or replace them if necessary before attempting to install the panel. Where assistance was required to remove a panel, make sure your assistant is on hand to install it.

Carefully settle the panel in place, following the instructions provided, and check that it engages correctly with its partners (where applicable) before tightening any of the fasteners. Where a panel engages another by means of tabs, be careful not to break the tab or its mating slot. Note that a small amount of lubricant (liquid soap or similar) applied to the mounting rubbers of the side panels will assist the panel retaining pegs to engage without the need for undue pressure.

Tighten the fasteners securely, but be careful not to overtighten any of them or the panel may break (not always immediately) due to the uneven stress.

2 Rear view mirrors - removal and installation

Removal

1 Unscrew the mirror using the lower nut on the base of the mirror mounting and remove it from the handlebar (see illustration).

Installation

2 Install the mirror into its mounting and screw it in until it is fully home and tight. To adjust the position of the mirror, counter-hold the lower nut and slacken the upper nut, then move the mirror until it is as required, then tighten the upper nut against the lower nut.

3 Seat - removal and installation

Removal

1 Insert the ignition key into the seat lock which is located under the left-hand side panel and turn it clockwise to unlock the seat (see illustration).

2.1 Unscrew the mirror using a spanner on the nut (arrowed)

3.1 Turn the key clockwise to unlock the seat

3.3 Locate the tab (arrowed) under the fuel tank

4.2 Each side panel is secured by three pegs (A)
which locate in the grommets (B)

2 Lift the rear of the seat and draw it back and away from the bike. Note how the tab at the front of the seat locates under the tank mounting bracket, and how the seat locates onto the locking rail.

Installation

3 Locate the tab at the front of the seat under the fuel tank mounting bracket (see illustration). Align the seat at the rear and push down on it to engage the latches.

4 Side panels -
removal and installation

Removal

1 Remove the seat (see Section 3).
2 Each side panel is secured by three pegs which are a press-fit into rubber grommets on the frame. Gently pull each panel away from the frame to release the pegs from the

grommets (see illustration). Do not force or bend the panel while removing it.

Installation

3 Installation is the reverse of removal.

 HAYNES HiNT *A smear of liquid soap applied to the mounting grommets will help the side panel and rear cover pegs engage without the need for undue pressure.*

5 Front mudguard -
removal and installation

Removal

1 Remove the front wheel for improved access, if required (see Chapter 6).
2 Carefully pull the press-fit brake hose

guides from the mudguard, where fitted (see illustration). Unscrew the four bolts securing the mudguard to the forks, noting the position of the brake hose and/or speedometer cable guide (see illustration). Carefully remove the mudguard from between the forks, noting how it fits.

Installation

3 Installation is the reverse of removal.

6 Chain guard -
removal and installation

Removal

1 Unscrew the three screws securing the chain guard to the swingarm and remove the guard, noting how it fits (see illustration).

Installation

2 Installation is the reverse of removal.

5.2a Pull the hose guides out of the mudguard

5.2b The mudguard is secured to each fork by two bolts

6.1 The chain guard is secured by three screws (arrowed)

7.2 The grab-rail is secured by two bolts (arrowed)

7.3a The rear cover is secured by two screws (arrowed) . . .

7.3b . . . and two pegs (A) which locate in the grommets (B)

7 Rear cover and grab-rail - removal and installation

Removal

1 Remove the seat (see Section 3).
2 On 750 models, remove the two bolts securing the passenger grab-rail, then remove the rail **(see illustration)**.

3 The rear cover is secured by two screws at the front ends, and by two pegs which are a press-fit into grommets on the top of the tail light assembly **(see illustrations)**. Remove the two screws, then carefully lift the cover off the tail light until the pegs are free.

Installation

4 Installation is the reverse of removal (see **Haynes Hint** on previous page).

Notes

Chapter 8
Electrical system

Contents

Degrees of difficulty

Easy, suitable for novice with little experience		Fairly easy, suitable for beginner with some experience		Fairly difficult, suitable for competent DIY mechanic		Difficult, suitable for experienced DIY mechanic		Very difficult, suitable for expert DIY or professional	

Specifications

Battery
Capacity
   ZR550 B1, B2, B3 and B4 models 12V, 12Ah
   All other models .... 12V, 10Ah MF (maintenance-free)
Electrolyte specific gravity - ZR550 B1, B2, B3 and B4 models ...... 1.280 at 20°C

Fuses
Main 30A
Headlight 10A
Tail light 10A
Turn signal (later models only) 10A
Ignition (later models only) 10A
Horn (later models only) 10A
Accessories
   ZR550 (all models), ZR750 C1, C2 (UK)
     and ZR750 C1 to C3 (US/Canada) 10A
   ZR750 C3, C4, C5, D1 (UK), ZR750 C4 (Canada) 15A

Bulbs
Headlight .... 60/55 W H4 halogen
Sidelight (UK only) 4W
Brake/taillight
   UK models 21/5W
   US models 27/8W
Turn signal lights
   UK models 21W
   US models 23/8W

Bulbs (continued)

Instrument lights - US ZR550 B1 and B2
 Speedometer and tachometer 3W
 Warning lights 3.4W
Instrument lights - all other models
 Speedometer 1.7W
 Tachometer and warning lights 3W

Fuel level sender

Resistance
 Fuel tank full .... 4 to 10 ohms
 Fuel tank empty .... 90 to 100 ohms

Carburettor heater system

Heater resistance .... 11 to 20 ohms
Atmospheric temperature sensor resistance
 Rising temperature .... from zero to infinite between 7 and 13°C
 Falling temperature .... from infinite to zero above 3°C
Oil temperature sensor resistance
 Rising temperature .... from zero to infinite between 37 and 43°C
 Falling temperature .... from infinite to zero above 33°C
Carburettor temperature sensor resistance
 at 9°C .... 2.9 K ohms
 at 10°C .... 2.2 to 5.2 K ohms
 at 12°C .... 3.0 to 7.2 K ohms
 at 25°C .... 43 K ohms

Starter motor

Brush length
 Standard .... 12.0 to 12.5 mm
 Service limit
  550 models .... 8.5 mm
  750 models .... 6.0 mm
Commutator diameter
 Standard .... 27.98 to 28.02 mm
 Service limit .... 27.0 mm

Alternator

Type .... Three phase ac
Rated current output
 550 models .... 17A at 10,000 rpm
 750 models .... 20A at 8000 rpm
Rated voltage output
 550 models .... min 45V at 4000 rpm
 750 models .... min 31V at 4000 rpm
Charging (regulated) voltage .... 14.0 to 15.0V
Stator coil resistance
 550 models .... 0.36 to 0.54 ohms
 750 models .... 0.05 to 0.70 ohms

Regulator/rectifier

Regulated voltage .... 14.0 to 15.0 V

Torque settings

Front brake master cylinder clamp bolts
 550 models .... 11 Nm
 750 models .... 8.8 Nm
Oil pressure switch .... 15 Nm
Neutral switch .... 15 Nm
Starter motor mounting bolts (750 models) .... 10 Nm
Alternator rotor bolt
 550 models .... 69 Nm
 750 models .... 125 Nm
Alternator stator bolts
 550 models .... 12 Nm
 750 models .... 8 Nm

1 General information

All models have a 12-volt electrical system. The components include a three-phase alternator unit and regulator/rectifier unit.

The regulator maintains the charging system output within the specified range to prevent overcharging, and the rectifier converts the ac (alternating current) output of the alternator to dc (direct current) to power the lights and other components and to charge the battery. The alternator rotor is mounted on the left-hand end of the crankshaft.

The starter motor is mounted on the crankcase behind the cylinders. The starting system includes the motor, the battery, the relay and the various wires and switches. If the engine stop switch and the ignition (main) switch are both in the "Run" or "On" position, the starter relay allows the starter motor to operate only if the transmission is in neutral (neutral switch on) or, if the transmission is in gear, if the clutch lever is pulled into the handlebar (clutch switch on) and the sidestand is up.

Note: *Keep in mind that electrical parts, once purchased, cannot be returned. To avoid any unnecessary expense, make very sure that the faulty component has been positively identified before buying a replacement part.*

2 Electrical fault finding

 Warning: To prevent the risk of short circuits, the ignition (main) switch must always be "OFF" and the battery negative (–) terminal should be disconnected before any of the bike's other electrical components are disturbed. Don't forget to reconnect the terminal securely once work is finished or if battery power is needed for circuit testing.

1 A typical electrical circuit consists of an electrical component, the switches, relays, etc. related to that component and the wiring and connectors that hook the component to both the battery and the frame. To aid in locating a problem in any electrical circuit, refer to the wiring diagrams at the end of this Chapter.

2 Before tackling any troublesome electrical circuit, first study the wiring diagram (see end of Chapter) thoroughly to get a complete picture of what makes up that individual circuit. Trouble spots, for instance, can often be narrowed down by noting if other components related to that circuit are operating properly or not. If several components or circuits fail at one time, chances are the fault lies in the fuse or earth connection, as several circuits often are routed through the same fuse and earth.

3 Electrical problems often stem from simple causes, such as loose or corroded connections or a blown fuse. Prior to any electrical fault finding, always visually check the condition of the fuse, wires and connections in the problem circuit. Intermittent failures can be especially frustrating, since you can't always duplicate the failure when it's convenient to test. In such situations, a good practice is to clean and check all of the connections in the affected circuit, whether or not they appear to be good. All of the connections and wires should also be wiggled to check for looseness which can cause intermittent failure.

4 If testing instruments are going to be utilised, use the wiring diagrams at the end of this Chapter to plan where you will make the necessary connections in order to accurately pinpoint the trouble spot.

5 The basic tools needed for electrical fault finding include a battery and bulb test circuit, a continuity tester, a test light, and a jumper wire. A multimeter capable of reading volts, ohms and amps is also very useful as an alternative to the above, and is necessary for performing more extensive tests and checks. Full details on the use of this test equipment are given in the *Fault Finding Equipment* section at the end of the manual.

3 Battery - removal, installation, inspection and maintenance

Caution: Be extremely careful when handling or working around the battery. The electrolyte is very caustic and an explosive gas (hydrogen) is given off when the battery is charging.

Removal and installation

1 Remove the seat (see Chapter 7). On 750 models, also remove the fuel tank and the tank bracket, then remove the two screws securing the air filter cover to the filter housing and lift off the cover (see Chapter 3) **(see illustration)**. On ZR550 B5 and B6 models, remove either of the side panels and unhook the rubber battery strap.

2 Unscrew the terminal screws and disconnect the leads from the battery, disconnecting the negative (–) terminal first, and noting that the positive (+) terminal has an insulating cover which must be pulled back **(see illustration)**. On ZR550 B1, B2, B3 and B4 models, disconnect the vent hose from the side of the battery. Unhook the rubber strap and lift the battery out of its box **(see illustrations)**.

3 On installation, clean the battery terminals and lead ends with a wire brush or knife and emery paper. Reconnect the leads, connecting the positive (+) terminal first, then

3.1 On 750 models, remove the air filter cover to access the battery

3.2a Pull back the insulating cover to access the positive (+) terminal

3.2b Unhook the strap . . .

3.2c . . . and remove the battery

fit the insulating cover over the positive (+) terminal **(see illustration 3.2a)**. On ZR550 B1, B2, B3 and B4 models, connect the vent hose to the side of the battery. Install the remaining components in a reverse of the removal procedure.

 HAYNES HiNT *Battery corrosion can be kept to a minimum by applying a layer of petroleum jelly to the terminals after the cables have been connected.*

Inspection and maintenance

4 The battery fitted to ZR550 B1, B2, B3 and B4 models is of the conventional lead/acid type, requiring regular checks of the electrolyte level (see Chapter 1) in addition to those detailed below. The battery fitted to all other models is of the maintenance-free (sealed) type, therefore requiring no regular checking/topping-up of the electrolyte level. However, the following checks should still be regularly performed.

5 Check the battery terminals and leads for tightness and corrosion. If corrosion is evident, unscrew the terminal screws and disconnect the leads from the battery, disconnecting the negative (–) terminal first, and clean the terminals and lead ends with a wire brush or knife and emery paper. Reconnect the leads, connecting the negative (–) terminal last, and apply a thin coat of petroleum jelly to the connections to slow further corrosion.

6 The battery case should be kept clean to prevent current leakage, which can discharge the battery over a period of time (especially when it sits unused). Wash the outside of the case with a solution of baking soda and water. Rinse the battery thoroughly, then dry it.

7 Look for cracks in the case and replace the battery if any are found. If acid has been spilled on the frame or battery holder, neutralise it with a baking soda and water solution, dry it thoroughly, then touch up any damaged paint. On ZR550 B1, B2, B3 and B4 models, make sure that the battery vent hose is routed correctly and is not kinked or pinched.

8 If the motorcycle sits unused for long periods of time, disconnect the cables from the battery terminals, negative (–) terminal first. Refer to Section 4 and charge the battery once every month to six weeks.

9 The condition of the battery can be assessed by measuring the voltage present at the battery terminals. Connect the voltmeter positive (+) probe to the battery positive (+) terminal and the negative (–) probe to the battery negative (–) terminal. When fully charged there should be more than 12.5 volts present. If the voltage falls below 12.0 volts the battery must be removed, disconnecting the negative (–) terminal first, and recharged as described below in Section 4.

4 Battery - charging

Caution: Be extremely careful when handling or working around the battery. The electrolyte is very caustic and an explosive gas (hydrogen) is given off when the battery is charging.

1 Remove the battery (see Section 3). Connect the charger to the battery, making sure that the positive (+) lead on the charger is connected to the positive (+) terminal on the battery, and the negative (–) lead is connected to the negative (–) terminal.

2 On ZR550 B1, B2, B3 and B4 models with a conventional battery, Kawasaki recommend that the battery is charged at a maximum rate of 1.2 amps for 10 hours. A specific gravity check can be made to determine when the battery is fully charged (refer to *Fault Finding Equipment* in the Reference section for details of specific gravity checks).

3 On all other models equipped with a sealed maintenance-free battery, Kawasaki recommend the battery is charged according to its current state. Use a multimeter set to dc volts to measure the voltage of the battery.

a) *If the voltage is 12.6 V or more, the battery does not need charging.*

b) *If the voltage is between 11.5 and 12.6 V, charge the battery at 1.2 A for between 10 and 5 hours, according to the voltage measured.*

c) *If the voltage is below 11.5 V, an initial high voltage input of about 25 V will be required for approximately five minutes before the battery will accept any charge. The charging current will drop, and the voltage should then be reduced until the charging current is as recommended. If the current does not drop, a new battery is required.*

4 Exceeding the figures can cause the battery to overheat, buckling the plates and rendering it useless. Few owners will have access to an expensive current-controlled charger, so if a normal domestic charger is used check that after a possible initial peak, the charge rate falls to a safe level **(see illustration)**. If the battery becomes hot during charging **stop**. Further charging will cause damage. On ZR550 B1, B2,

5.1 The junction box is under the seat

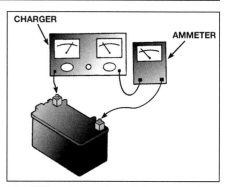

4.4 If the charger doesn't have ammeter built in, connect one in series as shown. DO NOT connect the ammeter between the battery terminals or it will be ruined

B3 and B4 models check the electrolyte level after charging and replenish if necessary (see Chapter 1). **Note:** *In emergencies the battery can be charged at a higher rate of around 4.0 or 5.0 amps for a period of 1 hour. However, this is not recommended and the low amp charge is by far the safer method of charging the battery.*

5 If the recharged battery discharges rapidly if left disconnected it is likely that an internal short caused by physical damage or sulphation has occurred. A new battery will be required. A sound item will tend to lose its charge at about 1% per day.

6 Install the battery (see Section 3).

7 If the motorcycle sits unused for long periods of time, charge the battery once every month to six weeks and leave it disconnected.

5 Fuses - check and replacement

1 The electrical system is protected by fuses of different ratings. All fuses are housed in the fusebox, which is located within the junction box under the seat **(see illustration)**. The junction box also contains the starter circuit relay and diode, and on US models the headlight relay, which should also be tested in the event of electrical problems (refer to Section 25).

2 To access the fuses, remove the seat (see Chapter 7) and unclip the fusebox lid **(see illustration)**.

5.2 Unclip the lid to access the fuses

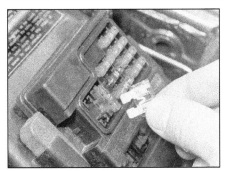

5.3a The fuses are a push fit

5.3b A blown fuse can be identified by a break in its element

5.5a Remove the junction box and disconnect the wiring connectors

10-Pin Connector   8-Pin Connector

Tester Connection	Tester Reading (Ω)
1 – 2	0
1 – 3 A/B	0
6 – 7	0
6 – 17	0
1 – 7	∞
8 – 17	∞

5.5b Fuse circuit testing - ZR550 B1 to B5 and ZR750 C1 to C4 models

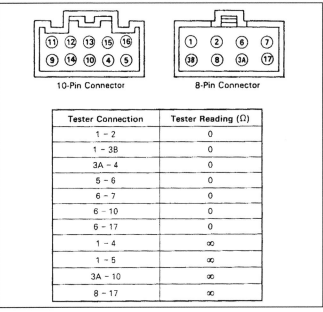

10-Pin Connector   8-Pin Connector

Tester Connection	Tester Reading (Ω)
1 – 2	0
1 – 3B	0
3A – 4	0
5 – 6	0
6 – 7	0
6 – 10	0
6 – 17	0
1 – 4	∞
1 – 5	∞
3A – 10	∞
8 – 17	∞

5.5c Fuse circuit testing - ZR550 B6, ZR750 C5 and D1 models

3 The fuses can be removed and checked visually. If you can't pull the fuse out with your fingertips, use a pair of needle-nose pliers **(see illustration)**. A blown fuse is easily identified by a break in the element **(see illustration)**. Each fuse is clearly marked with its rating and must only be replaced by a fuse of the correct rating. A spare fuse of each rating is housed in the fusebox. If a spare fuse is used, always replace it so that a spare of each rating is carried on the bike at all times. *Caution: Never put in a fuse of a higher rating or bridge the terminals with any other substitute, however temporary it may be. Serious damage may be done to the circuit, or a fire may start.*

4 If a fuse blows, be sure to check the wiring circuit very carefully for evidence of a short-circuit. Look for bare wires and chafed, melted or burned insulation. If the fuse is replaced before the cause is located, the new fuse will blow immediately.

5 Occasionally a fuse will blow or cause an open-circuit for no obvious reason. Corrosion of the fuse ends and fusebox terminals may

occur and cause poor fuse contact. If this happens, remove the corrosion with a wire brush or emery paper, then spray the fuse end and terminals with electrical contact cleaner. To determine whether any of the fusebox circuitry is faulty, slide the junction box out of its holder and disconnect the wiring connectors **(see illustration)**. Using the tables shown, check for continuity between the various terminals as indicated **(see illustrations)**.

6 Lighting system - check

1 The battery provides power for operation of the headlight, tail light, brake light and instrument cluster lights. If none of the lights operate, always check battery voltage before proceeding. Low battery voltage indicates either a faulty battery or a defective charging system. Refer to Section 3 for battery checks and Sections 32 and 33 for charging system tests. Also, check the condition of the fuses.

Headlight

2 If the headlight fails to work, first check the fuse with the ignition ON (see Section 5), and then the bulb (see Section 7). If they are both good, use jumper wires to connect the bulb directly to the battery terminals. If the light comes on, the problem lies in the wiring or one of the switches in the circuit. Refer to Section 20 for the switch testing procedures, and also the wiring diagrams at the end of this Chapter. On US models, a headlight relay is incorporated in the junction box circuitry, and there is no headlight switch incorporated in the handlebar switches. The headlight comes on automatically when the ignition is switched on and the engine is running, but will extinguish when the starter button is pressed. To check the headlight relay in the junction box, see Section 25.

Tail light

3 If the tail light fails to work, check the bulbs and the bulb terminals first, then the fuse, then check for battery voltage on the supply side of the tail light wiring connector. If

7.1a Remove the screw and its collar on each side of the headlight . . .

7.1b . . . and ease the rim out of the shell

voltage is present, check the earth (ground) circuit for an open or poor connection.

4 If no voltage is indicated, check the wiring between the tail light and the ignition switch, then check the switch. Also check the lighting switch on UK models.

Brake light

5 If the brake light fails to work, check the bulbs and the bulb terminals first, then the fuse, then check the brake light switch (see Section 14).

Neutral light

6 If the neutral light fails to operate when the transmission is in neutral, check the fuse and the bulb (see Sections 5 and 17). If they are in good condition, refer to Section 22 for the neutral switch check and replacement procedures.

Oil pressure warning light

7 If the oil pressure warning light fails to operate when the engine is not running, check the fuse and the bulb (see Sections 5 and 17). If they are in good condition, refer to Section 18 for the oil pressure switch check.

Instrument lights

8 See Section 17.

7 Headlight bulb and sidelight bulb - replacement

Note: *The headlight bulb is of the quartz-halogen type. Do not touch the bulb glass as skin acids will shorten the bulb's service life. If the bulb is accidentally touched, it should be wiped carefully when cold with a rag soaked in methylated spirit (stoddard solvent) and dried before fitting.*

 Warning: Allow the bulb time to cool before removing it if the headlight has just been on.

Headlight bulb

1 Remove the two screws securing the headlight rim to the headlight shell, and ease the rim out of the shell, noting how it fits **(see illustrations)**.

2 Disconnect the wiring connector and remove the rubber dust cover, noting how it fits **(see illustration)**.

3 Release the bulb retaining clip, noting how it fits, then remove the bulb **(see illustrations)**.

4 Fit the new bulb, bearing in mind the **Note** at the start of this Section. Ensure the tabs on the bulb fit correctly in the slots in the bulb housing, and secure it with the retaining clip.

7.2 Disconnect the headlight wiring connector and remove the rubber cover

7.3b . . . and remove the bulb

5 Install the dust cover, making sure it is correctly seated and with the TOP mark facing up, and connect the wiring connector **(see illustration)**.

6 Check the operation of the headlight, then install the rim into the shell and secure it with the screws **(see illustrations 7.1b and a)**.

Sidelight bulb

7 Remove the two screws securing the headlight rim to the headlight shell, and ease the rim out of the shell, noting how it fits **(see illustrations 7.1a and b)**.

7.3a Release the clip . . .

7.5 Fit the cover with the TOP mark uppermost

7.8a Pull the bulbholder out of the headlight . . .

7.8b . . . and remove the bulb

8 Pull the bulbholder out of its socket in the base of the headlight **(see illustration)**. Push the bulb down and twist it anti-clockwise to release it from the bulbholder **(see illustration)**.
9 Install the new bulb in the bulbholder, then install the bulbholder by pressing it in.
10 Check the operation of the sidelight, then install the headlight rim into the shell and secure it with the screws **(see illustrations 7.1b and a)**.

8 Headlight assembly - removal and installation

Removal

1 Remove the two screws securing the headlight rim to the headlight shell, and ease the rim out of the shell, noting how it fits **(see illustrations 7.1a and b)**.

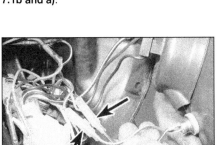

8.2 Disconnect the sidelight bulb wiring connectors (arrowed)

8.3a Remove the brake hose union bolts (arrowed) to release the headlight adjuster bracket

8.3b Unscrew the nuts and remove the bolts

8.4 The support frame is secured to the bottom yoke by a single bolt

2 Disconnect the wiring connectors from the headlight bulb **(see illustration 7.2)**, and the sidelight bulb **(see illustration)**.
3 To remove the headlight shell, first unscrew the bolts securing the brake hose union to the bottom yoke, thereby freeing the vertical beam adjuster **(see illustration)**. Free the wiring inside the shell from any clamps, then disconnect any wiring connectors necessary and ease the wiring out the back of the shell. Unscrew the nuts on the inside of the shell and remove the bolts securing the shell to the brackets and remove the shell **(see illustration)**.
4 If necessary, unscrew the bolts securing the brackets to the support frame and remove the brackets, with the turn signal assemblies attached or removed as required (Section 12). To remove the support frame, first remove the instrument cluster (see Section 15), then unscrew the bolt securing the frame to the bottom yoke and remove the frame, noting how it fits **(see illustration)**.

HAYNES HiNT *When disconnecting wiring, label the connectors to avoid confusion on reconnection.*

Installation

5 Installation is the reverse of removal. Make sure all the wiring is correctly connected and secured. Check the operation of the headlight and sidelight. Check the headlight aim (see Chapter 1).

9 Tail light bulbs - replacement

1 Unscrew the two screws securing the tail light lens and remove the lens **(see illustration)**.

9.1 The tail light lens is secured by two screws (arrowed)

2 Push the bulb in and twist it anti-clockwise to remove it **(see illustration)**. Check the socket terminals for corrosion and clean them if necessary. Line up the pins of the new bulb with the slots in the socket, then push the bulb in and turn it clockwise until it locks into place. **Note:** *The pins on the bulb are offset so it can only be installed one way. It is a good idea to use a paper towel or dry cloth when handling the new bulb to prevent injury if the bulb should break and to increase bulb life.*
3 Install the lens onto the tail light, making sure the sealing rubber is correctly seated, and secure it with the screws. Do not overtighten the lens screws as the lens is easily cracked.
4 Install the seat (see Chapter 7).

9.2 Push the bulb in and twist it anti-clockwise to remove it

10 Tail light assembly -
removal and installation

Removal

1 Remove the seat and the rear cover (see Chapter 7).
2 Trace the tail light wiring back from the tail light and disconnect it at the connector **(see illustration)**.
3 Unscrew the two nuts securing the tail light assembly and carefully remove it from the bike **(see illustration)**. Note the wiring clamp fitted with each nut.

Installation

4 Installation is the reverse of removal. Check the operation of the tail light and the brake light.

11 Turn signal bulbs -
replacement

1 Remove the two screws securing the lens to the turn signal assembly and remove the lens, noting which way round it fits **(see illustration)**. Remove the rubber gasket and check it for damage or deterioration. Replace it if necessary.
2 Push the bulb into the holder and twist it anti-clockwise to remove it **(see illustration)**. Check the socket terminals for corrosion and clean them if necessary. Line up the pins of the new bulb with the slots in the socket, then push the bulb in and turn it clockwise until it locks into place. **Note:** *It is a good idea to use a paper towel or dry cloth when handling the new bulb to prevent injury if the bulb should break and to increase bulb life.*
3 Install the lens back onto the cover, using a new gasket if required, and tighten the retaining screws **(see illustration)**. Take care not to overtighten the screws as the lens is easily cracked.

> **HAYNES HiNT** *If the socket contacts are dirty or corroded, scrape them clean and spray with electrical contact cleaner before a new bulb is installed.*

12 Turn signal assemblies -
removal and installation

Front

Removal

1 Remove the two screws securing the headlight rim to the headlight shell, and ease the rim out of the shell, noting how it fits **(see illustrations 7.1a and b)**.
2 Trace the turn signal wiring back from the turn signal and disconnect it at the connectors inside the headlight shell **(see illustration)**. Pull the wiring through to the turn signal mounting, noting its routing.

10.2 Disconnect the tail light wiring connector

10.3 The tail light assembly is secured by two nuts (arrowed)

11.1 The turn signal lens is secured by two screws (arrowed)

11.2 Push the bulb in and twist it anti-clockwise to remove it

11.3 Make sure the rubber gasket is properly seated when fitting the cover

12.2 The front turn signal wiring connectors are inside the headlight shell

12.3 The nut is on the inside of the headlight bracket

3 Unscrew the nut securing the turn signal assembly to the headlight bracket and carefully remove the assembly, taking care not to snag the wiring connectors as you draw them through the mounting hole **(see illustration)**.

Installation

4 Installation is the reverse of removal. Make sure the wiring is correctly routed and securely connected. Check the operation of the turn signals.

Rear

Removal

5 Remove the seat (see Chapter 7). Trace the turn signal wiring back from the turn signal and disconnect it at the connector **(see illustration)**. Pull the wiring through to the turn signal mounting, releasing it from any clips and noting its routing.
6 Unscrew the nut securing the turn signal assembly to the mudguard and carefully remove the assembly, taking care not to snag the wiring connectors as you draw them through the mounting hole **(see illustration)**.

Installation

7 Installation is the reverse of removal. Make sure the wiring is correctly routed and securely connected. Check the operation of the turn signals.

13 Turn signal circuit - check

1 The battery provides power for operation of the turn signal lights, so if they do not operate, always check the battery voltage first. Low battery voltage indicates either a faulty battery or a defective charging system. Refer to Section 3 for battery checks and Sections 32 and 33 for charging system tests. Also, check the fuse (see Section 5) and the switch (see Section 20).
2 Most turn signal problems are the result of a burned out bulb or corroded socket. This is especially true when the turn signals function properly in one direction, but fail to flash in the other direction. Check the bulbs and the sockets (see Section 11), and make sure that the bulbs are of the correct wattage.
3 If the bulbs and sockets are good, check the turn signal relay, which is mounted behind the left-hand side panel **(see illustration)**. Remove the side panel for access (see Chapter 7). Disconnect the relay wiring connector and check for voltage by connecting the positive (+) probe of a multimeter to the turn signal relay brown (early models) or orange/green (later models) wire, and the negative (–) probe to the

orange wire. With the ignition ON and the turn signal switch placed first to the right and then to the left side, there should be battery voltage in each case. Turn the ignition OFF when the check is complete. Also check for continuity between the relay terminals. There should be continuity (zero or close to zero resistance). If a resistance reading of more than a few ohms is shown, replace the relay.
4 If no power was present at the relay, check the wiring from the relay to the ignition (main) switch for continuity.
5 If power was present at the relay, using the appropriate wiring diagram at the end of this Chapter, check the wiring between the relay, turn signal switch and turn signal lights for continuity. If the wiring and switch are sound, replace the relay with a new one.

14 Brake light switches - check and replacement

Circuit check

1 Before checking any electrical circuit, check the bulb (see Section 9) and fuse (see Section 5).

12.5 Disconnect the turn signal wiring connectors

12.6 The nut (arrowed) is on the inside of the mudguard

13.3 The turn signal relay is behind the left-hand side panel

14.5 Disconnect the front brake switch wiring connectors (arrowed)

14.6 The switch is secured by a single screw (arrowed)

2 Using a multimeter or test light connected to a good earth (ground), check for voltage at the brake light switch wiring connector brown wire **(see illustration 14.5 or 14.8b)**. If there's no voltage present, check the wire between the switch and the ignition switch (see the *wiring diagrams* at the end of this Chapter).
3 If voltage is available, touch the probe of the test light to the other terminal (blue wire) of the switch, then pull the brake lever in or depress the brake pedal; the connector must be joined for this check. If no reading is obtained or the test light doesn't light up, replace the switch.
4 If a reading is obtained or the test light does light, check the wiring between the switch and the brake lights (see the *wiring diagrams* at the end of this Chapter).

Switch replacement

Front brake lever switch

5 Disconnect the wiring connectors from the switch **(see illustration)**.
6 Remove the single screw securing the switch to the bottom of the front brake master cylinder and remove the switch **(see illustration)**. It may be necessary to slacken the brake master cylinder lower clamp bolt and rotate the assembly on the handlebar until the screw is clear of the cables before it can be accessed with a screwdriver. If so, tighten the clamp bolt to the torque setting specified on completion.
7 Installation is the reverse of removal. The switch isn't adjustable.

Rear brake pedal switch

8 The switch is mounted on the inside of the frame above the master cylinder **(see illustration)**. Trace the wiring from the top of the switch and disconnect it at the wiring connector behind the right-hand side panel **(see illustration)**. Remove the side panel for access (see Chapter 7).
9 Detach the upper end of the switch spring from the switch, then unscrew the switch **(see illustration)**.
10 Installation is the reverse of removal. Make sure the brake light is activated just before the rear brake pedal takes effect. If adjustment is necessary, hold the switch and turn the adjusting nut on the switch body until the brake light is activated when required.

15 Instrument cluster and speedometer cable - removal and installation

Instrument cluster

Removal

1 Remove the two screws securing the headlight rim to the headlight shell, and ease the rim out of the shell, noting how it fits **(see illustrations 7.1a and b)**. Trace the wiring back from the instrument cluster and disconnect it at the connectors inside the headlight shell. Release the wiring from any clips or ties.
2 Unscrew the speedometer cable retaining ring from the back of the speedometer and detach the cable **(see illustration 15.5)**.
3 Unscrew the two nuts securing the instrument cluster to the underside of the top yoke and carefully remove the assembly from the yoke, taking care not to snag the wiring and noting its routing **(see illustration)**.

Installation

4 Installation is the reverse of removal. Make sure that the speedometer cable and wiring connectors are correctly routed and secured.

14.8a Rear brake light switch (arrowed)

14.8b Disconnect the wiring at the connector behind the right-hand side panel

14.9 Detach the spring from the switch

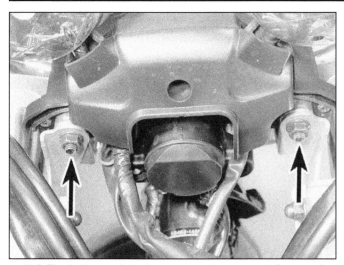

15.3 The instrument cluster is secured by two nuts (arrowed)

15.5 Unscrew the knurled ring securing the cable to the speedometer (arrowed) . . .

15.6 . . . and the drive housing (arrowed)

15.9 Make sure the inner cable locates correctly in the speedometer . . .

Speedometer cable

Removal

5 Unscrew the speedometer cable retaining ring from the rear of the instrument cluster and detach the cable **(see illustration)**.
6 Unscrew the retaining ring securing the lower end of the cable to the drive housing on the left-hand side of the front wheel **(see illustration)**.
7 Withdraw the cable from its guide(s) and remove it from the bike, noting its correct routing.

Installation

8 Route the cable correctly and install it in its retaining guide(s).
9 Connect the cable upper end to the instrument cluster and tighten the retaining ring securely **(see illustration)**.
10 Connect the cable lower end to the drive

housing and tighten the retaining ring securely **(see illustration)**.
11 Check that the cable doesn't restrict steering movement or interfere with any other components.

15.10 . . . and the drive housing

16 Instruments - check and replacement

Speedometer

Check

1 Special instruments are required to properly check the operation of this meter. If it is believed to be faulty, take the motorcycle to a Kawasaki dealer for assessment.

Replacement

2 Remove the instrument cluster (Section 15).
3 On US ZR550 B1 and B2 models, remove the screws securing the rear cover and remove the cover. Remove the nuts securing the mounting bracket and remove the bracket. Turn the odometer trip knob anti-

16.4a Remove the screw securing the rear cover

16.4b Speedometer mounting nut (A),
tachometer mounting nut (B)

clockwise and remove it from the front of the cluster. Remove the three screws on the back of the cluster which secure the front cover and remove the front cover. Remove the two screws securing the speedometer to the back cover and lift the speedometer out.

4 On all other models, remove the single screw securing the instrument cluster rear cover and remove the cover **(see illustration)**. Remove the nut securing the speedometer to the bracket and lift it off the bracket, noting how the small lug locates in the hole in the bracket **(see illustration)**. Unscrew the single screw securing the casing and withdraw the speedometer from the casing, then remove the bulbholders **(see illustrations 16.10a and b, and 17.1a)**.

5 Installation is the reverse of removal. Make sure the cable is correctly and securely connected.

Tachometer

Check

6 First check all the wiring in the tachometer circuit for faults (see the *wiring diagrams* at the end of this Chapter). If the wiring is all good, then the tachometer is probably faulty. Remove the fuel tank (see Chapter 3). Disconnect the

black wire from the primary circuit terminal on the ignition coil for nos. 1 and 4 cylinders. Turn the ignition switch ON. Connect an insulated jumper wire between the coil black wire and the positive (+) terminal of the battery. The tachometer needle should flick off its rest. If it doesn't. the tachometer is faulty.

7 Special instruments are required to properly check the operation of this meter. If it is believed to be faulty, take the motorcycle to a Kawasaki dealer for assessment.

Replacement

8 Remove the instrument cluster (Section 15). Disconnect the single wiring connector between the tachometer wiring and the warning light panel wiring.

9 On US ZR550 B1 and B2 models, remove the screws securing the rear cover and remove the cover. Remove the nuts securing the mounting bracket and remove the bracket. Turn the odometer trip knob anti-clockwise and remove it from the front of the cluster. Remove the tachometer wiring screws and detach the wires, carefully noting the position of each wire. Remove the three screws on the back of the cluster which secure the front cover and remove the front cover. Remove the screws securing the tachometer to the back cover and lift the tachometer out.

10 On all other models, remove the single screw securing the instrument cluster rear cover and remove the cover **(see illustration 16.4a)**. Remove the nut securing the tachometer to the bracket and lift it off the bracket, noting how the small lug locates in the hole in the bracket **(see illustration 16.4b)**. Unscrew the single screw securing the casing and withdraw the tachometer from the casing **(see illustrations)**. Remove the tachometer wiring screws and detach the wires, carefully noting the position of each wire. Also remove the bulbholders **(see illustration 17.1a)**.

11 Installation is the reverse of removal. Make sure the wires are correctly and securely connected.

Fuel gauge (all models except US ZR550 B1 and B2)

Check

12 Remove the seat (see Chapter 7). Trace the fuel level sender wiring from the underside of the fuel tank and disconnect it at the connector (remove the tank mounting bolts and raise the tank at the rear, or remove the tank for improved access if required - see Chapter 3) **(see illustration)**.

16.10a Remove the screw . . .

16.10b . . . and withdraw the instrument from the casing

16.12 Disconnect the fuel level sender wiring connector (arrowed)

17.1a Remove the bulbholder from the instrument . . .

17.1b . . . and pull the bulb from the holder

13 Connect an insulated jumper wire between the white/yellow and black/yellow terminals on the wiring loom side of the connector. With the ignition switched ON, the fuel gauge should read F (full), and with the ignition switched OFF it should read E (empty). If it doesn't, check the wiring between the connector and the gauge, and check for voltage at the brown wire on the back of the fuel gauge. If the wiring is good, then the gauge is faulty.

14 If the gauge reads correctly when tested, check the fuel level sender inside the fuel tank (see Section 26).

Replacement

15 The fuel gauge is integral with the tachometer. Refer to the tachometer replacement procedure above. If the fuel gauge is faulty, the entire tachometer must be replaced.

17 Instrument and warning light bulbs - replacement

Instrument bulbs

1 To replace the instrument illumination bulbs, remove the relevant instrument (see Section 16). Gently pull the bulbholder out of the instrument, then pull the bulb out of the bulbholder **(see illustrations)**. Carefully push the new bulb into the holder and the holder into the instrument, then install the instrument back into the casing or the casing onto the instrument (see Section 16).

Warning bulbs

2 To replace the warning light bulbs on US ZR550 B1 and B2 models, remove the instrument cluster (see Section 15), then remove the rear cover. Pull the relevant bulbholder out of the back of the panel. Gently pull the bulb out of the bulbholder. Carefully push the new bulb into position,

then push the bulbholder back into the rear of the panel.

3 To replace the warning light bulbs on all other models, remove the instrument cluster (see Section 15), then remove the single screw securing the rear cover **(see illustration 16.4a)**. Remove the three small screws securing the warning light panel to the cluster, then separate the panel, noting how the small lugs fit into the holes **(see illustrations)**. Pull the relevant bulbholder out of the back of panel, then gently pull the bulb out of the bulbholder **(see illustrations)**. Carefully push the new bulb into position, then push the bulbholder back into the rear of the panel.

18 Oil pressure switch - check, removal and installation

Check

1 The oil pressure warning light should come on when the ignition (main) switch is turned ON and extinguish a few seconds after the engine is started. If the oil pressure light comes on whilst the engine is running, stop the engine immediately and carry out an oil pressure check as described in Chapter 1.

2 If the oil pressure warning light does not

17.3a Remove the screws (arrowed) . . .

17.3b . . . and lift the panel off the cluster

17.3c Remove the bulbholder from the panel . . .

17.3d . . . and the bulb from the holder

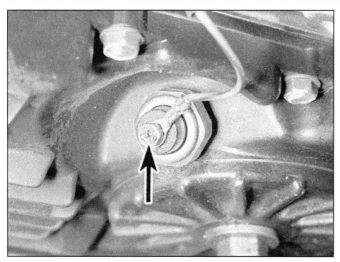

18.8 Oil pressure switch - 550 models except B4

19.8 The switch is secured by two Torx bolts (arrowed)

come on when the ignition is turned on, check the bulb (see Section 17) and fuse (see Section 5).

3 The oil pressure switch is screwed into the sump near the oil filter cover on all 550 models except UK B4 models **(see illustration 18.8)**, and into the right-hand side of the crankcase below the pulse generator assembly on 750 models and UK 550 B4 models - remove the pulse generator assembly cover for access. Remove the screw (where fitted) and detach the wiring connector from the switch. With the ignition switched ON, earth (ground) the wire on the crankcase and check that the warning light comes on. If the light comes on, the switch is defective and must be replaced.

4 If the light still does not come on, check for voltage at the wire terminal using a test light with the ignition switched ON. If there is no voltage present, check the wire between the switch, the instrument cluster and fusebox for continuity (see the *wiring diagrams* at the end of this Chapter).

5 If the warning light comes on whilst the engine is running, yet the oil pressure is satisfactory, remove the wire from the oil pressure switch. With the wire detached and the ignition switched ON the light should be out. If it is illuminated, the wire between the switch and instrument cluster must be earthed (grounded) at some point. If the wiring is good, the switch must be assumed faulty and replaced.

Removal

6 Drain the engine oil (see Chapter 1).

7 The oil pressure switch is screwed into the sump near the oil filter cover on all 550 models except UK B4 models, and into the right-hand side of the crankcase below the pulse generator assembly on 750 models and UK ZR550 B4 models - remove the pulse generator assembly cover for access. Discard the gasket as a new one must be used.

8 Detach the wiring connector from the switch **(see illustration)**.

9 Unscrew the oil pressure switch and withdraw it from the sump or crankcase.

Installation

10 Apply a suitable silicone sealant (Kawasaki Bond or equivalent) to the threads of the switch, then install it in the crankcase and tighten it to the torque setting specified at the beginning of the Chapter.

11 On 750 models and UK ZR550 B4 models, install the pulse generator assembly cover using a new gasket and tighten the bolts securely.

12 Fill the engine with the correct type and quantity of oil as described in Chapter 1.

19 Ignition (main) switch - check, removal and installation

Note: *To prevent the risk of short circuits, disconnect the battery negative (–) lead before making any ignition (main) switch checks.*

Check

1 Remove the two screws securing the headlight rim to the headlight shell, and ease the rim out of the shell **(see illustrations 7.1a and b)**. Trace the ignition (main) switch wiring back from the base of the switch and disconnect it at the connector in the headlight shell.

2 Using an ohmmeter or a continuity tester, check the continuity of the connector terminal pairs (see the *wiring diagrams* at the end of this Chapter). Continuity should exist between the terminals connected by a solid line on the diagram when the switch is in the indicated position.

3 If the switch fails any of the tests, replace it.

Removal

4 Remove the instrument cluster (Section 15).

5 Remove the handlebars (see Chapter 5).

6 Trace the ignition switch wiring and disconnect it at the connector (see Step 1).

7 Slacken the fork clamp bolts in the top yoke, then remove the steering stem bolt and washer. Lift the top yoke off the steering stem.

8 Remove the two Torx-head bolts to free the ignition switch from the top yoke **(see illustration)**. In the event that special security bolts have been used, which have shear-off heads, their heads must be drilled off.

Installation

9 Install the switch onto the top yoke. Using new special Torx bolts, tighten them until either the tool slips round on the bolt head, or until the bolt head sheers off.

10 The remainder of installation is the reverse of removal. Tighten the steering stem bolt and the fork clamp bolts in the top yoke to the torque settings specified at the beginning of Chapter 5. Make sure all wiring is correctly connected and secured by any clips or ties.

20 Handlebar switches - check

1 Generally speaking, the switches are reliable and trouble-free. Most troubles, when they do occur, are caused by dirty or corroded contacts, but wear and breakage of internal parts is a possibility that should not be overlooked. If breakage does occur, the entire switch and related wiring harness will have to be replaced with a new one, since individual parts are not available.

2 The switches can be checked for continuity using an ohmmeter or a continuity test light. Always disconnect the battery negative (–) cable, which will prevent the possibility of a short circuit, before making the checks.

3 Trace the wiring harness of the switch in question back to its connectors and

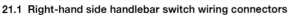

21.1 Right-hand side handlebar switch wiring connectors

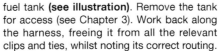

21.5 Left-hand side handlebar switch wiring connectors

disconnect them. The connectors located below the fuel tank. Remove the tank for access (see Chapter 3).

4 Using the ohmmeter or test light, check for continuity between the terminals of the switch harness with the switch in the various positions (ie switch off - no continuity, switch on - continuity) (see the *wiring diagrams* at the end of this Chapter).

5 If the continuity check indicates a problem exists, refer to Section 21, remove the switch and spray the switch contacts with electrical contact cleaner. If they are accessible, the contacts can be scraped clean with a knife or polished with crocus cloth. If switch components are damaged or broken, it will be obvious when the switch is disassembled.

21 Handlebar switches - removal and installation

Right-hand handlebar switch

Removal

1 If the switch is to be removed from the bike, rather than just displaced from the handlebar, trace the wiring harness back from the switch to the wiring connectors and disconnect them. The connectors are located below the

fuel tank **(see illustration)**. Remove the tank for access (see Chapter 3). Work back along the harness, freeing it from all the relevant clips and ties, whilst noting its correct routing.

2 Disconnect the two wires from the brake light switch **(see illustration 14.5)**.

3 Remove the throttle cables from the switch (see Chapter 3 - this procedure incorporates switch removal).

Installation

4 Installation is the reverse of removal. Make sure the locating pin in the front half of the switch fits into hole in the front of the handlebar. Refer to Chapter 3 for installation of the throttle cables.

Left-hand handlebar switch

Removal

5 If the switch is to be removed from the bike, rather than just displaced from the handlebar, trace the wiring harness back from the switch to the wiring connectors and disconnect them; the connectors are located below the fuel tank **(see illustration)**. Remove the tank for access (see Chapter 3). Work back along the harness, freeing it from all the relevant clips and ties, whilst noting its correct routing.

6 Disconnect the clutch switch wiring connector **(see illustration 24.2)**.

7 Remove the choke cable from the switch (see Chapter 3 - this procedure incorporates switch removal).

Installation

8 Installation is the reverse of removal. Make sure the locating pin in the front half of the switch fits into hole in the front of the handlebar. Refer to Chapter 3 for installation of the choke cable.

22 Neutral switch - check, removal and installation

Check

1 Before checking the electrical circuit, check the bulb (see Section 17) and fuse (see Section 5).

2 The switch is located in the left-hand side of the crankcase, behind the engine sprocket cover. Unscrew the gearchange linkage arm pinch bolt and remove the arm from the shaft, noting any alignment marks **(see illustration)**. If no marks are visible, make your own before removing the arm so that it can be correctly aligned with the shaft on installation. Unscrew the bolts securing the engine sprocket cover to the crankcase and remove the cover **(see illustrations)**. Detach the wiring connector

22.2a Remove the pinch bolt and slide the arm off the shaft

22.2b Engine sprocket cover bolts (arrowed) - 550 models

22.2c Engine sprocket cover bolts (arrowed) - 750 models

22.7 Disconnect the neutral switch wiring connector

23.2 Disconnect the sidestand switch wiring connector

from the neutral switch **(see illustration 22.7)**. Make sure the transmission is in neutral.

3 With the connector disconnected and the ignition switched ON, the neutral light should be out. If not, the wire between the connector and instrument cluster must be earthed (grounded) at some point.

4 Using an ohmmeter or continuity tester, check for continuity between the switch and the crankcase. With the transmission in neutral, there should be continuity. With the transmission in gear, there should be no continuity. If the tests prove otherwise, then either the switch is faulty or the neutral pin has been incorrectly installed in the selector drum (this is only likely if the gearchange selector drum pin holder plate has been removed).

5 If the continuity tests prove the switch is good, switch the ignition ON and check for voltage at the wire terminal using a test light. If there's no voltage present, check the wire between the switch, the instrument cluster and fusebox (see the *wiring diagrams* at the end of this Chapter). If the wiring is all good, remove the selector drum pin holder plate (see Chapter 2, Section 20) and check that the longer neutral pin is correctly positioned in the drum, and that the pin fits into the correct hole in the holder plate. With the transmission in neutral, the pin should align with the contact on the neutral switch.

Removal

6 Unscrew the gearchange linkage arm pinch bolt and remove the arm from the shaft, noting any alignment marks **(see illustration 22.2a)**. If no marks are visible, make your own before removing the arm so that it can be correctly aligned with the shaft on installation. Unscrew the engine sprocket cover bolts, and remove the cover **(see illustrations 22.2b and c)**.

7 Detach the wiring connector from the neutral switch **(see illustration)**. Make sure the transmission is in neutral.

8 Unscrew the switch and remove it.

Installation

9 Install the switch and tighten it to the specified torque.

10 Reconnect the switch wiring connector **(see illustration 22.7)**.

11 Check the operation of the neutral light.

12 Install the sprocket cover and the gearchange linkage arm, aligning the marks made on removal.

23 Sidestand switch -
check and replacement

Check

1 The sidestand switch is mounted on the frame just ahead of the sidestand pivot **(see illustration 23.8)**. The switch is part of the safety circuit which prevents or stops the engine running if the transmission is in gear whilst the sidestand is down, and prevents the engine from starting if the transmission is in gear unless the sidestand is up, and unless the clutch is pulled in. Before checking the electrical circuit, check the fuse (see Section 5).

2 Unscrew the gearchange linkage arm pinch bolt and remove the arm from the shaft, noting any alignment marks **(see illustration 22.2a)**. If no marks are visible, make your own before removing the arm so that it can be correctly aligned with the shaft on installation. Unscrew the bolts securing the engine sprocket cover to the crankcase and remove the cover **(see illustrations 22.2b or c)**. Trace the wiring back from the switch to its connector and disconnect it **(see illustration)**.

3 Check the operation of the switch using an ohmmeter or continuity test light. Connect the meter to the green/white and black/yellow wires on the switch side of the connector. With the sidestand up there should be continuity (zero resistance) between the terminals, and with the stand down there should be no continuity (infinite resistance).

4 If the switch does not perform as expected, it is defective and must be replaced.

5 If the switch is good, check the junction box and other components in the starter circuit as described in the relevant sections of this

Chapter. If all components are good, check the wiring between the various components (see the *wiring diagrams* at the end of this book).

> **HAYNES HiNT** *Sidestand switch troubles may be caused by a sticking switch plunger due to the ingress of road dirt - peel back the rubber gaiter and spray the plunger with a water dispersant aerosol.*

Replacement

6 The sidestand switch is mounted on the frame just ahead of the sidestand pivot. Unscrew the gearchange linkage arm pinch bolt and remove the arm from the shaft, noting any alignment marks **(see illustration 22.2a)**. If no marks are visible, make your own before removing the arm so that it can be correctly aligned with the shaft on installation. Unscrew the bolts securing the engine sprocket cover to the crankcase and remove the cover **(see illustrations 22.2b or c)**.

7 Trace the wiring back from the switch to its connector and disconnect it **(see illustration 23.2)**. Work back along the switch wiring, freeing it from any relevant retaining clips and ties, noting its correct routing.

8 Unscrew the two bolts securing the switch to the frame **(see illustration)**.

23.8 The sidestand switch is secured by two bolts (arrowed)

24.2 Disconnect the clutch switch wiring connector (arrowed)

9 Fit the new switch to the frame and install the retaining screws, tightening them securely.

10 Make sure the wiring is correctly routed up to the connector and retained by all the necessary clips and ties.

11 Reconnect the wiring connector and check the operation of the sidestand switch.

24 Clutch switch - check and replacement

Check

1 The clutch switch is situated on the base of the clutch lever bracket. The switch is part of the safety circuit which prevents or stops the engine running if the transmission is in gear whilst the sidestand is down, and prevents the engine from starting if the transmission is in gear unless the sidestand is up, and unless the clutch is pulled in.

2 To check the switch, disconnect the wiring connector from the switch **(see illustration)**. Connect the probes of an ohmmeter or a continuity test light to the black and black/yellow wire terminals on the switch. With the clutch lever pulled in, there should be continuity (zero resistance). With the clutch lever out, there should be no continuity (infinite resistance). Now connect the meter probes between the black and black/red wire terminals on the switch. With the clutch lever pulled in, there should be no continuity (infinite resistance). With the clutch lever out, there should be continuity (no resistance).

3 If the switch is good, check the junction box and other components in the starter circuit as described in the relevant sections of this Chapter. If all components are good, check the wiring between the various components (see the *wiring diagrams* at the end of this book).

Replacement

4 Disconnect the wiring connector from the clutch switch **(see illustration 24.2)**. Unscrew the two screws securing the switch to the bottom of the clutch lever bracket and remove the switch.

5 Installation is the reverse of removal. The switch isn't adjustable.

25 Junction box - check and replacement

25.2 Remove the junction box and disconnect the wiring connectors

Check

1 Remove the seat (see Chapter 7).

2 The junction box contains the starter circuit relay, the diodes, and on US models the headlight relay, as well as the fusebox. The starter circuit relay and diodes are part of the safety circuit which prevents or stops the engine running if the transmission is in gear whilst the sidestand is down, and prevents the engine from starting if the transmission is in gear unless the sidestand is up, and unless the clutch is pulled in. Slide the junction box out of its holder and disconnect the wiring connectors **(see illustration)**.

3 Using an ohmmeter or continuity tester and a 12 V battery with auxiliary leads, connect the meter probes and the battery leads (when specified) to the relay terminals on the junction box connectors as indicated **(see illustrations)**. Use an ohmmeter or continuity tester to check the diodes. If the results achieved after all terminal pairs have been tested as indicated do not agree with the results specified in the tables, the junction box is probably faulty - have your findings confirmed by a Kawasaki dealer before buying a replacement.

Relay Inspection (with the battery connected)

	Meter Connection	Battery Connection + −	Meter Reading (Ω)
Headlight Relay	*7 –8	*9 – 13	0
Starter Circuit Relay	11 – 13	11 – 12	0

(*) : U.S. and Canadian Models only

Relay Inspection (with the battery disconnected)

	Meter Connection	Meter Reading (Ω)
Headlight Relay	*7 – 8	∞
	*7 – 13	∞
Starter Circuit Relay	11 – 13	∞
	12 – 13	∞

25.3a Junction box tests - ZR550 B1 to B5 and ZR750 C1 to C4 models

Diode checks	8 to 13 (US/Canada only)	15 to 14
	9 to 13 (US/Canada only)	12 to 14	16 to 14

When testing diodes, the resistance reading should be low in one direction (continuity) and ten times as high (no continuity) when the meter probes are reversed. A diode which indicates high or low readings in each direction has failed.

10-Pin Connector

8-Pin Connector

Relay Inspection (with the battery connected)

	Meter Connection	Battery Connection +	Battery Connection −	Meter Reading (Ω)
Headlight Relay	*7 –8	*9	13	0
Starter Circuit Relay	11 – 13	11	12	0

(*) : U.S. and Canadian Models only

Relay Inspection (with the battery disconnected)

	Meter Connection	Meter Reading (Ω)
Headlight Relay	*7 – 8	∞
	*7 – 13	∞
Starter Circuit Relay	11 – 13	∞
	12 – 13	∞

25.3b Junction box tests - ZR550 B6, ZR750 C5 and D1 models

Diode checks

9 to 13 (US/Canada only)	8 to 13 (US/Canada only) 15 to 14
	12 to 14 16 to 14

When testing diodes, the resistance reading should be low in one direction (continuity) and ten times as high (no continuity) when the meter probes are reversed. A diode which indicates high or low readings in each direction has failed.

4 If the junction box is good, check the other components in the starter circuit as described in the relevant sections of this Chapter. If all the components are satisfactory, check the wiring between the various components (refer to the *wiring diagrams* at the end of this Chapter).

Replacement

5 Remove the seat (see Chapter 7).
6 Slide the junction box out of its holder and disconnect the wiring connectors **(see illustration 25.2)**. Install the new box and make sure the connectors are secure.
7 Install the seat (see Chapter 7).

26 Fuel level sender - check and replacement

> **Warning: Petrol (gasoline) is extremely flammable, so take extra precautions when you work on any part of the fuel system. Don't smoke or allow open flames or bare light bulbs near the work area, and don't work in a garage where a natural gas-type appliance is present. If you spill any fuel on your skin, rinse it off immediately with soap and water. When you perform any kind of work on the fuel system, wear safety glasses and have a fire extinguisher suitable for a class B type fire (flammable liquids) on hand.**

Check

1 Remove the seat (see Chapter 7). Trace the fuel level sender wiring from the underside of the fuel tank and disconnect it at the connector (remove the tank mounting bolts and raise the tank at the rear, or remove the tank for improved access if required - see Chapter 3) **(see illustration 16.12)**.
2 Using an ohmmeter set to ohms x 100 scale, connect the probes to the terminals on the sender side of the connector. Check the resistance reading with the tank empty and full. Compare the readings with those listed in the specifications at the beginning of the Chapter. Alternatively, remove the sender from the tank (see Steps 4 and 5 below) and, with the meter connected as above, manually move the float up and down to emulate the different positions **(see illustrations)**.
3 If the readings taken differ to those listed in the specifications, replace the sender.

Replacement

4 Drain and remove the fuel tank (see Chapter 3).
5 Prise off the sender cover using a flat-bladed screwdriver **(see illustration)**. Unscrew the bolts securing the sender to the base of the tank and withdraw it **(see illustration)**. Discard the gasket as a new one must be used.
6 Install the sender by reversing the removal process, using a new gasket **(see illustration)**.

26.2a Fuel level sender testing - FULL position

26.2b Fuel level sender testing - EMPTY position

26.5a Prise off the cover . . .

26.5b . . . then unscrew the bolts . . .   **26.5c . . . and withdraw the sender**   **26.6 Use a new gasket on installation**

**27.3a Atmospheric temperature sensor (arrowed)
and its wiring connector**

27.3b Carburettor temperature sensor (arrowed)

27 Carburettor heater system (UK later models only) - check and replacement

Check

1 The carburettor heater system fitted to UK ZR550 B4, B5 and B6 models, and to UK ZR750 C3, C4, C5 and D1 models incorporates a heater unit in each carburettor body, an atmospheric temperature sensor in the air filter housing and a relay. The ZR750 C3 and C4 models also have an oil temperature sensor and relay, and ZR550 B5 and B6 and ZR750 C5 and D1 models have a carburettor temperature sensor and a system control unit.

Heater unit

2 To check the heater unit in the carburettor, disconnect the wiring connector from the heater being tested and the black/yellow wire from the earth terminal. Using a multimeter set to the ohms x 10 scale, touch the positive (+) probe to the heater terminal and the negative (–) probe to the earth terminal on the carburettor body. If the reading obtained is not within the range specified at the beginning of the Chapter, replace the heater. Repeat the check for the remaining heaters.

Sensors

3 To check the atmospheric temperature sensor, the oil temperature sensor and the carburettor temperature sensor, disconnect the wiring connector and unscrew the sensor. The atmospheric temperature sensor is threaded into the front of the air filter housing **(see illustration)**, the oil temperature sensor is threaded into the crankcase below the pulse generator assembly cover, and the carburettor temperature sensor is threaded into the no. 2 carburettor in place of one of the joining bracket screws **(see illustration)**.
4 Fill a small heatproof container with water (for the atmospheric and carburettor sensors) or oil (for the oil temperature sensor) and place it on a stove. Using an ohmmeter, connect the positive (+) probe of the meter to the terminal on the sensor, and the negative (–) probe to the body of the sensor. Using some wire or other support suspend the sensor in the water or oil so that just the sensing portion and the threads are submerged. Also place a thermometer capable of reading temperatures up to 50°C in the water or oil so that its bulb is close to the sensor **(see illustration)**. **Note:** *None of the components should be allowed to directly touch the container.* Heat the water or oil over a low flame, stirring it gently. The

temperatures required for testing the sensor are not high, so avoid applying excessive heat.

⚠ *Warning: This must be done very carefully to avoid the risk of personal injury.*

5 Referring to the specifications at the beginning of the Chapter for the sensor being tested, check whether the resistance reading

27.4 Sensor test set-up
1 Sensor   2 Thermometer

27.7a Atmospheric temperature sensor relay test
Terminal numbers shown

27.7b Oil temperature sensor relay test
Terminal numbers shown

specified is obtained at the temperature specified. When the required temperature has been reached, turn off the heat and check that the correct reading is obtained as the temperature falls. If the meter readings obtained are different, or they are obtained at different temperatures, then the sensor is faulty and must be replaced.

Relay

6 To check the atmospheric temperature sensor and oil temperature sensor relay, disconnect the wiring connector from the relay and identify the terminal numbers which should be marked on the relay terminals. The relay is mounted behind the right-hand side

panel on 550 models, and under the fuel tank behind the regulator/rectifier on 750 models **(see illustrations 27.9a and b)**. Remove the side panel (see Chapter 7) or the fuel tank (see Chapter 3) for access.
7 Connect the probes of a continuity tester to terminals 3 and 4 of the relay. Using a fully-charged 12 volt battery and two insulated jumper wires, connect the positive (+) wire to terminal 1 and the negative (–) wire to terminal 2 **(see illustrations)**. The meter should show continuity (zero resistance) for the atmospheric temperature sensor, or no continuity (infinite resistance) for the oil temperature sensor. Disconnect the battery leads. The meter should now show no

continuity (infinite resistance) for the atmospheric temperature sensor, or continuity (zero resistance) for the oil temperature sensor. If the readings obtained differ, the sensor is faulty and should be replaced.

Control unit

8 To check the system control unit, which is mounted behind the ignition control unit on 550 models (necessitating its removal - see Chapter 4) and behind the left-hand side panel on 750 models, disconnect the wiring connector **(see illustrations 27.10a and b)**.
9 Using a multimeter set to the K ohms scale, connect the meter probes to each pair of terminals specified in the table **(see illustration)**. If any of the readings obtained differ from those specified in the table, the control unit is faulty and should be replaced.

Replacement

10 The carburettor heater system fitted to UK ZR550 B4, B5 and B6 models, and to UK ZR750 C3, C4, C5 and D1 models incorporates a heater unit in each carburettor body, an atmospheric temperature sensor in the air filter housing and a relay. ZR750 C3 and C4 models also have an oil temperature sensor and relay, and ZR550 B5 and B6 and ZR750 C5 and D1 models have a carburettor temperature sensor and a system control unit.
11 To remove the heater unit in the carburettor, disconnect the wiring connector from the heater being removed, then remove the screw securing the heater bracket and pull the heater out of the carburettor body **(see illustration)**.

(unit: kΩ)

		Tester (+) Lead Connection				
		1 (W/G)	2 (G)	3 (G/Y)	4 (BK/Y)	5 (BK)
Tester (–) Lead Connection	1 (W/G)	–	7 ~ 28	∞	6.5 ~ 28	17 ~ 80
	2 (G)	∞	–	∞	∞	∞
	3 (G/Y)	6 ~ 26	9.5 ~ 40	–	9.5 ~ 40	24 ~ 150
	4 (BK/Y)	4.4 ~ 19	1.4 ~ 6	∞	–	6.5 ~ 28
	5 (BK)	13 ~ 60	10 ~ 45	∞	6.5 ~ 28	–

27.9 System control unit test

27.11 Remove the bracket screw and withdraw the heater

27.13a Sensor relay - 550 models

27.13b Sensor relay - 750 models

27.13c Disconnect the relay wiring connector and remove the relay

27.14a System control unit - 550 models

27.14b System control unit - 750 models

12 The atmospheric temperature sensor is threaded into the front of the air filter housing **(see illustration 27.3a)**, the oil temperature sensor is threaded into the crankcase below the pulse generator assembly cover, and the carburettor temperature sensor is threaded into the no. 2 carburettor in place of one of the joining bracket screws **(see illustration 27.3b)**. Disconnect the wiring connector and unscrew the sensor (in the case of the oil temperature sensor, first drain the engine oil - see Chapter 1).

13 The relay is mounted behind the right-hand side panel on 550 models, and under the fuel tank behind the regulator/rectifier on 750 models **(see illustrations)**. Remove the side panel (see Chapter 7) or the fuel tank (see Chapter 3) for access. Disconnect the relay wiring connector and remove the relay **(see illustration)**.

14 The system control unit is mounted behind the ignition control unit on 550 models and behind the left-hand side panel on 750 models **(see illustrations)**. Remove the ignition control unit (see Chapter 4) or the side panel (see Chapter 7). Disconnect the wiring at the connector and pull the unit and its rubber sleeve off its mounting lugs.

15 Installation is the reverse of removal. Make sure all wiring connectors are secure.

Apply a silicone sealant to the threads of the oil temperature sensor.

28 Horn - check and replacement

Check

1 The horn is mounted in front of the engine below the steering head.
2 Unplug the wiring connectors from the horn **(see illustration)**. Using two jumper wires,

28.2 Disconnect the horn wiring connectors

apply battery voltage directly to the terminals on the horn. If the horn sounds, check the switch (see Section 21) and the wiring between the switch and the horn (see the *wiring diagrams* at the end of this Chapter).
3 If the horn doesn't sound, replace it.

Replacement

4 The horn is mounted in front of the engine below the steering head.
5 Unplug the wiring connectors from the horn **(see illustration 28.2)**, then unscrew the bolts securing the horn bracket and remove the horn from the bike **(see illustration)**.

28.5 The horn bracket is secured by two bolts (arrowed)

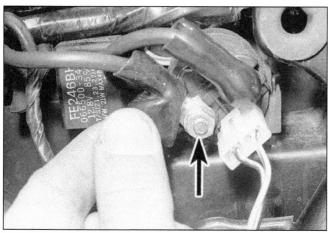

29.2 Detach the starter motor lead (arrowed) from the relay

29.4 Starter relay test meter (A) and battery (B) connections

6 Install the horn and securely tighten the bolts. Connect the wiring connectors to the horn.

29 Starter relay -
check and replacement

Check

1 If the starter circuit is faulty, first check the fuse (see Section 5).
2 The starter relay is located behind the left-hand side panel. Remove the side panel for access (see Chapter 7). Pull back the rubber cover on the starter motor lead, then unscrew the nut securing the starter motor lead to its terminal and disconnect the lead **(see illustration)**. Making sure that the disconnected lead is well clear of its terminal, switch the ignition ON and ensure the engine kill switch is in the RUN position, the transmission is in neutral and the clutch pulled in, then press the starter switch. The relay should click.
3 If the relay doesn't click, switch off the ignition and remove the relay as described below; test it as follows.
4 With the relay removed from the bike, set a multimeter to the ohms x 1 scale and connect it across the relay's starter motor and battery

lead terminals. Using a fully-charged 12 volt battery and two insulated jumper wires, connect the positive (+) terminal of the battery to the yellow/red wire terminal of the relay, and the negative (–) terminal to the black/yellow wire terminal of the relay **(see illustration)**. At this point the relay should click and the multimeter read 0 ohms (continuity). If this is the case the relay is proved good. If the relay does not click when battery voltage is applied and indicates no continuity (infinite resistance) across its terminals, it is faulty and must be replaced.
5 If the relay is good, check for battery voltage between the yellow/red wire and the black/yellow wire when the starter button is pressed. Check the other components in the starter circuit as described in the relevant sections of this Chapter. If all components are good, check the wiring between the various components (see the *wiring diagrams* at the end of this book).

Replacement

6 Remove the seat and the left-hand side panel (see Chapter 7).
7 Disconnect the battery terminals, remembering to disconnect the negative (–) terminal first.
8 Disconnect the relay wiring connector, then unscrew the two nuts securing the starter motor and battery leads to the relay and

detach the leads **(see illustration)**. Remove the relay with its rubber sleeve from its mounting lugs on the frame.
9 Installation is the reverse of removal, ensuring the terminal screws are securely tightened. Connect the negative (–) lead last when reconnecting the battery.

30 Starter motor -
removal and installation

Removal

1 Remove the seat (see Chapter 7). Disconnect the battery negative (–) lead.
2 On 550 models, unscrew the two bolts securing the starter motor top cover and lift off the cover **(see illustration)**. Slacken the upper starter motor mounting bolt, then remove the lower cover **(see illustration)**.
3 On 750 models, unscrew the gearchange linkage arm pinch bolt and remove the arm from the shaft, noting any alignment marks **(see illustration 22.2a)**. If no marks are visible, make your own before removing the arm so that it can be correctly aligned with the shaft on installation. Unscrew the bolts securing the engine sprocket cover to the crankcase and remove the cover **(see illustration 22.2c)**. Unscrew the two bolts

29.8 Disconnect the wiring connector (A), unscrew the nuts (B) and detach the leads

30.2a Unscrew the bolts (arrowed) and remove the top cover . . .

30.2b . . . then slacken the upper mounting bolt and remove the lower cover

30.3 Removing the top cover on 750 models

30.4 Unscrew the nut and detach the starter motor lead

30.5 Unscrew the mounting bolts . . .

30.6 . . . and remove the starter

securing the starter motor top cover, noting how the collar and rubber damper fit, and remove the cover **(see illustration)**.

4 Peel back the rubber cover and unscrew the nut securing the starter cable to the motor **(see illustration)**.

5 Unscrew the two bolts securing the starter motor to the crankcase **(see illustration)**.

6 Slide the starter motor out from the crankcase and remove it from the machine **(see illustration)**.

7 Remove the O-ring on the end of the starter motor and discard it; a new one must be used.

Installation

8 Install a new O-ring on the end of the starter motor and ensure it is seated in its groove **(see illustration)**. Apply a smear of engine oil to the O-ring to aid installation. Make sure that the mating surfaces between the starter motor mounting points and the crankcase are clean to ensure a good earth (ground).

9 Manoeuvre the motor into position and slide it into the crankcase **(see illustration 30.6)**. Ensure that the starter motor teeth mesh correctly with those of the starter idle/reduction gear.

10 Install the starter motor bolts. On 550 models, tighten only the lower bolt, leaving the upper one slack for the lower cover. On 750 models, tighten both bolts to the torque setting specified at the beginning of the Chapter.

11 Connect the starter cable to the motor and secure it with the nut **(see illustration 30.4)**. Make sure the rubber cover is correctly seated over the terminal.

12 On 550 models, install the lower cover so that the front mounting fits around the upper

starter motor bolt **(see illustration 30.2b)**. Tighten the bolt to secure the cover. Install the upper cover and tighten its bolts.

13 On 750 models, install the top cover, making sure the rubber damper and collar are correctly fitted, then install the bolts **(see illustration 30.3)**. Install the sprocket cover and the gearchange linkage arm, aligning the marks made previously, and tighten the pinch bolt securely **(see illustration)**.

14 Connect the battery negative (–) lead and install the seat.

30.8 Fit a new O-ring (arrowed)

30.13 Install the engine sprocket cover

31.2 Note the alignment marks between the main housing and the covers

31.3a Starter motor long bolts (arrowed) - 550 models

31.3b Starter motor long bolts (arrowed) - 750 models

31.6a Unscrew the nut (arrowed) and remove the washers . . .

31.6b . . . then remove the brushplate assembly

31 Starter motor - disassembly, inspection and reassembly

Disassembly

1 Remove the starter motor (see Section 30).
2 Note the alignment marks between the main housing and the front and rear covers as an aid to installation, or make some of your own if they are difficult to see **(see illustration)**. Also make a mark to identify which way up the housing fits.
3 Unscrew the two long bolts and withdraw them from the starter motor **(see illustrations)**. Discard their O-rings (550 models only) as new ones must be used. Remove the rear cover from the motor along with its O-ring. Discard the O-ring as a new one must be used. Remove the shims from the rear end of the armature shaft or from inside the rear cover.
4 Remove the front cover from the motor along with its O-ring. Discard the O-ring as a new one must be used. On 550 models, remove the washer(s) from the front end of the armature shaft and the seal protector from inside the front cover, noting their correct fitted locations **(see illustration 31.19a)**. On

750 models, remove the dividing plate, noting how the notch in its perimeter locates over the lug on the inside of the main housing **(see illustration 31.19c)**. Also note the locating pin between the ring gear and the front cover, and take care not to lose it **(see illustration 31.19d)**. The notch in the perimeter of the front cover also locates over the lug on the inside of the main housing. Remove the shims from the front end of the armature shaft.
5 Withdraw the armature from the main housing.
6 Noting the correct fitted location of each component, unscrew the terminal nut and remove the insulating washers **(see illustration)**. On US/Canada ZR750 C1, C2 and C3 models, remove the brushplate assembly and terminal bolt from the main housing. On all other models, remove the brushplate assembly and terminal bolt from the rear cover **(see illustration)**.
7 Lift the brush springs and slide the brushes out from their holders, noting how they fit.

Inspection

8 The parts of the starter motor that are most likely to require attention are the brushes. Measure the length of the brushes and compare the results to the brush length listed

in this Chapter's Specifications **(see illustration)**. If any of the brushes are worn beyond the service limit, replace the brush assembly with a new one. If the brushes are not worn excessively, nor cracked, chipped, or otherwise damaged, they may be re-used. Also check the brush springs, making sure they provide a firm pressure on the brush when installed.
9 Inspect the commutator bars on the armature for scoring, scratches and discoloration **(see illustration)**. The commutator can be cleaned and polished with crocus cloth, but do not use sandpaper or

31.8 Measure the length of each brush

31.9 Check the commutator bars as described

emery paper. After cleaning, wipe away any residue with a cloth soaked in electrical system cleaner or denatured alcohol. Clean out the mica grooves between the commutator bars. Measure the diameter of the commutator and compare it to the specifications. If the commutator has worn to below its service limit, the armature must be replaced.

10 Using an ohmmeter or a continuity test light, check for continuity between the commutator bars (see illustration). Continuity should exist between each bar and all of the

others. Also, check for continuity between the commutator bars and the armature shaft (see illustration). There should be no continuity (infinite resistance) between the commutator and the shaft. If the checks indicate otherwise, the armature is defective.

11 Check for continuity between each brush and the terminal bolt. There should be continuity (zero resistance). Check for continuity between the terminal bolt and the housing (when assembled). There should be no continuity (infinite resistance).

12 Check the front end of the armature shaft for worn, cracked, chipped and broken teeth. If the shaft is damaged or worn, replace the armature. On 750 models, similarly check the ring gear in the front cover and the drive pinion on the front of the cover. The drive pinion is secured by a circlip, and the chamfered side of the pinion teeth must face out (see illustration).

13 Inspect the end covers for signs of cracks or wear. Inspect the magnets in the main housing and the housing itself for cracks.

14 Inspect the insulating washers and front cover oil seal (550 models) for signs of damage and replace them if necessary.

Reassembly

15 Slide the brushes back into position in their holders on the brushplate and, on all except US ZR750 C1, C2 and C3 models, place the brush spring ends onto the brushes. On US ZR750 C1, C2 and C3 models, locate the spring end onto the top of the brush holder so that there is no pressure on the spring. This makes installation of the armature much easier.

16 Fit the inner rubber insulator on the terminal bolt, then insert the bolt through the rear cover (main housing on US ZR750 C1, C2 and C3 models) and install the brushplate assembly in the rear cover (main housing on US ZR750 C1, C2 and C3 models) making sure its tab is correctly located in the slot in the cover or housing (see illustration). Fit the O-ring and the washers over the terminal and secure it with the nut.

17 On all except US ZR750 C1, C2 and C3 models, slide the shims over the rear end of the armature shaft (see illustration). Insert the armature into the offset opening in the brushplate, locating the commutator bars against the brushes, then press the brushes back into the holders until the armature shaft

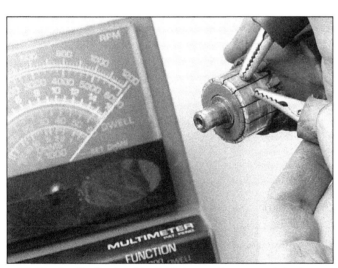

31.10a Continuity should exist between the commutator bars

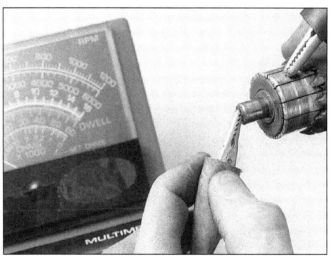

31.10b There should be no continuity between the commutator bars and the armature shaft

31.12 Check the drive pinion on 750 models

31.16 Install the brushplate and terminal bolt and fit the washers as shown

31.17a Fit the shims onto the shaft . . .

31.17b ... then install the armature in the rear housing ...

31.17c ... and locate the commutator against the brushes

31.18a Fit new O-rings onto the main housing ...

31.18b ... then fit the housing over the armature ...

31.18c ... aligning the marks noted or made on removal

31.19a On 550 models, fit the washers onto the shaft and the seal protector onto the front cover

end locates in its hole in the cover **(see illustrations)**. Take care not to damage the brushes. On US ZR750 C1, C2 and C3 models, insert the armature into the main housing, then locate the spring ends onto the brushes so that the brushes are pressed onto the commutator. On all models, check that each brush is securely pressed against the commutator by its spring and is free to move easily in its holder.

18 Fit a new O-ring onto each end of the main housing **(see illustration)**. On all except US ZR750 C1, C2 and C3 models, slide the housing over the armature, aligning the marks made on disassembly **(see illustration)**. On US ZR750 C1, C2 and C3 models, slide the shims over the rear end of the armature shaft, then fit the end cover onto the main housing, aligning the marks made on disassembly.

19 On 550 models, apply a smear of grease to the lips of the front cover oil seal. Fit the washer(s) onto the shaft and the seal protector onto the front cover, making sure that the tabs on the seal protector locate correctly **(see illustration)**. Install the cover, aligning the marks made on removal. On 750 models, fit the shims onto the front end of the armature shaft, then fit the dividing plate, locating the notch in its perimeter over the lug on the inside of the main housing. Check that the locating pin is installed in the notch between the perimeter of the ring gear and the front cover **(see illustration)**. Fit the front cover onto the housing, aligning the lug on the inside of the main housing with the notch in the perimeter of the ring gear **(see illustration)**.

31.19b On 750 models, fit the washers onto the shaft ...

31.19d Make sure the locating pin is in place ...

20 On 550 models, slide the lockwasher and a new O-ring onto each of the long bolts **(see illustration)**. On all models, check the marks

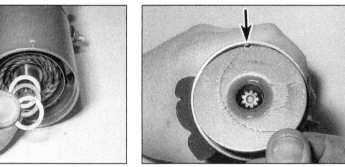

31.19c ... then install the dividing plate, aligning the notch with the lug (arrowed)

31.19e ... then fit the front cover, aligning the lug (A) with the notch (B)

made on removal are aligned, then install the long bolts and tighten them securely **(see illustration)**. On 550 models, make sure the

31.20a On 550 models, do not forget the O-ring and washer on each long bolt

flat side of the lockwasher locates correctly against the body of the rear cover **(see illustration 31.3a)**.
21 Install the starter motor (see Section 30).

32 Charging system testing - general information and precautions

1 If the performance of the charging system is suspect, the system as a whole should be checked first, followed by testing of the individual components. **Note:** *Before beginning the checks, make sure the battery is fully charged and that all system connections are clean and tight.*
2 Checking the output of the charging system and the performance of the various components within the charging system requires the use of a multimeter (with voltage, current and resistance checking facilities).
3 When making the checks, follow the procedures carefully to prevent incorrect connections or short circuits, as irreparable damage to electrical system components may result if short circuits occur.
4 If a multimeter is not available, the job of checking the charging system should be left to a Kawasaki dealer.

33.3 Checking the charging system leakage rate. Connect the meter as shown

31.20b On 750 models, the long bolts run outside the housing

33 Charging system - testing

1 If the machine's charging system is thought to be faulty, perform the following checks.

Leakage test

2 Remove the seat (see Chapter 7) and disconnect the lead from the battery negative (–) terminal.
3 Set the multimeter to the mA (milli Amps) function and connect its negative (–) probe to the battery negative (–) terminal, and positive (+) probe to the disconnected negative (–) lead **(see illustration)**. With the meter connected like this the reading should not exceed 0.1 mA.
4 If the reading exceeds the specified amount it is likely that there is a short circuit in the wiring. Thoroughly check the wiring between the various components (see the *wiring diagrams* at the end of this book).
5 If the reading is below the specified amount, the leakage rate is satisfactory. Disconnect the meter and reconnect the negative (–) lead to the battery, tightening it securely, Check the alternator output as described below.

Output test

Regulated output test

6 Remove the seat (see Chapter 7). Start the engine and warm it up to normal operating temperature then stop the engine.

33.10a Alternator wiring connectors (arrowed) - 550 models

7 Connect a multimeter set to the 0 - 20 volts dc scale (voltmeter) across the terminals of the battery (positive (+) lead to battery positive (+) terminal, negative (–) lead to battery negative (–) terminal). Start the engine, then turn on the lights (UK models) and note the reading obtained at idle speed - it should be just under battery voltage (12V). Increase engine speed and note the voltage reading - it should vary between 14 to 15V. Stop the engine and disconnect the meter when testing is complete. If the voltage is outside these limits, check the unregulated output of the alternator (see below), and the regulator (see Section 35). **Note:** *If the voltage is low, it is more likely that the alternator is faulty. If the voltage is above 15 volts, it is more likely that the regulator is faulty.*

> **HAYNES HiNT** *Clues to a faulty regulator are constantly blowing bulbs, with brightness varying considerably with engine speed, and battery overheating, necessitating frequent topping up of the electrolyte level.*

8 Carry out the above test with the headlight turned off and note the readings. On US/Canada the headlight wire connector must be detached from the back of the headlight unit to turn off the headlight.

Unregulated output test

9 Unscrew the gearchange linkage arm pinch bolt and remove the arm from the shaft, noting any alignment marks **(see illustration 22.2a)**. If no marks are visible, make your own before removing the arm so that it can be correctly aligned with the shaft on installation. Unscrew the bolts securing the engine sprocket cover to the crankcase and remove the cover **(see illustrations 22.2b or c)**.
10 Trace the alternator wiring from the base of the alternator cover and disconnect it at the connector(s) **(see illustrations)**. Using a multimeter set to 0 - 250 V ac range, connect the meter probes between two of the yellow wires from the alternator. Start the engine and increase its speed to 4000 rpm. Check the voltage output and compare it to the minimum specified at the beginning of the Chapter.

33.10b Alternator wiring connector (arrowed) - 750 models

33.14 Testing stator coil resistance

34.3 The alternator cover is secured by four bolts (arrowed)

11 Stop the engine, then connect the meter to another pair of yellow wires and repeat the test. Stop the engine then test across the remaining pair of yellow wires. If any of the three readings are below the minimum specified, check the stator coil resistance (see below). If the readings are good, check the regulator (see Section 35).

Alternator stator coil test

12 Unscrew the gearchange linkage arm pinch bolt and remove the arm from the shaft, noting any alignment marks **(see illustration 22.2a)**. If no marks are visible, make your own before removing the arm so that it can be correctly aligned with the shaft on installation. Unscrew the bolts securing the engine sprocket cover to the crankcase and remove the cover **(see illustrations 22.2b or c)**.
13 Trace the alternator wiring from the base of the alternator cover and disconnect it at the connector(s) **(see illustrations 33.9a or b)**.
14 Using multimeter set to the ohms x 1 scale, check the resistance between each of the wires on the alternator side of the connector, taking a total of three readings **(see illustration)**. Also check for continuity between each terminal and earth (ground). If the stator coil windings are in good condition there should be the resistance specified between each of the terminals, and no continuity (infinite resistance) between any of the terminals and ground (earth). If not, the alternator stator coil assembly is at fault and should be replaced. If the resistance readings are as specified but the alternator output is low when tested as above, the rotor magnets have probably weakened. **Note:** *Before condemning the stator coils, check the fault is not due to damaged wiring between the connector and coils.*

34 Alternator -
removal and installation

Removal

1 Unscrew the gearchange linkage arm pinch bolt and remove the arm from the shaft, noting any alignment marks **(see illustration 22.2a)**. If no marks are visible, make your own before removing the arm so that it can be correctly aligned with the shaft on installation. Unscrew the bolts securing the engine sprocket cover to the crankcase and remove the cover **(see illustrations 22.2b or c)**.
2 Trace the alternator wiring from the base of the alternator cover and disconnect it at the connector(s) **(see illustrations 33.10a or b)**. Release the wiring from any clips or ties.
3 Unscrew the alternator cover retaining bolts and lift the cover away from the engine **(see illustration)**. The stator is mounted inside the cover. Remove the gasket and discard it. Remove the two dowels from either the cover or the crankcase, if they are loose.
4 To remove the rotor bolt, the rotor must be held against rotation. If a rotor holding strap or tool is not available, place the transmission in gear and have an assistant apply the rear brake. Unscrew the bolt **(see illustration)**.

34.4 Alternator rotor bolt (arrowed)

5 To remove the rotor from the shaft it is necessary to use a rotor puller. The Kawasaki special tools (pt. no. 57001-1099 for 550 models, and pt. nos. 57001-1151 and 57001-1216 for 750 models), or a commercially available rotor puller can be used (making sure it has the correct thread on it). Screw the puller into the rotor thread, and using the method employed earlier to stop the rotor from turning, tighten the puller until the rotor is displaced from the shaft.

> **HAYNES HiNT** *A smart tap on the head of the puller will usually succeed in breaking any corrosion free between the rotor and crankshaft taper.*

6 To remove the stator from the crankcase cover, unscrew the three bolts securing the stator and the screws securing the wiring clamp, then remove the assembly from the cover, noting the routing of the wiring and how the rubber grommet fits **(see illustration)**.

Installation

7 De-grease the tapered portion of the crankshaft and the corresponding surface in the rotor using a suitable solvent. Make sure

34.6 Stator bolts (A), wiring clamp screws (B)

34.9 Install the cover using a new gasket

35.1a Regulator/rectifier wiring connector (arrowed) - later 550 models

35.1b Regulator/rectifier wiring connector (arrowed) - 750 models

that no metal objects have attached themselves to the magnet on the inside of the rotor then install the rotor onto the crankshaft. Install the rotor bolt and, using the method employed on removal to stop the rotor from turning, tighten it to the torque setting specified at the beginning of the Chapter.

8 Install the stator into the cover, aligning the rubber wiring grommet with the groove in the cover. Apply a suitable non-permanent thread-locking compound to the stator bolt threads, then install the bolts and tighten them to the specified torque setting. Apply a suitable sealant to the wiring grommet, then install it into the cutout in the cover. Install the wiring clamp and secure it with the screws **(see illustration 34.6)**.

9 Make sure the dowels are fitted, then install the alternator cover using a new gasket **(see illustration)**. Tighten the cover bolts evenly in a criss-cross sequence.

10 Reconnect the wiring at the connector(s), making sure it is correctly routed, and secure it with any clips or ties **(see illustrations 33.10a or b)**.

11 Install the sprocket cover and the gearchange lever, aligning the marks made on removal.

35 Regulator/rectifier unit - check and replacement

Check

1 The regulator/rectifier is mounted behind the right-hand side panel on early 550 models, below the battery tray above the front of the swingarm on later 550 models, and under the fuel tank on 750 models **(see illustrations 35.6a and b)**. Remove the right-hand side panel (see Chapter 7) or the fuel tank (see Chapter 3) as required. Trace the wiring from the regulator/rectifier unit and disconnect it at the connector, or disconnect the wiring connector from the unit, according to model **(see illustrations)**.

2 To test the rectifier circuit, use a multimeter set to the appropriate resistance scale and check the resistance between the various terminals of the regulator/rectifier connectors

as shown in the table **(see illustration)**. If the readings do not compare closely with those shown in the accompanying table the regulator/rectifier unit can be considered faulty. **Note:** *The use of certain multimeters could lead to false readings being obtained. Therefore, if the above check shows the regulator/rectifier unit to be faulty take the unit to a Kawasaki dealer for confirmation of its condition before replacing it.*

3 To test the regulator circuit, three fully charged 12 V batteries, each with a set of auxiliary leads, and a test light are required (see below). If these are not available, carry out a charging system test (see Section 33). If the conditions arise from that test that indicate a faulty regulator, take it to a Kawasaki dealer for further testing. Clues to a faulty regulator are constantly blowing bulbs, with brightness varying considerably with

No.	Connections		Reading	Meter
	Meter (+) to	Meter (−) to		Range
1	Y₁			
2	Y₂	W	∞	
3	Y₃			
4	Y₁			× 10 Ω
5	Y₂	BK/Y		or
6	Y₃		0 ~	× 100 Ω
7		Y₁	½ scale	
8	W	Y₂		
9		Y₃		
10		Y₁		
11	BK/Y	Y₂	∞	
12		Y₃		

35.2 Rectifier circuit test connections

35.4 Regulator circuit tests (see text)

35.6a Regulator/rectifier (arrowed) - later 550 models

35.6b Regulator/rectifier - 750 models

engine speed, and battery overheating, necessitating frequent topping up of the electrolyte level (where possible).

4 Referring to the three circuit diagrams shown, set each circuit up in turn (see illustration). Where dotted lines are shown to the yellow terminals on the connector, check the circuit for each of the terminals in turn using the same lead, thereby taking three readings for each circuit. In the first test circuit, the bulb should not light up. In the second test circuit, the bulb should not light up. In the third test circuit, the bulb should light up. If any of the tests prove otherwise, the regulator/rectifier is faulty and must be replaced.

5 The tests outlined above are not foolproof. If the test results indicate that the unit is good, and all other components in the charging circuit have been checked and proven good, but there is still a problem, the regulator/ rectifier may well be faulty. If this is the case, either take the unit to a Kawasaki dealer for testing, or substitute the suspect unit with one

that is known to be good and recheck the system.

Replacement

6 The regulator/rectifier is mounted behind the right-hand side panel on early 550 models, below the battery tray above the front of the swingarm on later 550 models, and under the fuel tank on 750 models (see illustrations). Remove the right-hand side panel (see Chapter 7) or the fuel tank (see Chapter 3) as required. Trace the wiring from the regulator/rectifier unit and disconnect it at the connector, or disconnect the wiring connector from the unit, according to model (see illustrations 34.1a or b).

7 Unscrew the two bolts or screws securing the unit and remove it.

8 Install the new unit and tighten its mountings securely. Connect the wiring at the connector.

9 Install the right-hand side panel (see Chapter 7) or fuel tank (see Chapter 3) as required.

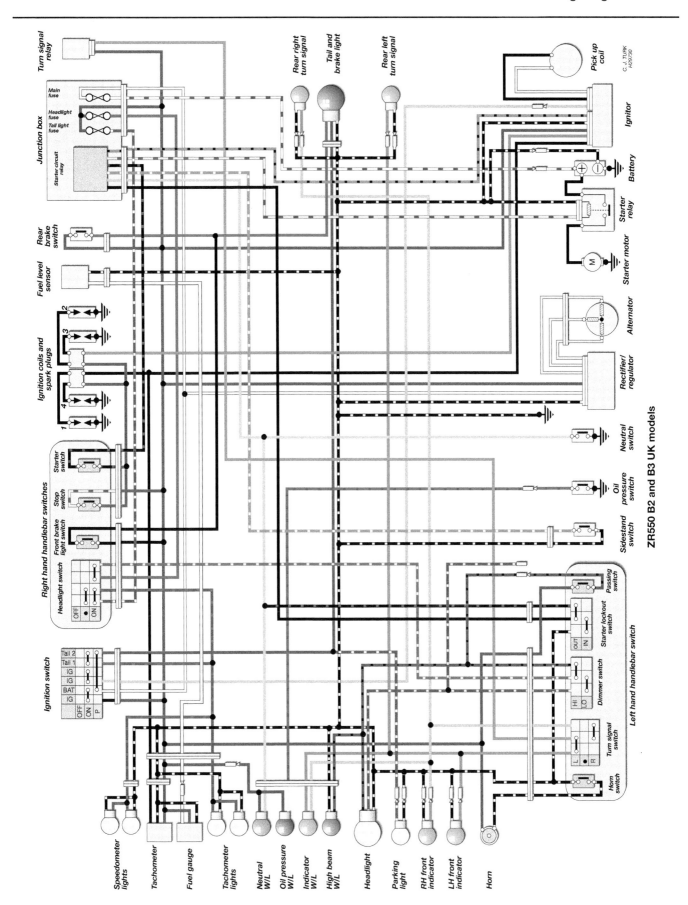

Turn signal relay

Junction box
Main fuse
Headlight fuse
Tail light fuse
Starter circuit relay

Rear brake switch

Fuel level sensor

Ignition coils and spark plugs

Right hand handlebar switches
Starter switch
Stop switch
Front brake light switch
Headlight switch
OFF
ON

Ignition switch
Tail 2
Tail 1
IG
IG
BAT
IG
OFF
ON
P

Speedometer lights

Tachometer

Fuel gauge

Tachometer lights

Neutral W/L

Oil pressure W/L

Indicator W/L

High beam W/L

Headlight

Parking light

RH front indicator

LH front indicator

Horn

Rear right turn signal

Tail and brake light

Rear left turn signal

Pick up coil

Ignitor

Battery

Starter relay

Starter motor

Alternator

Rectifier/ regulator

Neutral

Oil pressure switch

Sidestand switch

Passing switch

Starter lockout switch
OUT
IN

Dimmer switch
HI
LO

Turn signal switch
L
R

Horn switch

Left hand handlebar switch

ZR550 B2 and B3 UK models

C. J. TURK
H29130

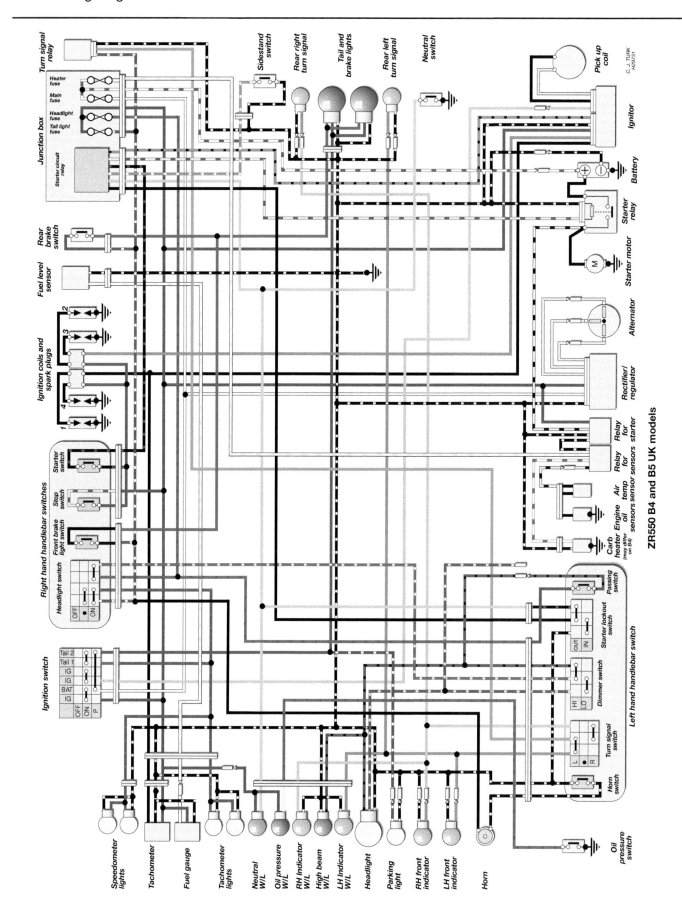

Turn signal relay

Heater fuse
Main fuse
Headlight fuse
Tail light fuse

Junction box

Starter circuit relay

Rear brake switch

Fuel level sensor

Ignition coils and spark plugs

Right hand handlebar switches

Starter switch
Stop switch
Front brake light switch

Headlight switch

OFF · ON

Ignition switch

Tail 2
Tail 1
IG
IG
BAT
IG

OFF · ON · P

Sidestand switch

Rear right turn signal

Tail and brake lights

Rear left turn signal

Neutral switch

Pick up coil

Ignitor

Battery

Starter relay

Starter motor

Alternator

Rectifier/ regulator

Relay for starter

Relay for sensors

Engine sensors

Air temp

Oil

Carb heater (may differ on B4)

Passing switch

Starter lockout switch

OUT · IN

Dimmer switch

HI · LO

Turn signal switch

L · R

Horn switch

Left hand handlebar switch

Speedometer lights
Tachometer
Fuel gauge
Tachometer lights
Neutral W/L
Oil pressure W/L
RH Indicator W/L
High beam W/L
LH Indicator W/L
Headlight
Parking light
RH front indicator
LH front indicator
Horn
Oil pressure switch

ZR550 B4 and B5 UK models

C.J.TURK
H29731

ZR550 B6 UK models

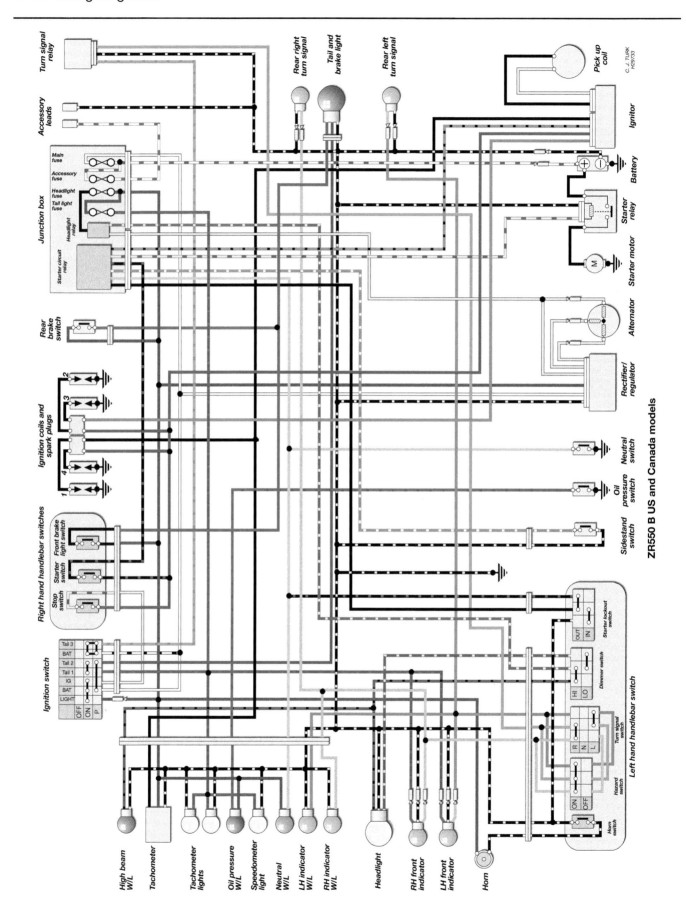

ZR550 B US and Canada models

Turn signal relay

Main fuse
Headlight fuse
Tail light fuse

Junction box

Starter circuit relay

Rear brake switch

Fuel level sensor

Ignition coils and spark plugs

Right hand handlebar switches

Starter switch
Stop switch
Front brake light switch
Headlight switch
OFF
ON

Ignition switch
Tail 2
Tail 1
IG
IG
BAT
IG
OFF
ON
P

Rear right turn signal
Tail and brake light
Rear left turn signal
Pick up coil

C. J. TURK
H29734

Ignitor

Battery

Starter relay

Starter motor

Alternator

Rectifier/ regulator

Neutral switch

Oil pressure switch

Sidestand switch

ZR750 C1 and C2 UK models

Passing switch
Starter lockout switch
OUT
IN
Dimmer switch
HI
LO
Turn signal switch
L
R
Horn switch

Left hand handlebar switch

Speedometer lights
Tachometer
Fuel gauge
Tachometer lights
Neutral W/L
Oil pressure W/L
Indicator W/L
High beam W/L
Headlight
Parking light
RH front indicator
LH front indicator
Horn

ZR750 C3 UK models

ZR750 C4 UK model

ZR750 C5 and D1 UK models

Turn signal relay

Accessory leads
−
+

Junction box
Main fuse
Accessory fuse
Headlight fuse
Tail light fuse
Headlight relay
Starter circuit relay

Rear brake switch

Fuel level sensor

Ignition coils and spark plugs
2
3
4
1

Right hand handlebar switches
Starter switch
Stop switch
Front brake light switch

Ignition switch
Tail 2
Tail 1
IG
IG
BAT
IG
OFF ON P

Speedometer lights

Tachometer

Fuel gauge

Tachometer lights

Neutral W/L

Oil pressure W/L

Indicator W/L

High beam W/L

Headlight

RH front indicator

LH front indicator

Horn

Rear right turn signal

Tail and brake light

Rear left turn signal

Pick up coil

Ignitor

Battery

Starter relay

Starter motor

Alternator

Rectifier/ regulator

Neutral switch

Oil pressure switch

Sidestand switch

Starter lockout switch

Dimmer switch
HI
LO

Turn signal switch
L off R

Horn switch

Left hand handlebar switch

ZR750 C US and Canada models

C.J.TURK
H29738

Dimensions and Weights

550 models

Wheelbase
    UK models . . . . .1435 mm
    US models . . . . 1440 mm
Overall length
    UK models . . . . .2080 mm
    US models . . . . .2100 mm
Overall width . . . . .755 mm
Overall height . . . . .1095 mm
Seat height . . . . .770 mm
Minimum ground clearance . . . . .120 mm
Weight (dry)
    UK models . . . . .179 kg
    US models . . . . .178 kg

750 models

Wheelbase . . . . .1455 mm
Overall length . . . . .2105 mm
Overall width . . . . .770 mm
Overall height . . . . .1095 mm
Seat height . . . . .780 mm
Minimum ground clearance . . . . .150 mm
Weight (dry)
    C models . . . . .201 kg
    D models . . . . .212 kg

Buying tools

A toolkit is a fundamental requirement for servicing and repairing a motorcycle. Although there will be an initial expense in building up enough tools for servicing, this will soon be offset by the savings made by doing the job yourself. As experience and confidence grow, additional tools can be added to enable the repair and overhaul of the motorcycle. Many of the specialist tools are expensive and not often used so it may be preferable to hire them, or for a group of friends or motorcycle club to join in the purchase.

As a rule, it is better to buy more expensive, good quality tools. Cheaper tools are likely to wear out faster and need to be renewed more often, nullifying the original saving.

Warning: To avoid the risk of a poor quality tool breaking in use, causing injury or damage to the component being worked on, always aim to purchase tools which meet the relevant national safety standards.

The following lists of tools do not represent the manufacturer's service tools, but serve as a guide to help the owner decide which tools are needed for this level of work. In addition, items such as an electric drill, hacksaw, files, soldering iron and a workbench equipped with a vice, may be needed. Although not classed as tools, a selection of bolts, screws, nuts, washers and pieces of tubing always come in useful.

For more information about tools, refer to the Haynes *Motorcycle Workshop Practice TechBook* (Bk. No. 3470).

Manufacturer's service tools

Inevitably certain tasks require the use of a service tool. Where possible an alternative tool or method of approach is recommended, but sometimes there is no option if personal injury or damage to the component is to be avoided. Where required, service tools are referred to in the relevant procedure.

Service tools can usually only be purchased from a motorcycle dealer and are identified by a part number. Some of the commonly-used tools, such as rotor pullers, are available in aftermarket form from mail-order motorcycle tool and accessory suppliers.

Maintenance and minor repair tools

1 Set of flat-bladed screwdrivers
2 Set of Phillips head screwdrivers
3 Combination open-end and ring spanners
4 Socket set (3/8 inch or 1/2 inch drive)
5 Set of Allen keys or bits

6 Set of Torx keys or bits
7 Pliers, cutters and self-locking grips (Mole grips)
8 Adjustable spanners
9 C-spanners
10 Tread depth gauge and tyre pressure gauge

11 Cable oiler clamp
12 Feeler gauges
13 Spark plug gap measuring tool
14 Spark plug spanner or deep plug sockets
15 Wire brush and emery paper

16 Calibrated syringe, measuring vessel and funnel
17 Oil filter adapters
18 Oil drainer can or tray
19 Pump type oil can
20 Grease gun

21 Straight-edge and steel rule
22 Continuity tester
23 Battery charger
24 Hydrometer (for battery specific gravity check)
25 Anti-freeze tester (for liquid-cooled engines)

Repair and overhaul tools

1 Torque wrench
   (small and mid-ranges)
2 Conventional, plastic or
   soft-faced hammers
3 Impact driver set

4 Vernier gauge
5 Circlip pliers (internal and
   external, or combination)
6 Set of cold chisels
   and punches

7 Selection of pullers
8 Breaker bars
9 Chain breaking/
   riveting tool set

10 Wire stripper and
    crimper tool
11 Multimeter (measures
    amps, volts and ohms)
12 Stroboscope (for
    dynamic timing checks)

13 Hose clamp
    (wingnut type shown)
14 Clutch holding tool
15 One-man brake/clutch
    bleeder kit

Specialist tools

1 Micrometers
   (external type)
2 Telescoping gauges
3 Dial gauge

4 Cylinder
   compression gauge
5 Vacuum gauges (left) or
   manometer (right)
6 Oil pressure gauge

7 Plastigauge kit
8 Valve spring compressor
   (4-stroke engines)
9 Piston pin drawbolt tool

10 Piston ring removal and
    installation tool
11 Piston ring clamp
12 Cylinder bore hone
    (stone type shown)

13 Stud extractor
14 Screw extractor set
15 Bearing driver set

1 Workshop equipment and facilities

The workbench

● Work is made much easier by raising the bike up on a ramp - components are much more accessible if raised to waist level. The hydraulic or pneumatic types seen in the dealer's workshop are a sound investment if you undertake a lot of repairs or overhauls (see illustration 1.1).

1.1 Hydraulic motorcycle ramp

● If raised off ground level, the bike must be supported on the ramp to avoid it falling. Most ramps incorporate a front wheel locating clamp which can be adjusted to suit different diameter wheels. When tightening the clamp, take care not to mark the wheel rim or damage the tyre - use wood blocks on each side to prevent this.
● Secure the bike to the ramp using tie-downs (see illustration 1.2). If the bike has only a sidestand, and hence leans at a dangerous angle when raised, support the bike on an auxiliary stand.

1.2 Tie-downs are used around the passenger footrests to secure the bike

● Auxiliary (paddock) stands are widely available from mail order companies or motorcycle dealers and attach either to the wheel axle or swingarm pivot (see illustration 1.3). If the motorcycle has a centrestand, you can support it under the crankcase to prevent it toppling whilst either wheel is removed (see illustration 1.4).

1.3 This auxiliary stand attaches to the swingarm pivot

1.4 Always use a block of wood between the engine and jack head when supporting the engine in this way

Fumes and fire

● Refer to the Safety first! page at the beginning of the manual for full details. Make sure your workshop is equipped with a fire extinguisher suitable for fuel-related fires (Class B fire - flammable liquids) - it is not sufficient to have a water-filled extinguisher.
● Always ensure adequate ventilation is available. Unless an exhaust gas extraction system is available for use, ensure that the engine is run outside of the workshop.
● If working on the fuel system, make sure the workshop is ventilated to avoid a build-up of fumes. This applies equally to fume build-up when charging a battery. Do not smoke or allow anyone else to smoke in the workshop.

Fluids

● If you need to drain fuel from the tank, store it in an approved container marked as suitable for the storage of petrol (gasoline) (see illustration 1.5). Do not store fuel in glass jars or bottles.

1.5 Use an approved can only for storing petrol (gasoline)

● Use proprietary engine degreasers or solvents which have a high flash-point, such as paraffin (kerosene), for cleaning off oil, grease and dirt - never use petrol (gasoline) for cleaning. Wear rubber gloves when handling solvent and engine degreaser. The fumes from certain solvents can be dangerous - always work in a well-ventilated area.

Dust, eye and hand protection

● Protect your lungs from inhalation of dust particles by wearing a filtering mask over the nose and mouth. Many frictional materials still contain asbestos which is dangerous to your health. Protect your eyes from spouts of liquid and sprung components by wearing a pair of protective goggles (see illustration 1.6).

1.6 A fire extinguisher, goggles, mask and protective gloves should be at hand in the workshop

● Protect your hands from contact with solvents, fuel and oils by wearing rubber gloves. Alternatively apply a barrier cream to your hands before starting work. If handling hot components or fluids, wear suitable gloves to protect your hands from scalding and burns.

What to do with old fluids

● Old cleaning solvent, fuel, coolant and oils should not be poured down domestic drains or onto the ground. Package the fluid up in old oil containers, label it accordingly, and take it to a garage or disposal facility. Contact your local authority for location of such sites or ring the oil care hotline.

OIL CARE
FOLLOW THE CODE

OIL BANK LINE
0800 66 33 66

Note: It is antisocial and illegal to dump oil down the drain. To find the location of your local oil recycling bank, call this number free.

In the USA, note that any oil supplier must accept used oil for recycling.

2 Fasteners -
screws, bolts and nuts

Fastener types and applications

Bolts and screws

● Fastener head types are either of hexagonal, Torx or splined design, with internal and external versions of each type **(see illustrations 2.1 and 2.2)**; splined head fasteners are not in common use on motorcycles. The conventional slotted or Phillips head design is used for certain screws. Bolt or screw length is always measured from the underside of the head to the end of the item **(see illustration 2.11)**.

2.1 Internal hexagon/Allen (A), Torx (B) and splined (C) fasteners, with corresponding bits

2.2 External Torx (A), splined (B) and hexagon (C) fasteners, with corresponding sockets

● Certain fasteners on the motorcycle have a tensile marking on their heads, the higher the marking the stronger the fastener. High tensile fasteners generally carry a 10 or higher marking. Never replace a high tensile fastener with one of a lower tensile strength.

Washers **(see illustration 2.3)**

● Plain washers are used between a fastener head and a component to prevent damage to the component or to spread the load when torque is applied. Plain washers can also be used as spacers or shims in certain assemblies. Copper or aluminium plain washers are often used as sealing washers on drain plugs.

2.3 Plain washer (A), penny washer (B), spring washer (C) and serrated washer (D)

● The split-ring spring washer works by applying axial tension between the fastener head and component. If flattened, it is fatigued and must be renewed. If a plain (flat) washer is used on the fastener, position the spring washer between the fastener and the plain washer.

● Serrated star type washers dig into the fastener and component faces, preventing loosening. They are often used on electrical earth (ground) connections to the frame.

● Cone type washers (sometimes called Belleville) are conical and when tightened apply axial tension between the fastener head and component. They must be installed with the dished side against the component and often carry an OUTSIDE marking on their outer face. If flattened, they are fatigued and must be renewed.

● Tab washers are used to lock plain nuts or bolts on a shaft. A portion of the tab washer is bent up hard against one flat of the nut or bolt to prevent it loosening. Due to the tab washer being deformed in use, a new tab washer should be used every time it is disturbed.

● Wave washers are used to take up endfloat on a shaft. They provide light springing and prevent excessive side-to-side play of a component. Can be found on rocker arm shafts.

Nuts and split pins

● Conventional plain nuts are usually six-sided **(see illustration 2.4)**. They are sized by thread diameter and pitch. High tensile nuts carry a number on one end to denote their tensile strength.

2.4 Plain nut (A), shouldered locknut (B), nylon insert nut (C) and castellated nut (D)

● Self-locking nuts either have a nylon insert, or two spring metal tabs, or a shoulder which is staked into a groove in the shaft - their advantage over conventional plain nuts is a resistance to loosening due to vibration. The nylon insert type can be used a number of times, but must be renewed when the friction of the nylon insert is reduced, ie when the nut spins freely on the shaft. The spring tab type can be reused unless the tabs are damaged. The shouldered type must be renewed every time it is disturbed.

● Split pins (cotter pins) are used to lock a castellated nut to a shaft or to prevent slackening of a plain nut. Common applications are wheel axles and brake torque arms. Because the split pin arms are deformed to lock around the nut a new split pin must always be used on installation - always fit the correct size split pin which will fit snugly in the shaft hole. Make sure the split pin arms are correctly located around the nut **(see illustrations 2.5 and 2.6)**.

2.5 Bend split pin (cotter pin) arms as shown (arrows) to secure a castellated nut

2.6 Bend split pin (cotter pin) arms as shown to secure a plain nut

Caution: If the castellated nut slots do not align with the shaft hole after tightening to the torque setting, tighten the nut until the next slot aligns with the hole - never slacken the nut to align its slot.

● R-pins (shaped like the letter R), or slip pins as they are sometimes called, are sprung and can be reused if they are otherwise in good condition. Always install R-pins with their closed end facing forwards **(see illustration 2.7)**.

**2.7 Correct fitting of R-pin.
Arrow indicates forward direction**

Circlips (see illustration 2.8)

● Circlips (sometimes called snap-rings) are used to retain components on a shaft or in a housing and have corresponding external or internal ears to permit removal. Parallel-sided (machined) circlips can be installed either way round in their groove, whereas stamped circlips (which have a chamfered edge on one face) must be installed with the chamfer facing away from the direction of thrust load **(see illustration 2.9)**.

2.8 External stamped circlip (A), internal stamped circlip (B), machined circlip (C) and wire circlip (D)

● Always use circlip pliers to remove and install circlips; expand or compress them just enough to remove them. After installation, rotate the circlip in its groove to ensure it is securely seated. If installing a circlip on a splined shaft, always align its opening with a shaft channel to ensure the circlip ends are well supported and unlikely to catch **(see illustration 2.10)**.

THRUST LOAD

THRUST WASHER

SHARP EDGE

0650H

CHAMFERED EDGE

2.9 Correct fitting of a stamped circlip

**2.10 Align circlip opening
with shaft channel**

● Circlips can wear due to the thrust of components and become loose in their grooves, with the subsequent danger of becoming dislodged in operation. For this reason, renewal is advised every time a circlip is disturbed.
● Wire circlips are commonly used as piston pin retaining clips. If a removal tang is provided, long-nosed pliers can be used to dislodge them, otherwise careful use of a small flat-bladed screwdriver is necessary. Wire circlips should be renewed every time they are disturbed.

Thread diameter and pitch

● Diameter of a male thread (screw, bolt or stud) is the outside diameter of the threaded portion **(see illustration 2.11)**. Most motorcycle manufacturers use the ISO (International Standards Organisation) metric system expressed in millimetres, eg M6 refers to a 6 mm diameter thread. Sizing is the same for nuts, except that the thread diameter is measured across the valleys of the nut.
● Pitch is the distance between the peaks of the thread **(see illustration 2.11)**. It is expressed in millimetres, thus a common bolt size may be expressed as 6.0 x 1.0 mm (6 mm thread diameter and 1 mm pitch). Generally pitch increases in proportion to thread diameter, although there are always exceptions.
● Thread diameter and pitch are related for conventional fastener applications and the accompanying table can be used as a guide. Additionally, the AF (Across Flats), spanner or socket size dimension of the bolt or nut **(see illustration 2.11)** is linked to thread and pitch specification. Thread pitch can be measured with a thread gauge **(see illustration 2.12)**.

AF

L

D

P

2.11 Fastener length (L), thread diameter (D), thread pitch (P) and head size (AF)

**2.12 Using a thread gauge
to measure pitch**

AF size	Thread diameter x pitch (mm)
8 mm	M5 x 0.8
8 mm	M6 x 1.0
10 mm	M6 x 1.0
12 mm	M8 x 1.25
14 mm	M10 x 1.25
17 mm	M12 x 1.25

● The threads of most fasteners are of the right-hand type, ie they are turned clockwise to tighten and anti-clockwise to loosen. The reverse situation applies to left-hand thread fasteners, which are turned anti-clockwise to tighten and clockwise to loosen. Left-hand threads are used where rotation of a component might loosen a conventional right-hand thread fastener.

Seized fasteners

● Corrosion of external fasteners due to water or reaction between two dissimilar metals can occur over a period of time. It will build up sooner in wet conditions or in countries where salt is used on the roads during the winter. If a fastener is severely corroded it is likely that normal methods of removal will fail and result in its head being ruined. When you attempt removal, the fastener thread should be heard to crack free and unscrew easily - if it doesn't, stop there before damaging something.
● A smart tap on the head of the fastener will often succeed in breaking free corrosion which has occurred in the threads **(see illustration 2.13)**.
● An aerosol penetrating fluid (such as WD-40) applied the night beforehand may work its way down into the thread and ease removal. Depending on the location, you may be able to make up a Plasticine well around the fastener head and fill it with penetrating fluid.

2.13 A sharp tap on the head of a fastener will often break free a corroded thread

● If you are working on an engine internal component, corrosion will most likely not be a problem due to the well lubricated environment. However, components can be very tight and an impact driver is a useful tool in freeing them **(see illustration 2.14)**.

2.14 Using an impact driver to free a fastener

● Where corrosion has occurred between dissimilar metals (eg steel and aluminium alloy), the application of heat to the fastener head will create a disproportionate expansion rate between the two metals and break the seizure caused by the corrosion. Whether heat can be applied depends on the location of the fastener - any surrounding components likely to be damaged must first be removed **(see illustration 2.15)**. Heat can be applied using a paint stripper heat gun or clothes iron, or by immersing the component in boiling water - wear protective gloves to prevent scalding or burns to the hands.

2.15 Using heat to free a seized fastener

● As a last resort, it is possible to use a hammer and cold chisel to work the fastener head unscrewed **(see illustration 2.16)**. This will damage the fastener, but more importantly extreme care must be taken not to damage the surrounding component.

Caution: Remember that the component being secured is generally of more value than the bolt, nut or screw - when the fastener is freed, do not unscrew it with force, instead work the fastener back and forth when resistance is felt to prevent thread damage.

2.16 Using a hammer and chisel to free a seized fastener

Broken fasteners and damaged heads

● If the shank of a broken bolt or screw is accessible you can grip it with self-locking grips. The knurled wheel type stud extractor tool or self-gripping stud puller tool is particularly useful for removing the long studs which screw into the cylinder mouth surface of the crankcase or bolts and screws from which the head has broken off **(see illustration 2.17)**. Studs can also be removed by locking two nuts together on the threaded end of the stud and using a spanner on the lower nut **(see illustration 2.18)**.

2.17 Using a stud extractor tool to remove a broken crankcase stud

2.18 Two nuts can be locked together to unscrew a stud from a component

● A bolt or screw which has broken off below or level with the casing must be extracted using a screw extractor set. Centre punch the fastener to centralise the drill bit, then drill a hole in the fastener **(see illustration 2.19)**. Select a drill bit which is approximately half to three-quarters the

2.19 When using a screw extractor, first drill a hole in the fastener . . .

diameter of the fastener and drill to a depth which will accommodate the extractor. Use the largest size extractor possible, but avoid leaving too small a wall thickness otherwise the extractor will merely force the fastener walls outwards wedging it in the casing thread.

● If a spiral type extractor is used, thread it anti-clockwise into the fastener. As it is screwed in, it will grip the fastener and unscrew it from the casing **(see illustration 2.20)**.

2.20 . . . then thread the extractor anti-clockwise into the fastener

● If a taper type extractor is used, tap it into the fastener so that it is firmly wedged in place. Unscrew the extractor (anti-clockwise) to draw the fastener out.

> ⚠ **Warning: Stud extractors are very hard and may break off in the fastener if care is not taken - ask an engineer about spark erosion if this happens.**

● Alternatively, the broken bolt/screw can be drilled out and the hole retapped for an oversize bolt/screw or a diamond-section thread insert. It is essential that the drilling is carried out squarely and to the correct depth, otherwise the casing may be ruined - if in doubt, entrust the work to an engineer.
● Bolts and nuts with rounded corners cause the correct size spanner or socket to slip when force is applied. Of the types of spanner/socket available always use a six-point type rather than an eight or twelve-point type - better grip

2.21 Comparison of surface drive ring spanner (left) with 12-point type (right)

is obtained. Surface drive spanners grip the middle of the hex flats, rather than the corners, and are thus good in cases of damaged heads **(see illustration 2.21)**.

● Slotted-head or Phillips-head screws are often damaged by the use of the wrong size screwdriver. Allen-head and Torx-head screws are much less likely to sustain damage. If enough of the screw head is exposed you can use a hacksaw to cut a slot in its head and then use a conventional flat-bladed screwdriver to remove it. Alternatively use a hammer and cold chisel to tap the head of the fastener around to slacken it. Always replace damaged fasteners with new ones, preferably Torx or Allen-head type.

HAYNES HINT

A dab of valve grinding compound between the screw head and screw-driver tip will often give a good grip.

Thread repair

● Threads (particularly those in aluminium alloy components) can be damaged by overtightening, being assembled with dirt in the threads, or from a component working loose and vibrating. Eventually the thread will fail completely, and it will be impossible to tighten the fastener.

● If a thread is damaged or clogged with old locking compound it can be renovated with a thread repair tool (thread chaser) **(see illustrations 2.22 and 2.23)**; special thread

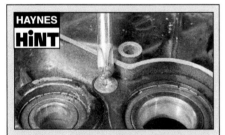

2.22 A thread repair tool being used to correct an internal thread

2.23 A thread repair tool being used to correct an external thread

chasers are available for spark plug hole threads. The tool will not cut a new thread, but clean and true the original thread. Make sure that you use the correct diameter and pitch tool. Similarly, external threads can be cleaned up with a die or a thread restorer file **(see illustration 2.24)**.

2.24 Using a thread restorer file

● It is possible to drill out the old thread and retap the component to the next thread size. This will work where there is enough surrounding material and a new bolt or screw can be obtained. Sometimes, however, this is not possible - such as where the bolt/screw passes through another component which must also be suitably modified, also in cases where a spark plug or oil drain plug cannot be obtained in a larger diameter thread size.

● The diamond-section thread insert (often known by its popular trade name of Heli-Coil) is a simple and effective method of renewing the thread and retaining the original size. A kit can be purchased which contains the tap, insert and installing tool **(see illustration 2.25)**. Drill out the damaged thread with the size drill specified **(see illustration 2.26)**. Carefully retap the thread **(see illustration 2.27)**. Install the

2.25 Obtain a thread insert kit to suit the thread diameter and pitch required

2.26 To install a thread insert, first drill out the original thread . . .

2.27 . . . tap a new thread . . .

2.28 . . . fit insert on the installing tool . . .

2.29 . . . and thread into the component . . .

2.30 . . . break off the tang when complete

insert on the installing tool and thread it slowly into place using a light downward pressure **(see illustrations 2.28 and 2.29)**. When positioned between a 1/4 and 1/2 turn below the surface withdraw the installing tool and use the break-off tool to press down on the tang, breaking it off **(see illustration 2.30)**.

● There are epoxy thread repair kits on the market which can rebuild stripped internal threads, although this repair should not be used on high load-bearing components.

Thread locking and sealing compounds

● Locking compounds are used in locations where the fastener is prone to loosening due to vibration or on important safety-related items which might cause loss of control of the motorcycle if they fail. It is also used where important fasteners cannot be secured by other means such as lockwashers or split pins.

● Before applying locking compound, make sure that the threads (internal and external) are clean and dry with all old compound removed. Select a compound to suit the component being secured - a non-permanent general locking and sealing type is suitable for most applications, but a high strength type is needed for permanent fixing of studs in castings. Apply a drop or two of the compound to the first few threads of the fastener, then thread it into place and tighten to the specified torque. Do not apply excessive thread locking compound otherwise the thread may be damaged on subsequent removal.

● Certain fasteners are impregnated with a dry film type coating of locking compound on their threads. Always renew this type of fastener if disturbed.

● Anti-seize compounds, such as copper-based greases, can be applied to protect threads from seizure due to extreme heat and corrosion. A common instance is spark plug threads and exhaust system fasteners.

3 Measuring tools and gauges

Feeler gauges

● Feeler gauges (or blades) are used for measuring small gaps and clearances (see illustration 3.1). They can also be used to measure endfloat (sideplay) of a component on a shaft where access is not possible with a dial gauge.

● Feeler gauge sets should be treated with care and not bent or damaged. They are etched with their size on one face. Keep them clean and very lightly oiled to prevent corrosion build-up.

3.1 Feeler gauges are used for measuring small gaps and clearances - thickness is marked on one face of gauge

● When measuring a clearance, select a gauge which is a light sliding fit between the two components. You may need to use two gauges together to measure the clearance accurately.

Micrometers

● A micrometer is a precision tool capable of measuring to 0.01 or 0.001 of a millimetre. It should always be stored in its case and not in the general toolbox. It must be kept clean and never dropped, otherwise its frame or measuring anvils could be distorted resulting in inaccurate readings.

● External micrometers are used for measuring outside diameters of components and have many more applications than internal micrometers. Micrometers are available in different size ranges, eg 0 to 25 mm, 25 to 50 mm, and upwards in 25 mm steps; some large micrometers have interchangeable anvils to allow a range of measurements to be taken. Generally the largest precision measurement you are likely to take on a motorcycle is the piston diameter.

● Internal micrometers (or bore micrometers) are used for measuring inside diameters, such as valve guides and cylinder bores. Telescoping gauges and small hole gauges are used in conjunction with an external micro-meter, whereas the more expensive internal micrometers have their own measuring device.

External micrometer

Note: *The conventional analogue type instrument is described. Although much easier to read, digital micrometers are considerably more expensive.*

● Always check the calibration of the micrometer before use. With the anvils closed (0 to 25 mm type) or set over a test gauge (for

3.2 Check micrometer calibration before use

the larger types) the scale should read zero **(see illustration 3.2)**; make sure that the anvils (and test piece) are clean first. Any discrepancy can be adjusted by referring to the instructions supplied with the tool. Remember that the micrometer is a precision measuring tool - don't force the anvils closed, use the ratchet (4) on the end of the micrometer to close it. In this way, a measured force is always applied.

● To use, first make sure that the item being measured is clean. Place the anvil of the micrometer (1) against the item and use the thimble (2) to bring the spindle (3) lightly into contact with the other side of the item **(see illustration 3.3)**. Don't tighten the thimble down because this will damage the micrometer - instead use the ratchet (4) on the end of the micrometer. The ratchet mechanism applies a measured force preventing damage to the instrument.

● The micrometer is read by referring to the linear scale on the sleeve and the annular scale on the thimble. Read off the sleeve first to obtain the base measurement, then add the fine measurement from the thimble to obtain the overall reading. The linear scale on the sleeve represents the measuring range of the micrometer (eg 0 to 25 mm). The annular scale

3.3 Micrometer component parts

| 1 Anvil | 3 Spindle | 5 Frame |
| 2 Thimble | 4 Ratchet | 6 Locking lever |

on the thimble will be in graduations of 0.01 mm (or as marked on the frame) - one full revolution of the thimble will move 0.5 mm on the linear scale. Take the reading where the datum line on the sleeve intersects the thimble's scale. Always position the eye directly above the scale otherwise an inaccurate reading will result.

In the example shown the item measures 2.95 mm (see illustration 3.4):

Linear scale	2.00 mm
Linear scale	0.50 mm
Annular scale	0.45 mm
Total figure	**2.95 mm**

3.5 Micrometer reading of 46.99 mm on linear and annular scales . . .

3.7 Expand the telescoping gauge in the bore, lock its position . . .

3.4 Micrometer reading of 2.95 mm

3.6 . . . and 0.004 mm on vernier scale

3.8 . . . then measure the gauge with a micrometer

Most micrometers have a locking lever (6) on the frame to hold the setting in place, allowing the item to be removed from the micrometer.
● Some micrometers have a vernier scale on their sleeve, providing an even finer measurement to be taken, in 0.001 increments of a millimetre. Take the sleeve and thimble measurement as described above, then check which graduation on the vernier scale aligns with that of the annular scale on the thimble **Note:** *The eye must be perpendicular to the scale when taking the vernier reading - if necessary rotate the body of the micrometer to ensure this.* Multiply the vernier scale figure by 0.001 and add it to the base and fine measurement figures.

In the example shown the item measures 46.994 mm (see illustrations 3.5 and 3.6):

Linear scale (base)	46.000 mm
Linear scale (base)	00.500 mm
Annular scale (fine)	00.490 mm
Vernier scale	00.004 mm
Total figure	**46.994 mm**

Internal micrometer

● Internal micrometers are available for measuring bore diameters, but are expensive and unlikely to be available for home use. It is suggested that a set of telescoping gauges and small hole gauges, both of which must be used with an external micrometer, will suffice for taking internal measurements on a motorcycle.
● Telescoping gauges can be used to

measure internal diameters of components. Select a gauge with the correct size range, make sure its ends are clean and insert it into the bore. Expand the gauge, then lock its position and withdraw it from the bore **(see illustration 3.7)**. Measure across the gauge ends with a micrometer **(see illustration 3.8)**.
● Very small diameter bores (such as valve guides) are measured with a small hole gauge. Once adjusted to a slip-fit inside the component, its position is locked and the gauge withdrawn for measurement with a micrometer **(see illustrations 3.9 and 3.10)**.

Vernier caliper

Note: *The conventional linear and dial gauge type instruments are described. Digital types are easier to read, but are far more expensive.*
● The vernier caliper does not provide the precision of a micrometer, but is versatile in being able to measure internal and external diameters. Some types also incorporate a depth gauge. It is ideal for measuring clutch plate friction material and spring free lengths.
● To use the conventional linear scale vernier, slacken off the vernier clamp screws (1) and set its jaws over (2), or inside (3), the item to be measured **(see illustration 3.11)**. Slide the jaw into contact, using the thumbwheel (4) for fine movement of the sliding scale (5) then tighten the clamp screws (1). Read off the main scale (6) where the zero on the sliding scale (5) intersects it, taking the whole number to the left of the zero; this provides the base measurement. View along the sliding scale and select the division which

3.9 Expand the small hole gauge in the bore, lock its position . . .

3.10 . . . then measure the gauge with a micrometer

lines up exactly with any of the divisions on the main scale, noting that the divisions usually represents 0.02 of a millimetre. Add this fine measurement to the base measurement to obtain the total reading.

3.11 Vernier component parts (linear gauge)

1 Clamp screws   3 Internal jaws   5 Sliding scale   7 Depth gauge
2 External jaws   4 Thumbwheel   6 Main scale

In the example shown the item measures 55.92 mm **(see illustration 3.12)**:

Base measurement	55.00 mm
Fine measurement	00.92 mm
Total figure	**55.92 mm**

3.12 Vernier gauge reading of 55.92 mm

3.13 Vernier component parts (dial gauge)

1 Clamp screw   5 Main scale
2 External jaws   6 Sliding scale
3 Internal jaws   7 Dial gauge
4 Thumbwheel

● Some vernier calipers are equipped with a dial gauge for fine measurement. Before use, check that the jaws are clean, then close them fully and check that the dial gauge reads zero. If necessary adjust the gauge ring accordingly. Slacken the vernier clamp screw (1) and set its jaws over (2), or inside (3), the item to be measured **(see illustration 3.13)**. Slide the jaws into contact, using the thumbwheel (4) for fine movement. Read off the main scale (5) where the edge of the sliding scale (6) intersects it, taking the whole number to the left of the zero; this provides the base measurement. Read off the needle position on the dial gauge (7) scale to provide the fine measurement; each division represents 0.05 of a millimetre. Add this fine measurement to the base measurement to obtain the total reading.

In the example shown the item measures 55.95 mm **(see illustration 3.14)**:

Base measurement	55.00 mm
Fine measurement	00.95 mm
Total figure	**55.95 mm**

3.14 Vernier gauge reading of 55.95 mm

Plastigauge

● Plastigauge is a plastic material which can be compressed between two surfaces to measure the oil clearance between them. The width of the compressed Plastigauge is measured against a calibrated scale to determine the clearance.

● Common uses of Plastigauge are for measuring the clearance between crankshaft journal and main bearing inserts, between crankshaft journal and big-end bearing inserts, and between camshaft and bearing surfaces. The following example describes big-end oil clearance measurement.

● Handle the Plastigauge material carefully to prevent distortion. Using a sharp knife, cut a length which corresponds with the width of the bearing being measured and place it carefully across the journal so that it is parallel with the shaft **(see illustration 3.15)**. Carefully install both bearing shells and the connecting rod. Without rotating the rod on the journal tighten its bolts or nuts (as applicable) to the specified torque. The connecting rod and bearings are then disassembled and the crushed Plastigauge examined.

3.15 Plastigauge placed across shaft journal

● Using the scale provided in the Plastigauge kit, measure the width of the material to determine the oil clearance **(see illustration 3.16)**. Always remove all traces of Plastigauge after use using your fingernails.

> *Caution: Arriving at the correct clearance demands that the assembly is torqued correctly, according to the settings and sequence (where applicable) provided by the motorcycle manufacturer.*

3.16 Measuring the width of the crushed Plastigauge

Dial gauge or DTI (Dial Test Indicator)

● A dial gauge can be used to accurately measure small amounts of movement. Typical uses are measuring shaft runout or shaft endfloat (sideplay) and setting piston position for ignition timing on two-strokes. A dial gauge set usually comes with a range of different probes and adapters and mounting equipment.
● The gauge needle must point to zero when at rest. Rotate the ring around its periphery to zero the gauge.
● Check that the gauge is capable of reading the extent of movement in the work. Most gauges have a small dial set in the face which records whole millimetres of movement as well as the fine scale around the face periphery which is calibrated in 0.01 mm divisions. Read off the small dial first to obtain the base measurement, then add the measurement from the fine scale to obtain the total reading.

In the example shown the gauge reads 1.48 mm (see illustration 3.17):

Base measurement	1.00 mm
Fine measurement	0.48 mm
Total figure	**1.48 mm**

3.17 Dial gauge reading of 1.48 mm

● If measuring shaft runout, the shaft must be supported in vee-blocks and the gauge mounted on a stand perpendicular to the shaft. Rest the tip of the gauge against the centre of the shaft and rotate the shaft slowly whilst watching the gauge reading (see illustration 3.18). Take several measurements along the length of the shaft and record the

3.18 Using a dial gauge to measure shaft runout

maximum gauge reading as the amount of runout in the shaft. **Note:** *The reading obtained will be total runout at that point - some manufacturers specify that the runout figure is halved to compare with their specified runout limit.*
● Endfloat (sideplay) measurement requires that the gauge is mounted securely to the surrounding component with its probe touching the end of the shaft. Using hand pressure, push and pull on the shaft noting the maximum endfloat recorded on the gauge (see illustration 3.19).

3.19 Using a dial gauge to measure shaft endfloat

● A dial gauge with suitable adapters can be used to determine piston position BTDC on two-stroke engines for the purposes of ignition timing. The gauge, adapter and suitable length probe are installed in the place of the spark plug and the gauge zeroed at TDC. If the piston position is specified as 1.14 mm BTDC, rotate the engine back to 2.00 mm BTDC, then slowly forwards to 1.14 mm BTDC.

Cylinder compression gauges

● A compression gauge is used for measuring cylinder compression. Either the rubber-cone type or the threaded adapter type can be used. The latter is preferred to ensure a perfect seal against the cylinder head. A 0 to 300 psi (0 to 20 Bar) type gauge (for petrol/gasoline engines) will be suitable for motorcycles.
● The spark plug is removed and the gauge either held hard against the cylinder head (cone type) or the gauge adapter screwed into the cylinder head (threaded type) (see illustration 3.20). Cylinder compression is measured with the engine turning over, but not running - carry out the compression test as described in

3.20 Using a rubber-cone type cylinder compression gauge

Fault Finding Equipment. The gauge will hold the reading until manually released.

Oil pressure gauge

● An oil pressure gauge is used for measuring engine oil pressure. Most gauges come with a set of adapters to fit the thread of the take-off point (see illustration 3.21). If the take-off point specified by the motorcycle manufacturer is an external oil pipe union, make sure that the specified replacement union is used to prevent oil starvation.

3.21 Oil pressure gauge and take-off point adapter (arrow)

● Oil pressure is measured with the engine running (at a specific rpm) and often the manufacturer will specify pressure limits for a cold and hot engine.

Straight-edge and surface plate

● If checking the gasket face of a component for warpage, place a steel rule or precision straight-edge across the gasket face and measure any gap between the straight-edge and component with feeler gauges (see illustration 3.22). Check diagonally across the component and between mounting holes (see illustration 3.23).

3.22 Use a straight-edge and feeler gauges to check for warpage

3.23 Check for warpage in these directions

● Checking individual components for warpage, such as clutch plain (metal) plates, requires a perfectly flat plate or piece or plate glass and feeler gauges.

4 Torque and leverage

What is torque?

● Torque describes the twisting force about a shaft. The amount of torque applied is determined by the distance from the centre of the shaft to the end of the lever and the amount of force being applied to the end of the lever; distance multiplied by force equals torque.

● The manufacturer applies a measured torque to a bolt or nut to ensure that it will not slacken in use and to hold two components securely together without movement in the joint. The actual torque setting depends on the thread size, bolt or nut material and the composition of the components being held.

● Too little torque may cause the fastener to loosen due to vibration, whereas too much torque will distort the joint faces of the component or cause the fastener to shear off. Always stick to the specified torque setting.

Using a torque wrench

● Check the calibration of the torque wrench and make sure it has a suitable range for the job. Torque wrenches are available in Nm (Newton-metres), kgf m (kilograms-force metre), lbf ft (pounds-feet), lbf in (inch-pounds). Do not confuse lbf ft with lbf in.

● Adjust the tool to the desired torque on the scale (see illustration 4.1). If your torque wrench is not calibrated in the units specified, carefully convert the figure (see Conversion Factors). A manufacturer sometimes gives a torque setting as a range (8 to 10 Nm) rather than a single figure - in this case set the tool midway between the two settings. The same torque may be expressed as 9 Nm ± 1 Nm. Some torque wrenches have a method of locking the setting so that it isn't inadvertently altered during use.

4.1 Set the torque wrench index mark to the setting required, in this case 12 Nm

● Install the bolts/nuts in their correct location and secure them lightly. Their threads must be clean and free of any old locking compound. Unless specified the threads and flange should be dry - oiled threads are necessary in certain circumstances and the manufacturer will take this into account in the specified torque figure. Similarly, the manufacturer may also specify the application of thread-locking compound.

● Tighten the fasteners in the specified sequence until the torque wrench clicks, indicating that the torque setting has been reached. Apply the torque again to double-check the setting. Where different thread diameter fasteners secure the component, as a rule tighten the larger diameter ones first.

● When the torque wrench has been finished with, release the lock (where applicable) and fully back off its setting to zero - do not leave the torque wrench tensioned. Also, do not use a torque wrench for slackening a fastener.

Angle-tightening

● Manufacturers often specify a figure in degrees for final tightening of a fastener. This usually follows tightening to a specific torque setting.

● A degree disc can be set and attached to the socket (see illustration 4.2) or a protractor can be used to mark the angle of movement on the bolt/nut head and the surrounding casting (see illustration 4.3).

4.2 Angle tightening can be accomplished with a torque-angle gauge . . .

4.3 . . . or by marking the angle on the surrounding component

Loosening sequences

● Where more than one bolt/nut secures a component, loosen each fastener evenly a little at a time. In this way, not all the stress of the joint is held by one fastener and the components are not likely to distort.

● If a tightening sequence is provided, work in the REVERSE of this, but if not, work from the outside in, in a criss-cross sequence (see illustration 4.4).

4.4 When slackening, work from the outside inwards

Tightening sequences

● If a component is held by more than one fastener it is important that the retaining bolts/nuts are tightened evenly to prevent uneven stress build-up and distortion of sealing faces. This is especially important on high-compression joints such as the cylinder head.

● A sequence is usually provided by the manufacturer, either in a diagram or actually marked in the casting. If not, always start in the centre and work outwards in a criss-cross pattern (see illustration 4.5). Start off by securing all bolts/nuts finger-tight, then set the torque wrench and tighten each fastener by a small amount in sequence until the final torque is reached. By following this practice,

4.5 When tightening, work from the inside outwards

the joint will be held evenly and will not be distorted. Important joints, such as the cylinder head and big-end fasteners often have two- or three-stage torque settings.

Applying leverage

● Use tools at the correct angle. Position a socket wrench or spanner on the bolt/nut so that you pull it towards you when loosening. If this can't be done, push the spanner without curling your fingers around it **(see illustration 4.6)** - the spanner may slip or the fastener loosen suddenly, resulting in your fingers being crushed against a component.

4.6 If you can't pull on the spanner to loosen a fastener, push with your hand open

● Additional leverage is gained by extending the length of the lever. The best way to do this is to use a breaker bar instead of the regular length tool, or to slip a length of tubing over the end of the spanner or socket wrench.
● If additional leverage will not work, the fastener head is either damaged or firmly corroded in place (see *Fasteners*).

5 Bearings

Bearing removal and installation

Drivers and sockets

● Before removing a bearing, always inspect the casing to see which way it must be driven out - some casings will have retaining plates or a cast step. Also check for any identifying markings on the bearing and if installed to a certain depth, measure this at this stage. Some roller bearings are sealed on one side - take note of the original fitted position.
● Bearings can be driven out of a casing using a bearing driver tool (with the correct size head) or a socket of the correct diameter. Select the driver head or socket so that it contacts the outer race of the bearing, not the balls/rollers or inner race. Always support the casing around the bearing housing with wood blocks, otherwise there is a risk of fracture. The bearing is driven out with a few blows on the driver or socket from a heavy mallet. Unless access is severely restricted (as with wheel bearings), a pin-punch is not recommended unless it is moved around the bearing to keep it square in its housing.

● The same equipment can be used to install bearings. Make sure the bearing housing is supported on wood blocks and line up the bearing in its housing. Fit the bearing as noted on removal - generally they are installed with their marked side facing outwards. Tap the bearing squarely into its housing using a driver or socket which bears only on the bearing's outer race - contact with the bearing balls/rollers or inner race will destroy it **(see illustrations 5.1 and 5.2)**.
● Check that the bearing inner race and balls/rollers rotate freely.

5.1 Using a bearing driver against the bearing's outer race

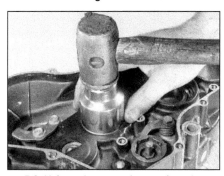

5.2 Using a large socket against the bearing's outer race

Pullers and slide-hammers

● Where a bearing is pressed on a shaft a puller will be required to extract it **(see illustration 5.3)**. Make sure that the puller clamp or legs fit securely behind the bearing and are unlikely to slip out. If pulling a bearing

5.3 This bearing puller clamps behind the bearing and pressure is applied to the shaft end to draw the bearing off

off a gear shaft for example, you may have to locate the puller behind a gear pinion if there is no access to the race and draw the gear pinion off the shaft as well **(see illustration 5.4)**.

> *Caution: Ensure that the puller's centre bolt locates securely against the end of the shaft and will not slip when pressure is applied. Also ensure that puller does not damage the shaft end.*

5.4 Where no access is available to the rear of the bearing, it is sometimes possible to draw off the adjacent component

● Operate the puller so that its centre bolt exerts pressure on the shaft end and draws the bearing off the shaft.
● When installing the bearing on the shaft, tap only on the bearing's inner race - contact with the balls/rollers or outer race with destroy the bearing. Use a socket or length of tubing as a drift which fits over the shaft end **(see illustration 5.5)**.

5.5 When installing a bearing on a shaft use a piece of tubing which bears only on the bearing's inner race

● Where a bearing locates in a blind hole in a casing, it cannot be driven or pulled out as described above. A slide-hammer with knife-edged bearing puller attachment will be required. The puller attachment passes through the bearing and when tightened expands to fit firmly behind the bearing **(see illustration 5.6)**. By operating the slide-hammer part of the tool the bearing is jarred out of its housing **(see illustration 5.7)**.
● It is possible, if the bearing is of reasonable weight, for it to drop out of its housing if the casing is heated as described opposite. If this

5.6 Expand the bearing puller so that it locks behind the bearing . . .

5.7 . . . attach the slide hammer to the bearing puller

method is attempted, first prepare a work surface which will enable the casing to be tapped face down to help dislodge the bearing - a wood surface is ideal since it will not damage the casing's gasket surface. Wearing protective gloves, tap the heated casing several times against the work surface to dislodge the bearing under its own weight **(see illustration 5.8)**.

5.8 Tapping a casing face down on wood blocks can often dislodge a bearing

● Bearings can be installed in blind holes using the driver or socket method described above.

Drawbolts

● Where a bearing or bush is set in the eye of a component, such as a suspension linkage arm or connecting rod small-end, removal by drift may damage the component. Furthermore, a rubber bushing in a shock absorber eye cannot successfully be driven out of position. If access is available to a engineering press, the task is straightforward. If not, a drawbolt can be fabricated to extract the bearing or bush.

5.9 Drawbolt component parts assembled on a suspension arm

1 Bolt or length of threaded bar
2 Nuts
3 Washer (external diameter greater than tubing internal diameter)
4 Tubing (internal diameter sufficient to accommodate bearing)
5 Suspension arm with bearing
6 Tubing (external diameter slightly smaller than bearing)
7 Washer (external diameter slightly smaller than bearing)

5.10 Drawing the bearing out of the suspension arm

● To extract the bearing/bush you will need a long bolt with nut (or piece of threaded bar with two nuts), a piece of tubing which has an internal diameter larger than the bearing/bush, another piece of tubing which has an external diameter slightly smaller than the bearing/ bush, and a selection of washers **(see illustrations 5.9 and 5.10)**. Note that the pieces of tubing must be of the same length, or longer, than the bearing/bush.
● The same kit (without the pieces of tubing) can be used to draw the new bearing/bush back into place **(see illustration 5.11)**.

5.11 Installing a new bearing (1) in the suspension arm

Temperature change

● If the bearing's outer race is a tight fit in the casing, the aluminium casing can be heated to release its grip on the bearing. Aluminium will expand at a greater rate than the steel bearing outer race. There are several ways to do this, but avoid any localised extreme heat (such as a blow torch) - aluminium alloy has a low melting point.
● Approved methods of heating a casing are using a domestic oven (heated to 100°C) or immersing the casing in boiling water **(see illustration 5.12)**. Low temperature range localised heat sources such as a paint stripper heat gun or clothes iron can also be used **(see illustration 5.13)**. Alternatively, soak a rag in boiling water, wring it out and wrap it around the bearing housing.

> ⚠ **Warning: All of these methods require care in use to prevent scalding and burns to the hands. Wear protective gloves when handling hot components.**

5.12 A casing can be immersed in a sink of boiling water to aid bearing removal

5.13 Using a localised heat source to aid bearing removal

● If heating the whole casing note that plastic components, such as the neutral switch, may suffer - remove them beforehand.
● After heating, remove the bearing as described above. You may find that the expansion is sufficient for the bearing to fall out of the casing under its own weight or with a light tap on the driver or socket.
● If necessary, the casing can be heated to aid bearing installation, and this is sometimes the recommended procedure if the motorcycle manufacturer has designed the housing and bearing fit with this intention.

● Installation of bearings can be eased by placing them in a freezer the night before installation. The steel bearing will contract slightly, allowing easy insertion in its housing. This is often useful when installing steering head outer races in the frame.

Bearing types and markings

● Plain shell bearings, ball bearings, needle roller bearings and tapered roller bearings will all be found on motorcycles (see illustrations 5.14 and 5.15). The ball and roller types are usually caged between an inner and outer race, but uncaged variations may be found.

5.14 Shell bearings are either plain or grooved. They are usually identified by colour code (arrow)

5.15 Tapered roller bearing (A), needle roller bearing (B) and ball journal bearing (C)

● Shell bearings (often called inserts) are usually found at the crankshaft main and connecting rod big-end where they are good at coping with high loads. They are made of a phosphor-bronze material and are impregnated with self-lubricating properties.
● Ball bearings and needle roller bearings consist of a steel inner and outer race with the balls or rollers between the races. They require constant lubrication by oil or grease and are good at coping with axial loads. Taper roller bearings consist of rollers set in a tapered cage set on the inner race; the outer race is separate. They are good at coping with axial loads and prevent movement along the shaft - a typical application is in the steering head.
● Bearing manufacturers produce bearings to ISO size standards and stamp one face of the bearing to indicate its internal and external diameter, load capacity and type (see illustration 5.16).
● Metal bushes are usually of phosphor-bronze material. Rubber bushes are used in suspension mounting eyes. Fibre bushes have also been used in suspension pivots.

5.16 Typical bearing marking

Bearing fault finding

● If a bearing outer race has spun in its housing, the housing material will be damaged. You can use a bearing locking compound to bond the outer race in place if damage is not too severe.
● Shell bearings will fail due to damage of their working surface, as a result of lack of lubrication, corrosion or abrasive particles in the oil (see illustration 5.17). Small particles of dirt in the oil may embed in the bearing material whereas larger particles will score the bearing and shaft journal. If a number of short journeys are made, insufficient heat will be generated to drive off condensation which has built up on the bearings.

5.17 Typical bearing failures

● Ball and roller bearings will fail due to lack of lubrication or damage to the balls or rollers. Tapered-roller bearings can be damaged by overloading them. Unless the bearing is sealed on both sides, wash it in paraffin (kerosene) to remove all old grease then allow it to dry. Make a visual inspection looking to dented balls or rollers, damaged cages and worn or pitted races (see illustration 5.18).
● A ball bearing can be checked for wear by listening to it when spun. Apply a film of light oil to the bearing and hold it close to the ear - hold the outer race with one hand and spin the inner

5.18 Example of ball journal bearing with damaged balls and cages

5.19 Hold outer race and listen to inner race when spun

race with the other hand (see illustration 5.19). The bearing should be almost silent when spun; if it grates or rattles it is worn.

6 Oil seals

Oil seal removal and installation

● Oil seals should be renewed every time a component is dismantled. This is because the seal lips will become set to the sealing surface and will not necessarily reseal.
● Oil seals can be prised out of position using a large flat-bladed screwdriver (see illustration 6.1). In the case of crankcase seals, check first that the seal is not lipped on the inside, preventing its removal with the crankcases joined.

6.1 Prise out oil seals with a large flat-bladed screwdriver

● New seals are usually installed with their marked face (containing the seal reference code) outwards and the spring side towards the fluid being retained. In certain cases, such as a two-stroke engine crankshaft seal, a double lipped seal may be used due to there being fluid or gas on each side of the joint.

● Use a bearing driver or socket which bears only on the outer hard edge of the seal to install it in the casing - tapping on the inner edge will damage the sealing lip.

Oil seal types and markings

● Oil seals are usually of the single-lipped type. Double-lipped seals are found where a liquid or gas is on both sides of the joint.
● Oil seals can harden and lose their sealing ability if the motorcycle has been in storage for a long period - renewal is the only solution.
● Oil seal manufacturers also conform to the ISO markings for seal size - these are moulded into the outer face of the seal (see illustration 6.2).

6.2 These oil seal markings indicate inside diameter, outside diameter and seal thickness

7 Gaskets and sealants

Types of gasket and sealant

● Gaskets are used to seal the mating surfaces between components and keep lubricants, fluids, vacuum or pressure contained within the assembly. Aluminium gaskets are sometimes found at the cylinder joints, but most gaskets are paper-based. If the mating surfaces of the components being joined are undamaged the gasket can be installed dry, although a dab of sealant or grease will be useful to hold it in place during assembly.
● RTV (Room Temperature Vulcanising) silicone rubber sealants cure when exposed to moisture in the atmosphere. These sealants are good at filling pits or irregular gasket faces, but will tend to be forced out of the joint under very high torque. They can be used to replace a paper gasket, but first make sure that the width of the paper gasket is not essential to the shimming of internal components. RTV sealants should not be used on components containing petrol (gasoline).
● Non-hardening, semi-hardening and hard setting liquid gasket compounds can be used with a gasket or between a metal-to-metal joint. Select the sealant to suit the application: universal non-hardening sealant can be used on virtually all joints; semi-hardening on joint faces which are rough or damaged; hard setting sealant on joints which require a permanent bond and are subjected to high temperature and pressure. **Note:** *Check first if the paper gasket has a bead of sealant*

impregnated in its surface before applying additional sealant.
● When choosing a sealant, make sure it is suitable for the application, particularly if being applied in a high-temperature area or in the vicinity of fuel. Certain manufacturers produce sealants in either clear, silver or black colours to match the finish of the engine. This has a particular application on motorcycles where much of the engine is exposed.
● Do not over-apply sealant. That which is squeezed out on the outside of the joint can be wiped off, whereas an excess of sealant on the inside can break off and clog oilways.

Breaking a sealed joint

● Age, heat, pressure and the use of hard setting sealant can cause two components to stick together so tightly that they are difficult to separate using finger pressure alone. Do not resort to using levers unless there is a pry point provided for this purpose (see illustration 7.1) or else the gasket surfaces will be damaged.
● Use a soft-faced hammer (see illustration 7.2) or a wood block and conventional hammer to strike the component near the mating surface. Avoid hammering against cast extremities since they may break off. If this method fails, try using a wood wedge between the two components.

Caution: If the joint will not separate, double-check that you have removed all the fasteners.

7.1 If a pry point is provided, apply gently pressure with a flat-bladed screwdriver

7.2 Tap around the joint with a soft-faced mallet if necessary - don't strike cooling fins

Removal of old gasket and sealant

● Paper gaskets will most likely come away complete, leaving only a few traces stuck on

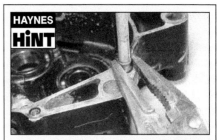

Most components have one or two hollow locating dowels between the two gasket faces. If a dowel cannot be removed, do not resort to gripping it with pliers - it will almost certainly be distorted. Install a close-fitting socket or Phillips screwdriver into the dowel and then grip the outer edge of the dowel to free it.

the sealing faces of the components. It is imperative that all traces are removed to ensure correct sealing of the new gasket.
● Very carefully scrape all traces of gasket away making sure that the sealing surfaces are not gouged or scored by the scraper (see illustrations 7.3, 7.4 and 7.5). Stubborn deposits can be removed by spraying with an aerosol gasket remover. Final preparation of

7.3 Paper gaskets can be scraped off with a gasket scraper tool . . .

7.4 . . . a knife blade . . .

7.5 . . . or a household scraper

7.6 Fine abrasive paper is wrapped around a flat file to clean up the gasket face

7.7 A kitchen scourer can be used on stubborn deposits

the gasket surface can be made with very fine abrasive paper or a plastic kitchen scourer **(see illustrations 7.6 and 7.7)**.
● Old sealant can be scraped or peeled off components, depending on the type originally used. Note that gasket removal compounds are available to avoid scraping the components clean; make sure the gasket remover suits the type of sealant used.

8 Chains

Breaking and joining final drive chains

● Drive chains for all but small bikes are continuous and do not have a clip-type connecting link. The chain must be broken using a chain breaker tool and the new chain securely riveted together using a new soft rivet-type link. Never use a clip-type connecting link instead of a rivet-type link, except in an emergency. Various chain breaking and riveting tools are available, either as separate tools or combined as illustrated in the accompanying photographs - read the instructions supplied with the tool carefully.

⚠️ **Warning: The need to rivet the new link pins correctly cannot be overstressed - loss of control of the motorcycle is very likely to result if the chain breaks in use.**

● Rotate the chain and look for the soft link. The soft link pins look like they have been

8.1 Tighten the chain breaker to push the pin out of the link . . .

8.2 . . . withdraw the pin, remove the tool . . .

8.3 . . . and separate the chain link

deeply centre-punched instead of peened over like all the other pins **(see illustration 8.9)** and its sideplate may be a different colour. Position the soft link midway between the sprockets and assemble the chain breaker tool over one of the soft link pins **(see illustration 8.1)**. Operate the tool to push the pin out through the chain **(see illustration 8.2)**. On an O-ring chain, remove the O-rings **(see illustration 8.3)**. Carry out the same procedure on the other soft link pin.

Caution: Certain soft link pins (particularly on the larger chains) may require their ends to be filed or ground off before they can be pressed out using the tool.

● Check that you have the correct size and strength (standard or heavy duty) new soft link - do not reuse the old link. Look for the size marking on the chain sideplates **(see illustration 8.10)**.
● Position the chain ends so that they are engaged over the rear sprocket. On an O-ring

8.4 Insert the new soft link, with O-rings, through the chain ends . . .

8.5 . . . install the O-rings over the pin ends . . .

8.6 . . . followed by the sideplate

chain, install a new O-ring over each pin of the link and insert the link through the two chain ends **(see illustration 8.4)**. Install a new O-ring over the end of each pin, followed by the sideplate (with the chain manufacturer's marking facing outwards) **(see illustrations 8.5 and 8.6)**. On an unsealed chain, insert the link through the two chain ends, then install the sideplate with the chain manufacturer's marking facing outwards.
● Note that it may not be possible to install the sideplate using finger pressure alone. If using a joining tool, assemble it so that the plates of the tool clamp the link and press the sideplate over the pins **(see illustration 8.7)**. Otherwise, use two small sockets placed over

8.7 Push the sideplate into position using a clamp

8.8 Assemble the chain riveting tool over one pin at a time and tighten it fully

8.9 Pin end correctly riveted (A), pin end unriveted (B)

the rivet ends and two pieces of the wood between a G-clamp. Operate the clamp to press the sideplate over the pins.

● Assemble the joining tool over one pin (following the maker's instructions) and tighten the tool down to spread the pin end securely **(see illustrations 8.8 and 8.9)**. Do the same on the other pin.

 Warning: Check that the pin ends are secure and that there is no danger of the sideplate coming loose. If the pin ends are cracked the soft link must be renewed.

Final drive chain sizing

● Chains are sized using a three digit number, followed by a suffix to denote the chain type **(see illustration 8.10)**. Chain type is either standard or heavy duty (thicker sideplates), and also unsealed or O-ring/X-ring type.

● The first digit of the number relates to the pitch of the chain, ie the distance from the centre of one pin to the centre of the next pin **(see illustration 8.11)**. Pitch is expressed in eighths of an inch, as follows:

8.10 Typical chain size and type marking

8.11 Chain dimensions

| Sizes commencing with a 4 (eg 428) have a pitch of 1/2 inch (12.7 mm) |
| Sizes commencing with a 5 (eg 520) have a pitch of 5/8 inch (15.9 mm) |
| Sizes commencing with a 6 (eg 630) have a pitch of 3/4 inch (19.1 mm) |

● The second and third digits of the chain size relate to the width of the rollers, again in imperial units, eg the 525 shown has 5/16 inch (7.94 mm) rollers **(see illustration 8.11)**.

9   Hoses

Clamping to prevent flow

● Small-bore flexible hoses can be clamped to prevent fluid flow whilst a component is worked on. Whichever method is used, ensure that the hose material is not permanently distorted or damaged by the clamp.

a) A brake hose clamp available from auto accessory shops **(see illustration 9.1)**.
b) A wingnut type hose clamp **(see illustration 9.2)**.

9.1 Hoses can be clamped with an automotive brake hose clamp . . .

9.2 . . . a wingnut type hose clamp . . .

c) Two sockets placed each side of the hose and held with straight-jawed self-locking grips **(see illustration 9.3)**.
d) Thick card each side of the hose held between straight-jawed self-locking grips **(see illustration 9.4)**.

9.3 . . . two sockets and a pair of self-locking grips . . .

9.4 . . . or thick card and self-locking grips

Freeing and fitting hoses

● Always make sure the hose clamp is moved well clear of the hose end. Grip the hose with your hand and rotate it whilst pulling it off the union. If the hose has hardened due to age and will not move, slit it with a sharp knife and peel its ends off the union **(see illustration 9.5)**.

● Resist the temptation to use grease or soap on the unions to aid installation; although it helps the hose slip over the union it will equally aid the escape of fluid from the joint. It is preferable to soften the hose ends in hot water and wet the inside surface of the hose with water or a fluid which will evaporate.

9.5 Cutting a coolant hose free with a sharp knife

Conversion Factors

Length (distance)

Inches (in)	x 25.4	= Millimetres (mm)	x 0.0394	= Inches (in)	
Feet (ft)	x 0.305	= Metres (m)	x 3.281	= Feet (ft)	
Miles	x 1.609	= Kilometres (km)	x 0.621	= Miles	

Volume (capacity)

Cubic inches (cu in; in^3)	x 16.387	= Cubic centimetres (cc; cm^3)	x 0.061	= Cubic inches (cu in; in^3)	
Imperial pints (Imp pt)	x 0.568	= Litres (l)	x 1.76	= Imperial pints (Imp pt)	
Imperial quarts (Imp qt)	x 1.137	= Litres (l)	x 0.88	= Imperial quarts (Imp qt)	
Imperial quarts (Imp qt)	x 1.201	= US quarts (US qt)	x 0.833	= Imperial quarts (Imp qt)	
US quarts (US qt)	x 0.946	= Litres (l)	x 1.057	= US quarts (US qt)	
Imperial gallons (Imp gal)	x 4.546	= Litres (l)	x 0.22	= Imperial gallons (Imp gal)	
Imperial gallons (Imp gal)	x 1.201	= US gallons (US gal)	x 0.833	= Imperial gallons (Imp gal)	
US gallons (US gal)	x 3.785	= Litres (l)	x 0.264	= US gallons (US gal)	

Mass (weight)

Ounces (oz)	x 28.35	= Grams (g)	x 0.035	= Ounces (oz)	
Pounds (lb)	x 0.454	= Kilograms (kg)	x 2.205	= Pounds (lb)	

Force

Ounces-force (ozf; oz)	x 0.278	= Newtons (N)	x 3.6	= Ounces-force (ozf; oz)	
Pounds-force (lbf; lb)	x 4.448	= Newtons (N)	x 0.225	= Pounds-force (lbf; lb)	
Newtons (N)	x 0.1	= Kilograms-force (kgf; kg)	x 9.81	= Newtons (N)	

Pressure

Pounds-force per square inch (psi; lbf/in^2; lb/in^2)	x 0.070	= Kilograms-force per square centimetre (kgf/cm^2; kg/cm^2)	x 14.223	= Pounds-force per square inch (psi; lbf/in^2; lb/in^2)	
Pounds-force per square inch (psi; lbf/in^2; lb/in^2)	x 0.068	= Atmospheres (atm)	x 14.696	= Pounds-force per square inch (psi; lbf/in^2; lb/in^2)	
Pounds-force per square inch (psi; lbf/in^2; lb/in^2)	x 0.069	= Bars	x 14.5	= Pounds-force per square inch (psi; lbf/in^2; lb/in^2)	
Pounds-force per square inch (psi; lbf/in^2; lb/in^2)	x 6.895	= Kilopascals (kPa)	x 0.145	= Pounds-force per square inch (psi; lbf/in^2; lb/in^2)	
Kilopascals (kPa)	x 0.01	= Kilograms-force per square centimetre (kgf/cm^2; kg/cm^2)	x 98.1	= Kilopascals (kPa)	
Millibar (mbar)	x 100	= Pascals (Pa)	x 0.01	= Millibar (mbar)	
Millibar (mbar)	x 0.0145	= Pounds-force per square inch (psi; lbf/in^2; lb/in^2)	x 68.947	= Millibar (mbar)	
Millibar (mbar)	x 0.75	= Millimetres of mercury (mmHg)	x 1.333	= Millibar (mbar)	
Millibar (mbar)	x 0.401	= Inches of water (inH$_2$O)	x 2.491	= Millibar (mbar)	
Millimetres of mercury (mmHg)	x 0.535	= Inches of water (inH$_2$O)	x 1.868	= Millimetres of mercury (mmHg)	
Inches of water (inH$_2$O)	x 0.036	= Pounds-force per square inch (psi; lbf/in^2; lb/in^2)	x 27.68	= Inches of water (inH$_2$O)	

Torque (moment of force)

Pounds-force inches (lbf in; lb in)	x 1.152	= Kilograms-force centimetre (kgf cm; kg cm)	x 0.868	= Pounds-force inches (lbf in; lb in)	
Pounds-force inches (lbf in; lb in)	x 0.113	= Newton metres (Nm)	x 8.85	= Pounds-force inches (lbf in; lb in)	
Pounds-force inches (lbf in; lb in)	x 0.083	= Pounds-force feet (lbf ft; lb ft)	x 12	= Pounds-force inches (lbf in; lb in)	
Pounds-force feet (lbf ft; lb ft)	x 0.138	= Kilograms-force metres (kgf m; kg m)	x 7.233	= Pounds-force feet (lbf ft; lb ft)	
Pounds-force feet (lbf ft; lb ft)	x 1.356	= Newton metres (Nm)	x 0.738	= Pounds-force feet (lbf ft; lb ft)	
Newton metres (Nm)	x 0.102	= Kilograms-force metres (kgf m; kg m)	x 9.804	= Newton metres (Nm)	

Power

Horsepower (hp)	x 745.7	= Watts (W)	x 0.0013	= Horsepower (hp)	

Velocity (speed)

Miles per hour (miles/hr; mph)	x 1.609	= Kilometres per hour (km/hr; kph)	x 0.621	= Miles per hour (miles/hr; mph)	

Fuel consumption*

Miles per gallon (mpg)	x 0.354	= Kilometres per litre (km/l)	x 2.825	= Miles per gallon (mpg)	

Temperature

Degrees Fahrenheit = (°C x 1.8) + 32   Degrees Celsius (Degrees Centigrade; °C) = (°F - 32) x 0.56

It is common practice to convert from miles per gallon (mpg) to litres/100 kilometres (l/100km), where mpg x l/100 km = 282

A number of chemicals and lubricants are available for use in motorcycle maintenance and repair. They include a wide variety of products ranging from cleaning solvents and degreasers to lubricants and protective sprays for rubber, plastic and vinyl.

● **Contact point/spark plug cleaner** is a solvent used to clean oily film and dirt from points, grime from electrical connectors and oil deposits from spark plugs. It is oil free and leaves no residue. It can also be used to remove gum and varnish from carburettor jets and other orifices.

● **Carburettor cleaner** is similar to contact point/spark plug cleaner but it usually has a stronger solvent and may leave a slight oily reside. It is not recommended for cleaning electrical components or connections.

● **Brake system cleaner** is used to remove grease or brake fluid from brake system components (where clean surfaces are absolutely necessary and petroleum-based solvents cannot be used); it also leaves no residue.

● **Silicone-based lubricants** are used to protect rubber parts such as hoses and grommets, and are used as lubricants for hinges and locks.

● **Multi-purpose grease** is an all purpose lubricant used wherever grease is more practical than a liquid lubricant such as oil. Some multi-purpose grease is coloured white and specially formulated to be more resistant to water than ordinary grease.

● **Gear oil** (sometimes called gear lube) is a specially designed oil used in transmissions and final drive units, as well as other areas where high friction, high temperature lubrication is required. It is available in a number of viscosities (weights) for various applications.

● **Motor oil**, of course, is the lubricant specially formulated for use in the engine. It normally contains a wide variety of additives to prevent corrosion and reduce foaming and wear. Motor oil comes in various weights (viscosity ratings) of from 5 to 80. The recommended weight of the oil depends on the seasonal temperature and the demands on the engine. Light oil is used in cold climates and under light load conditions; heavy oil is used in hot climates and where high loads are encountered. Multi-viscosity oils are designed to have characteristics of both light and heavy oils and are available in a number of weights from 5W-20 to 20W-50.

● **Petrol additives** perform several functions, depending on their chemical makeup. They usually contain solvents that help dissolve gum and varnish that build up on carburettor and inlet parts. They also serve to break down carbon deposits that form on the inside surfaces of the combustion chambers. Some additives contain upper cylinder lubricants for valves and piston rings.

● **Brake and clutch fluid** is a specially formulated hydraulic fluid that can withstand the heat and pressure encountered in brake/clutch systems. Care must be taken that this fluid does not come in contact with painted surfaces or plastics. An opened container should always be resealed to prevent contamination by water or dirt.

● **Chain lubricants** are formulated especially for use on motorcycle final drive chains. A good chain lube should adhere well and have good penetrating qualities to be effective as a lubricant inside the chain and on the side plates, pins and rollers. Most chain lubes are either the foaming type or quick drying type and are usually marketed as sprays. Take care to use a lubricant marked as being suitable for O-ring chains.

● **Degreasers** are heavy duty solvents used to remove grease and grime that may accumulate on engine and frame components. They can be sprayed or brushed on and, depending on the type, are rinsed with either water or solvent.

● **Solvents** are used alone or in combination with degreasers to clean parts and assemblies during repair and overhaul. The home mechanic should use only solvents that are non-flammable and that do not produce irritating fumes.

● **Gasket sealing compounds** may be used in conjunction with gaskets, to improve their sealing capabilities, or alone, to seal metal-to-metal joints. Many gasket sealers can withstand extreme heat, some are impervious to petrol and lubricants, while others are capable of filling and sealing large cavities. Depending on the intended use, gasket sealers either dry hard or stay relatively soft and pliable. They are usually applied by hand, with a brush, or are sprayed on the gasket sealing surfaces.

● **Thread locking compound** is an adhesive locking compound that prevents threaded fasteners from loosening because of vibration. It is available in a variety of types for different applications.

● **Moisture dispersants** are usually sprays that can be used to dry out electrical components such as the fuse block and wiring connectors. Some types can also be used as treatment for rubber and as a lubricant for hinges, cables and locks.

● **Waxes and polishes** are used to help protect painted and plated surfaces from the weather. Different types of paint may require the use of different types of wax polish. Some polishes utilise a chemical or abrasive cleaner to help remove the top layer of oxidised (dull) paint on older vehicles. In recent years, many non-wax polishes (that contain a wide variety of chemicals such as polymers and silicones) have been introduced. These non-wax polishes are usually easier to apply and last longer than conventional waxes and polishes.

About the MOT Test

In the UK, all vehicles more than three years old are subject to an annual test to ensure that they meet minimum safety requirements. A current test certificate must be issued before a machine can be used on public roads, and is required before a road fund licence can be issued. Riding without a current test certificate will also invalidate your insurance.

For most owners, the MOT test is an annual cause for anxiety, and this is largely due to owners not being sure what needs to be checked prior to submitting the motorcycle for testing. The simple answer is that a fully roadworthy motorcycle will have no difficulty in passing the test.

This is a guide to getting your motorcycle through the MOT test. Obviously it will not be possible to examine the motorcycle to the same standard as the professional MOT tester, particularly in view of the equipment required for some of the checks. However, working through the following procedures will enable you to identify any problem areas before submitting the motorcycle for the test.

It has only been possible to summarise the test requirements here, based on the regulations in force at the time of printing. Test standards are becoming increasingly stringent, although there are some exemptions for older vehicles. More information about the MOT test can be obtained from the TSO publications, *How Safe is your Motorcycle* and *The MOT Inspection Manual for Motorcycle Testing*.

Many of the checks require that one of the wheels is raised off the ground. If the motorcycle doesn't have a centre stand, note that an auxiliary stand will be required. Additionally, the help of an assistant may prove useful.

Certain exceptions apply to machines under 50 cc, machines without a lighting system, and Classic bikes - if in doubt about any of the requirements listed below seek confirmation from an MOT tester prior to submitting the motorcycle for the test.

Check that the frame number is clearly visible.

> **HAYNES HiNT**
>
> *If a component is in borderline condition, the tester has discretion in deciding whether to pass or fail it. If the motorcycle presented is clean and evidently well cared for, the tester may be more inclined to pass a borderline component than if the motorcycle is scruffy and apparently neglected.*

Electrical System

Lights, turn signals, horn and reflector

✔ With the ignition on, check the operation of the following electrical components. **Note:** *The electrical components on certain small-capacity machines are powered by the generator, requiring that the engine is run for this check.*

a) *Headlight and tail light. Check that both illuminate in the low and high beam switch positions.*

b) *Position lights. Check that the front position light (or sidelight) and tail light illuminate in this switch position.*

c) *Turn signals. Check that all flash at the correct rate, and that the warning light(s) function correctly. Check that the turn signal switch works correctly.*

d) *Hazard warning system (where fitted). Check that all four turn signals flash in this switch position.*

e) *Brake stop light. Check that the light comes on when the front and rear brakes are independently applied. Models first used on or after 1st April 1986 must have a brake light switch on each brake.*

f) *Horn. Check that the sound is continuous and of reasonable volume.*

✔ Check that there is a red reflector on the rear of the machine, either mounted separately or as part of the tail light lens.

✔ Check the condition of the headlight, tail light and turn signal lenses.

Headlight beam height

✔ The MOT tester will perform a headlight beam height check using specialised beam setting equipment **(see illustration 1)**. This equipment will not be available to the home mechanic, but if you suspect that the headlight is incorrectly set or may have been maladjusted in the past, you can perform a rough test as follows.

✔ Position the bike in a straight line facing a brick wall. The bike must be off its stand, upright and with a rider seated. Measure the height from the ground to the centre of the headlight and mark a horizontal line on the wall at this height. Position the motorcycle 3.8 metres from the wall and draw a vertical

Headlight beam height checking equipment

line up the wall central to the centreline of the motorcycle. Switch to dipped beam and check that the beam pattern falls slightly lower than the horizontal line and to the left of the vertical line **(see illustration 2)**.

3·8 m

90°

90°

H29003

Home workshop beam alignment check

Exhaust System and Final Drive

Exhaust

✔ Check that the exhaust mountings are secure and that the system does not foul any of the rear suspension components.
✔ Start the motorcycle. When the revs are increased, check that the exhaust is neither holed nor leaking from any of its joints. On a linked system, check that the collector box is not leaking due to corrosion.

✔ Note that the exhaust decibel level ("loudness" of the exhaust) is assessed at the discretion of the tester. If the motorcycle was first used on or after 1st January 1985 the silencer must carry the BSAU 193 stamp, or a marking relating to its make and model, or be of OE (original equipment) manufacture. If the silencer is marked NOT FOR ROAD USE, RACING USE ONLY or similar, it will fail the MOT.

Final drive

✔ On chain or belt drive machines, check that the chain/belt is in good condition and does not have excessive slack. Also check that the sprocket is securely mounted on the rear wheel hub. Check that the chain/belt guard is in place.
✔ On shaft drive bikes, check for oil leaking from the drive unit and fouling the rear tyre.

Steering and Suspension

Steering

✔ With the front wheel raised off the ground, rotate the steering from lock to lock. The handlebar or switches must not contact the fuel tank or be close enough to trap the rider's hand. Problems can be caused by damaged lock stops on the lower yoke and frame, or by the fitting of non-standard handlebars.
✔ When performing the lock to lock check, also ensure that the steering moves freely without drag or notchiness. Steering movement can be impaired by poorly routed cables, or by overtight head bearings or worn bearings. The tester will perform a check of the steering head bearing lower race by mounting the front wheel on a surface plate, then performing a lock to

lock check with the weight of the machine on the lower bearing **(see illustration 3)**.
✔ Grasp the fork sliders (lower legs) and attempt to push and pull on the forks **(see**

Front wheel mounted on a surface plate for steering head bearing lower race check

illustration 4). Any play in the steering head bearings will be felt. Note that in extreme cases, wear of the front fork bushes can be misinterpreted for head bearing play.
✔ Check that the handlebars are securely mounted.
✔ Check that the handlebar grip rubbers are secure. They should by bonded to the bar left end and to the throttle cable pulley on the right end.

Front suspension

✔ With the motorcycle off the stand, hold the front brake on and pump the front forks up and down **(see illustration 5)**. Check that they are adequately damped.

Checking the steering head bearings for freeplay

Hold the front brake on and pump the front forks up and down to check operation

Inspect the area around the fork dust seal for oil leakage (arrow)

Bounce the rear of the motorcycle to check rear suspension operation

Checking for rear suspension linkage play

✔ Inspect the area above and around the front fork oil seals **(see illustration 6)**. There should be no sign of oil on the fork tube (stanchion) nor leaking down the slider (lower leg). On models so equipped, check that there is no oil leaking from the anti-dive units.
✔ On models with swingarm front suspension, check that there is no freeplay in the linkage when moved from side to side.

Rear suspension

✔ With the motorcycle off the stand and an assistant supporting the motorcycle by its handlebars, bounce the rear suspension **(see illustration 7)**. Check that the suspension components do not foul on any of the cycle parts and check that the shock absorber(s) provide adequate damping.
✔ Visually inspect the shock absorber(s) and check that there is no sign of oil leakage from its damper. This is somewhat restricted on certain single shock models due to the location of the shock absorber.
✔ With the rear wheel raised off the ground, grasp the wheel at the highest point and attempt to pull it up **(see illustration 8)**. Any play in the swingarm pivot or suspension linkage bearings will be felt as movement. **Note:** *Do not confuse play with actual suspension movement*. Failure to lubricate suspension linkage bearings can lead to bearing failure **(see illustration 9)**.
✔ With the rear wheel raised off the ground, grasp the swingarm ends and attempt to move the swingarm from side to side and forwards and backwards - any play indicates wear of the swingarm pivot bearings **(see illustration 10)**.

Worn suspension linkage pivots (arrows) are usually the cause of play in the rear suspension

Grasp the swingarm at the ends to check for play in its pivot bearings

Brake pad wear can usually be viewed without removing the caliper. Most pads have wear indicator grooves (1) and some also have indicator tangs (2)

On drum brakes, check the angle of the operating lever with the brake fully applied. Most drum brakes have a wear indicator pointer and scale.

Brakes, Wheels and Tyres

Brakes

✔ With the wheel raised off the ground, apply the brake then free it off, and check that the wheel is about to revolve freely without brake drag.

✔ On disc brakes, examine the disc itself. Check that it is securely mounted and not cracked.

✔ On disc brakes, view the pad material through the caliper mouth and check that the pads are not worn down beyond the limit (see illustration 11).

✔ On drum brakes, check that when the brake is applied the angle between the operating lever and cable or rod is not too great (see illustration 12). Check also that the operating lever doesn't foul any other components.

✔ On disc brakes, examine the flexible hoses from top to bottom. Have an assistant hold the brake on so that the fluid in the hose is under pressure, and check that there is no sign of fluid leakage, bulges or cracking. If there are any metal brake pipes or unions, check that these are free from corrosion and damage. Where a brake-linked anti-dive system is fitted, check the hoses to the anti-dive in a similar manner.

✔ Check that the rear brake torque arm is secure and that its fasteners are secured by self-locking nuts or castellated nuts with split-pins or R-pins (see illustration 13).

✔ On models with ABS, check that the self-check warning light in the instrument panel works.

✔ The MOT tester will perform a test of the motorcycle's braking efficiency based on a calculation of rider and motorcycle weight. Although this cannot be carried out at home, you can at least ensure that the braking systems are properly maintained. For hydraulic disc brakes, check the fluid level, lever/pedal feel (bleed of air if its spongy) and pad material. For drum brakes, check adjustment, cable or rod operation and shoe lining thickness.

Wheels and tyres

✔ Check the wheel condition. Cast wheels should be free from cracks and if of the built-up design, all fasteners should be secure. Spoked wheels should be checked for broken, corroded, loose or bent spokes.

✔ With the wheel raised off the ground, spin the wheel and visually check that the tyre and wheel run true. Check that the tyre does not foul the suspension or mudguards.

✔ With the wheel raised off the ground, grasp the wheel and attempt to move it about the axle (spindle) (see illustration 14). Any play felt here indicates wheel bearing failure.

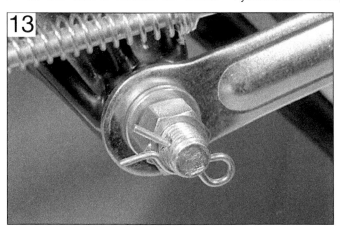

Brake torque arm must be properly secured at both ends

Check for wheel bearing play by trying to move the wheel about the axle (spindle)

Checking the tyre tread depth

Tyre direction of rotation arrow can be found on tyre sidewall

Castellated type wheel axle (spindle) nut must be secured by a split pin or R-pin

Two straightedges are used to check wheel alignment

✔ Check the tyre tread depth, tread condition and sidewall condition **(see illustration 15)**.
✔ Check the tyre type. Front and rear tyre types must be compatible and be suitable for road use. Tyres marked NOT FOR ROAD USE, COMPETITION USE ONLY or similar, will fail the MOT.

✔ If the tyre sidewall carries a direction of rotation arrow, this must be pointing in the direction of normal wheel rotation **(see illustration 16)**.
✔ Check that the wheel axle (spindle) nuts (where applicable) are properly secured. A self-locking nut or castellated nut with a split-pin or R-pin can be used **(see illustration 17)**.
✔ Wheel alignment is checked with the motorcycle off the stand and a rider seated. With the front wheel pointing straight ahead, two perfectly straight lengths of metal or wood and placed against the sidewalls of both tyres **(see illustration 18)**. The gap each side of the front tyre must be equidistant on both sides. Incorrect wheel alignment may be due to a cocked rear wheel (often as the result of poor chain adjustment) or in extreme cases, a bent frame.

General checks and condition

✔ Check the security of all major fasteners, bodypanels, seat, fairings (where fitted) and mudguards.

✔ Check that the rider and pillion footrests, handlebar levers and brake pedal are securely mounted.

✔ Check for corrosion on the frame or any load-bearing components. If severe, this may affect the structure, particularly under stress.

Sidecars

A motorcycle fitted with a sidecar requires additional checks relating to the stability of the machine and security of attachment and swivel joints, plus specific wheel alignment (toe-in) requirements. Additionally, tyre and lighting requirements differ from conventional motorcycle use. Owners are advised to check MOT test requirements with an official test centre.

Preparing for storage

Before you start

If repairs or an overhaul is needed, see that this is carried out now rather than left until you want to ride the bike again.

Give the bike a good wash and scrub all dirt from its underside. Make sure the bike dries completely before preparing for storage.

Engine

● Remove the spark plug(s) and lubricate the cylinder bores with approximately a teaspoon of motor oil using a spout-type oil can **(see illustration 1)**. Reinstall the spark plug(s). Crank the engine over a couple of times to coat the piston rings and bores with oil. If the bike has a kickstart, use this to turn the engine over. If not, flick the kill switch to the OFF position and crank the engine over on the starter **(see illustration 2)**. If the nature on the ignition system prevents the starter operating with the kill switch in the OFF position,

remove the spark plugs and fit them back in their caps; ensure that the plugs are earthed (grounded) against the cylinder head when the starter is operated **(see illustration 3)**.

⚠️ **Warning: It is important that the plugs are earthed (grounded) away from the spark plug holes otherwise there is a risk of atomised fuel from the cylinders igniting.**

HAYNES HINT *On a single cylinder four-stroke engine, you can seal the combustion chamber completely by positioning the piston at TDC on the compression stroke.*

● Drain the carburettor(s) otherwise there is a risk of jets becoming blocked by gum deposits from the fuel **(see illustration 4)**.

● If the bike is going into long-term storage, consider adding a fuel stabiliser to the fuel in the tank. If the tank is drained completely, corrosion of its internal surfaces may occur if left unprotected for a long period. The tank can be treated with a rust preventative especially for this purpose. Alternatively, remove the tank and pour half a litre of motor oil into it, install the filler cap and shake the tank to coat its internals with oil before draining off the excess. The same effect can also be achieved by spraying WD40 or a similar water-dispersant around the inside of the tank via its flexible nozzle.

● Make sure the cooling system contains the correct mix of antifreeze. Antifreeze also contains important corrosion inhibitors.

● The air intakes and exhaust can be sealed off by covering or plugging the openings. Ensure that you do not seal in any condensation; run the engine until it is hot,

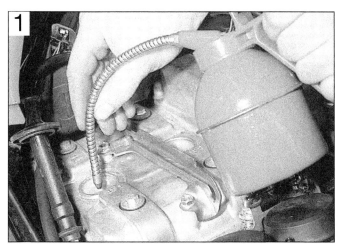

Squirt a drop of motor oil into each cylinder

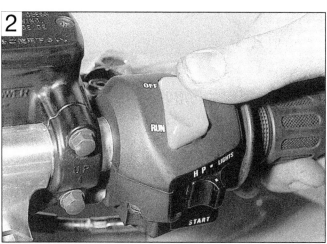

Flick the kill switch to OFF . . .

. . . and ensure that the metal bodies of the plugs (arrows) are earthed against the cylinder head

Connect a hose to the carburettor float chamber drain stub (arrow) and unscrew the drain screw

Exhausts can be sealed off with a plastic bag

Disconnect the negative lead (A) first, followed by the positive lead (B)

Use a suitable battery charger - this kit also assess battery condition

then switch off and allow to cool. Tape a piece of thick plastic over the silencer end(s) **(see illustration 5)**. Note that some advocate pouring a tablespoon of motor oil into the silencer(s) before sealing them off.

Battery

● Remove it from the bike - in extreme cases of cold the battery may freeze and crack its case **(see illustration 6)**.

● Check the electrolyte level and top up if necessary (conventional refillable batteries). Clean the terminals.
● Store the battery off the motorcycle and away from any sources of fire. Position a wooden block under the battery if it is to sit on the ground.
● Give the battery a trickle charge for a few hours every month **(see illustration 7)**.

Tyres

● Place the bike on its centrestand or an auxiliary stand which will support the motorcycle in an upright position. Position wood blocks under the tyres to keep them off the ground and to provide insulation from damp. If the bike is being put into long-term storage, ideally both tyres should be off the ground; not only will this protect the tyres, but will also ensure that no load is placed on the steering head or wheel bearings.
● Deflate each tyre by 5 to 10 psi, no more or the beads may unseat from the rim, making subsequent inflation difficult on tubeless tyres.

Pivots and controls

● Lubricate all lever, pedal, stand and footrest pivot points. If grease nipples are fitted to the rear suspension components, apply lubricant to the pivots.
● Lubricate all control cables.

Cycle components

● Apply a wax protectant to all painted and plastic components. Wipe off any excess, but don't polish to a shine. Where fitted, clean the screen with soap and water.
● Coat metal parts with Vaseline (petroleum jelly). When applying this to the fork tubes, do not compress the forks otherwise the seals will rot from contact with the Vaseline.
● Apply a vinyl cleaner to the seat.

Storage conditions

● Aim to store the bike in a shed or garage which does not leak and is free from damp.
● Drape an old blanket or bedspread over the bike to protect it from dust and direct contact with sunlight (which will fade paint). This also hides the bike from prying eyes. Beware of tight-fitting plastic covers which may allow condensation to form and settle on the bike.

Getting back on the road

Engine and transmission

● Change the oil and replace the oil filter. If this was done prior to storage, check that the oil hasn't emulsified - a thick whitish substance which occurs through condensation.
● Remove the spark plugs. Using a spout-type oil can, squirt a few drops of oil into the cylinder(s). This will provide initial lubrication as the piston rings and bores comes back into contact. Service the spark plugs, or fit new ones, and install them in the engine.

● Check that the clutch isn't stuck on. The plates can stick together if left standing for some time, preventing clutch operation. Engage a gear and try rocking the bike back and forth with the clutch lever held against the handlebar. If this doesn't work on cable-operated clutches, hold the clutch lever back against the handlebar with a strong elastic band or cable tie for a couple of hours **(see illustration 8)**.
● If the air intakes or silencer end(s) were blocked off, remove the bung or cover used.
● If the fuel tank was coated with a rust

Hold clutch lever back against the handlebar with elastic bands or a cable tie preventative, oil or a stabiliser added to the fuel, drain and flush the tank and dispose of the fuel sensibly. If no action was taken with the fuel tank prior to storage, it is advised that the old fuel is disposed of since it will go off over a period of time. Refill the fuel tank with fresh fuel.

Frame and running gear

● Oil all pivot points and cables.
● Check the tyre pressures. They will definitely need inflating if pressures were reduced for storage.
● Lubricate the final drive chain (where applicable).
● Remove any protective coating applied to the fork tubes (stanchions) since this may well destroy the fork seals. If the fork tubes weren't protected and have picked up rust spots, remove them with very fine abrasive paper and refinish with metal polish.
● Check that both brakes operate correctly. Apply each brake hard and check that it's not possible to move the motorcycle forwards, then check that the brake frees off again once released. Brake caliper pistons can stick due to corrosion around the piston head, or on the sliding caliper types, due to corrosion of the slider pins. If the brake doesn't free after repeated operation, take the caliper off for examination. Similarly drum brakes can stick

due to a seized operating cam, cable or rod linkage.
● If the motorcycle has been in long-term storage, renew the brake fluid and clutch fluid (where applicable).
● Depending on where the bike has been stored, the wiring, cables and hoses may have been nibbled by rodents. Make a visual check and investigate disturbed wiring loom tape.

Battery

● If the battery has been previously removal and given top up charges it can simply be reconnected. Remember to connect the positive cable first and the negative cable last.
● On conventional refillable batteries, if the battery has not received any attention, remove it from the motorcycle and check its electrolyte level. Top up if necessary then charge the battery. If the battery fails to hold a charge and a visual checks show heavy white sulphation of the plates, the battery is probably defective and must be renewed. This is particularly likely if the battery is old. Confirm battery condition with a specific gravity check.
● On sealed (MF) batteries, if the battery has not received any attention, remove it from the motorcycle and charge it according to the information on the battery case - if the battery fails to hold a charge it must be renewed.

Starting procedure

● If a kickstart is fitted, turn the engine over a couple of times with the ignition OFF to distribute oil around the engine. If no kickstart is fitted, flick the engine kill switch OFF and the ignition ON and crank the engine over a couple of times to work oil around the upper cylinder components. If the nature of the ignition system is such that the starter won't work with the kill switch OFF, remove the spark plugs, fit them back into their caps and earth (ground) their bodies on the cylinder head. Reinstall the spark plugs afterwards.
● Switch the kill switch to RUN, operate the choke and start the engine. If the engine won't start don't continue cranking the engine - not only will this flatten the battery, but the starter motor will overheat. Switch the ignition off and try again later. If the engine refuses to start, go through the fault finding procedures in this manual. **Note:** *If the bike has been in storage for a long time, old fuel or a carburettor blockage may be the problem. Gum deposits in carburettors can block jets - if a carburettor cleaner doesn't prove successful the carburettors must be dismantled for cleaning.*

● Once the engine has started, check that the lights, turn signals and horn work properly.

● Treat the bike gently for the first ride and check all fluid levels on completion. Settle the bike back into the maintenance schedule.

This Section provides an easy reference-guide to the more common faults that are likely to afflict your machine. Obviously, the opportunities are almost limitless for faults to occur as a result of obscure failures, and to try and cover all eventualities would require a book. Indeed, a number have been written on the subject.

Successful troubleshooting is not a mysterious 'black art' but the application of a bit of knowledge combined with a systematic and logical approach to the problem. Approach any troubleshooting by first accurately identifying the symptom and then checking through the list of possible causes, starting with the simplest or most obvious and progressing in stages to the most complex.

Take nothing for granted, but above all apply liberal quantities of common sense.

The main symptom of a fault is given in the text as a major heading below which are listed the various systems or areas which may contain the fault. Details of each possible cause for a fault and the remedial action to be taken are given, in brief, in the paragraphs below each heading. Further information should be sought in the relevant Chapter.

1 Engine doesn't start or is difficult to start

- ☐ Starter motor doesn't rotate
- ☐ Starter motor rotates but engine does not turn over
- ☐ Starter works but engine won't turn over (seized)
- ☐ No fuel flow
- ☐ Engine flooded
- ☐ No spark or weak spark
- ☐ Compression low
- ☐ Stalls after starting
- ☐ Rough idle

2 Poor running at low speed

- ☐ Spark weak
- ☐ Fuel/air mixture incorrect
- ☐ Compression low
- ☐ Poor acceleration

3 Poor running or no power at high speed

- ☐ Firing incorrect
- ☐ Fuel/air mixture incorrect
- ☐ Compression low
- ☐ Knocking or pinking
- ☐ Miscellaneous causes

4 Overheating

- ☐ Engine overheats
- ☐ Firing incorrect
- ☐ Fuel/air mixture incorrect
- ☐ Compression too high
- ☐ Engine load excessive
- ☐ Lubrication inadequate
- ☐ Miscellaneous causes

5 Clutch problems

- ☐ Clutch slipping
- ☐ Clutch not disengaging completely

6 Gearchanging problems

- ☐ Doesn't go into gear, or lever doesn't return
- ☐ Jumps out of gear
- ☐ Overshifts

7 Abnormal engine noise

- ☐ Knocking or pinking
- ☐ Piston slap or rattling
- ☐ Valve noise
- ☐ Other noise

8 Abnormal driveline noise

- ☐ Clutch noise
- ☐ Transmission noise
- ☐ Final drive noise

9 Abnormal frame and suspension noise

- ☐ Front end noise
- ☐ Shock absorber noise
- ☐ Brake noise

10 Oil pressure light comes on

- ☐ Engine lubrication system
- ☐ Electrical system

11 Excessive exhaust smoke

- ☐ White smoke
- ☐ Black smoke
- ☐ Brown smoke

12 Poor handling or stability

- ☐ Handlebar hard to turn
- ☐ Handlebar shakes or vibrates excessively
- ☐ Handlebar pulls to one side
- ☐ Poor shock absorbing qualities

13 Braking problems

- ☐ Brakes are spongy, don't hold
- ☐ Brake lever or pedal pulsates
- ☐ Brakes drag

14 Electrical problems

- ☐ Battery dead or weak
- ☐ Battery overcharged

1 Engine doesn't start or is difficult to start

Starter motor doesn't rotate

- [ ] Engine kill switch OFF.
- [ ] Fuse blown. Check fuse (Chapter 8).
- [ ] Battery voltage low. Check and recharge battery (Chapter 8).
- [ ] Starter motor defective. Make sure the wiring to the starter is secure. Make sure the starter relay clicks when the start button is pushed. If the relay clicks, then the fault is in the wiring or motor.
- [ ] Starter relay faulty. Check it using the procedure in Chapter 8.
- [ ] Starter switch not contacting. The contacts could be wet, corroded or dirty. Disassemble and clean the switch (Chapter 8).
- [ ] Wiring open or shorted. Check all wiring connections and harnesses to make sure that they are dry, tight and not corroded. Also check for broken or frayed wires that can cause a short to ground (earth) (see wiring diagram, Chapter 8).
- [ ] Ignition (main) switch defective. Check the switch according to the procedure in Chapter 8. Replace the switch with a new one if it is defective.
- [ ] Engine kill switch defective. Check for wet, dirty or corroded contacts. Clean or replace the switch as necessary (Chapter 8).
- [ ] Faulty neutral or side stand switch. Check the wiring to each switch and the switch itself according to the procedures in Chapter 8.
- [ ] Faulty starter circuit relay or diode. Check the junction box according to the procedure in Chapter 8.

Starter motor rotates but engine does not turn over

- [ ] Starter clutch defective. Inspect and repair or replace (Chapter 2).
- [ ] Damaged idle/reduction gear or starter gears. Inspect and replace the damaged parts (Chapter 2).

Starter works but engine won't turn over (seized)

- [ ] Seized engine caused by one or more internally damaged components. Failure due to wear, abuse or lack of lubrication. Damage can include seized valves, followers, camshafts, pistons, crankshaft, connecting rod bearings, or transmission gears or bearings. Refer to Chapter 2 for engine disassembly.

No fuel flow

- [ ] No fuel in tank.
- [ ] Main fuel cock filter clogged. Remove the fuel cock and clean it and the filter (Chapter 3).
- [ ] Fuel line clogged. Pull the fuel line loose and carefully blow through it.
- [ ] Float needle valve clogged. For both of the valves to be clogged, either a very bad batch of fuel with an unusual additive has been used, or some other foreign material has entered the tank. Many times after a machine has been stored for many months without running, the fuel turns to a varnish-like liquid and forms deposits on the inlet needle valves and jets. The carburettors should be removed and overhauled if draining the float chambers doesn't solve the problem (Chapter 3).

Engine flooded

- [ ] Float height incorrect. Check and adjust as necessary (Chapter 3).
- [ ] Float needle valve worn or stuck open. A piece of dirt, rust or other debris can cause the valve to seat improperly, causing excess fuel to be admitted to the float chamber. In this case, the float chamber should be cleaned and the needle valve and seat inspected. If the needle and seat are worn, then the leaking will persist and the parts should be replaced with new ones (Chapter 3).
- [ ] Starting technique incorrect. Under normal circumstances (i.e., if all the carburettor functions are sound) the machine should start with little or no throttle. When the engine is cold, the choke should be operated and the engine started without opening the throttle.

When the engine is at operating temperature, only a very slight amount of throttle should be necessary. If the engine is flooded hold the throttle open while cranking the engine. This will allow additional air to reach the cylinders.

No spark or weak spark

- [ ] Ignition switch OFF.
- [ ] Engine kill switch turned to the OFF position.
- [ ] Battery voltage low. Check and recharge the battery as necessary (Chapter 8).
- [ ] Spark plugs dirty, defective or worn out. Locate reason for fouled plugs using spark plug condition chart and follow the plug maintenance procedures (Chapter 1).
- [ ] Spark plug caps or secondary (HT) wiring faulty. Check condition. Replace either or both components if cracks or deterioration are evident (Chapter 4).
- [ ] Spark plug caps not making good contact. Make sure that the plug caps fit snugly over the plug ends.
- [ ] Ignition control unit defective. Check the unit, referring to Chapter 4 for details.
- [ ] Pulse generator coil defective. Check the coil, referring to Chapter 4 for details.
- [ ] Ignition HT coil(s) defective. Check the coils, referring to Chapter 4 for details.
- [ ] Ignition or kill switch shorted. This is usually caused by water, corrosion, damage or excessive wear. The switches can be disassembled and cleaned with electrical contact cleaner. If cleaning does not help, replace the switches (Chapter 8).
- [ ] Wiring shorted or broken between:
    - a) Ignition (main) switch and engine kill switch (or blown fuse)
    - b) Ignition control unit and engine kill switch
    - c) Ignition control unit and ignition HT coils
    - d) Ignition HT coils and spark plugs
    - e) Ignition control unit and pulse generator coil
- [ ] Make sure that all wiring connections are clean, dry and tight. Look for chafed and broken wires (Chapters 4 and 8).

Compression low

- [ ] Spark plugs loose. Remove the plugs and inspect their threads. Reinstall and tighten to the specified torque (Chapter 1).
- [ ] Cylinder head not sufficiently tightened down. If the cylinder head is suspected of being loose, then there's a chance that the gasket or head is damaged if the problem has persisted for any length of time. The head bolts should be tightened to the proper torque in the correct sequence (Chapter 2).
- [ ] Improper valve clearance. This means that the valve is not closing completely and compression pressure is leaking past the valve. Check and adjust the valve clearances (Chapter 1).
- [ ] Cylinder and/or piston worn. Excessive wear will cause compression pressure to leak past the rings. This is usually accompanied by worn rings as well. A top-end overhaul is necessary (Chapter 2).
- [ ] Piston rings worn, weak, broken, or sticking. Broken or sticking piston rings usually indicate a lubrication or carburation problem that causes excess carbon deposits or seizures to form on the pistons and rings. Top-end overhaul is necessary (Chapter 2).
- [ ] Piston ring-to-groove clearance excessive. This is caused by excessive wear of the piston ring lands. Piston replacement is necessary (Chapter 2).
- [ ] Cylinder head gasket damaged. If the head is allowed to become loose, or if excessive carbon build-up on the piston crown and combustion chamber causes extremely high compression, the head gasket may leak. Retorquing the head is not always sufficient to restore the seal, so gasket replacement is necessary (Chapter 2).

1 Engine doesn't start or is difficult to start (continued)

☐ Cylinder head warped. This is caused by overheating or improperly tightened head bolts. Machine shop resurfacing or head replacement is necessary (Chapter 2).

☐ Valve spring broken or weak. Caused by component failure or wear; the springs must be replaced (Chapter 2).

☐ Valve not seating properly. This is caused by a bent valve (from over-revving or improper valve adjustment), burned valve or seat (improper carburation) or an accumulation of carbon deposits on the seat (from carburation or lubrication problems). The valves must be cleaned and/or replaced and the seats serviced if possible (Chapter 2).

Stalls after starting

☐ Improper choke action. Make sure the choke linkage shaft is getting a full stroke and staying in the out position (Chapter 3).

☐ Ignition malfunction (Chapter 4).

☐ Carburettor malfunction (Chapter 3).

☐ Fuel contaminated. The fuel can be contaminated with either dirt or water, or can change chemically if the machine is allowed to sit for several months or more. Drain the tank and float chambers (Chapter 3).

☐ Intake air leak. Check for loose carburettor-to-intake manifold connections, loose or missing vacuum gauge adapter caps, or loose carburettor tops (Chapter 3).

☐ Engine idle speed incorrect. Turn idle adjusting screw until the engine idles at the specified rpm (Chapter 1).

Rough idle

☐ Ignition malfunction (Chapter 4).

☐ Idle speed incorrect (Chapter 1).

☐ Carburettors not synchronised. Adjust carburettors with vacuum gauge or manometer set (Chapter 1).

☐ Carburettor malfunction (Chapter 3).

☐ Fuel contaminated. The fuel can be contaminated with either dirt or water, or can change chemically if the machine is allowed to sit for several months or more. Drain the tank and float chambers (Chapter 3).

☐ Intake air leak. Check for loose carburettor-to-intake manifold connections, loose or missing vacuum gauge adapter caps, or loose carburettor tops (Chapter 3).

☐ Air filter clogged. Replace the air filter element (Chapter 1).

2 Poor running at low speeds

Spark weak

☐ Battery voltage low. Check and recharge battery (Chapter 8).

☐ Spark plugs fouled, defective or worn out (Chapter 1)

☐ Spark plug cap or HT wiring defective (Chapters 1 and 4).

☐ Spark plug caps not making contact.

☐ Incorrect spark plugs. Wrong type, heat range or cap configuration. Check and install correct plugs (Chapter 1).

☐ Ignition control defective (Chapter 4).

☐ Pulse generator coil defective (Chapter 4).

☐ Ignition HT coil(s) defective (Chapter 4).

Fuel/air mixture incorrect

☐ Pilot screws out of adjustment (Chapter 3).

☐ Pilot jet or air passage clogged. Remove and overhaul the carburettors (Chapter 3).

☐ Air bleed holes clogged. Remove carburettor and blow out all passages (Chapter 3).

☐ Air filter clogged, poorly sealed or missing (Chapter 1).

☐ Air filter housing poorly sealed. Look for cracks, holes or loose clamps and replace or repair defective parts (Chapter 3).

☐ Fuel level too high or too low. Check the float height (Chapter 3).

☐ Carburettor intake manifolds loose. Check for cracks, breaks, tears or loose clamps. Replace the rubber intake manifold joints if split or perished (Chapter 3).

Compression low

☐ Spark plugs loose. Remove the plugs and inspect their threads. Reinstall and tighten to the specified torque (Chapter 1).

☐ Cylinder head not sufficiently tightened down. If the cylinder head is suspected of being loose, then there's a chance that the gasket or head is damaged if the problem has persisted for any length of time. The head bolts should be tightened to the proper torque in the correct sequence (Chapter 2).

☐ Improper valve clearance. This means that the valve is not closing completely and compression pressure is leaking past the valve. Check and adjust the valve clearances (Chapter 1).

☐ Cylinder and/or piston worn. Excessive wear will cause compression pressure to leak past the rings. This is usually accompanied by worn rings as well. A top-end overhaul is necessary (Chapter 2).

☐ Piston rings worn, weak, broken, or sticking. Broken or sticking piston rings usually indicate a lubrication or carburation problem that causes excess carbon deposits or seizures to form on the pistons and rings. Top-end overhaul is necessary (Chapter 2).

☐ Piston ring-to-groove clearance excessive. This is caused by excessive wear of the piston ring lands. Piston replacement is necessary (Chapter 2).

☐ Cylinder head gasket damaged. If the head is allowed to become loose, or if excessive carbon build-up on the piston crown and combustion chamber causes extremely high compression, the head gasket may leak. Retorquing the head is not always sufficient to restore the seal, so gasket replacement is necessary (Chapter 2).

☐ Cylinder head warped. This is caused by overheating or improperly tightened head bolts. Machine shop resurfacing or head replacement is necessary (Chapter 2).

☐ Valve spring broken or weak. Caused by component failure or wear; the springs must be replaced (Chapter 2).

☐ Valve not seating properly. This is caused by a bent valve (from over-revving or improper valve adjustment), burned valve or seat (improper carburation) or an accumulation of carbon deposits on the seat (from carburation or lubrication problems). The valves must be cleaned and/or replaced and the seats serviced if possible (Chapter 2).

Poor acceleration

☐ Carburettors leaking or dirty. Overhaul the carburettors (Chapter 3).

☐ Timing not advancing. Faulty pulse generator coil or ignitor unit (Chapter 4).

☐ Carburettors not synchronised. Adjust them with a vacuum gauge set or manometer (Chapter 1).

☐ Engine oil viscosity too high. Using a heavier oil than that recommended in Chapter 1 can damage the oil pump or lubrication system and cause drag on the engine.

☐ Brakes dragging. Usually caused by debris which has entered the brake piston seals, or from a warped disc or bent axle. Repair as necessary (Chapter 6).

3 Poor running or no power at high speed

Firing incorrect

- ☐ Air filter restricted. Clean or replace filter (Chapter 1).
- ☐ Spark plugs fouled, defective or worn out (Chapter 1).
- ☐ Spark plug cap or HT wiring defective (Chapters 1 and 4).
- ☐ Spark plug caps not making contact. Make sure they are properly connected.
- ☐ Incorrect spark plugs. Wrong type, heat range or cap configuration. Check and install correct plugs (Chapter 1).
- ☐ Ignition control unit defective (Chapter 4).
- ☐ Pulse generator coil defective (Chapter 4).
- ☐ Ignition HT coil(s) defective (Chapter 4).

Fuel/air mixture incorrect

- ☐ Air bleed holes clogged. Remove carburettor and blow out all passages (Chapter 3).
- ☐ Air filter clogged, poorly sealed or missing (Chapter 1).
- ☐ Air filter housing poorly sealed. Look for cracks, holes or loose clamps and replace or repair defective parts (Chapter 3).
- ☐ Fuel level too high or too low. Check the float height (Chapter 3).
- ☐ Carburettor intake manifolds loose. Check for cracks, breaks, tears or loose clamps. Replace the rubber intake manifold joints if split or perished (Chapter 3).
- ☐ Jet needle incorrectly positioned or worn Check and adjust or replace (Chapter 3).
- ☐ Main jet clogged. Dirt, water or other contaminants can clog the main jets. Clean the fuel tap filter, the in-line filter, the float chamber area, and the jets and carburettor orifices (Chapter 3).
- ☐ Main jet wrong size. The standard jetting is for sea level atmospheric pressure and oxygen content. Check jet size (Chapter 3).
- ☐ Throttle shaft-to-carburettor body clearance excessive. Overhaul carburettors, replacing worn parts or complete carburettor if necessary (Chapter 3).

Compression low

- ☐ Spark plugs loose. Remove the plugs and inspect their threads. Reinstall and tighten to the specified torque (Chapter 1).
- ☐ Cylinder head not sufficiently tightened down. If the cylinder head is suspected of being loose, then there's a chance that the gasket or head is damaged if the problem has persisted for any length of time. The head bolts should be tightened to the proper torque in the correct sequence (Chapter 2).
- ☐ Improper valve clearance. This means that the valve is not closing completely and compression pressure is leaking past the valve. Check and adjust the valve clearances (Chapter 1).
- ☐ Cylinder and/or piston worn. Excessive wear will cause compression pressure to leak past the rings. This is usually accompanied by worn rings as well. A top-end overhaul is necessary (Chapter 2).
- ☐ Piston rings worn, weak, broken, or sticking. Broken or sticking piston rings usually indicate a lubrication or carburation problem that causes excess carbon deposits or seizures to form on the pistons and rings. Top-end overhaul is necessary (Chapter 2).
- ☐ Piston ring-to-groove clearance excessive. This is caused by excessive wear of the piston ring lands. Piston replacement is necessary (Chapter 2).
- ☐ Cylinder head gasket damaged. If the head is allowed to become loose, or if excessive carbon build-up on the piston crown and combustion chamber causes extremely high compression, the head gasket may leak. Retorquing the head is not always sufficient to restore the seal, so gasket replacement is necessary (Chapter 2).
- ☐ Cylinder head warped. This is caused by overheating or improperly tightened head bolts. Machine shop resurfacing or head replacement is necessary (Chapter 2).
- ☐ Valve spring broken or weak. Caused by component failure or wear; the springs must be replaced (Chapter 2).
- ☐ Valve not seating properly. This is caused by a bent valve (from over-revving or improper valve adjustment), burned valve or seat (improper carburation) or an accumulation of carbon deposits on the seat (from carburation or lubrication problems). The valves must be cleaned and/or replaced and the seats serviced if possible (Chapter 2).

Knocking or pinging

- ☐ Carbon build-up in combustion chamber. Use of a fuel additive that will dissolve the adhesive bonding the carbon particles to the crown and chamber is the easiest way to remove the build-up. Otherwise, the cylinder head will have to be removed and decarbonized (Chapter 2).
- ☐ Incorrect or poor quality fuel. Old or improper grades of fuel can cause detonation. This causes the piston to rattle, thus the knocking or pinging sound. Drain old fuel and always use the recommended fuel grade (Chapter 3).
- ☐ Spark plug heat range incorrect. Uncontrolled detonation indicates the plug heat range is too hot. The plug in effect becomes a glow plug, raising cylinder temperatures. Install the proper heat range plug (Chapter 1).
- ☐ Improper air/fuel mixture. This will cause the cylinder to run hot, which leads to detonation. Clogged jets or an air leak can cause this imbalance (Chapter 3).

Miscellaneous causes

- ☐ Throttle valve doesn't open fully. Adjust the throttle grip freeplay (Chapter 1).
- ☐ Clutch slipping. May be caused by loose or worn clutch components. Overhaul clutch (Chapter 2).
- ☐ Timing not advancing. Ignition control unit faulty (Chapter 4).
- ☐ Engine oil viscosity too high. Using a heavier oil than the one recommended in Chapter 1 can damage the oil pump or lubrication system and cause drag on the engine.
- ☐ Brakes dragging. Usually caused by debris which has entered the brake piston seals, or from a warped disc or bent axle. Repair as necessary.

4 Overheating

Firing incorrect

☐ Spark plugs fouled, defective or worn out (Chapter 1).
☐ Incorrect spark plugs (Chapter 1).
☐ Faulty ignition HT coils (Chapter 4).

Fuel/air mixture incorrect

☐ Main jet clogged. Dirt, water and other contaminants can clog the main jets. Clean the fuel tap filter, the fuel pump in-line filter, the float chamber area and the jets and carburettor orifices (Chapter 3).
☐ Main jet wrong size. The standard jetting is for sea level atmospheric pressure and oxygen content. Check jet size (Chapter 3).
☐ Air filter clogged, poorly sealed or missing (Chapter 1).
☐ Air filter housing poorly sealed. Look for cracks, holes or loose clamps and replace or repair (Chapter 3).
☐ Fuel level too low. Check float height (Chapter 3).
☐ Carburettor intake manifolds loose. Check for cracks, breaks, tears or loose clamps. Replace the rubber intake manifold joints if split or perished (Chapter 3).

Compression too high

☐ Carbon build-up in combustion chamber. Use of a fuel additive that will dissolve the adhesive bonding the carbon particles to the piston crown and chamber is the easiest way to remove the build-up. Otherwise, the cylinder head will have to be removed and decarbonized (Chapter 2).
☐ Improperly machined head surface or installation of incorrect gasket during engine assembly (Chapter 2).

Engine load excessive

☐ Clutch slipping. Can be caused by damaged, loose or worn clutch components. Overhaul clutch (Chapter 2).

☐ Engine oil level too high. The addition of too much oil will cause pressurisation of the crankcase and inefficient engine operation. Check Specifications and drain to proper level (Chapter 1).
☐ Engine oil viscosity too high. Using a heavier oil than the one recommended in Chapter 1 can damage the oil pump or lubrication system as well as cause drag on the engine.
☐ Brakes dragging. Usually caused by debris which has entered the brake piston seals, or from a warped disc or bent axle. Repair as necessary.
☐ Excessive friction in moving engine parts due to inadequate lubrication, worn bearings or incorrect assembly. Overhaul engine (Chapter 2).

Lubrication inadequate

☐ Engine oil level too low. Friction caused by intermittent lack of lubrication or from oil that is overworked can cause overheating. The oil provides a definite cooling function in the engine. Check the oil level (Chapter 1).
☐ Poor quality engine oil or incorrect viscosity or type. Oil is rated not only according to viscosity but also according to type. Some oils are not rated high enough for use in this engine. Check the Specifications section and change to the correct oil (Chapter 1).
☐ Worn oil pump or clogged oil passages. Check oil pump and clean passages (Chapter 2).

Miscellaneous causes

☐ Engine cooling fins clogged with debris.
☐ Modification to exhaust system. Most aftermarket exhaust systems cause the engine to run leaner, which make them run hotter. When installing an accessory exhaust system, always rejet the carburettors.

5 Clutch problems

Clutch slipping

☐ Cable freeplay insufficient. Check and adjust cable (Chapter 1).
☐ Friction plates worn or warped. Overhaul the clutch assembly (Chapter 2).
☐ Plain plates warped (Chapter 2).
☐ Clutch springs broken or weak. Old or heat-damaged (from slipping clutch) springs should be replaced with new ones (Chapter 2).
☐ Clutch release mechanism defective. Replace any defective parts (Chapter 2).
☐ Clutch centre or housing unevenly worn. This causes improper engagement of the plates. Replace the damaged or worn parts (Chapter 2).

Clutch not disengaging completely

☐ Cable freeplay excessive. Check and adjust cable (Chapter 1).
☐ Clutch plates warped or damaged. This will cause clutch drag, which in turn will cause the machine to creep. Overhaul the clutch assembly (Chapter 2).

☐ Clutch spring tension uneven. Usually caused by a sagged or broken spring. Check and replace the springs as a set (Chapter 2).
☐ Engine oil deteriorated. Old, thin, worn out oil will not provide proper lubrication for the plates, causing the clutch to drag. Replace the oil and filter (Chapter 1).
☐ Engine oil viscosity too high. Using a heavier oil than recommended in Chapter 1 can cause the plates to stick together, putting a drag on the engine. Change to the correct weight oil (Chapter 1).
☐ Clutch housing seized on mainshaft. Lack of lubrication, severe wear or damage can cause the guide to seize on the shaft. Overhaul of the clutch, and perhaps transmission, may be necessary to repair the damage (Chapter 2).
☐ Clutch release mechanism defective. Overhaul the clutch cover components (Chapter 2).
☐ Loose clutch centre nut. Causes drum and centre misalignment putting a drag on the engine. Engagement adjustment continually varies. Overhaul the clutch assembly (Chapter 2).

6 Gearchanging problems

Doesn't go into gear or lever doesn't return

- [ ] Clutch not disengaging. See above.
- [ ] Selector fork(s) bent or seized. Often caused by dropping the machine or from lack of lubrication. Overhaul the transmission (Chapter 2).
- [ ] Gear(s) stuck on shaft. Most often caused by a lack of lubrication or excessive wear in transmission bearings and bushings. Overhaul the transmission (Chapter 2).
- [ ] Gear selector drum binding. Caused by lubrication failure or excessive wear. Replace the drum and bearing (Chapter 2).
- [ ] Gearchange lever return spring weak or broken (Chapter 2).
- [ ] Gearchange lever or linkage arm broken. Splines stripped out of lever or shaft, caused by allowing the lever to get loose or from dropping the machine. Replace necessary parts (Chapter 2).

- [ ] Gearchange mechanism stopper arm broken or worn. Full engagement and rotary movement of shift drum results. Replace the arm (Chapter 2).
- [ ] Selector/stopper arm spring broken. Allows arms to float, causing sporadic shift operation. Replace spring (Chapter 2).

Jumps out of gear

- [ ] Selector fork(s) worn. Overhaul the transmission (Chapter 2).
- [ ] Gear groove(s) worn. Overhaul the transmission (Chapter 2).
- [ ] Gear dogs or dog slots worn or damaged. The gears should be inspected and replaced. No attempt should be made to service the worn parts (Chapter 2).

Overshifts

- [ ] Selector/stopper arm spring weak or broken (Chapter 2).
- [ ] Gearchange shaft return spring post broken or distorted (Chapter 2).

7 Abnormal engine noise

Knocking or pinging

- [ ] Carbon build-up in combustion chamber. Use of a fuel additive that will dissolve the adhesive bonding the carbon particles to the piston crown and chamber is the easiest way to remove the build-up. Otherwise, the cylinder head will have to be removed and decarbonized (Chapter 2).
- [ ] Incorrect or poor quality fuel. Old or improper fuel can cause detonation. This causes the pistons to rattle, thus the knocking or pinging sound. Drain the old fuel and always use the recommended grade fuel (Chapter 3).
- [ ] Spark plug heat range incorrect. Uncontrolled detonation indicates that the plug heat range is too hot. The plug in effect becomes a glow plug, raising cylinder temperatures. Install the proper heat range plug (Chapter 1).
- [ ] Improper air/fuel mixture. This will cause the cylinders to run hot and lead to detonation. Clogged jets or an air leak can cause this imbalance (Chapter 3).

Piston slap or rattling

- [ ] Cylinder-to-piston clearance excessive. Caused by improper assembly. Inspect and overhaul top-end parts (Chapter 2).
- [ ] Connecting rod bent. Caused by over-revving, trying to start a badly flooded engine or from ingesting a foreign object into the combustion chamber. Replace the damaged parts (Chapter 2).
- [ ] Piston pin or piston pin bore worn or seized from wear or lack of lubrication. Replace damaged parts (Chapter 2).
- [ ] Piston ring(s) worn, broken or sticking. Overhaul the top-end (Chapter 2).
- [ ] Piston seizure damage. Usually from lack of lubrication or overheating. Replace the pistons and bore the cylinders, as necessary (Chapter 2).

- [ ] Connecting rod upper or lower end clearance excessive. Caused by excessive wear or lack of lubrication. Replace worn parts (Chapter 2).

Valve noise

- [ ] Incorrect valve clearances. Adjust the clearances (Chapter 1).
- [ ] Valve spring broken or weak. Check and replace weak valve springs (Chapter 2).
- [ ] Camshaft or cylinder head worn or damaged. Lack of lubrication at high rpm is usually the cause of damage. Insufficient oil or failure to change the oil at the recommended intervals are the chief causes. Since there are no replaceable bearings in the head, the head itself will have to be replaced if there is excessive wear or damage (Chapter 2).

Other noise

- [ ] Cylinder head gasket leaking (Chapter 1).
- [ ] Exhaust pipe leaking at cylinder head connection. Caused by improper fit of pipe(s) or loose exhaust flange. All exhaust fasteners should be tightened evenly and carefully. Failure to do this will lead to a leak (Chapter 3).
- [ ] Crankshaft runout excessive. Caused by a bent crankshaft (from over-revving) or damage from an upper cylinder component failure. Can also be attributed to dropping the machine on either of the crankshaft ends (Chapter 2).
- [ ] Engine mounting bolts loose. Tighten all engine mount bolts (Chapter 2).
- [ ] Crankshaft bearings worn (Chapter 2).
- [ ] Cam chain tensioner defective. Replace (Chapter 2).
- [ ] Cam chain, sprockets or guides worn (Chapter 2).

8 Abnormal driveline noise

Clutch noise

- ☐ Clutch housing/friction plate clearance excessive (Chapter 2).
- ☐ Loose or damaged clutch pressure plate and/or bolts (Chapter 2).

Transmission noise

- ☐ Bearings worn. Also includes the possibility that the shafts are worn. Overhaul the transmission (Chapter 2).
- ☐ Gears worn or chipped (Chapter 2).
- ☐ Metal chips jammed in gear teeth. Probably pieces from a broken clutch, gear or shift mechanism that were picked up by the gears. This will cause early bearing failure (Chapter 2).

- ☐ Engine oil level too low. Causes a howl from transmission. Also affects engine power and clutch operation (Chapter 1).

Final drive noise

- ☐ Chain not adjusted properly (Chapter 1).
- ☐ Front or rear sprocket loose. Tighten fasteners (Chapter 5).
- ☐ Sprockets worn. Replace sprockets (Chapter 5).
- ☐ Rear sprocket warped. Replace sprockets (Chapter 5).
- ☐ Wheel coupling damper worn. Replace damper (Chapter 5).

9 Abnormal frame and suspension noise

Front end noise

- ☐ Low fluid level or improper viscosity oil in forks. This can sound like spurting and is usually accompanied by irregular fork action (Chapter 5).
- ☐ Spring weak or broken. Makes a clicking or scraping sound. Fork oil, when drained, will have a lot of metal particles in it (Chapter 5).
- ☐ Steering head bearings loose or damaged. Clicks when braking. Check and adjust or replace as necessary (Chapters 1 and 5).
- ☐ Fork yokes loose. Make sure all clamp pinch bolts are tight (Chapter 5).
- ☐ Fork tube bent. Good possibility if machine has been dropped. Replace tube with a new one (Chapter 5).
- ☐ Front axle or axle clamp bolt loose. Tighten them to the specified torque (Chapter 6).

Shock absorber noise

- ☐ Fluid level incorrect. Indicates a leak caused by defective seal. Shock will be covered with oil. Replace shock or seek advice on repair from a Kawasaki dealer (Chapter 5).
- ☐ Defective shock absorber with internal damage. This is in the body of the shock and can't be remedied. The shock must be replaced with a new one (Chapter 5).

- ☐ Bent or damaged shock body. Replace the shock with a new one (Chapter 5).
- ☐ Loose or worn mountings. Check and replace as needed (Chapter 5).

Brake noise

- ☐ Squeal caused by pad shim not installed or positioned correctly (Chapter 6).
- ☐ Squeal caused by dust on brake pads. Usually found together with glazed pads. Clean using brake cleaning solvent (Chapter 6).
- ☐ Contamination of brake pads. Oil, brake fluid or dirt causing brake to chatter or squeal. Clean or replace pads (Chapter 6).
- ☐ Pads glazed. Caused by excessive heat from prolonged use or from contamination. Do not use sandpaper, emery cloth, carborundum cloth or any other abrasive to roughen the pad surfaces as abrasives will stay in the pad material and damage the disc. A very fine flat file can be used, but pad replacement is suggested as a cure (Chapter 6).
- ☐ Disc warped. Can cause a chattering, clicking or intermittent squeal. Usually accompanied by a pulsating lever and uneven braking. Replace the disc (Chapter 6).
- ☐ Loose or worn wheel bearings. Check and replace as needed (Chapter 6).

10 Oil pressure light comes on

Engine lubrication system

- ☐ Engine oil pump defective, blocked oil strainer gauze or failed relief valve. Carry out oil pressure check (Chapter 2).
- ☐ Engine oil level low. Inspect for leak or other problem causing low oil level and add recommended oil (Chapter 1).
- ☐ Engine oil viscosity too low. Very old, thin oil or an improper weight of oil used in the engine. Change to correct oil (Chapter 1).
- ☐ Camshaft or journals worn. Excessive wear causing drop in oil pressure. Replace cam and/or cylinder head. Abnormal wear

could be caused by oil starvation at high rpm from low oil level or improper weight or type of oil (Chapter 1).
- ☐ Crankshaft and/or bearings worn. Same problems as paragraph 4. Check and replace crankshaft and/or bearings (Chapter 2).

Electrical system

- ☐ Oil pressure switch defective. Check the switch according to the procedure in Chapter 8. Replace it if it is defective.
- ☐ Oil pressure indicator light circuit defective. Check for pinched, shorted, disconnected or damaged wiring (Chapter 8).

11 Excessive exhaust smoke

White smoke

- [ ] Piston oil ring worn. The ring may be broken or damaged, causing oil from the crankcase to be pulled past the piston into the combustion chamber. Replace the rings with new ones (Chapter 2).
- [ ] Cylinders worn, cracked, or scored. Caused by overheating or oil starvation. The cylinders will have to be rebored and new pistons installed (Chapter 2).
- [ ] Valve oil seal damaged or worn. Replace oil seals with new ones (Chapter 2).
- [ ] Valve guide worn. Perform a complete valve job (Chapter 2).
- [ ] Engine oil level too high, which causes the oil to be forced past the rings. Drain oil to the proper level (Chapter 1).
- [ ] Head gasket broken between oil return and cylinder. Causes oil to be pulled into the combustion chamber. Replace the head gasket and check the head for warpage (Chapter 2).
- [ ] Abnormal crankcase pressurisation, which forces oil past the rings. Clogged ventilation system or breather hose (Chapter 2).

Black smoke

- [ ] Air filter clogged. Clean or replace the element (Chapter 1).

- [ ] Main jet too large or loose. Compare the jet size to the Specifications (Chapter 3).
- [ ] Choke cable or linkage shaft stuck, causing fuel to be pulled through choke circuit (Chapter 3).
- [ ] Fuel level too high. Check and adjust the float height(s) as necessary (Chapter 3).
- [ ] Float needle valve held off needle seat. Clean the float chambers and fuel line and replace the needles and seats if necessary (Chapter 3).

Brown smoke

- [ ] Main jet too small or clogged. Lean condition caused by wrong size main jet or by a restricted orifice. Clean float chambers and jets and compare jet size to Specifications (Chapter 3).
- [ ] Fuel flow insufficient. Float needle valve stuck closed due to chemical reaction with old fuel. Float height incorrect. Restricted fuel line. Clean line and float chamber and adjust floats if necessary (Chapter 3).
- [ ] Carburettor intake manifold clamps loose (Chapter 3).
- [ ] Air filter poorly sealed or not installed (Chapter 1).

12 Poor handling or stability

Handlebar hard to turn

- [ ] Steering head bearing adjuster nut too tight. Check adjustment (Chapter 1).
- [ ] Bearings damaged. Roughness can be felt as the bars are turned from side-to-side. Replace bearings and races (Chapter 5).
- [ ] Races dented or worn. Denting results from wear in only one position (e.g., straight ahead), from a collision or hitting a pothole or from dropping the machine. Replace races and bearings (Chapter 5).
- [ ] Steering stem lubrication inadequate. Causes are grease getting hard from age or being washed out by high pressure car washes. Disassemble steering head and repack bearings (Chapter 5).
- [ ] Steering stem bent. Caused by a collision, hitting a pothole or by dropping the machine. Replace damaged part. Don't try to straighten the steering stem (Chapter 5).
- [ ] Front tire air pressure too low (Chapter 1).

Handlebar shakes or vibrates excessively

- [ ] Tyres worn or out of balance (Chapter 6).
- [ ] Swingarm bearings worn. Replace worn bearings (Chapter 5).
- [ ] Rim(s) warped or damaged. Inspect wheels for runout (Chapter 6).
- [ ] Wheel bearings worn. Worn front or rear wheel bearings can cause poor tracking. Worn front bearings will cause wobble (Chapter 6).
- [ ] Handlebar clamp bolts loose (Chapter 5).
- [ ] Fork yoke bolts loose. Tighten them to the specified torque (Chapter 5).
- [ ] Engine mounting bolts loose. Will cause excessive vibration with increased engine rpm (Chapter 2).

Handlebar pulls to one side

- [ ] Frame bent. Definitely suspect this if the machine has been dropped. May or may not be accompanied by cracking near the bend. Replace the frame (Chapter 5).
- [ ] Wheels out of alignment. Caused by improper location of axle spacers or from bent steering stem or frame (Chapter 5).
- [ ] Swingarm bent or twisted. Caused by age (metal fatigue) or impact damage. Replace the arm (Chapter 5).
- [ ] Steering stem bent. Caused by impact damage or by dropping the motorcycle. Replace the steering stem (Chapter 5).
- [ ] Fork tube bent. Disassemble the forks and replace the damaged parts (Chapter 5).
- [ ] Fork oil level uneven. Check, add or drain as necessary (Chapter 1).

Poor shock absorbing qualities

- [ ] Too hard:
  - a) Fork oil level excessive (Chapter 5).
  - b) Fork oil viscosity too high. Use a lighter oil (see the Specifications in Chapter 5).
  - c) Fork tube bent. Causes a harsh, sticking feeling (Chapter 5).
  - d) Shock shaft or body bent or damaged (Chapter 5).
  - e) Fork internal damage (Chapter 5).
  - f) Shock internal damage.
  - g) Tire pressure too high (Chapter 1).
- [ ] Too soft:
  - a) Fork or shock oil insufficient and/or leaking (Chapter 5).
  - b) Fork oil level too low (Chapter 5).
  - c) Fork oil viscosity too light (Chapter 5).
  - d) Fork springs weak or broken (Chapter 5).
  - e) Shock internal damage or leakage (Chapter 5).

13 Braking problems

Brakes are spongy, don't hold

- ☐ Air in brake line. Caused by inattention to master cylinder fluid level or by leakage. Locate problem and bleed brakes (Chapter 6).
- ☐ Pad or disc worn (Chapters 1 and 6).
- ☐ Brake fluid leak. Causes air in brake line. Locate problem and bleed brakes (Chapter 6).
- ☐ Contaminated pads. Caused by contamination with oil, grease, brake fluid, etc. Clean or replace pads. Clean disc thoroughly with brake cleaner (Chapter 6).
- ☐ Brake fluid deteriorated. Fluid is old or contaminated. Drain system, replenish with new fluid and bleed the system (Chapter 6).
- ☐ Master cylinder internal parts worn or damaged causing fluid to bypass (Chapter 6).
- ☐ Master cylinder bore scratched by foreign material or broken spring. Repair or replace master cylinder (Chapter 6).
- ☐ Disc warped. Replace disc (Chapter 6).

Brake lever or pedal pulsates

- ☐ Disc warped. Replace disc (Chapter 6).

- ☐ Axle bent. Replace axle (Chapter 6).
- ☐ Brake caliper bolts loose (Chapter 6).
- ☐ Brake caliper sliders damaged or sticking, causing caliper to bind. Lubricate the sliders or replace them if they are corroded or bent (Chapter 6).
- ☐ Wheel warped or otherwise damaged (Chapter 6).
- ☐ Wheel bearings damaged or worn (Chapter 6).

Brakes drag

- ☐ Master cylinder piston seized. Caused by wear or damage to piston or cylinder bore (Chapter 6).
- ☐ Lever balky or stuck. Check pivot and lubricate (Chapter 6).
- ☐ Brake caliper binds. Caused by inadequate lubrication or damage to caliper sliders (Chapter 6).
- ☐ Brake caliper piston seized in bore. Caused by wear or ingestion of dirt past deteriorated seal (Chapter 6).
- ☐ Brake pad damaged. Pad material separated from backing plate. Usually caused by faulty manufacturing process or from contact with chemicals. Replace pads (Chapter 6).
- ☐ Pads improperly installed (Chapter 6).

14 Electrical problems

Battery dead or weak

- ☐ Battery faulty. Caused by sulphated plates which are shorted through sedimentation. Also, broken battery terminal making only occasional contact (Chapter 8).
- ☐ Battery cables making poor contact (Chapter 1).
- ☐ Load excessive. Caused by addition of high wattage lights or other electrical accessories.
- ☐ Ignition (main) switch defective. Switch either grounds (earths) internally or fails to shut off system. Replace the switch (Chapter 8).
- ☐ Regulator/rectifier defective (Chapter 8).

- ☐ Alternator stator coil open or shorted (Chapter 8).
- ☐ Wiring faulty. Wiring grounded (earthed) or connections loose in ignition, charging or lighting circuits (Chapter 8).

Battery overcharged

- ☐ Regulator/rectifier defective. Overcharging is noticed when battery gets excessively warm (Chapter 8).
- ☐ Battery defective. Replace battery with a new one (Chapter 8).
- ☐ Battery amperage too low, wrong type or size. Install manufacturer's specified amp-hour battery to handle charging load (Chapter 8).

Checking engine compression

● Low compression will result in exhaust smoke, heavy oil consumption, poor starting and poor performance. A compression test will provide useful information about an engine's condition and if performed regularly, can give warning of trouble before any other symptoms become apparent.

● A compression gauge will be required, along with an adapter to suit the spark plug hole thread size. Note that the screw-in type gauge/adapter set up is preferable to the rubber cone type.

● Before carrying out the test, first check the valve clearances as described in Chapter 1.

1 Run the engine until it reaches normal operating temperature, then stop it and remove the spark plug(s), taking care not to scald your hands on the hot components.

2 Install the gauge adapter and compression gauge in No. 1 cylinder spark plug hole **(see illustration 1)**.

Screw the compression gauge adapter into the spark plug hole, then screw the gauge into the adapter

3 On kickstart-equipped motorcycles, make sure the ignition switch is OFF, then open the throttle fully and kick the engine over a couple of times until the gauge reading stabilises.

4 On motorcycles with electric start only, the procedure will differ depending on the nature of the ignition system. Flick the engine kill switch (engine stop switch) to OFF and turn the ignition switch ON; open the throttle fully and crank the engine over on the starter motor for a couple of revolutions until the gauge reading stabilises. If the starter will not operate with the kill switch OFF, turn the ignition switch OFF and refer to the next paragraph.

5 Install the spark plugs back into their suppressor caps and arrange the plug electrodes so that their metal bodies are earthed (grounded) against the cylinder head; this is essential to prevent damage to the ignition system as the engine is spun over **(see illustration 2)**. Position the plugs well

All spark plugs must be earthed (grounded) against the cylinder head

away from the plug holes otherwise there is a risk of atomised fuel escaping from the combustion chambers and igniting. As a safety precaution, cover the top of the valve cover with rag. Now turn the ignition switch ON and kill switch ON, open the throttle fully and crank the engine over on the starter motor for a couple of revolutions until the gauge reading stabilises.

6 After one or two revolutions the pressure should build up to a maximum figure and then stabilise. Take a note of this reading and on multi-cylinder engines repeat the test on the remaining cylinders.

7 The correct pressures are given in Chapter 2 Specifications. If the results fall within the specified range and on multi-cylinder engines all are relatively equal, the engine is in good condition. If there is a marked difference between the readings, or if the readings are lower than specified, inspection of the top-end components will be required.

8 Low compression pressure may be due to worn cylinder bores, pistons or rings, failure of the cylinder head gasket, worn valve seals, or poor valve seating.

9 To distinguish between cylinder/piston wear and valve leakage, pour a small quantity of oil into the bore to temporarily seal the piston rings, then repeat the compression tests **(see illustration 3)**. If the readings show

Bores can be temporarily sealed with a squirt of motor oil

a noticeable increase in pressure this confirms that the cylinder bore, piston, or rings are worn. If, however, no change is indicated, the cylinder head gasket or valves should be examined.

10 High compression pressure indicates excessive carbon build-up in the combustion chamber and on the piston crown. If this is the case the cylinder head should be removed and the deposits removed. Note that excessive carbon build-up is less likely with the used on modern fuels.

Checking battery open-circuit voltage

 Warning: The gases produced by the battery are explosive - never smoke or create any sparks in the vicinity of the battery. Never allow the electrolyte to contact your skin or clothing - if it does, wash it off and seek immediate medical attention.

Measuring open-circuit battery voltage

Float-type hydrometer for measuring battery specific gravity

● Before any electrical fault is investigated the battery should be checked.

● You'll need a dc voltmeter or multimeter to check battery voltage. Check that the leads are inserted in the correct terminals on the meter, red lead to positive (+ve), black lead to negative (-ve). Incorrect connections can damage the meter.

● A sound fully-charged 12 volt battery should produce between 12.3 and 12.6 volts across its terminals (12.8 volts for a maintenance-free battery). On machines with a 6 volt battery, voltage should be between 6.1 and 6.3 volts.

1 Set a multimeter to the 0 to 20 volts dc range and connect its probes across the battery terminals. Connect the meter's positive (+ve) probe, usually red, to the battery positive (+ve) terminal, followed by the meter's negative (-ve) probe, usually black, to the battery negative terminal (-ve) (see illustration 4).

2 If battery voltage is low (below 10 volts on a 12 volt battery or below 4 volts on a six volt battery), charge the battery and test the voltage again. If the battery repeatedly goes flat, investigate the motorcycle's charging system.

Checking battery specific gravity (SG)

 Warning: The gases produced by the battery are explosive - never smoke or create any sparks in the vicinity of the battery. Never allow the electrolyte to contact your skin or clothing - if it does, wash it off and seek immediate medical attention.

● The specific gravity check gives an indication of a battery's state of charge.

● A hydrometer is used for measuring specific gravity. Make sure you purchase one

which has a small enough hose to insert in the aperture of a motorcycle battery.

● Specific gravity is simply a measure of the electrolyte's density compared with that of water. Water has an SG of 1.000 and fully-charged battery electrolyte is about 26% heavier, at 1.260.

● Specific gravity checks are not possible on maintenance-free batteries. Testing the open-circuit voltage is the only means of determining their state of charge.

1 To measure SG, remove the battery from the motorcycle and remove the first cell cap. Draw

Digital multimeter can be used for all electrical tests

some electrolyte into the hydrometer and note the reading (see illustration 5). Return the electrolyte to the cell and install the cap.

2 The reading should be in the region of 1.260 to 1.280. If SG is below 1.200 the battery needs charging. Note that SG will vary with temperature; it should be measured at 20°C (68°F). Add 0.007 to the reading for every 10°C above 20°C, and subtract 0.007 from the reading for every 10°C below 20°C. Add 0.004 to the reading for every 10°F above 68°F, and subtract 0.004 from the reading for every 10°F below 68°F.

3 When the check is complete, rinse the hydrometer thoroughly with clean water.

Checking for continuity

● The term continuity describes the uninterrupted flow of electricity through an electrical circuit. A continuity check will determine whether an open-circuit situation exists.

● Continuity can be checked with an ohmmeter, multimeter, continuity tester or battery and bulb test circuit (see illustrations 6, 7 and 8).

Battery-powered continuity tester

Battery and bulb test circuit

Continuity check of front brake light switch using a meter - note split pins used to access connector terminals

Continuity check of rear brake light switch using a continuity tester

● All of these instruments are self-powered by a battery, therefore the checks are made with the ignition OFF.

● As a safety precaution, always disconnect the battery negative (-ve) lead before making checks, particularly if ignition switch checks are being made.

● If using a meter, select the appropriate ohms scale and check that the meter reads infinity (∞). Touch the meter probes together and check that meter reads zero; where necessary adjust the meter so that it reads zero.

● After using a meter, always switch it OFF to conserve its battery.

Switch checks

1 If a switch is at fault, trace its wiring up to the wiring connectors. Separate the wire connectors and inspect them for security and condition. A build-up of dirt or corrosion here will most likely be the cause of the problem - clean up and apply a water dispersant such as WD40.

2 If using a test meter, set the meter to the ohms x 10 scale and connect its probes across the wires from the switch **(see illustration 9)**. Simple ON/OFF type switches, such as brake light switches, only have two

wires whereas combination switches, like the ignition switch, have many internal links. Study the wiring diagram to ensure that you are connecting across the correct pair of wires. Continuity (low or no measurable resistance - 0 ohms) should be indicated with the switch ON and no continuity (high resistance) with it OFF.

3 Note that the polarity of the test probes doesn't matter for continuity checks, although care should be taken to follow specific test procedures if a diode or solid-state component is being checked.

4 A continuity tester or battery and bulb circuit can be used in the same way. Connect its probes as described above **(see illustration 10)**. The light should come on to indicate continuity in the ON switch position, but should extinguish in the OFF position.

Wiring checks

● Many electrical faults are caused by damaged wiring, often due to incorrect routing or chaffing on frame components.

● Loose, wet or corroded wire connectors can also be the cause of electrical problems, especially in exposed locations.

1 A continuity check can be made on a single length of wire by disconnecting it at each end

and connecting a meter or continuity tester across both ends of the wire **(see illustration 11)**.

2 Continuity (low or no resistance - 0 ohms) should be indicated if the wire is good. If no continuity (high resistance) is shown, suspect a broken wire.

Checking for voltage

● A voltage check can determine whether current is reaching a component.

● Voltage can be checked with a dc voltmeter, multimeter set on the dc volts scale, test light or buzzer **(see illustrations 12 and 13)**. A meter has the advantage of being able to measure actual voltage.

● When using a meter, check that its leads are inserted in the correct terminals on the meter, red to positive (+ve), black to negative (-ve). Incorrect connections can damage the meter.

● A voltmeter (or multimeter set to the dc volts scale) should always be connected in parallel (across the load). Connecting it in series will destroy the meter.

● Voltage checks are made with the ignition ON.

Continuity check of front brake light switch sub-harness

A simple test light can be used for voltage checks

A buzzer is useful for voltage checks

Checking for voltage at the rear brake light power supply wire using a meter . . .

1 First identify the relevant wiring circuit by referring to the wiring diagram at the end of this manual. If other electrical components share the same power supply (ie are fed from the same fuse), take note whether they are working correctly - this is useful information in deciding where to start checking the circuit.

2 If using a meter, check first that the meter leads are plugged into the correct terminals on the meter (see above). Set the meter to the dc volts function, at a range suitable for the battery voltage. Connect the meter red probe (+ve) to the power supply wire and the black probe to a good metal earth (ground) on the motorcycle's frame or directly to the battery negative (-ve) terminal **(see illustration 14)**. Battery voltage should be shown on the meter

A selection of jumper wires for making earth (ground) checks

. . . or a test light - note the earth connection to the frame (arrow)

with the ignition switched ON.

3 If using a test light or buzzer, connect its positive (+ve) probe to the power supply terminal and its negative (-ve) probe to a good earth (ground) on the motorcycle's frame or directly to the battery negative (-ve) terminal **(see illustration 15)**. With the ignition ON, the test light should illuminate or the buzzer sound.

4 If no voltage is indicated, work back towards the fuse continuing to check for voltage. When you reach a point where there is voltage, you know the problem lies between that point and your last check point.

Checking the earth (ground)

● Earth connections are made either directly to the engine or frame (such as sensors, neutral switch etc. which only have a positive feed) or by a separate wire into the earth circuit of the wiring harness. Alternatively a short earth wire is sometimes run directly from the component to the motorcycle's frame.
● Corrosion is often the cause of a poor earth connection.
● If total failure is experienced, check the security of the main earth lead from the

negative (-ve) terminal of the battery and also the main earth (ground) point on the wiring harness. If corroded, dismantle the connection and clean all surfaces back to bare metal.

1 To check the earth on a component, use an insulated jumper wire to temporarily bypass its earth connection **(see illustration 16)**. Connect one end of the jumper wire between the earth terminal or metal body of the component and the other end to the motorcycle's frame.

2 If the circuit works with the jumper wire installed, the original earth circuit is faulty. Check the wiring for open-circuits or poor connections. Clean up direct earth connections, removing all traces of corrosion and remake the joint. Apply petroleum jelly to the joint to prevent future corrosion.

Tracing a short-circuit

● A short-circuit occurs where current shorts to earth (ground) bypassing the circuit components. This usually results in a blown fuse.

● A short-circuit is most likely to occur where the insulation has worn through due to wiring chafing on a component, allowing a direct path to earth (ground) on the frame.

1 Remove any bodypanels necessary to access the circuit wiring.
2 Check that all electrical switches in the circuit are OFF, then remove the circuit fuse and connect a test light, buzzer or voltmeter (set to the dc scale) across the fuse terminals. No voltage should be shown.
3 Move the wiring from side to side whilst observing the test light or meter. When the test light comes on, buzzer sounds or meter shows voltage, you have found the cause of the short. It will usually shown up as damaged or burned insulation.
4 Note that the same test can be performed on each component in the circuit, even the switch.

A

ABS (Anti-lock braking system) A system, usually electronically controlled, that senses incipient wheel lockup during braking and relieves hydraulic pressure at wheel which is about to skid.

Aftermarket Components suitable for the motorcycle, but not produced by the motorcycle manufacturer.

Allen key A hexagonal wrench which fits into a recessed hexagonal hole.

Alternating current (ac) Current produced by an alternator. Requires converting to direct current by a rectifier for charging purposes.

Alternator Converts mechanical energy from the engine into electrical energy to charge the battery and power the electrical system.

Ampere (amp) A unit of measurement for the flow of electrical current. Current = Volts ÷ Ohms.

Ampere-hour (Ah) Measure of battery capacity.

Angle-tightening A torque expressed in degrees. Often follows a conventional tightening torque for cylinder head or main bearing fasteners **(see illustration)**.

Angle-tightening cylinder head bolts

Antifreeze A substance (usually ethylene glycol) mixed with water, and added to the cooling system, to prevent freezing of the coolant in winter. Antifreeze also contains chemicals to inhibit corrosion and the formation of rust and other deposits that would tend to clog the radiator and coolant passages and reduce cooling efficiency.

Anti-dive System attached to the fork lower leg (slider) to prevent fork dive when braking hard.

Anti-seize compound A coating that reduces the risk of seizing on fasteners that are subjected to high temperatures, such as exhaust clamp bolts and nuts.

API American Petroleum Institute. A quality standard for 4-stroke motor oils.

Asbestos A natural fibrous mineral with great heat resistance, commonly used in the composition of brake friction materials. Asbestos is a health hazard and the dust created by brake systems should never be inhaled or ingested.

ATF Automatic Transmission Fluid. Often used in front forks.

ATU Automatic Timing Unit. Mechanical device for advancing the ignition timing on early engines.

ATV All Terrain Vehicle. Often called a Quad.

Axial play Side-to-side movement.

Axle A shaft on which a wheel revolves. Also known as a spindle.

B

Backlash The amount of movement between meshed components when one component is held still. Usually applies to gear teeth.

Ball bearing A bearing consisting of a hardened inner and outer race with hardened steel balls between the two races.

Bearings Used between two working surfaces to prevent wear of the components and a build-up of heat. Four types of bearing are commonly used on motorcycles: plain shell bearings, ball bearings, tapered roller bearings and needle roller bearings.

Bevel gears Used to turn the drive through 90º. Typical applications are shaft final drive and camshaft drive **(see illustration)**.

Bevel gears are used to turn the drive through 90°

BHP Brake Horsepower. The British measurement for engine power output. Power output is now usually expressed in kilowatts (kW).

Bias-belted tyre Similar construction to radial tyre, but with outer belt running at an angle to the wheel rim.

Big-end bearing The bearing in the end of the connecting rod that's attached to the crankshaft.

Bleeding The process of removing air from an hydraulic system via a bleed nipple or bleed screw.

Bottom-end A description of an engine's crankcase components and all components contained there-in.

BTDC Before Top Dead Centre in terms of piston position. Ignition timing is often expressed in terms of degrees or millimetres BTDC.

Bush A cylindrical metal or rubber component used between two moving parts.

Burr Rough edge left on a component after machining or as a result of excessive wear.

C

Cam chain The chain which takes drive from the crankshaft to the camshaft(s).

Canister The main component in an evaporative emission control system (California market only); contains activated charcoal granules to trap vapours from the fuel system rather than allowing them to vent to the atmosphere.

Castellated Resembling the parapets along the top of a castle wall. For example, a castellated wheel axle or spindle nut.

Catalytic converter A device in the exhaust system of some machines which converts certain pollutants in the exhaust gases into less harmful substances.

Charging system Description of the components which charge the battery, ie the alternator, rectifer and regulator.

Circlip A ring-shaped clip used to prevent endwise movement of cylindrical parts and shafts. An internal circlip is installed in a groove in a housing; an external circlip fits into a groove on the outside of a cylindrical piece such as a shaft. Also known as a snap-ring.

Clearance The amount of space between two parts. For example, between a piston and a cylinder, between a bearing and a journal, etc.

Coil spring A spiral of elastic steel found in various sizes throughout a vehicle, for example as a springing medium in the suspension and in the valve train.

Compression Reduction in volume, and increase in pressure and temperature, of a gas, caused by squeezing it into a smaller space.

Compression damping Controls the speed the suspension compresses when hitting a bump.

Compression ratio The relationship between cylinder volume when the piston is at top dead centre and cylinder volume when the piston is at bottom dead centre.

Continuity The uninterrupted path in the flow of electricity. Little or no measurable resistance.

Continuity tester Self-powered bleeper or test light which indicates continuity.

Cp Candlepower. Bulb rating commonly found on US motorcycles.

Crossply tyre Tyre plies arranged in a criss-cross pattern. Usually four or six plies used, hence 4PR or 6PR in tyre size codes.

Cush drive Rubber damper segments fitted between the rear wheel and final drive sprocket to absorb transmission shocks **(see illustration)**.

Cush drive rubbers dampen out transmission shocks

D

Degree disc Calibrated disc for measuring piston position. Expressed in degrees.

Dial gauge Clock-type gauge with adapters for measuring runout and piston position. Expressed in mm or inches.

Diaphragm The rubber membrane in a master cylinder or carburettor which seals the upper chamber.

Diaphragm spring A single sprung plate often used in clutches.

Direct current (dc) Current produced by a dc generator.

Decarbonisation The process of removing carbon deposits - typically from the combustion chamber, valves and exhaust port/system.

Detonation Destructive and damaging explosion of fuel/air mixture in combustion chamber instead of controlled burning.

Diode An electrical valve which only allows current to flow in one direction. Commonly used in rectifiers and starter interlock systems.

Disc valve (or rotary valve) A induction system used on some two-stroke engines.

Double-overhead camshaft (DOHC) An engine that uses two overhead camshafts, one for the intake valves and one for the exhaust valves.

Drivebelt A toothed belt used to transmit drive to the rear wheel on some motorcycles. A drivebelt has also been used to drive the camshafts. Drivebelts are usually made of Kevlar.

Driveshaft Any shaft used to transmit motion. Commonly used when referring to the final driveshaft on shaft drive motorcycles.

E

Earth return The return path of an electrical circuit, utilising the motorcycle's frame.

ECU (Electronic Control Unit) A computer which controls (for instance) an ignition system, or an anti-lock braking system.

EGO Exhaust Gas Oxygen sensor. Sometimes called a Lambda sensor.

Electrolyte The fluid in a lead-acid battery.

EMS (Engine Management System) A computer controlled system which manages the fuel injection and the ignition systems in an integrated fashion.

Endfloat The amount of lengthways movement between two parts. As applied to a crankshaft, the distance that the crankshaft can move side-to-side in the crankcase.

Endless chain A chain having no joining link. Common use for cam chains and final drive chains.

EP (Extreme Pressure) Oil type used in locations where high loads are applied, such as between gear teeth.

Evaporative emission control system Describes a charcoal filled canister which stores fuel vapours from the tank rather than allowing them to vent to the atmosphere. Usually only fitted to California models and referred to as an EVAP system.

Expansion chamber Section of two-stroke engine exhaust system so designed to improve engine efficiency and boost power.

F

Feeler blade or gauge A thin strip or blade of hardened steel, ground to an exact thickness, used to check or measure clearances between parts.

Final drive Description of the drive from the transmission to the rear wheel. Usually by chain or shaft, but sometimes by belt.

Firing order The order in which the engine cylinders fire, or deliver their power strokes, beginning with the number one cylinder.

Flooding Term used to describe a high fuel level in the carburettor float chambers, leading to fuel overflow. Also refers to excess fuel in the combustion chamber due to incorrect starting technique.

Free length The no-load state of a component when measured. Clutch, valve and fork spring lengths are measured at rest, without any preload.

Freeplay The amount of travel before any action takes place. The looseness in a linkage, or an assembly of parts, between the initial application of force and actual movement. For example, the distance the rear brake pedal moves before the rear brake is actuated.

Fuel injection The fuel/air mixture is metered electronically and directed into the engine intake ports (indirect injection) or into the cylinders (direct injection). Sensors supply information on engine speed and conditions.

Fuel/air mixture The charge of fuel and air going into the engine. See **Stoichiometric ratio**.

Fuse An electrical device which protects a circuit against accidental overload. The typical fuse contains a soft piece of metal which is calibrated to melt at a predetermined current flow (expressed as amps) and break the circuit.

G

Gap The distance the spark must travel in jumping from the centre electrode to the side electrode in a spark plug. Also refers to the distance between the ignition rotor and the pickup coil in an electronic ignition system.

Gasket Any thin, soft material - usually cork, cardboard, asbestos or soft metal - installed between two metal surfaces to ensure a good seal. For instance, the cylinder head gasket seals the joint between the block and the cylinder head.

Gauge An instrument panel display used to monitor engine conditions. A gauge with a movable pointer on a dial or a fixed scale is an analogue gauge. A gauge with a numerical readout is called a digital gauge.

Gear ratios The drive ratio of a pair of gears in a gearbox, calculated on their number of teeth.

Glaze-busting see Honing

Grinding Process for renovating the valve face and valve seat contact area in the cylinder head.

Gudgeon pin The shaft which connects the connecting rod small-end with the piston. Often called a piston pin or wrist pin.

H

Helical gears Gear teeth are slightly curved and produce less gear noise that straight-cut gears. Often used for primary drives.

Installing a Helicoil thread insert in a cylinder head

Helicoil A thread insert repair system. Commonly used as a repair for stripped spark plug threads **(see illustration)**.

Honing A process used to break down the glaze on a cylinder bore (also called glaze-busting). Can also be carried out to roughen a rebored cylinder to aid ring bedding-in.

HT (High Tension) Description of the electrical circuit from the secondary winding of the ignition coil to the spark plug.

Hydraulic A liquid filled system used to transmit pressure from one component to another. Common uses on motorcycles are brakes and clutches.

Hydrometer An instrument for measuring the specific gravity of a lead-acid battery.

Hygroscopic Water absorbing. In motorcycle applications, braking efficiency will be reduced if DOT 3 or 4 hydraulic fluid absorbs water from the air - care must be taken to keep new brake fluid in tightly sealed containers.

I

lbf ft Pounds-force feet. An imperial unit of torque. Sometimes written as ft-lbs.

lbf in Pound-force inch. An imperial unit of torque, applied to components where a very low torque is required. Sometimes written as in-lbs.

IC Abbreviation for Integrated Circuit.

Ignition advance Means of increasing the timing of the spark at higher engine speeds. Done by mechanical means (ATU) on early engines or electronically by the ignition control unit on later engines.

Ignition timing The moment at which the spark plug fires, expressed in the number of crankshaft degrees before the piston reaches the top of its stroke, or in the number of millimetres before the piston reaches the top of its stroke.

Infinity (∞) Description of an open-circuit electrical state, where no continuity exists.

Inverted forks (upside down forks) The sliders or lower legs are held in the yokes and the fork tubes or stanchions are connected to the wheel axle (spindle). Less unsprung weight and stiffer construction than conventional forks.

J

JASO Quality standard for 2-stroke oils.

Joule The unit of electrical energy.

Journal The bearing surface of a shaft.

K

Kickstart Mechanical means of turning the engine over for starting purposes. Only usually fitted to mopeds, small capacity motorcycles and off-road motorcycles.

Kill switch Handebar-mounted switch for emergency ignition cut-out. Cuts the ignition circuit on all models, and additionally prevent starter motor operation on others.

km Symbol for kilometre.

kmh Abbreviation for kilometres per hour.

L

Lambda (λ) sensor A sensor fitted in the exhaust system to measure the exhaust gas oxygen content (excess air factor).

Lapping see **Grinding**.
LCD Abbreviation for Liquid Crystal Display.
LED Abbreviation for Light Emitting Diode.
Liner A steel cylinder liner inserted in a aluminium alloy cylinder block.
Locknut A nut used to lock an adjustment nut, or other threaded component, in place.
Lockstops The lugs on the lower triple clamp (yoke) which abut those on the frame, preventing handlebar-to-fuel tank contact.
Lockwasher A form of washer designed to prevent an attaching nut from working loose.
LT Low Tension Description of the electrical circuit from the power supply to the primary winding of the ignition coil.

M

Main bearings The bearings between the crankshaft and crankcase.
Maintenance-free (MF) battery A sealed battery which cannot be topped up.
Manometer Mercury-filled calibrated tubes used to measure intake tract vacuum. Used to synchronise carburettors on multi-cylinder engines.
Micrometer A precision measuring instrument that measures component outside diameters **(see illustration)**.

Tappet shims are measured with a micrometer

MON (Motor Octane Number) A measure of a fuel's resistance to knock.
Monograde oil An oil with a single viscosity, eg SAE80W.
Monoshock A single suspension unit linking the swingarm or suspension linkage to the frame.
mph Abbreviation for miles per hour.
Multigrade oil Having a wide viscosity range (eg 10W40). The W stands for Winter, thus the viscosity ranges from SAE10 when cold to SAE40 when hot.
Multimeter An electrical test instrument with the capability to measure voltage, current and resistance. Some meters also incorporate a continuity tester and buzzer.

N

Needle roller bearing Inner race of caged needle rollers and hardened outer race. Examples of uncaged needle rollers can be found on some engines. Commonly used in rear suspension applications and in two-stroke engines.
Nm Newton metres.
NOx Oxides of Nitrogen. A common toxic pollutant emitted by petrol engines at higher temperatures.

O

Octane The measure of a fuel's resistance to knock.
OE (Original Equipment) Relates to components fitted to a motorcycle as standard or replacement parts supplied by the motorcycle manufacturer.
Ohm The unit of electrical resistance. Ohms = Volts ÷ Current.
Ohmmeter An instrument for measuring electrical resistance.
Oil cooler System for diverting engine oil outside of the engine to a radiator for cooling purposes.
Oil injection A system of two-stroke engine lubrication where oil is pump-fed to the engine in accordance with throttle position.
Open-circuit An electrical condition where there is a break in the flow of electricity - no continuity (high resistance).
O-ring A type of sealing ring made of a special rubber-like material; in use, the O-ring is compressed into a groove to provide the sealing action.
Oversize (OS) Term used for piston and ring size options fitted to a rebored cylinder.
Overhead cam (sohc) engine An engine with single camshaft located on top of the cylinder head.
Overhead valve (ohv) engine An engine with the valves located in the cylinder head, but with the camshaft located in the engine block or crankcase.
Oxygen sensor A device installed in the exhaust system which senses the oxygen content in the exhaust and converts this information into an electric current. Also called a Lambda sensor.

P

Plastigauge A thin strip of plastic thread, available in different sizes, used for measuring clearances. For example, a strip of Plastigauge is laid across a bearing journal. The parts are assembled and dismantled; the width of the crushed strip indicates the clearance between journal and bearing.
Polarity Either negative or positive earth (ground), determined by which battery lead is connected to the frame (earth return). Modern motorcycles are usually negative earth.
Pre-ignition A situation where the fuel/air mixture ignites before the spark plug fires. Often due to a hot spot in the combustion chamber caused by carbon build-up. Engine has a tendency to 'run-on'.
Pre-load (suspension) The amount a spring is compressed when in the unloaded state. Preload can be applied by gas, spacer or mechanical adjuster.
Premix The method of engine lubrication on older two-stroke engines. Engine oil is mixed with the petrol in the fuel tank in a specific ratio. The fuel/oil mix is sometimes referred to as "petroil".
Primary drive Description of the drive from the crankshaft to the clutch. Usually by gear or chain.
PS Pfedestärke - a German interpretation of BHP.
PSI Pounds-force per square inch. Imperial measurement of tyre pressure and cylinder pressure measurement.
PTFE Polytetrafluoroethylene. A low friction substance.

Pulse secondary air injection system A process of promoting the burning of excess fuel present in the exhaust gases by routing fresh air into the exhaust ports.

Q

Quartz halogen bulb Tungsten filament surrounded by a halogen gas. Typically used for the headlight **(see illustration)**.

Quartz halogen headlight bulb construction

R

Rack-and-pinion A pinion gear on the end of a shaft that mates with a rack (think of a geared wheel opened up and laid flat). Sometimes used in clutch operating systems.
Radial play Up and down movement about a shaft.
Radial ply tyres Tyre plies run across the tyre (from bead to bead) and around the circumference of the tyre. Less resistant to tread distortion than other tyre types.
Radiator A liquid-to-air heat transfer device designed to reduce the temperature of the coolant in a liquid cooled engine.
Rake A feature of steering geometry - the angle of the steering head in relation to the vertical **(see illustration)**.

Steering geometry

Rebore Providing a new working surface to the cylinder bore by boring out the old surface. Necessitates the use of oversize piston and rings.

Rebound damping A means of controlling the oscillation of a suspension unit spring after it has been compressed. Resists the spring's natural tendency to bounce back after being compressed.

Rectifier Device for converting the ac output of an alternator into dc for battery charging.

Reed valve An induction system commonly used on two-stroke engines.

Regulator Device for maintaining the charging voltage from the generator or alternator within a specified range.

Relay A electrical device used to switch heavy current on and off by using a low current auxiliary circuit.

Resistance Measured in ohms. An electrical component's ability to pass electrical current.

RON (Research Octane Number) A measure of a fuel's resistance to knock.

rpm revolutions per minute.

Runout The amount of wobble (in-and-out movement) of a wheel or shaft as it's rotated. The amount a shaft rotates 'out-of-true'. The out-of-round condition of a rotating part.

S

SAE (Society of Automotive Engineers) A standard for the viscosity of a fluid.

Sealant A liquid or paste used to prevent leakage at a joint. Sometimes used in conjunction with a gasket.

Service limit Term for the point where a component is no longer useable and must be renewed.

Shaft drive A method of transmitting drive from the transmission to the rear wheel.

Shell bearings Plain bearings consisting of two shell halves. Most often used as big-end and main bearings in a four-stroke engine. Often called bearing inserts.

Shim Thin spacer, commonly used to adjust the clearance or relative positions between two parts. For example, shims inserted into or under tappets or followers to control valve clearances. Clearance is adjusted by changing the thickness of the shim.

Short-circuit An electrical condition where current shorts to earth (ground) bypassing the circuit components.

Skimming Process to correct warpage or repair a damaged surface, eg on brake discs or drums.

Slide-hammer A special puller that screws into or hooks onto a component such as a shaft or bearing; a heavy sliding handle on the shaft bottoms against the end of the shaft to knock the component free.

Small-end bearing The bearing in the upper end of the connecting rod at its joint with the gudgeon pin.

Spalling Damage to camshaft lobes or bearing journals shown as pitting of the working surface.

Specific gravity (SG) The state of charge of the electrolyte in a lead-acid battery. A measure of the electrolyte's density compared with water.

Straight-cut gears Common type gear used on gearbox shafts and for oil pump and water pump drives.

Stanchion The inner sliding part of the front forks, held by the yokes. Often called a fork tube.

Stoichiometric ratio The optimum chemical air/fuel ratio for a petrol engine, said to be 14.7 parts of air to 1 part of fuel.

Sulphuric acid The liquid (electrolyte) used in a lead-acid battery. Poisonous and extremely corrosive.

Surface grinding (lapping) Process to correct a warped gasket face, commonly used on cylinder heads.

T

Tapered-roller bearing Tapered inner race of caged needle rollers and separate tapered outer race. Examples of taper roller bearings can be found on steering heads.

Tappet A cylindrical component which transmits motion from the cam to the valve stem, either directly or via a pushrod and rocker arm. Also called a cam follower.

TCS Traction Control System. An electronically-controlled system which senses wheel spin and reduces engine speed accordingly.

TDC Top Dead Centre denotes that the piston is at its highest point in the cylinder.

Thread-locking compound Solution applied to fastener threads to prevent slackening. Select type to suit application.

Thrust washer A washer positioned between two moving components on a shaft. For example, between gear pinions on gearshaft.

Timing chain See **Cam Chain.**

Timing light Stroboscopic lamp for carrying out ignition timing checks with the engine running.

Top-end A description of an engine's cylinder block, head and valve gear components.

Torque Turning or twisting force about a shaft.

Torque setting A prescribed tightness specified by the motorcycle manufacturer to ensure that the bolt or nut is secured correctly. Undertightening can result in the bolt or nut coming loose or a surface not being sealed. Overtightening can result in stripped threads, distortion or damage to the component being retained.

Torx key A six-point wrench.

Tracer A stripe of a second colour applied to a wire insulator to distinguish that wire from another one with the same colour insulator. For example, Br/W is often used to denote a brown insulator with a white tracer.

Trail A feature of steering geometry. Distance from the steering head axis to the tyre's central contact point.

Triple clamps The cast components which extend from the steering head and support the fork stanchions or tubes. Often called fork yokes.

Turbocharger A centrifugal device, driven by exhaust gases, that pressurises the intake air. Normally used to increase the power output from a given engine displacement.

TWI Abbreviation for Tyre Wear Indicator. Indicates the location of the tread depth indicator bars on tyres.

U

Universal joint or U-joint (UJ) A double-pivoted connection for transmitting power from a driving to a driven shaft through an angle. Typically found in shaft drive assemblies.

Unsprung weight Anything not supported by the bike's suspension (ie the wheel, tyres, brakes, final drive and bottom (moving) part of the suspension).

V

Vacuum gauges Clock-type gauges for measuring intake tract vacuum. Used for carburettor synchronisation on multi-cylinder engines.

Valve A device through which the flow of liquid, gas or vacuum may be stopped, started or regulated by a moveable part that opens, shuts or partially obstructs one or more ports or passageways. The intake and exhaust valves in the cylinder head are of the poppet type.

Valve clearance The clearance between the valve tip (the end of the valve stem) and the rocker arm or tappet/follower. The valve clearance is measured when the valve is closed. The correct clearance is important - if too small the valve won't close fully and will burn out, whereas if too large noisy operation will result.

Valve lift The amount a valve is lifted off its seat by the camshaft lobe.

Valve timing The exact setting for the opening and closing of the valves in relation to piston position.

Vernier caliper A precision measuring instrument that measures inside and outside dimensions. Not quite as accurate as a micrometer, but more convenient.

VIN Vehicle Identification Number. Term for the bike's engine and frame numbers.

Viscosity The thickness of a liquid or its resistance to flow.

Volt A unit for expressing electrical "pressure" in a circuit. Volts = current x ohms.

W

Water pump A mechanically-driven device for moving coolant around the engine.

Watt A unit for expressing electrical power. Watts = volts x current.

Wear limit see **Service limit**

Wet liner A liquid-cooled engine design where the pistons run in liners which are directly surrounded by coolant **(see illustration)**.

Wet liner arrangement

Wheelbase Distance from the centre of the front wheel to the centre of the rear wheel.

Wiring harness or loom Describes the electrical wires running the length of the motorcycle and enclosed in tape or plastic sheathing. Wiring coming off the main harness is usually referred to as a sub harness.

Woodruff key A key of semi-circular or square section used to locate a gear to a shaft. Often used to locate the alternator rotor on the crankshaft.

Wrist pin Another name for gudgeon or piston pin.

Note: *References throughout this index are in the form - "Chapter number" • "page number"*

Preserving Our Motoring Heritage

< *The Model J Duesenberg Derham Tourster. Only eight of these magnificent cars were ever built – this is the only example to be found outside the United States of America*

Almost every car you've ever loved, loathed or desired is gathered under one roof at the Haynes Motor Museum. Over 300 immaculately presented cars and motorbikes represent every aspect of our motoring heritage, from elegant reminders of bygone days, such as the superb Model J Duesenberg to curiosities like the bug-eyed BMW Isetta. There are also many old friends and flames. Perhaps you remember the 1959 Ford Popular that you did your courting in? The magnificent 'Red Collection' is a spectacle of classic sports cars including AC, Alfa Romeo, Austin Healey, Ferrari, Lamborghini, Maserati, MG, Riley, Porsche and Triumph.

A Perfect Day Out

Each and every vehicle at the Haynes Motor Museum has played its part in the history and culture of Motoring. Today, they make a wonderful spectacle and a great day out for all the family. Bring the kids, bring Mum and Dad, but above all bring your camera to capture those golden memories for ever. You will also find an impressive array of motoring memorabilia, a comfortable 70 seat video cinema and one of the most extensive transport book shops in Britain. The Pit Stop Cafe serves everything from a cup of tea to wholesome, home-made meals or, if you prefer, you can enjoy the large picnic area nestled in the beautiful rural surroundings of Somerset.

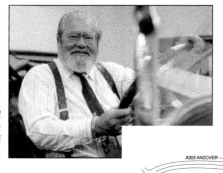

> *John Haynes O.B.E., Founder and Chairman of the museum at the wheel of a Haynes Light 12.*

< *The 1936 490cc sohc-engined International Norton – well known for its racing success*

The Museum is situated on the A359 Yeovil to Frome road at Sparkford, just off the A303 in Somerset. It is about 40 miles south of Bristol, and 25 minutes drive from the M5 intersection at Taunton.

Open 9.30am - 5.30pm (10.00am - 4.00pm Winter) 7 days a week, *except Christmas Day, Boxing Day and New Years Day*

Special rates available for schools, coach parties and outings Charitable Trust No. 292048